A Free Corrector

A Free Corrector

Colin Gunton and the Legacy of Augustine

Joshua McNall

Fortress Press
Minneapolis

A FREE CORRECTOR

Colin Gunton and the Legacy of Augustine

Copyright © 2015 Fortress Press. All rights reserved. Except for brief quotations in critical articles or reviews, no part of this book may be reproduced in any manner without prior written permission from the publisher. Visit http://www.augsburgfortress.org/copyrights/ or write to Permissions, Augsburg Fortress, Box 1209, Minneapolis, MN 55440.

Cover design: Alisha Lofgren

Library of Congress Cataloging-in-Publication Data is available

Paperback ISBN: 978-1-4514-8796-1

Hardcover ISBN: 978-1-4514-9974-2

eBook ISBN: 978-1-4514-9664-2

The paper used in this publication meets the minimum requirements of American National Standard for Information Sciences — Permanence of Paper for Printed Library Materials, ANSI Z329.48-1984.

Manufactured in the U.S.A.

This book was produced using PressBooks.com, and PDF rendering was done by PrinceXML.

To Brianna, and the growing family God has given us.

Contents

Acknowledgements		ix
Abbreviations		xi
1.	A Free Corrector: Colin Gunton on the Trinity, Creation, and the Legacy of Augustine	*1*
2.	Critiques Of Colin Gunton: Challenges on the Trinity, Creation, and the Legacy of Augustine	*29*
3.	Gunton and Augustine's God: The Question of Monistic Imbalance in Augustine's Trinitarianism	*53*
4.	Gunton and Augustine's World: The Question of Dualism in Augustine's Doctrine of Creation	*93*
5.	Gunton and Augustine's Medieval Afterlife (Part One)	*133*
6.	Gunton and Augustine's Medieval Afterlife (Part Two)	*165*
7.	Gunton and Augustine's Reformation Afterlife	*189*
8.	Gunton and Augustine's Modern Afterlife	*215*

9.	Gunton and the Triune Corrective (Part One): Irenaeus as an "Antidote" to Certain Augustinian Imbalances	*233*
10.	Gunton and the Triune Corrective (Part Two): The Cappadocian Fathers as the "Antidote" to Certain Augustinian Imbalances	*259*
11.	On "Fruit" and Free Correctors: Conclusions on Colin Gunton and the Legacy of Augustine	*281*
	Bibliography	*297*
	Index	*325*

Acknowledgements

Colin Gunton liked to claim that *ALL THINGS* are the result of *mutually constitutive relationships*. This book is like that.

The subsequent pages, which began as my doctoral thesis at The University of Manchester (UK), would not have been possible without the guidance of my supervisor, Dr. Thomas A. Noble. From the beginning Dr. Noble was a model of both scholarship and Christian encouragement. Thus I could not have asked for a better guide.

Many others also offered insights and assistance. Because I never met the late Colin Gunton, I benefited from conversations with one of his final students, Dr. David Rainey. Likewise, Dr. Bradley Green—although he literally "wrote the book" on Gunton and Augustine—was willing to encourage my research at an early stage. My employer, Oklahoma Wesleyan University, provided me with time and financial assistance to pursue this work, and my colleagues offered their support. Stephanie Leupp tracked down dozens of books for me through interlibrary loan, and she was always eager to help me access those sources that were especially difficult to find. In England, Joseph Wood patiently put up my incessant emails as I attempted to adhere to all the submission guidelines for a British PhD, even while living "across the pond." I am sure he is glad to be done with that, but he never showed it. In addition, Nazarene Theological College (Manchester) was gracious in welcoming me into their community every summer; I will remember fondly the time spent there in Didsbury.

In the transition to publication, my thanks go to the extraordinary staff at Fortress Press. Michael Gibson, Carolyn Halvorson, Marissa Wold, and the rest of the Fortress family were a delight to work with.

Thanks also go to my parents, Greg and Bonita McNall, and to my wife's parents, Brian and Janette Maydew. Since my doctoral work required me to spend several weeks in England every summer, the assistance of our parents (especially with our children) was invaluable.

This book is dedicated to my wife, Brianna, and the growing family God has given us. In the end, I suspect that Augustine was right in thinking that there are no true analogies for the Trinity. Yet marriage is a metaphor for something (Ephesians 5), and it is through our loving union that I have learned much of what it means to be "one," while still retaining our particularity. As Augustine wrote:

Uides trinitatem si caritatem uides (*De Trinitate*, 8.8.12).

Abbreviations

AH	Irenaeus, *Against Heresies*
An. et or.	Augustine, *De anima et eius orgine*
c. ep. Man.	Augustine, *Contra epistulam Manichaei quam vocant fundamenti*
CD	Karl Barth, *Church Dogmatics*
Civ.	Augustine, *De Civitate Dei*
Conf.	Augustine, *Confessiones*
Con. Iul.	Augustine, *Contra Julianum*
Corrept.	Augustine, *De correptione et gratia*
CT	Jaroslav Pelikan, *The Christian Tradition*
Dem.	Irenaeus, *Demonstration of Apostolic Preaching*
div. qu.	Augustine, *De diversis quaestionibus octoginta tribus*
Doctr. chr.	Augustine, *De doctrina Christiana*
en. Ps.	Augustine, *Enarrationes in Psalmos*
Ench.	Augustine, *Enchiridion de fide, spe et caritate*
Ep.	Augustine, *Epistulae*
Exp. Prop. Rm.	Augustine, *Expositio quarundam propositionum ex epistula Apostoli ad Romanos*
f. et symb.	Augustine, *De fide et symbolo*
Gn. adv. man.	Augustine, *De Genesi adversus Manicheos*

Gn. litt.	Augustine, *De Genesi ad Litteram*
Gn. litt. imp.	Augustine, *De Genesi ad litteram imperfectus liber*
Jo. ev. tr.	Augustine, *In Johannis Evangelium Tractatus*
Lib. arb	Augustine, *De Libero Arbitrio*
Mor.	Augustine, *De moribus ecclesiae catholicae et de moribus Manichaeorum*
nat. b.	Augustine, *De natura boni*
orig. an.	Augustine, *On the Origin of the Soul*
Retract.	Augustine, *Retractationes*
Soliloq.	Augustine, *Soliloquia*
Trin.	Augustine, *De Trinitate*
Vera rel.	Augustine, *De Vera Religione*

1

A Free Corrector: Colin Gunton on the Trinity, Creation, and the Legacy of Augustine

Saint Augustine once wrote that when it came to his legacy, he desired "not only a pious reader but a free corrector."[1] It may be argued that he got his wish in Colin Gunton (1941–2003).

Perhaps as much as any modern theologian, Gunton sought to provide a rectification to the supposed consequences of Augustine's massive influence. His basic argument, as we will see, was that a monistic imbalance in Augustine's doctrine of God was connected to a damaging dualism in Augustine's doctrine of creation. Thus, over time, the triune God was allegedly distanced from the economy of salvation, and modernity both reaped the consequences and reacted

---

1. Augustine, *Trin.* 3. preface, 2. This translation is that of the *Nicene and Post-Nicene Fathers*, trans. Arthur Haddan, revised and annotated by W. G. T. Shedd, series 1, vol. 3 (New York: Cosimo Classics, 1887, 2007). Subsequent citations are from this same translation unless otherwise noted.

violently to this theological fragmentation. In all of this, Gunton was indeed, a *very* "free corrector" of the man from Hippo Regius. Yet a crucial question still remains: Was Gunton's reading of this history (to use Augustine's word) a "pious" one? Was it fair?

For at least one scholar who disagrees with Gunton's Augustinian narrative, it is important to note that even his harshest critiques were grounded in a commitment to the gospel. As Stephen Holmes remembers, "[Gunton's] chief glory as a teacher was that, somehow, he communicated . . . how to think . . . about theological questions in a way that hazarded all on the gospel, that can cut through the faithless games and apparently *pious* evasions."[2] For Gunton, to be a truly "pious reader" meant to question the received tradition in such a way that the gospel might again ring clear. Yet unlike Augustine, who lived long enough to sum up his literary project in the *Retractationes*, Gunton's sudden death in 2003 left what was meant to be his magnum opus (a three volume dogmatic theology) still unfinished.[3] Thus, as we have now eclipsed the ten-year anniversary of his passing, it is Gunton's work that is receiving "free correction."

In time, the eulogies give way (as they no doubt should) to scholarly critique. Trends change within theology, and while the twentieth century brought a so-called renaissance of Trinitarian thought, more recent years have brought a stiff critique of those modern theologians who might move too quickly from the inner life of God to certain social, ethical, or ecclesial applications.[4] Along these lines, Gunton's work has sometimes been included in the now

---

2. Stephen Holmes, in introduction to the posthumous publication of Colin Gunton, *The Barth Lectures*, ed. P.H. Brazier (London: T&T Clark, 2007), 7–8. Emphasis mine.
3. The first volume of this project exists only in draft form as *A Christian Dogmatic Theology*, vol. 1, *The Triune God: A Doctrine of the Trinity as Though Jesus Makes a Difference*, 2003, unpublished typescript. Cited in Robert Jenson, "A Decision Tree of Colin Gunton's Thinking," in *The Theology of Colin Gunton*, ed. Lincoln Harvey (London: T&T Clark, 2010), 16.
4. See, for instance, Stephen Holmes, *The Quest for the Trinity: The Doctrine of God in Scripture, History, and Modernity* (Downers Grove, IL: IVP Academic), 2012.

widespread critique of those theologies that may be broadly labeled as *social Trinitarianism*.[5] Thus a recent journal article even went so far as to proclaim the *failure* of Gunton's entire theological project.[6] Likewise, on the subject of Gunton and Augustine, Bradley Green has provided the lengthiest critique of Gunton's particular arguments, while drawing heavily upon the contemporary Augustine scholarship of Lewis Ayres and others.[7] Despite the value of these prior studies, it will be our contention that there is more to be said of Gunton's theological legacy. Thus the objective of this book will be to provide a *fresh* evaluation of perhaps the most disputed element of his work, the treatment of Augustine's *legacy* on the doctrine of the Trinity and the doctrine of creation.

How though will this study stand distinct from prior scholarship? While Green confined his monograph to Gunton and Augustine, the present work goes further in examining Gunton's claims regarding Augustine's "afterlife" (that is, the diverse appropriations of Augustine's thought by various medieval and early modern thinkers). To do so, while remaining within the confines of a single volume, presents a daunting challenge. Augustine's corpus is massive, and when one moves on to survey those later thinkers who have been greatly influenced by him, the amount of primary and secondary source literature quickly balloons to even more gargantuan proportions. To mitigate this considerable difficulty, we will seek the help of a noted church historian, Jaroslav Pelikan, who along with other specialists, will help us gain some perspective on Augustine's numerous intellectual descendants. The reason for selecting Pelikan

---

5. See, for instance, the lumping together of Gunton's work with that of Jürgen Moltmann. Karen Kilby, "Is an Apophatic Trinitarianism Possible?" in *International Journal of Systematic Theology*, 12, no. 1 (Jan., 2010), 65n1.
6. Bernhard Nausner, "The Failure of a Laudable Project: Gunton, the Trinity and Human Self-Understanding," *The Scottish Journal of Theology*, 62, no. 4 (2009): 403–20.
7. Bradley G. Green, *Colin Gunton and the Failure of Augustine: The Theology of Colin Gunton in Light of Augustine* (Eugene, OR: Pickwick, 2011).

rests not merely on the breadth of his historical scholarship,⁸ but also on the fact that Augustine specialist James J. O'Donnell can refer to him as the "best guide" to Augustine's massive influence upon the subsequent centuries.⁹ With this evaluation in mind, Pelikan will serve as a kind of primary arbiter between Gunton and his critics when the subject turns to Augustine's theological legacy.

In the end, the basic argument will be as follows: *while Gunton was indeed unfair to Saint Augustine, not all his claims about Augustine's "afterlife" may be so easily dismissed.* In turning especially to Augustine's intellectual descendants, we will see that certain points in Gunton's argument remain viable, albeit in more limited respects. Most notably, we will see that Gunton was justified to contend that Augustine's "inward turn" (that is, his decision to look inward in order to encounter truth, or the divine)[10] would contribute to certain problems as this notion filtered through the subsequent centuries. Ideas have unintended consequences; they evolve, and one cannot control the unique ways in which one's thought may be adapted by the subsequent tradition. Thus while one goal of this book is to defend Augustine against Gunton's often overblown critiques, another goal will be to show how Gunton was partly right in noting the way in which Augustine's "inward turn" would unwittingly contribute to a certain rationalism, individualism, and subjective introspection within the modern ethos.

Before this final verdict may be rendered, however, a more basic task must be accomplished within this opening chapter. Our purpose here will be to provide an introductory sketch of Gunton's basic claims on the (1) Trinity, (2) creation, and (3) the influence of

---

8. In the words of Mark Noll, Pelikan "chronicled the history of Christian doctrine . . . on a scale no one has attempted in the twentieth century." Mark A. Noll, "The Doctrine Doctor," in *Christianity Today*, Sept. 10, 1990, 17–8.
9. James J. O'Donnell, *Augustine: A New Biography* (New York: Harper, 2005), 336.
10. See especially Augustine, *Conf.*, 7.10. Ch. 3 will explore this move in detail.

Augustine upon these central doctrines. What exactly did Gunton claim with regard to these subjects, and how did his thinking develop in interaction with others? While the following sketch must remain brief, its placement will provide some necessary context for the more detailed work to come.

In terms of method, our approach within this opening chapter will be consistent with one of Gunton's most basic arguments: "As human persons," he wrote, "we are, in large measure, what *others* have made us."[11] We are, in Gunton's view, the result of "mutually constitutive relationships."[12] Since this was Gunton's claim, it seems fitting that an introduction to his own *project* would deal also with those *persons* who served to shape his thought. Thus we will introduce the relevant portions of Gunton's work by highlighting some (though certainly not all) of the "constitutive relationships" that helped to spawn his most distinctive theological insights.

The Trinity

We begin with the Trinity, and three figures (Barth, Coleridge, and Zizioulas) who would prove formative for Gunton's thought. From each of these constitutive relations he would both modify and selectively appropriate certain insights that would go on to characterize his constructive doctrine of the Trinity. Thus in chronicling these influences one comes to see again that Gunton's project was indeed a mixture of *retrieval* and *revision*.[13]

---

11. Colin Gunton, *The Promise of Trinitarian Theology* (London: T&T Clark, 1991), 83. Emphasis mine.
12. Ibid., 152; cf. Colin Gunton, *The Triune Creator: A Historical and Systematic Study* (Grand Rapids: Eerdmans, 1998), 208–9.
13. See Bradley Green, "Gunton and the Theological Origin of Modernity," in Harvey, *Theology of Colin Gunton*, 165–81.

Karl Barth and the Revelatory Trinity

Across the breadth of Gunton's corpus, the story starts (and almost ends) with Karl Barth (1886–1968). Gunton's own doctoral thesis, begun under the guidance of Robert Jenson,[14] examined the doctrine of God as seen in Barth and Hartshorne.[15] And while Gunton died before the task could be accomplished, he would speak in later years of a desire to write a final book on Barth, perhaps upon retirement from King's College London.[16] Sadly, this never happened, and the posthumous publication of Gunton's *Barth Lectures* is as close as we can get to Gunton's final thoughts on the great Swiss-German theologian.

Most importantly, Gunton learned from Barth that theology begins only after "God reveals himself."[17] Thus for both men, *revelation* must be granted preeminence over any system of human *reason*.[18] With regard to the Trinity, this truth is essential because if the God revealed is the Father, Son, and Holy Spirit, then the Trinity is, as Gunton put it, "[not] merely a dogma to be believed," but "the living focus of life and thought."[19] In the view of many commentators, the resurgence of Trinitarian theology within the twentieth century can be largely traced to Barth's substantial

---

14. For the importance of Jenson to Gunton's thinking, see especially Gunton's comments in "Creation and Mediation in the Theology of Robert W. Jenson: An Encounter and a Convergence," in *Trinity, Time, and Church: A Response to the Theology of Robert W. Jenson*, ed. Colin Gunton (Grand Rapids: Eerdmans, 2000), 81.
15. Colin Gunton, *Becoming and Being: The Doctrine of God in Charles Hartshorne and Karl Barth*, new ed. (London: SCM, 2001).
16. See Paul Brazier's preface to Gunton, *Barth Lectures*, xv.
17. Gunton, *Becoming and Being*, 128. See Karl Barth, *Church Dogmatics*, ed. G. W. Bromiley and T. F. Torrance, trans. G. T. Thomson and Harold Knight, vol. 1/1 (Edinburgh: T&T Clark, 1956), 296–98. Hereafter: *CD*, by volume and page number.
18. While Gunton recognized the importance of reason, his qualm was in giving it a "capital R" and allowing it to determine what theology could or could not say about God. See Gunton's posthumously published classroom lectures on this subject, *Revelation and Reason*, ed. P. H. Brazier (London: T&T Clark, 2008), 12–13; cf. *Barth Lectures*, 52.
19. Gunton, *Promise of Trinitarian Theology*, 3.

influence.[20] For Gunton, this can be glimpsed in the headings used within his own doctoral thesis. Here Hartshorne's "Neoclassical Theism" was to be contrasted with Barth's "*Trinitarian* Theology."[21]

Over time, Gunton would become increasingly dissatisfied with the *content* of Barth's theology, even while affirming the *method* of beginning with God's gracious self-revelation. In particular, he came to believe that Barth followed Augustine and "the West" in failing to be sufficiently Trinitarian in his view of God. By this, he meant that Barth sometimes displayed a tendency to (1) play time against eternity, (2) to deemphasize the full-humanity of Jesus, and (3) to neglect the role of the Holy Spirit as the *Perfector* of the project of creation.[22] While the relative merits of such claims cannot detain us here, we will return to such charges frequently when examining Gunton's claims against Augustine and his supposed influence. In the first place, Gunton took from Barth the profound conviction that belief in the Trinity should structure the way one does theology.[23]

Second, Gunton also took from Barth what may be seen as a Trinitarian polemic against the alienating effects of certain currents within modern culture.[24] As Holmes notes, "Barth, alone among the truly great theologians in [Gunton's] opinion, is one of us, he is modern, and does theology while conscious of that."[25] As will become clear, Gunton was no fan of modern Western individualism, yet this was not merely because it produced what he viewed as a fragmented, and ironically homogenized,[26] society. For Gunton, the

---

20. So says Stanley J. Grenz, *The Social God and the Relational Self: A Trinitarian Theology of the Imago Dei* (Louisville: Westminster John Knox, 2001), 4.
21. See the table of contents in Gunton, *Becoming and Being*. Emphasis mine.
22. See Gunton, *Barth Lectures*, and the 2001 epilogue to *Becoming and Being*, 225–45.
23. Stephen Holmes, "Towards the 'Analogia Personae et Relationis': Developments in Gunton's Trinitarian Thinking," in Harvey, *The Theology of Colin Gunton*, 34.
24. See Colin Gunton, *Enlightenment and Alienation: An Essay towards a Trinitarian Theology* (Grand Rapids: Eerdmans, 1985).
25. Gunton, *Revelation and Reason*, 9. For further elucidation of how Barth's doctrine of the Trinity impacted Barth's treatment of creation, see Holmes, *The Quest for the Trinity*, 6–7.

ultimate problem with an individualistic ontology is that it remains out of touch with *reality* as structured by the triune God.[27] And with this, we mark a further step in Gunton's Trinitarian development.

Samuel Taylor Coleridge and the Triune Transcendentals

If Barth provides the revelatory foundation for Gunton's doctrine of the Trinity, then a flash of applicatory inspiration came from the effusive pen of Samuel Taylor Coleridge (1772–1834).[28] Upon appointment in 1985 to the chair of Christian doctrine at King's College, Gunton gave an inaugural lecture in which he credited Coleridge for suggesting a Trinitarian hermeneutic as the *only* alternative to monistic and dualistic readings of reality.[29] Seven years later, this insight would be developed into what has been described as Gunton's most "magisterial"[30] work: *The One, the Three and the Many*.[31]

In this book, Gunton seized upon Coleridge's hint that the Trinity is the *idea idearum*, the idea that sheds light on all aspects of reality. By claiming this, Gunton sought to highlight some ways in which created being (whether things or persons) may be seen to bear the abiding marks of the Trinity. As Gunton wrote, "Of the universe as a whole we should conclude that it is marked by relationality. . . . All things are what they are by being particulars constituted by many and

---

26. See Colin Gunton, *The One, the Three and the Many: God, Creation and the Culture of Modernity* (Cambridge: Cambridge University Press, 1993), ch. 1.
27. Ibid., ch. 8; cf. Gunton, *Promise of Trinitarian Theology*, ch. 5.
28. For the crucial text, see Samuel Taylor Coleridge, "On the Prometheus of Aeschylus," *Complete Works*, ed. W. G. T. Shedd, vol. 4 (New York: Harper and Brothers, 1853), 344–65. Cited in Gunton, *Triune Creator*, 137.
29. Colin Gunton, "The One, the Three and the Many: An Inaugural Lecture in the Chair of Christian Doctrine" (London: King's College London, 1985). Cited in Holmes, "Analogia Personae," 38.
30. Stephen Holmes, "Obituary: Rev. Professor Colin E. Gunton," *Guardian*, June 3, 2003.
31. The italics distinguish the 1992 Bampton Lecture (*One, the Three and the Many*) from the 1985 lecture that preceded it.

various forms of relation. . . . All created people and things are marked by their coming from and returning to the God who is himself, in his essential and inmost being, a being in relation."[32]

For Gunton, a crucial goal behind this endeavor was to bring both diagnosis and healing to certain modern ills.[33] His claim was that only a Trinitarian perspective on all of reality can give due weight to both the One and the Many.[34] In his view, all other starting points must eventually collapse our interactions into either an individualistic pluralism or a totalitarian monism.[35] For Gunton, such false choices obliterated the "trinitarian transcendentals" (those universal marks of being) that God both embodies and, to a lesser extent, bestows upon creation. Such transcendentals were identified by Gunton as (1) *relationality,* the fact that all things are inextricably related to God, humanity and the created order;[36] (2) *particularity* (or "substantiality"),[37] the fact that all things are irreducibly and distinctly what they are;[38] and (3) *perichoresis,* the analogical means by which relationality and particularity are held together through a kind of mutual, though imperfect, reciprocity.[39]

Given his impending critique of Augustine, it is important to note what Gunton saw to be a distinction between his "triune transcendentals" and the Augustinian search for the *vestigia trinitatis.* While both methods found traces of the Trinity within created being, Gunton's charge was that Augustine focused on mathematical patterns of "three-in-one-ness" within the individual human person.

---

32. Gunton, *One, the Three and the Many,* 229.
33. Ibid., 2.
34. See also Colin Gunton, *A Brief Theology of Revelation* (Edinburgh: T&T Clark, 1995), 62.
35. Gunton, *One, the Three and the Many,* 7.
36. Ibid., ch. 6.
37. Ibid., 195. Here Gunton explains his synonymous usage of the two terms (*particularity* and *substantiality*). To avoid confusion, we will hereafter refer to *particularity* because Gunton makes use of it more frequently.
38. Ibid., ch. 7.
39. Ibid., 163–79.

Thus Augustine would devote much time, especially in the latter books of *De Trinitate*, to locating the presence of sacred triads within the inner realm of the individual human mind.[40] In response to this allegedly individual focus, Gunton believed that the search for such internal *vestigia* "obscure[d] the real possibilities for a relational ontology,"[41] while the transcendentals do just the opposite by highlighting how all of creation bears the indelible marks of a triune Maker.[42] We shall have to examine the viability of this claim.

Despite this search for "transcendentals" within *The One, the Three and the Many*, Gunton would also admit that this project had led him into the "perilous" territory of theological "speculation."[43] His critics seize upon this fact,[44] and there is evidence that Gunton himself would later move beyond this enterprise. With the 1992 Bampton Lectures behind him, Holmes noted that "the hermeneutical deployment of the doctrine of the Trinity . . . would cease to figure prominently in [Gunton's] work."[45] With this shift noted, we may now transition from Gunton's Trinitarian perspective on the *universe*, to his Trinitarian perspective on human *personhood*.

John Zizioulas and the Cappadocian Achievement

Even while Gunton was engaged in the metaphysical employment of the Trinity in order to unearth the triune transcendentals, another key relationship was forming. From the Greek Orthodox bishop John Zizioulas (b. 1931), he was introduced to what he would come to see as an Eastern corrective to Western (often spoken of as

---

40. See ch. 3.
41. Gunton, *One, the Three and the Many*, 144n23. Gunton was exposed to at least one critique of Augustine's *vestigia* through Barth. See Gunton, *Becoming and Being*, 136.
42. See Holmes, "Analogia Personae," 39.
43. Gunton, *One, the Three and the Many*, 167.
44. See ch. 2.
45. See Holmes, "Analogia Personae," 39.

"Augustinian") theological errors.[46] While Gunton had initially shared Barth's squeamishness regarding the language of triune "persons,"[47] Zizioulas would later mediate the work of the Cappadocian Fathers to him, which would demonstrate, at least in Gunton's mind, that the "personal" is indeed *primordial* in terms of God's being.[48]

Here God's unity was not to be found, as it supposedly would be after Augustine, in some underlying divine substance, but rather in the *koinonia* of particular and perichoretic *persons*.[49] As Gunton wrote,

> It is, of course, to the Cappadocians and particularly to Basil that the real development of a relational conception of the person is owed. By giving priority to the concept of person in their doctrine of God, they transform at once the meaning of both concepts [*ousia/hypostasis*]. The being of God is not now understood in the way characteristic of Greek metaphysics, but in terms of communion. God *is* "a sort of continuous and indivisible community" says the letter usually attributed to Basil of Caesarea.... The being of God consists in the community of *hypostaseis* who give and receive their reality to and from one another.[50]

In all of this we will see that Gunton's claims have been profoundly challenged.[51] Yet for now, we merely note how Gunton's

---

46. See Colin Gunton, "Persons and Particularity," in *The Theology of John Zizioulas: Personhood and the Church*, ed. Douglas Knight (Burlington, VT: Ashgate, 2007).
47. See the 2001 epilogue to *Becoming and Being*; cf. Gunton, *Enlightenment and Alienation*, 141.
48. Gunton, "Persons and Particularity," 100. This dovetails with the notion that personhood is both an eschatological and a "protological" concept. On the latter, Gunton cites Graham McFarlane's research as illustrative of this point. See Gunton, *Promise of Trinitarian Theology*, 115.
49. Cf. John Zizioulas, *Being as Communion*, 88. Cited in Gunton, "Persons and Particularity," 100. In contrast to Zizioulas, Gunton was wary of what he saw to be an Eastern overemphasis upon the priority of the Father as the "source" of the Trinity. See Gunton, "Persons and Particularity," 103. For evidence that Gunton was moving toward Zizioulas in even this regard, see Paul Cumin's comments on Gunton's partially completed dogmatics. Cumin, "The Taste of Cake," in Harvey, *Theology of Colin Gunton*.
50. Gunton, *Promise of Trinitarian Theology*, 94.
51. See ch. 2.

understanding of triune persons came to shed new light on his view of human personhood.

By selectively retrieving and revising Trinitarian insights from the likes of Barth, Coleridge, and Zizioulas, Gunton could now state that "it is in our relatedness to *others* that our being human consists."[52] In this, he distanced himself from any attempt to identify the *imago Dei* as an individual possession. That was the alleged fault of Augustine, and in Gunton's view, the West had never recovered from this theological error. As he argued, the human mind was not an image of the Trinity, rather human persons are, for "to be a person is to be distinct from other persons, and yet inextricably bound up with them."[53]

In this way, Gunton came to view the concept of *human personhood* in the light of the triune God.[54] Yet for him, this link was made possible only through the embodiment of the one who is indeed the true "image of the invisible God" (Col. 1:15).[55] Because creation was formed "in" the Son (Col. 1:16), it was, for Gunton, the person of Christ, as sustained by the Holy Spirit, who allowed for a relation between a holy God and a fallen world.[56] And with this christological bridge in place, we are now prepared to provide a brief introduction to Gunton's distinctive doctrine of creation.

---

52. Colin Gunton, "Trinity, Ontology and Anthropology: Towards a Renewal of the Doctrine of the *Imago Dei*," in *Persons, Divine and Human: King's College Essays in Theological Anthropology*, ed. Christoph Schwöbel and Colin Gunton (Edinburgh: T&T Clark, 1991), 58. Italics mine.
53. Colin Gunton, *The Christian Faith: An Introduction to Christian Doctrine* (Oxford: Blackwell, 2002), 43.
54. Gunton, *Triune Creator*, 209.
55. Subsequent biblical citations from the NIV (2011), unless otherwise noted.
56. Gunton, *Triune Creator*, 140–43. Gunton's emphasis on creation "in the Son" rather than "in God" *simpliciter* distinguishes his Trinitarian doctrine of creation from the panentheism of Moltmann and others. See Gunton, *Triune Creator*, 141–43.

Creation (and Mediation)

For Gunton, an understanding of God's triune *being* was inextricably related to God's mediated *action* within history.[57] Thus, as we turn from the doctrine of the Trinity to the doctrine of creation, we find yet another set of constitutive relationships. First, in the imagery of Irenaeus, Gunton spoke of creation (and mediation) by virtue of God's "two hands," the Son and Holy Spirit. And secondly, through the help of John Owen and Edward Irving, Gunton's pneumatology came to emphasize the Spirit's role in perfecting both the sonship of Jesus and the project of creation. We turn now to survey these facets of Gunton's theology.

Irenaeus and the "Hands" Of God

Gunton would refer to Irenaeus (c. 140–202 AD) as "the church's greatest theologian of creation,"[58] and among his favorite references to the second-century bishop stood the metaphor of God and his "two hands."[59] For Gunton, this imagery revealed how God could act within, while remaining distinct from, the universe itself. As he wrote, "I do not think we can do better than to hold to Irenaeus' straightforward characterization of God's action in the world: The Father works . . . by means of his two hands, the Son and the Spirit. . . . In sum: all divine action, whether in creation, salvation or final

---

57. Thus the title of Gunton's Trinitarian reappropriation of the divine attributes: *Act and Being: Towards a Theology of the Divine Attributes* (London: SCM Press, 2002).
58. Gunton, *Christian Faith*, 10.
59. See Irenaeus, *Against the Heresies* [hereafter, *AH*] 4.20.1: "It was not angels . . . who made us, nor who formed us . . . nor anyone else, except the Word of the Lord. . . . For God did not stand in need of these [beings] . . . as if He did not possess His own hands . . . the Son and the Spirit, by whom and in whom, freely and spontaneously, He made all things." Unless otherwise noted, subsequent citations from the *Ante-Nicene Fathers*, ed. A. Robertson, J. Donaldson, A.C. Cox, trans. Dominic J. Unger, vol. 1 (Grand Rapids: Eerdmans, 1987).

redemption is the action of God the Father . . . brought about by his two hands."[60]

In the dualism of Irenaeus's gnostic opponents, Gunton saw a mirror image of the modern West: "Whereas ancient thought tended to abstract Jesus Christ from history by eternalizing him . . . modern thought tends to abstract him from eternity by making his temporality absolute."[61] From this perspective, so-called Platonic dualisms were "from above," whereas so-called Enlightenment dualisms were "from below."[62] Despite their differences, Gunton believed that both paradigms resulted in a kind of "schizophrenia" regarding the relationship between Christ and creation.

The glory of Irenaeus, at least in Gunton's view, was that while "philosopher-theologians"[63] (often typified by Augustine) sought to connect God to creation by such things as (1) the conduit of the rational mind, (2) the assistance of angelic intermediaries, (3) the appeal to general revelation or (4) the retreat to divine omnipotence, Irenaeus pointed to the *divine economy*.[64] Here God was seen as relating personally to the world by virtue of the Son and Spirit. Thus, for Gunton, both ancient and modern dualisms must be overcome by a theology of triune mediation.[65]

It is important to note that Gunton used the language of *mediation* in two distinct, though related, ways.[66] First, in reference to the

---

60. Colin Gunton, *Father, Son, and Holy Spirit: Toward a Fully Trinitarian Theology* (London: T&T Clark, 2003), 79–80.
61. Colin Gunton, *Yesterday and Today: A Study of Continuities of Christology* (Grand Rapids: Eerdmans, 1983), 53.
62. See Schwöbel, "The Shape of Colin Gunton's Theology," in Harvey, *Theology of Colin Gunton*, 187.
63. Gunton uses this pejorative in *Yesterday and Today*, 42.
64. By the *economy*, Gunton meant "God's actions taking place in time according to the biblical account." *Triune Creator*, 77.
65. Gunton, *Yesterday and Today*, 95.
66. This insight comes by way of David Höhne, *Spirit and Sonship: Colin Gunton's Theology of Particularity and the Holy Spirit* (Burlington, VT: Ashgate, 2010), 29.

Irenaean image of God and his "two hands," Gunton emphasized how the Father acts through the Son immanently, while acting through the Spirit transcendently to bring creation to its appointed end.[67] In keeping with this metaphor, the Son and Spirit are the means by which God is present in creation, while at the same time giving the creation space to be itself. Gunton would again refer to this concept of distinctness-in-relation as the notion of "particularity." Thus a proper account of mediation allows one to avoid the twin evils of both a pantheistic monism and a distant deism in which God becomes a kind of absentee landlord. Second, and in relation to the life of Jesus, Gunton also used the language of *mediation* to describe how God upholds the humanity of Christ through the Spirit, which enables Jesus to fulfill his salvific mission.[68] Yet to understand fully this pneumatological development in Gunton's thinking, we must note how the work of John Owen (1616–1683) and Edward Irving (1792–1834) would prove essential in showing how the Spirit enables the sonship of Jesus and perfects the project of creation.

John Owen and Edward Irving: The Perfecting Spirit

Before addressing the pneumatological advance that Gunton found in Owen and Irving, we must first address the supposed theological error that he desired to correct by virtue of it. Gunton had long decried what he saw as a "docetic tendency" within many orthodox Christologies.[69] It was this concern that would even lead him to distance himself from the Definition of Chalcedon as it pertained to the "two natures" of Christ. As Gunton wrote, "Another cause

---

67. See Gunton, *Triune Creator*, 192.
68. See Gunton, *Christian Faith*, 101–2.
69. Colin Gunton, *Christ and Creation*, the Didsbury Lectures, 1990 (Eugene, OR: Wipf and Stock, 2005), 70. See also *Yesterday and Today*, 15.

for offence in the modern world is the doctrine of 'two natures': that Christ was, according to the language of the tradition 'one person in two natures.' This has sometimes led to the appearance of a kind of hybrid being, two contrary realities stitched together, like a centaur, suggesting two persons rather than one person in two natures."[70] As evidence of this "centaur Christology," Gunton pointed to the tendency to ascribe certain actions (for instance, weeping and fatigue) to the humanity of Jesus, while assigning others (for instance, miracles and forgiveness) to his divinity.[71] For Gunton, this represented "the judgment of Solomon" as the personhood of Christ was effectively cut in two.[72]

To avoid such dichotomies, Gunton adopted the position known as *monothelitism*: the belief that Christ had but one will.[73] By this, he sought to emphasize both the unity and the humanity of the Messiah. As Gunton argued, "There are not two wills within Jesus, only two at work in his career, his will and the will of his Father."[74] Yet herein lies a crucial question: How is it possible to maintain the full divinity of Jesus, which Gunton saw as essential, without recourse to either the language of Chalcedon or the logic of modern kenoticism?[75] Gunton's answer was a pneumatological one.

Taking cues from Basil of Caesarea, Gunton recognized the Spirit as the *perfecting cause* within the Trinity.[76] Yet it was the influence of John Owen and Edward Irving that would put this pneumatological insight to its christological use.[77] From Owen, Gunton found

---

70. Gunton, *Christian Faith*, 78–9.
71. Ibid., 79; also, *Christ and Creation*, 81. For Augustine's employment of this tactic, see *Trin.* 1.
72. Gunton, *Yesterday and Today*, 180.
73. Monothelitism was condemned at the seventh-century Council of Constantinople.
74. Gunton, *Christian Faith*, 109–10; See also *Act and Being*, 29–30.
75. Gunton saw modern kenotic theories to be "essentially dualistic," while arguing that one may speak of a "self-emptying" of God, "only if it is understood in such a way as to be an *expression* rather than a 'retraction' of his deity." *Yesterday and Today*, 172. Emphasis his.
76. Basil, *On the Holy Spirit*, 15, 36, 38. Cited in Gunton, *Father, Son, and Holy Spirit*, 81.
77. See Gunton, *Brief Theology of Revelation*, 28.

resistance to the notion that the human Jesus was "pushed around" by his divine nature.[78] This false option supposedly presented Christ's humanity as something "preprogrammed," either by the transcendent *Logos asarkos*, or by the innate possession of the Holy Spirit from the time of his conception.[79] For Gunton, both alternatives presented a Jesus who was a kind of *tertium quid*, a hybrid being, who was not, as Hebrews presents him, like us in every way, apart from sin (Heb. 4:15).[80]

In the face of these supposedly faulty options, Gunton found in Irving a controversial corrective.[81] As he would come to argue, it was by free submission to the Spirit that the *fallen* humanity of Jesus was sustained and perfected. As Gunton wrote, "[Jesus] is not only fully human, but in some way also shares our fallen condition. . . . The Son is—we might say—enabled to be the Son by virtue of the way the Spirit realizes and perfects the love between him and the Father. Only so are the three truly one God."[82] In all of this, Gunton's goal was to show that "Christ is not only Lord of creation, but also part of it,"[83] even to the point of sharing in our fallenness.[84]

As we will see, this view of Jesus is yet another aspect of Gunton's theology that has been challenged.[85] Yet in his own mind, this brand of "Spirit-enabled Christology" showed once again how the triune God works *within*, while respecting the particularity *of*, the created

---

78. See Gunton, *Christian Faith*, 103; cf. *Promise of Trinitarian Theology*, 69. Gunton credited Alan Spence for directing him to key references in Owen. See *Promise of Trinitarian Theology*, 69.
79. This was Augustine's view (see *Trin.* 15.46). For Gunton, this resulted in a Jesus whose actions were "predetermined" by the Holy Spirit as a kind of "automatic pilot." *Christ and Creation*, 49.
80. Gunton, *Christ and Creation*, 34.
81. See Gunton, "Two Dogmas Revisited: Edward Irving's Christology," in *The Scottish Journal of Theology* 41 (1988): 359–76.
82. Gunton, *Christian Faith*, 101. Here Gunton appeals to Rom. 8:3: God sent his Son "in the likeness of sinful flesh."
83. Gunton, *Christ and Creation*, 25.
84. See Gunton, *Triune Creator*, 192, 223–24; See also *The Actuality of Atonement: A Study of Metaphor, Rationality, and the Christian Tradition* (Grand Rapids: Eerdmans, 1989), 131.
85. See ch. 2.

order. Thus for Gunton, one must never abstract the topic of creation from that of Christ.[86]

Gunton's Constructive Theology of the Triune Creator

In gathering the strands from these and other constitutive relations, Gunton developed his distinctive doctrine of creation. Here, the Edenic habitation was not a *paradise*, but a *project* that was meant to culminate in something even better than a yet-to-be-fully tended garden.[87] As an unnecessitated (and *ex nihilo*) project, the created order was granted intrinsic value.[88] And as the project of a God who "takes his time" (as evidenced by the language of days in Genesis 1), there was no basis for eschewing either temporal being or goodness.[89]

For Gunton, such truths should have allayed the fears of both ancient Platonists and modern fundamentalists, who, in different ways, approached the creation narratives with faulty presuppositions.[90] Through his own theology, Gunton sought to correct such errors, yet in doing so, he increasingly found himself in conflict with a pervasive and (allegedly) problematic force: the massive influence of Augustine. Thus we turn now to a final, and ironically "constitutive" relationship.

Augustine's "Honied Poison"

It was from Barth that Gunton picked up a rather unflattering description of Augustine's theological influence. In certain regards,

---

86. See Gunton, *Triune Creator*, 192.
87. Gunton, *Triune Creator*, 12, 197, 202; cf. *Christian Faith*, 25, 29. It was for this reason that Gunton adopted the view of John Duns Scotus that there would have been an incarnation even if Adam had not fallen (*Triune Creator*, 121).
88. Gunton, *Triune Creator*, 9–10.
89. See especially Gunton, *Triune Creator*, ch. 4.
90. Provided that we affirm God as Creator, Gunton sees the discussion of evolution as irrelevant to Christian belief. See *Triune Creator*, 87.

Augustine's brilliant and voluminous writings were to be seen *not* as the triumph of orthodox theology, but as "honied poison."[91] Nowhere was this evaluation more accurate, in Gunton's mind, than in the previously surveyed doctrines of the Trinity and creation.

To be sure, Gunton was hardly alone in his critique of Augustine on such points.[92] As Neil Ormerod claims, Augustine became "the whipping boy of much modern Trinitarian theology."[93] Yet in Gunton's work especially, it would sometimes seem that Augustine was "not [only] a whipping boy but the whip"(!) by which subsequent thinkers were marked out as problematic.[94] With this in mind, our goal here is merely to outline very briefly Gunton's indictments against Augustine and his influence. We begin with the doctrine of the Trinity.

Augustine and the Trinity

Whereas Gunton learned from Barth that a triune model of revelation must take preeminence over any system of human reason, he claimed to find the corruption of this notion in Augustine. Thus, in the unrestrained context of the lecture hall, Gunton could allege that in Augustine

---

91. Or "sweet poison" (*süβes Gift*). See Gunton, *Father, Son, and Holy Spirit,* 41. For an example of Barth using the epithet in print, see Karl Barth, *The Holy Spirit and the Christian Life: The Theological Basis of Ethics,* trans. R. Birch Hoyle (Louisville: Westminster John Knox Press, 1993), 22. Most notably, Barth used the phrase in reference to Augustine's tendency toward determinism. See also T. F. Torrance, *Karl Barth, Biblical and Evangelical Theologian* (Edinburgh: T&T Clark, 1990), 122. Credit goes to my doctoral supervisor Thomas A. Noble for first introducing me to this colorful phrase.
92. For a historical survey of somewhat similar critiques against Augustine, including those of Harnack, Barth, Boff, Moltmann, Charles Taylor, Robert Jenson and John Zizioulas, see Bradley Green, *Gunton and the Failure of Augustine,* ch. 1.
93. Neil Ormerod, "Augustine and the Trinity: Whose Crisis?" in *Pacifica* 16, Feb., 2003, 17.
94. This phrase is used to describe the pro-Nicene treatment of Arius and subsequent "Arians." Maurice Wiles, "Attitudes to Arius in the Arian Controversy," in *Arianism after Arius,* ed. M. R. Barnes and D. H. Williams (Edinburgh: T&T Clark, 2000), 43.

we have a combination of Hebrew Revelation and Greek reason. This is a difficult "marriage" because in Revelation you are taught, whereas in reason you find out for yourself. Yes, that's a generalization, and although we should avoid generalizations I think it is one that is fair. . . . Augustine fused them, combined them, and he combines what we might call the rational quest for God and situation where God meets us halfway.[95]

While taking into account the fact that few, if any, instructors might like for their impromptu classroom comments to be committed to print upon their death, the above excerpt reveals something of the problem Gunton saw in Augustine's use of revelation and human reason.

Second, whereas Gunton found in Coleridge a way of seeing all reality as bearing the abiding marks of the Trinity, he came to reject what he saw as Augustine's habit of connecting the *vestigia trinitatis* to the internal qualities of the rational human mind.[96] As Gunton wrote, "The crucial analogy for Augustine is between the inner structure of the human mind and the inner being of God, because it is in the former that the latter is made known . . . more really than in the 'outer' economy of grace."[97] Here in the so-called psychological analogies of *De Trinitate*, where Augustine found a certain "image" of the Trinity within himself,[98] Gunton saw a tendency toward an inward-facing monistic imbalance. Thus, as he put it, there was "in Augustine, and in most Western theology after him, a tendency towards modalism."[99] This suspicion of a monistic and modalistic view of God was then confirmed, for Gunton, by Augustine's alleged

---

95. Gunton, *Revelation and Reason*, 108–9.
96. It is possible that Gunton was also influenced by Barth in this critique. See Barth, *CD*, 1/1, 335–36.
97. Gunton, *Promise of Trinitarian Theology*, 45.
98. See, for instance, Augustine, *Trin.* 9.12.18. A detailed exploration of these mental similitudes must await ch. 3.
99. Gunton, *Promise of Trinitarian Theology*, 42.

inability to grasp what Zizioulas noted as the Cappadocian achievement in Trinitarian theology.

Third, while the Cappadocians supposedly emphasized the *koinonia* of divine persons, Augustine famously admitted that he did not know what distinction "the Greeks" had wished to make between the one *ousia* and the three *hypostases*.[100] In this, Gunton saw an abiding failure to give due weight to the particularity of the Father, Son and Holy Spirit. As he wrote,

> [Augustine's] relatively brief and sketchy discussion of the ontological status of the three persons in God shows him asking a different kind of question from that asked by the Cappadocians: not, What kind of being is this, that God is to be found in the relations of Father, Son and Spirit? But, What kind of sense can be made of the apparent logical oddity of the threeness of the one God in terms of Aristotelian subject-predicate logic?[101]

In terms of the Trinity, these beliefs led Gunton to a bold conclusion: Augustine's brilliant and influential writings had bequeathed to his descendants a view of God that was skewed toward monism, modalism, and an otherwise unhealthy overemphasis upon the divine unity.[102] Future chapters will evaluate this sweeping charge, yet for now, we turn to its corollary.

Augustine and Creation

While Gunton sensed a monistic imbalance in Augustine's doctrine of the Trinity, he saw a damaging *dualism* in his treatment of creation.[103] The roots of this problem were to be traced "in every case" to Augustine's "continuing adherence to platonic ways of

---

100. Augustine, *Trin.* 5.10.
101. Gunton, *Promise of Trinitarian Theology*, 40–41.
102. See Gunton, *One, the Three and the Many*, 138; *Act and Being*, 134–5; *Father, Son, and Holy Spirit*, 33.
103. See, for instance, Gunton, *One, the Three and the Many*, 2–3, 55.

thought."[104] As Gunton put it, "With the platonists, [Augustine] found it difficult to believe that the material and sensible realm could either be truly real or the object or the vehicle of knowledge."[105] The specifics of this claim, including the controversial question of Augustine's "Platonism," must be taken up in later chapters.[106] For now, however, we will merely note what Gunton saw to be the evidence of Augustine's failure. In his view, Augustine's problem was to be evidenced in a deficient treatment of (1) time, (2) matter, and (3) triune mediation.

(1) Augustine and Time

For Gunton, an Irenaean emphasis on the divine economy revealed a God who "takes his time" in perfecting the project of creation. Yet in Augustine there was a decision to replace the days of Genesis 1 with a view of creation as an instantaneous act. Indeed, as Augustine argued, the language of days was only used as a concession to "weaker souls." In reality, God created all things instantaneously.[107] In this move, Gunton sensed a Platonic tendency to elevate the *timeless* at the expense of the *temporal*. Thus the specific strand of dualism to be seen here was an undue opposition between time and eternity. As Gunton wrote, "To be in time is, for Augustine, despite his confidence in the good divine creation, to be in a sphere of existence *finally lacking in reality*. Here lies the ambiguity, the two-headedness, that was to

---

104. Gunton, *Triune Creator*, 74.
105. Gunton, *Promise of Trinitarian Theology*, 33.
106. With regard to terminology, I will follow Lewis Ayres in consciously using the wider term *Platonism* to "designate ideas that are found in a range of Christian and non-Christian authors beyond the bounds of neo-Platonism as such." In this way, *Neoplatonism* will be restricted to those areas in which men like Plotinus (and, at times, Augustine) stood notably apart from earlier Platonic traditions. See Lewis Ayres, *Augustine and the Trinity* (Cambridge: Cambridge University Press, 2010), 13n3.
107. Here Gunton cites Augustine's *Unfinished Literal Commentary on Genesis* (*Gn. litt. imp.*), 3.7. Unfortunately, Gunton confusingly cites this work as Augustine's *Literal Interpretation* (*Triune Creator*, 77). For the sake of clarity, we will use the more precise title.

fly apart so disastrously . . . some thousand years later."[108] In this, Gunton traced a scarlet thread from Augustine to Kant and the idea that temporal realities may be but a projection of the human mind.[109]

(2) Augustine and Matter

Similarly, in the treatment of *materiality*, Gunton saw an abiding tension between Augustine's various statements. On the one hand, as he matured, Augustine's denunciations of his youthful (Manichaen) dualism became more pronounced. Yet for Gunton, this was not sufficient. As he put it, "Augustine continued to be marked by the scars of the Manichaeism from which he was so desperate to be healed."[110] In reference to the *Confessions,* Gunton wrote, "We cannot emphasise this too strongly. Matter is not 'very good,' but 'close to being nothing' [*Conf.* 12.7]."[111] The cause of this, in Gunton's view, was that in contrast to Irenaeus, "Augustine is not moving from the incarnation to the goodness of the created order. He is defending a position once established by that means, but now tends to leave them firmly in the background."[112] In terms of Augustine's legacy, Gunton believed that this devaluing of the material world would contribute to an eschatology of escapism within the West, in which the ultimate desire was not for a kingdom come on earth, but for a portion of humanity to be taken happily to heaven.[113]

---

108. Gunton, *Yesterday and Today*, 109–10. Italics original.
109. Ibid., 110. Here Gunton refers to *Conf.* 12.8 to show Augustine wondering whether time might be but an extension of his mind. For the connection to Kant, see Gunton, *One, the Three and the Many*, ch. 3.
110. Gunton, *Triune Creator*, 79.
111. Ibid., 78.
112. Ibid., 74.
113. Gunton, *Promise of Trinitarian Theology*, 172–73.

(3) Augustine and Triune Mediation

For Gunton, these previous oppositions (between time and eternity and matter and spirit) could have been averted by a greater emphasis upon the (Spirit-empowered) christological mediation of God's good creation. Thus while the subject of triune mediation does not represent a third dualism, it does, for Gunton, illustrate the profound consequences of Augustine's ill-formed doctrine of creation. Gunton's charge was that if one cannot think rightly about time and matter, then one is destined to think wrongly about the most central of Christian doctrines: the incarnation.[114]

While acknowledging the centrality of the incarnation for Augustine ("For Augustine, that doctrine was central"),[115] Gunton believed that the need to refute certain Arian opponents[116] led Augustine to make Christ's divinity "more important" than his humanity.[117] Thus the Spirit-enabled mediatorship of the *incarnate* Christ was allegedly impinged upon by other *nonphysical* mediators: most notably (1) the angels, (2) the naked will of God, (3) the *Logos asarkos*, and (4) the immaterial human soul. Later chapters must examine these contentions, yet for now our goal is merely to introduce the charge that Augustine's failure with regard to mediation was linked to a dualistic elevation of mind over matter,

---

114. Ibid., 34; we will return to this theme in ch. 4.
115. Ibid., 33.
116. Recent patristic specialists have pointed out the danger in using the heresiological label "Arian" to describe subsequent thinkers who subscribed to some version of a "Homoian" Christology. As Lewis Ayres notes, "it is virtually impossible to identify a school of thought dependent on Arius' specific theology, and certainly impossible to show that even a bare majority of Arians had any extensive knowledge of Arius' writing." While this is indeed a helpful historical reminder, the present book will, with some hesitation, continue to employ the Arian label, not as a genealogical term which indicates allegiance and full agreement with Arius himself, but as a commonly recognized theological label that allows us to point to the diverse array of thinkers who denied (in some way) that the Son (or *Logos*) was eternally *homoousios* with the Father and thus fully divine. See Ayres, *Nicaea and its Legacy: An Approach to Fourth-Century Trinitarian Theology* (Oxford: Oxford University Press, 2004), 2–3.
117. Gunton, *Promise of Trinitarian Theology*, 34.

and a drift toward modern inwardness and individualism.[118] In all of this, Augustine's supposed errors in the doctrine of the Trinity were linked to other errors in his treatment of created being.

Some Partial Praise for Augustine

Given the breadth of the above critiques, a further question now presents itself: Did Gunton ever praise Augustine? In fact, he did find value in certain aspects of Augustine's thought. First, Gunton conceded that Augustine did *sometimes* speak of God's relation to the world in christological terms. Most notably, he affirmed Augustine's defense of creation *ex nihilo* on the christological ground that any other view (for instance, emanation) must posit a preexisting substance that would then be equal to God's Son in terms of eternality.[119] In the same vein, Gunton also spoke positively about the christological orientation of Augustine's sacramental theology. Here the fruit of creation (bread and wine) became, in Augustine, "visible words," which bore a relation to the *Word* made flesh.[120] In these instances Christ and creation were related positively, and Gunton praised Augustine for it.

Second, with regard to epistemology, Gunton applauded Augustine's notion that all knowledge is a gift of grace. As Augustine put it, "Unless you believe you will not understand."[121] For Gunton, this dictum could be seen as a source for Anselm's *fides quaerens intellectum*,[122] and an inauguration of a "post-critical philosophy"[123] that would inspire the likes of Barth and Polanyi.[124] Third, Gunton

---

118. Ibid., 43; cf. Gunton, *One, the Three and the Many*, 203.
119. See Augustine, *Conf.* 12.7. Of this passage, Gunton states, "This is one of the rare places where Augustine treats the doctrine of creation Christologically." *Triune Creator*, 75.
120. Gunton, *Christian Faith*, 130.
121. See Gunton, *Enlightenment and Alienation*, 3, 51, 131.
122. Gunton, *Barth Lectures*, 64–5.
123. Gunton, *Enlightenment and Alienation*, 51.

also spoke positively of Augustine's foresight in avoiding wooden literalism in his treatment of the creation narratives (although the supposed Platonic motivation for this symbolic reading remained troublesome for Gunton).[125] And fourth, in terms of temporality, Gunton affirmed Augustine for asserting that the world was created *with* and not *in* time, as the latter would again imply that something else existed eternally alongside God.[126]

Yet on the whole, these partial agreements with Augustine were not the focus of Gunton's attention. In fact, as we have seen already, Gunton's true focus was never on Augustine at all, but upon the supposed modern and medieval repercussions of Augustine's influence. Thus in the unrestrained context of the classroom, Gunton would even go so far as to claim that "in a sense all Western thought is a variation on Augustine."[127] This was no compliment. And as we might expect, such sweeping statements have left Gunton open to withering critiques. These will be the topic of the following chapter. Within this opening chapter, our aim has been merely to introduce the basic shape of Gunton's arguments on the Trinity, creation, and the supposedly baneful Augustine upon these doctrines.

Conclusion

Our claim has been that distinctive elements of Gunton's project may be introduced through some of the "constitutive relations" that served

---

124. See Karl Barth, *Fides Quaerens Intellectum. Anselm's Proof of the Existence of God in the Context of His Theological Scheme*, trans. I. W. Robertson (London: SCM Press, 1960), 25–26. Also, Michael Polanyi, *Personal Knowledge. Towards a Post-Critical Philosophy* (London: Routledge, 1962). Cited in Gunton, *Enlightenment and Alienation*, 51.
125. Gunton, *Enlightenment and Alienation*, 81. On this point, Gunton cites Augustine against modern fundamentalist "creationism."
126. See Augustine, *De Civitate Dei*, 11.6; hereafter *Civ.* Cited in Gunton, *Triune Creator*, 82.
127. Gunton, *Revelation and Reason*, 42. As seen in other classroom lectures, Gunton could openly admit that his offhand statements on Augustine were prone to "bias" and "generalisation." *Barth Lectures*, 96.

to shape his thought. On the one hand, this may seem a rather strange approach. We have perhaps been taught that a person's uniqueness (their "particularity") is best understood in the ways that they stand utterly apart from others. Yet Gunton fought against this notion. Thus the *form* of this chapter has been connected to the *content* of his work.

First, by selectively retrieving insights from the likes of Barth, Coleridge, and Zizioulas, Gunton sought to orient all of Christian thought "under the heading of trinitarian theology."[128] Second, by coupling his view of the Trinity with an emphasis on creation and mediation, Gunton sought to show how our understanding of God's *triune being* is directly related to his *mediated action* within the divine economy. Thus, "the project of creation is realized," only "as the Holy Spirit offers it, perfected, to the Father through the Son."[129]

Yet finally, in this process of retrieval, we also noted Gunton's propensity for *revision*. Most notably in Augustine, Gunton saw a devastating movement toward *monism* in the doctrine of God, and *dualism* in the doctrine of creation. As these false emphases supposedly filtered through the centuries, Gunton claimed that in Augustine we have "the Achilles' heel of all Western theology."[130] As such statements illustrate, Gunton was at times a very "free corrector" of Augustine's legacy. Yet to offer free critique is also to invite it. Thus having introduced these elements of Gunton's theology, we turn next to see how they have been profoundly challenged.

---

128. So says Christoph Schwöbel, "The Shape of Colin Gunton's Theology," 182.
129. Gunton, *Promise of Trinitarian Theology*, 91.
130. Gunton, *Becoming and Being*, 238 (2001 epilogue).

2

Critiques Of Colin Gunton: Challenges on the Trinity, Creation, and the Legacy of Augustine

While the prior chapter introduced Gunton's treatment of the Trinity, creation, and the legacy of Augustine, the present chapter will show how these aspects of his work have been profoundly challenged. We will begin by surveying the various critiques of Gunton on the subject of Augustine and his supposed influence. Next, we will turn to Gunton's constructive doctrine of the Trinity, and to the charge of *projectionism* as leveled against his "Cappadocian alternative" to Augustine's purported errors. Finally, we will turn to Gunton's "neo-Irenaean"[1] doctrine of creation, and to the charge that in his rush to distance himself from Augustine's supposed dualism,

---

1. See Lincoln Harvey's use of this designation in his introduction to *The Theology of Colin Gunton*, ed. Lincoln Harvey (London: T&T Clark, 2010), 2.

Gunton may have wrongfully identified the incarnate Christ with a *fallen* world.

In all of this, our survey of various arguments must again remain brief. The goal of this chapter is therefore merely to elucidate the content of a given charge, to note the relevant literature behind it, and to highlight important questions that will demand attention at a later time. In so doing, we will demonstrate that aspects of Gunton's project stand in need of further examination, and we will also note how the remainder of this work will allow us to evaluate many of the charges highlighted in this chapter. We begin with Saint Augustine.

Critiques of Gunton on Augustine

As Holmes notes, "[Gunton] was master of the grand historical narrative, and would tell big stories spanning centuries to illustrate what he regarded as the key historical developments."[2] This broadbrushed telling of theological history reportedly gave his students the sense that ideas matter, yet it also left Gunton open to the charge of historical distortion.[3] On the subject of Augustine, even some of Gunton's relative allies were forced to acknowledge that their friend had a tendency to "overdo it."[4] For John Webster, Gunton's judgments on Augustine were "breathtakingly tendentious,"[5] while Christoph Schwöbel says that they were "unfair perhaps" and wishes that readers could see the good-natured smile that would often accompany Gunton's most sweeping critiques. As Schwöbel writes, "In his lectures Gunton could be disconcertingly open about his prejudices, as for example, when he admits that the view he has just

---

2. Holmes, in his introduction to *Revelation and Reason*, ed. P. H. Brazier (London: T&T Clark, 2008), 7.
3. Ibid., 7–8.
4. Jenson, "A Decision Tree of Colin Gunton's Thinking," in Harvey, *Theology of Colin Gunton*, 11–12.
5. Webster, "Gunton and Barth," in Harvey, *Theology of Colin Gunton*, 18.

developed 'is a biased one because I don't like Augustine. I think he is the fountainhead of our troubles.'"[6]

As seen previously, the fullest engagement with Gunton's specific arguments on Augustine has come by way of Bradley Green. In the published version of his doctoral dissertation (*Colin Gunton and the Failure of Augustine*), Green draws frequently upon the Augustine scholarship of Lewis Ayres and Michel René Barnes in order to acquit Augustine of Gunton's most sweeping allegations.[7]

The Doctrine of Creation

On the doctrine of creation, Green acknowledges that there is indeed a limited dualism within Augustine's thought, yet his charge is that Gunton makes too much of this reality. As he puts it, "While Augustine does affirm a type of matter-spirit dualism . . . it is important to see that . . . this is a limited dualism. Both matter *and* spirit are good, although Augustine sees the spiritual as superior."[8] In a related argument, Green also claims that in accusing Augustine of a Platonic downgrading of materiality, Gunton failed to recognise the extent to which *De Trinitate* actually esteems matter by showing that there can be no understanding of the triune God apart from "the concrete sacrificial act of Christ."[9] To support this notion, Green cites the work of Michel Barnes to show that, far from being a purely exploratory and irenic work, parts of *De Trinitate* actually represent

---

6. Schwöbel, in his preface to *The Barth Lectures*, ed. P.H. Brazier (London: T&T Clark, 2007), xxii–xxiii (citing Gunton, *Barth Lectures*, 96).
7. See also Green, "The Protomodern Augustine? Colin Gunton and the Failure of Augustine," *International Journal of Systematic Theology* 9, no. 3 (July, 2009): 328–41; Green, "Colin Gunton and the Theological Origin of Modernity," in Harvey, *Theology of Colin Gunton*.
8. Bradley G. Green, *Colin Gunton and the Failure of Augustine: The Theology of Colin Gunton in Light of Augustine* (Eugene, OR: Pickwick, 2011), 132.
9. Green is quoting Earl C. Muller, "Rhetorical and Theological Issues in the Structuring of Augustine's *De Trinitate*," in *Studia Patristica* 27, ed. E. A. Livingstone (Leuven: Peeters Press, 1993), 359. Cited in Green, "The Protomodern Augustine," 339. This critique is seconded by Michael Hanby, *Augustine and Modernity* (New York: Routledge, 2003), 15.

an anti-Neoplatonic polemic.[10] As Green argues, "The relevance of all this to Gunton's position should be clear. If Augustine is engaged in an anti-Neoplatonic polemic, and if he is trying to show that the only way to God is through a crucified, bloody, physical man, then Augustine seems to have a rather high view of this material, created world."[11]

Yet is this necessarily the case?

While leaving conclusions for a later time, it is important to note that Gunton was not claiming that Augustine rejected the basic tenet of the incarnation. Nor was he claiming that Augustine lacked an appreciation for the cross. It is, of course, possible to maintain a robust affirmation of such doctrines while simultaneously evidencing a pervasive matter-spirit dualism. As evidence, one might point to the example of Origen, who wrote that "although we proclaim the Son of God to be *Logos* we do not bring forward as evidence a pure and holy *Logos*, but a man who was arrested most disgracefully and crucified."[12] Here in Origen, we see a theologian who, although famous for his matter-spirit dualism, still managed to celebrate the crucified Messiah. Along these lines, Gunton's argument was not that Augustine rejected the cross or incarnation (who would seriously claim this!?) but that his "contributions to the doctrine of creation are so various that it is difficult to know which of them to stress."[13] As we will see in chapter 4, this statement is essentially an accurate one. Beyond this, Gunton also argued that Augustine's dualism was

---

10. See Michel René Barnes, "The Arians of Book V and the Genre of *De Trinitate*," *Journal of Theological Studies* NS 44 (1993): 185–95; Michel René Barnes, "Exegesis and Polemic in Augustine's *De Trinitate* I," *Augustinian Studies* 30 (1999): 43–59. Cited in Green, "The Protomodern Augustine," 338.
11. Green, "The Protomodern Augustine," 338.
12. Origen, *Against Celsus*, 2.31.
13. Gunton, *The Triune Creator: A Historical and Systematic Study* (Grand Rapids: Eerdmans, 1998), 73.

in fact "more dangerous" (that is, more enduring) because it was "controlled" enough to avoid a widespread condemnation.[14]

In light of this, our own research will go on to argue that Green's appeal to Augustine's obvious belief in the cross and incarnation is not enough to acquit him of Gunton's more substantial charge of an influential dualism, exaggerated though it was.[15] Thus, as Robert Jenson argues, Green's critique, though "more cautious and polite than some," is not entirely convincing: "Did Gunton overdo it? Probably. . . . But was Gunton just wrong? I think not."[16]

The Doctrine of the Trinity

On the Trinity, the rebuttal to Gunton's argument centers on the idea that Augustine avoids a monistic imbalance by safeguarding the irreducible particularity of the Father, Son, and Holy Spirit.[17] As Green argues, this fact can be seen first in Augustine's *relational* treatment of God's eternal processions and temporal missions.[18] Here, as Edmund Hill describes it, "The sendings of the Son and the Holy Spirit reveal their eternal processions from the Father . . . and thus reveal the inner trinitarian mystery of God."[19] Because the sendings mirror the processions, the triune mystery is therefore seen to be profoundly relational, and in no way monistic. As Green argues,

> In Augustine's trinitarian theology it is completely legitimate to call *relationship* a *substance-word*. This is a claim which is not worked out

---

14. Ibid., 76.
15. See especially chs. 4 and 6.
16. Jenson, "A Decision Tree," in Harvey, *Theology of Colin Gunton*, 11.
17. For an introduction to Augustine's treatment of the "irreducibility" of the Father, Son and Spirit, see Lewis Ayres, "The Fundamental Grammar of Augustine's Trinitarian Theology," in *Augustine and His Critics*, ed. R. Dodaro and G. Lawless (New York: Routledge, 2000), 51–76.
18. Here Gunton's previously cited critics (Green, Barnes, Hanby, and Ayres) are joined by Scott A. Dunham, *The Trinity and Creation in Augustine: An Ecological Analysis* (SUNY: Albany, NY, 2008), 37.
19. Edmund Hill, *The Mystery of the Trinity* (London: Chapman, 1985), 89. Cited in Green, "The Protomodern Augustine," 338.

> thoroughly in *De Trinitate*, but it is a claim which is completely consistent with the arguments Augustine proffers in the work. . . . The analogies from the human mind, particularly the mind remembering itself, understanding itself, and loving itself are fundamentally *active* and *relational* analogies. . . . Stated differently, at the heart of what it means to be a human person is the Trinity and relationship.[20]

In addition to this line of argument, Gunton's critics also take issue with his judgment that Augustine founded a mode of Trinitarian inquiry that began with a focus upon God's one-ness (*De Deo Uno*), while at the same time giving short shrift to the "particularity" of the Father, Son and Holy Spirit (*De Deo Trino*).[21] In this scheme, Gunton alleged that God's "being [was] not communion, but something underlying it."[22] In response to this so-called Greek/Latin paradigm (with the Cappadocian "East" beginning with the three *hypostases*, while the Augustinian "West" began with the one substance of God), it has now been widely argued that this entire schema is the product of a nineteenth-century historian: Theodore de Régnon.[23] Thus as Sarah Coakley argues, "To have the 'West' attacked by the 'East' on a reading of the Cappadocians that was ultimately spawned by a French Jesuit [de Régnon] is a strange irony."[24] Future chapters must evaluate this claim as it pertains to Gunton's Augustinian narrative.

Yet lest we too quickly dismiss all that Gunton said about Augustine's doctrine of the Trinity, here again is Robert Jenson's more sympathetic evaluation:

---

20. Green, "The Protomodern Augustine," 340. Emphasis in original.
21. See Gunton, *The Promise of Trinitarian Theology* (London: T&T Clark, 1991), 31.
22. Ibid., 10–11.
23. See especially Michel René Barnes, "Augustine in Contemporary Trinitarian Theology," *Theological Studies* 56 (1995): 237–50; "De Régnon Reconsidered," in *Augustinian Studies* 26, no. 2 (1995), 51–79; Theodore de Régnon, SJ, *Études de thélogie positive sur la Sainte Trinité*, four vols. in three (Paris: Victor Retaux, 1892, 1998). We will return to this subject momentarily in our treatment of the critiques against Gunton's reading of the Cappadocians.
24. Sarah Coakley, "Re-Thinking Gregory of Nyssa: Introduction—Gender, Trinitarian Analogies, and the Pedagogy of *The Song*," in *Modern Theology* 18, no. 4 (Oct., 2002): 434.

Augustine *did* in fact emphatically and insistently lay down propositions that became maxims of subsequent Western theology. He *did* in fact say that the Cappadocian distinction of *ousia/hypostasis*—the very distinction that enabled the creedal doctrine of the Trinity—could be no more than a purely linguistic device. . . . He *did* treat the works of God in the economy . . . as indivisible . . . thereby destroying the whole basis on which the immanent Trinity could be affirmed in the first place. He *did* say that it is absurd, as violating the divine simplicity, to think that the Father could not be what he is apart from the Son, and vice versa. . . . Augustine, alas, did in fact say these things, and they have been a curse on Western theology ever since.[25]

Once again, the future chapters of this work will have to evaluate the viability of Jenson's claim. For now, we move from Gunton's reading of Augustine, to his reading of Augustine's "afterlife."

Augustine's Legacy

In turning to Augustine's influence upon the subsequent tradition, Michael Hanby has constructed what is perhaps the most extensive critique of Gunton's modern genealogy.[26] Here he joins others in challenging the link between Augustine's interiority and the rational introspection of such later thinkers as René Descartes.[27] While agreeing with Gunton that the crisis of modern Western individualism and inwardness was, in part, the result of Trinitarian deficiencies,[28] Hanby rejects the attempt to blame these problems (in *any* way) upon Augustine's thought. As he argues, "Descartes'

---

25. Jenson, "A Decision Tree," 12.
26. See Hanby, *Augustine and Modernity*, esp. ch. 1.
27. See also the related critiques of Gunton by such figures as Rowan Williams and Matthew Drever. Williams, "*Sapientia* and the Trinity: Reflections on the *De Trinitate*," in *Collectanea Augustiniana: Mélanges T. J. Van Bavel*, ed. B. Brunning, M. Lamberigts and J. Van Houtem (Leuven: Leuven University Press, 1990), 316–32; Drever, "Redeeming Creation: *Creatio ex nihilo* and the *Imago Dei* in Augustine," in the *International Journal of Systematic Theology* 15, no. 2 (April, 2013): 136–53; Drever, "The Self before God? Rethinking Augusitne's Trinitarian Thought," in *The Harvard Theological Review* 100, no. 2 (2007): 233–42.
28. Hanby, *Augustine and Modernity*, 18.

res cogitans, thought to issue naturally from the seed of Augustine's thought, is a bastard offspring whose other parent is a stoic voluntarism that Augustine had once contested in the name of Christ and the Trinity."[29] In a related critique, Lewis Ayres claims that Gunton made "an important hermeneutical error in equating Augustine's understanding of 'turning inwards' with some modern understandings of self-hood."[30] Likewise, Rowan Williams argues that Augustine's "introspective method" stands distinct from modern forms of inwardness, because it was "designed to 'demythologise' the solitary human ego by establishing the life of the mind firmly in relation to God—and what is more, to God understood as self-gift."[31]

In all of this, our own discussion of Augustine's influence must seek to differentiate clearly between the character of Augustine's own thought, and the many ways in which his insights would be developed by later thinkers. While some ideas may have unintended consequences as they are taken up and retooled by the subsequent tradition, this does not justify the simplistic identification of the earlier idea with all its subsequent adaptations. The need for such a differentiation is made more acute by Ayres's contention that while Gunton's work "was marked by an increasing willingness to admit the complexity of Augustine's thought," he did "not draw any developed distinction between Augustine himself and the subsequent traditions of interpretation."[32] Our own research must seek to avoid this error.

In turning to Gunton's way of doing history, another critique pertains to Gunton's claim that modernity was in many respects a *rightful rejection* of ill-formed Christian doctrines.[33] While Green

---

29. Ibid., 3.
30. Lewis Ayres, review of *The One, the Three and the Many*, by Colin E. Gunton, *Augustinian Studies*, 26, no. 2 (1995): 131.
31. Williams, "*Sapientia* and the Trinity," 331.
32. Ayres, review of *The One, the Three and the Many*, 131.

concedes that aspects of modernity *were* shaped by theological errors, his claim is that Gunton's way of telling the story displays an insufficient emphasis upon the noetic effects of sin.

> Gunton sees modernity generally in terms of getting the ideas or concepts *wrong*, and then naturally tends to see the healing of modernity as primarily a matter of getting the ideas or concepts *right*. . . . I want to change things a bit and suggest that . . . more attention should be given to the cognitive and noetic effects of sinfulness, and how mistaken intellectual developments should be seen *at least in part* as rooted in the reality of human sinfulness.[34]

This critique maintains that whereas Paul spoke of humanity recoiling from *truth* (Rom. 1:25), Gunton often spoke of humanity as recoiling from *poor theological constructs*.[35] One example of this can be seen in a passage that, though not cited by Green, is nonetheless indicative of his argument. As Gunton argued, "We can say that as a historical phenomenon, modernity can be understood as the era which arises out of Christendom by making against its predecessor a charge of hypocrisy: that its freedom is a cloak for tyranny, its creed a pretext for the suppression of the authentic human quest for truth."[36] While acknowledging the likelihood that "Christendom" was often hypocritical, Green contends that Gunton paints too rosy a picture of those "authentic truth-seekers" known as moderns. Thus he asks how this portrayal of humanity relates to those premodern persons who rejected Jesus. As John notes, these individuals rejected truth, not because they were presented with a hypocritical gospel that failed

---

33. As Gunton claimed, while "Christianity is indeed offensive to the natural human mind," it has been "made offensive by its representatives for the wrong reasons." *The One, the Three and the Many: God, Creation and the Culture of Modernity* (Cambridge: Cambridge University Press, 1993), 1.
34. Bradley Green, "Theological Origin of Modernity," 171. Emphasis his.
35. Ibid., 172. Emphasis mine.
36. Gunton, *One, the Three and the Many*, 123.

to account for the concept of "particularity," but because they loved darkness instead of the light (John 3:19).[37]

In fairness, Green acknowledges that Gunton did, at times, speak strongly of the effects of human sinfulness. He bemoaned, for instance, the Enlightenment's "demonic . . . self-confidence and lack of a doctrine of sin."[38] Yet as Green alleges, this sentiment was not sufficiently *emphasized* in Gunton's account of Western intellectual history.[39] Thus again, the allegation is that the "Augustinian tradition" receives a disproportionate amount of blame. In the end, this charge is in some ways a restatement of Gunton's admitted tendency toward historical reduction.[40] Thus, as John Webster argues, Gunton's "diagnosis of a doctrine's history . . . suggests that too much ground is covered too quickly."[41] And, as Stephen Holmes observes of Gunton's classroom lectures, "[His] telling of intellectual history is often enough impressionistic, offering heightened contrasts, bold colours and stark lines; like a great painting, however, if it distorted the appearance of reality somewhat it was only to reveal more clearly the essence of what was being looked at."[42] As a

---

37. See Green, "Theological Origin of Modernity," 174, 177.
38. Gunton, *The Actuality of Atonement: A Study of Metaphor, Rationality, and the Christian Tradition* (Grand Rapids: Eerdmans, 1989), 176. Cited in Green, "Theological Origin of Modernity," 173.
39. This contention therefore leads us to a related question: What was Gunton's position on the matter of *original sin*? Not surprisingly, he refused to accept what he saw as an overly "Augustinian" position (Gunton, *The Christian Faith: An Introduction to Christian Doctrine* [Oxford: Blackwell, 2002], 60) which would involve the seminal transmission of ignorance, concupiscence, and death from Adam to his offspring. For Augustine's view on this, see Paul Rigby, "Original Sin," in *Augustine through the Ages: An Encyclopedia*, ed. Allan Fitzgerald (Grand Rapids: Eerdmans, 1999), 607–14. For Gunton, while unregenerate humans are not "pre-programmed" to sin, they do exist in a web of fallen relations that, apart from God's grace-driven intervention, makes sin inevitable (see Gunton, *Christ and Creation*, the Didsbury Lectures, 1990 [Eugene, OR: Wipf and Stock, 2005], 45–46). Thus while Gunton rejected some of the specifics in Augustine's doctrine, he could still speak of both "original sin" (Gunton, *Christian Faith*, 45), and "total depravity" (*Christian Faith*, 62).
40. For Gunton's admission of this tendency in his own thought, see *The Barth Lectures*, 96.
41. John Webster, "Systematic Theology after Barth: Jüngel, Jenson and Gunton," in *The Modern Theologians: An Introduction to Christian Theology since 1918*, ed. David Ford and Rachel Muers (Oxford: Blackwell, 2005), 261.
42. Holmes, in his introduction to *Revelation and Reason*, 5.

dogmatician, Gunton sought to emphasize the consequences of ill-formed Christian doctrines, yet our own research must evaluate the extent to which this dogmatic concern may have resulted in historical inaccuracies.

For now, we turn from Augustine to what Gunton saw as the triune corrective to certain Augustinian imbalances. This shift is relevant because, as we will see, it is possible to allege that Gunton's claims against Augustine can be partly traced to the "inconsistencies and inadequacies" within his own handling of the Trinity and creation.[43]

Critiques of Gunton's Doctrine of the Trinity

One of Gunton's great laments was that belief in the Trinity has often been *irrelevant* for the life of the church.[44] Thus his project sought to highlight ways in which the Trinity is a doctrine with profound implications for all of life. With this as a goal, it should perhaps be unsurprising that one critique of Gunton's Trinitarian theology is that it entails a *projection* of outside agendas upon both the Godhead, and upon the work of some of Gunton's heroes: the Cappadocian Fathers.

Projection from and for the Culture

In *The One, The Three and the Many*, Gunton made the case that only a fresh understanding of a Creator who is both unity and plurality can begin to heal a culture torn between the Scylla of individualism and the Charybdis of collectivism.[45] In response, few have argued with the claim that "salient aspects of modern culture are predicated on

---

43. So says Neil Ormerod, "Augustine and the Trinity: Whose Crisis?" in *Pacifica* 16, Feb., 2003, 17–32.
44. See, for instance, Gunton, *Promise of Trinitarian Theology*, 198.
45. Gunton, *One, the Three and the Many*, 7.

the denial of the Christian gospel."⁴⁶ Yet it is precisely the relevance of Gunton's project that has led some to suspect that his work was shaped more by an assessment of perceived cultural needs than by a more objective reflection upon the Christian faith.⁴⁷

To help us understand this charge, here is Karen Kilby's attempted deconstruction of what Gunton and others are really up to:

> We have here something like a three stage process. First, a concept, [say] perichoresis, is used to name what is not understood, to name whatever it is that makes the three Persons one. Secondly, the concept is filled out rather suggestively with notions borrowed from our own experience of relationships and relatedness. And then finally, it is presented as an exciting resource [that] Christian theology has to offer the wider world in its reflections upon relationships and relatedness.⁴⁸

Herein lies the charge of *cultural projection* as leveled against the so-called renewal of Trinitarian theology within the twentieth-century.⁴⁹ Yet what may be said to contextualize this charge as it pertains specifically to Gunton?

First, it should be acknowledged that Gunton would *agree* with Kilby on the inherent projectionism of certain "social doctrines" of the Trinity. In a revised preface to *The Promise of Trinitarian Theology*, he even highlighted two kinds of projectionism deriving, ironically, from opposite tendencies. The first, he argued, can be seen in the work of Ted Peters and Catherine LaCugna, who, in rejecting any

---

46. Ibid., 1.
47. Variations of this critique can be seen in Bernhard Nausner, "The Failure of a Laudable Project: Gunton, the Trinity and Human Self-Understanding," *The Scottish Journal of Theology* 62, no. 4 (2009): 403–20; Karen Kilby, "Perichoresis and Projection: Problems with Social Doctrines of the Trinity," *New Blackfriars* 81 (2000): 432–45; Richard Fermer, "The Limits of Trinitarian Theology as a Methodological Paradigm," *Neue Zeitschrift für Systematische Theologie und Religionsphilosophie* 41 (1999): 158–86; J. P. Mackey, "Are There Christian Alternatives to Trinitarian Thinking?," in *The Christian Understanding of God Today*, ed. J. M. Byrne (Dublin: Columbia Press, 1996).
48. Kilby, "Perichoresis and Projection," 442.
49. For broad critique of this "revival," see Holmes, *The Quest for the Trinity: The Doctrine of God in Scripture, History, and Modernity* (Downers Grove, IL: IVP Academic).

appeal to an immanent (or ontological) Trinity, come dangerously near to a form of pantheism that brings God and the world too close. For Gunton, a second form of projectionism emerges from those social theorists who begin with an understanding of the immanent Trinity as a kind of straightforward principle of explanation and ethics: "Because God is like this, it is argued, then the world is, or ought to be, like that."[50] While acknowledging that his own theology sought certain analogies between divine and human relations, Gunton also urged caution, stating that "arguments from analogy tread a slippery slope towards mere projection."[51] With statements like this, Gunton sought to avoid the charge of cultural projection that he leveled against the work of others.

Where though is the evidence that Gunton failed at this endeavor? For Bernhard Nausner, who recently heralded the *failure* of Gunton's theological project, the first piece of evidence can be seen in the way Gunton sometimes began his treatment of the Trinity from a "cultural critical starting point." Here Nausner cites the stinging critique of modernity that comes at the beginning of *The One, The Three and the Many*.[52] His claim is that with such obvious biases against modern individualism, Gunton could not help but find in the divine community what he saw as lacking in the culture. Likewise, Lewis Ayres has argued that Gunton's triune ontology owes "far more to modern social preoccupations than to actual strands in the complex history of theological metaphors."[53]

---

50. Gunton, *Promise of Trinitarian Theology*, xviii–xx.
51. Gunton, *Father, Son, and Holy Spirit: Toward a Fully Trinitarian Theology* (London: T&T Clark, 2003), xiii; cf. Gunton, *Promise of Trinitarian Theology*, xix. While Nausner cites this same quotation, he wrongly asserts that these words are directed toward Peters and LuCugna. In fact, Gunton has moved on to address a second kind of projectionism as we have noted above. See Nausner, "Failure of a Laudable Project," 406.
52. Nausner, "Failure of a Laudable Project," 403.
53. Lewis Ayres, review of *The Promise of Trinitarian Theology*, by Colin Gunton, *Journal of Theological Studies* 43 (1992): 782.

In response, it should be noted that this suspicion (however justified) is not the same as solid proof. While Gunton's desire to bring healing to an individualistic and alienating culture may lead us to *suspect* a form of projection, it is not enough to validate the charge. Perhaps sensing this, Nausner finds stronger evidence of this error in Gunton's preoccupation with the discovery of so-called Trinitarian transcendentals. As we have seen, Gunton viewed these "open transcendentals" as universal marks of being. There were "open" (as in *open to revision*) because their discovery was necessarily rooted not only in an evaluation of divine revelation, but also in a fallible examination of the social and material world.[54] Nevertheless, in Gunton's view, such open transcendentals may be of service as we attempt to make some sense of both divine and creaturely existence. For Gunton, a Christian grasp of (1) relationality, (2) particularity, and (3) perichoresis can help prevent our interactions from collapsing into the individualistic pluralism of Heraclitus or the totalitarian monism of Parmenides.[55]

On this subject, Nausner's claim is that by highlighting "relationality" over any "positive reconceptualisation of the notion of individualism," Gunton unduly projects his disdain for modern individualism onto both divine and human persons.[56] In response to Nausner's argument, it should again be noted that there is an element of this charge that lies beyond the realm of quantifiable evaluation. After all, one cannot easily prove the extent to which an underlying motive has led to certain intellectual conclusions, and for

---

54. In addition to the discussion of the transcendentals in the previous chapter, see Gunton, *One, the Three and the Many*, 134–35. In his epistemology, Gunton would take frequent cues from Michael Polanyi. See Polanyi's *Personal Knowledge: Towards a Post-Critical Philosophy*, 2nd ed. (London: Routledge, 1962).
55. See the second half of Gunton, *One, the Three and the Many*.
56. Nausner, "Failure of a Laudable Project," 419. Emphasis mine.

his own part, Gunton would refer to this tactic as the disgraceful "Freudianizing of one's opponents."[57]

How then should we proceed? In the end, perhaps the most effective way of detecting a form of "cultural projectionism" will involve the very process of the present study. If Gunton's overarching historical arguments are simply wrong, most notably with regard to Augustine and his inheritors, then it seems more likely that his own theology involves a tendency toward cultural projection. Thus while we have now introduced this critique of Gunton's doctrine of the Trinity, we must now connect it to his Augustinian narrative.

Projection and the Cappadocian Fathers

As we have seen, one of Gunton's arguments was that Augustine squandered the "ontological achievement" of his Eastern predecessors: Gregory of Nyssa, Gregory of Nazianzus, and especially Basil the Great.[58] For Gunton, it was the Cappadocians who guarded the Trinity from the clutches of a monistic imbalance, emphasized the Spirit's outward function in perfecting creation, and were so unfortunately overshadowed by the brilliant man from Hippo Regius.[59] In response to Gunton's claims, perhaps the most common critique is that he adopted a flawed view of the Cappadocians, most often from the influential work of John Zizioulas. This charge has several facets.

First, the allegation of Richard Fermer and Bernhard Nausner is that both Zizioulas and Gunton do something that the Cappadocians never do when they "reduce the concept of *ousia* (essence / substance) . . . to the concept of *koinonia* (communion)."[60] As Nausner argues,

---

57. Gunton, *Revelation and Reason*, 87.
58. See Gunton, *Promise of Trinitarian Theology*, 10–11.
59. See again ch. 1.
60. Fermer, "Limits of Trinitarian Theology," 165.

the Cappadocians held these terms together in a "balanced dialectic," while Gunton conflates them in order to support his social and theological agenda.[61]

Second, other scholars have now questioned whether the likes of Gunton and Zizioulas fairly represent the Cappadocian use of *hypostasis* within their triune vocabulary.[62] As Gunton argued, the Cappadocians, and Basil in particular, gave "priority to the concept of person in their doctrine of God,"[63] while Augustine evidenced a monistic overemphasis upon the unity of the divine nature.[64] In response to this claim, Lucian Turcescu argues that it is incorrect to assert that the Cappadocians viewed "person as a category [that] is ontologically prior to substance."[65] Similarly, Stephen Holmes asserts that "the patristic inheritance, East and West, essentially spoke with one voice," and "Augustine [was] the most capable interpreter of Cappadocian Trinitarianism."[66]

Third, in turning also to the talk of human *hypostases*, Holmes contends that it is simply wrong to cite the Cappadocians as "seeing personhood as univocal, or at least as very closely analogical, when applied to divine persons and human people."[67] At this point, the charge is that both Gunton and others fail to take seriously enough the Cappadocian use of *epinoia*, which speaks to the need for greater caution when applying a human "conception" (*epinoia*) to divine

---

61. Nausner, "Failure of a Laudable Project," 414.
62. See Sarah Coakley, "'Persons' in the 'Social' Doctrine of the Trinity: A Critique of Current Analytic Discussion," in *The Trinity: An Interdisciplinary Symposium on the Trinity*, ed. Stephen T. Davis, Daniel Kendall, and Gerald O'Collins (Oxford: Oxford University Press, 1999), 132; Lewis Ayres, "On Not Three People: The Fundamental Themes of Gregory of Nyssa's Trinitarian Theology as Seen in *To Ablabius: On Not Three Gods*," in *Modern Theology* 18, no. 4 (Oct., 2002); Lucian Turcescu, "'Person' Versus 'Individual,' and Other Modern Misreadings of Gregory of Nyssa," in *Modern Theology* 18, no. 4 (Oct., 2002): 527–39.
63. Gunton, *Promise of Trinitarian Theology*, 94.
64. Ibid., 31–32.
65. Turcescu, "'Person' Versus 'Individual'," 528, 530.
66. Holmes, *The Quest for the Trinity*, 144 and 146 respectively.
67. Ibid., 29; cf. Holmes, "Analogia Personae," in Harvey, *Theology of Colin Gunton*, 44.

realities.⁶⁸ If this is true, then Gunton's Augustinian narrative must also be revised, for as we have seen, his claim was that Augustine "failed to appropriate the ontological achievement of his Eastern colleagues."⁶⁹

In fairness to Gunton, it should again be clarified that his goal was never merely to replicate a "Cappadocian theology," or even to say that such a monolithic entity exists in a technical sense. As his peers have noted, Gunton was far too much of a dissenter, and a restlessly constructive theologian, to content himself with reproducing the work of Basil or his peers. In Webster's words, Gunton "never evaded theological responsibility by hiding in the skirts of a tradition,"⁷⁰ and as Jenson points out, Gunton could also critique the Eastern tradition (and Zizioulas himself) when he felt it to be necessary.⁷¹ Thus it seems possible that Gunton would not be overly concerned with the charge that he somehow failed to duplicate the Cappadocian doctrine of the Trinity. Still, the fact remains that Gunton did make historical claims regarding the contrast between Augustine and the Cappadocians. Thus our work must also evaluate his Cappadocian argument so far as it pertains to his Augustinian narrative.

Critiques of Gunton's Doctrine of Creation

For now, we turn from the critiques of Gunton's doctrine of the Trinity to the claims against his doctrine of creation.

---

68. See John Behr's treatment of *epinoia* in *The Nicene Faith*, part 2 (Crestwood, NY: St. Vladimir's Seminary Press, 2004), 282–90.
69. Gunton, *Promise of Trinitarian Theology*, 10–11.
70. Webster, "Gunton and Barth," 27.
71. See Jenson, "A Decision Tree," 13; Holmes, "Analogia Personae," 43. See also Schwöbel's illuminating footnote on this subject in "Shape of Colin Gunton's Theology," in Harvey, *Theology of Colin Gunton*, 207n59.

Gunton's Use of Irenaeus

If the Cappadocians might have helped Augustine understand the Trinity, then Gunton viewed Irenaeus as a potential antidote to Augustine's supposedly dualistic treatment of created being.[72] As we will see (in chapter 9), Augustine did read Irenaeus,[73] yet Gunton's claim was that he failed to appropriate the possibilities within the Irenaean treatment of matter, time, and mediation.[74]

Yet just as with the Cappadocians, Gunton's attempt to reappropriate the work of Irenaeus has also been critiqued. As a second century-thinker, Irenaeus was addressing different challenges from those of his post-Nicene successors; thus Alan Spence has raised concerns about Gunton's ability to repristinate the Irenaean treatment of various theological issues: "Can [Gunton] as a modern man enter Irenaeus' world, a worldview unshaped by the formulations of Nicaea and Chalcedon, and practice his theology with integrity within an intellectual framework that is not yet determined by the *homoousion* or the challenge of the Arians?"[75] While the question is a valid one, its focus is not upon a misreading of Irenaeus per se, but upon Gunton's supposed desire to practice theology in a world that no longer exists, a world not yet conditioned by the threat of Arianism or the conclusions of later councils. In light of this, our work must examine whether such later developments alter the extent to which Irenaeus may be seen as a viable alternative to Augustine's supposed dualism.[76]

---

72. See, for instance, Gunton, *One, the Three and the Many*, 205.
73. See Augustine, *Con. Iul.* 1.3.5.
74. See again ch. 1; also Gunton, *One, the Three and the Many*, 151; *Triune Creator*, 74.
75. Spence, "The Person as Willing Agent: Classifying Gunton's Christology," in Harvey, *Theology of Colin Gunton*, 60.
76. See ch. 7.

On Christ and "Fallen" Creation

Like Irenaeus, Gunton stressed the strong connection between Christ and his creation. In so doing, he drew from Irving (and others) in order to speak even of the "fallen" humanity of Jesus.[77] The motive behind this move was to show that Christ was like us in every way, apart from sin. Yet as we will see, this connection between Jesus and a fallen world has also drawn critique. Thus while Gunton chided Augustine for a "docetic tendency" in his Christology,[78] it may be argued that this allegation merely reveals a deficiency within Gunton's own account of Christ.

The basis for Gunton's linkage between Christ and fallen creation was both ontological and soteriological in nature.[79] For Gunton, because Jesus' humanity was not an *ex nihilo* creation of the Father, it must be seen as coming from the material of the fallen created order. Thus he drew approvingly from Irving when he wrote that "the Father sends the Spirit to form a body for his Son out of the only material available to hand: the *soiled flesh* of the created order which he comes to redeem."[80] Here we see the move from ontology to soteriology. For Gunton, if Christ does not enter fully into our fallen state, then he cannot bring salvation to it.[81] As Nazianzen wrote,

---

77. See Gunton, "Two Dogmas Revisited: Edward Irving's Christology," in *The Scottish Journal of Theology* 41 (1988): 359–76.
78. See ch. 1.
79. See E. Jerome Van Kuiken, "On Falling Forward: The World, the Flesh, and the Spirit in Colin Gunton's Christology," an unpublished paper presented on Oct., 2, 2009 at the Wesleyan-Free Methodist Graduate Students's Theological Seminar. For support, see also Alan Spence, "The Person as Willing Agent,"49–64.
80. Gunton, *Triune Creator*, 223. Emphasis added. Gunton is drawing upon *The Collected Writings of Edward Irving in Five Volumes*, ed. G. Carlyle, vol. 5 (London: Alexander Strachan, 1865), 115–16.
81. Van Kuiken, "Falling Forward," 7.

"The unassumed is the unhealed."[82] Hence, for Gunton, Christ took up our fallen flesh, but without succumbing to temptation.

The question, however, is how Jesus can be both *fallen* and *sinless*. Gunton's answer was not an appeal to the "divine side" of Christ's supposedly dual natures. For him, as we have seen already, such talk of "dual natures" invariably led "to the appearance of a kind of hybrid being . . . a centaur, suggesting two persons rather than one."[83] Instead, Gunton's emphasis was upon the Holy Spirit as the one who empowered Jesus to live up to his divine calling. As Gunton claimed, "In shaping from the clay of earth a body for the Son, the Spirit enables this part of earth to be fully itself, to move to perfection rather than dissolution."[84] Yet what must be said in response to this aspect of Gunton's work?

In fairness, Gunton did attempt to distinguish himself from that which was deemed heretical in Irving. While Irving sometimes spoke of Christ's sinful flesh, Gunton preferred to speak of Christ's humanity as merely "fallen."[85] Despite this, it is not always clear that Gunton could disentangle the two terms. In *Christ and Creation*, he wrote that "both literally and metaphorically to be fallen is to pollute and to be polluted."[86] Likewise, he claimed that Jesus both "exacerbated as much as healed" the social conditions under which he lived, thus contributing to their fallenness.[87] All this raises the question as to whether one can both "pollute" the world and

---

82. Gregory of Nazianzus, "Epistle 101," in *Christology of the Later Fathers*, ed. Edward R. Hardy (Philadelphia: Westminster, 1954), 218.
83. Gunton, *Christian Faith*, 77–78.
84. Gunton, *Christ and Creation*, 52; cf. *Christian Faith*, 105–6. Gunton claimed that it was a private letter from Geoffrey Nuttal that first pointed him toward the need for a stronger pneumatological relationship in his Christology. *Christ and Creation*, 11. This was an emphasis that Gunton would later see to be lacking in such earlier works as *Yesterday and Today: A Study of Continuities of Christology* (Grand Rapids: Eerdmans, 1983).
85. Gunton, *Christian Faith*, 36.
86. Gunton, *Christ and Creation*, 58; cf. *Actuality of Atonement*, 131.
87. Gunton, *Christian Faith*, 101. This point is drawn out by Van Kuiken in "Falling Forward," 8.

"contribute to the fallenness" of others while somehow remaining free from guilt and sin. At this point, both Jerome Van Kuiken and Alan Spence have raised concerns that Gunton's ambiguous language may be almost as problematic as that of Irving.[88]

One example of this may be seen in Gunton's contention that Christ's humanity came "from the soil of *sinful* earth."[89] As Van Kuiken notes, Gunton's language seems careless at best, for "the earth is not a moral agent";[90] it is fallen; it is not sinful. Likewise, Webster questions whether Gunton has been "beguiled into believing that Jesus' humanity needs somehow to be protected from the determination of the Word if it is to have integrity."[91] While the present book is not a study on the viability of Gunton's constructive Christology, these charges must be acknowledged for the simple reason that they raise questions, and provide some further context, for Gunton's rigorous critique of the "dualistic"[92] and "docetic"[93] tendencies of both Augustine and the subsequent Western tradition. Put simply, if Gunton's own view of Christ and creation is seen to be aberrant, then his charges against Augustine on such matters are potentially more suspect.

Yet in surveying this final critique of Gunton's Christology, we should note that for one, Robert Jenson remained strangely optimistic that had Gunton lived longer, he would have rethought and retooled this aspect of his theology.[94] On the one hand, Jenson's optimism may seem improbable. We live, after all, in a world where *all people*, not least theologians, are tempted to "stick to their guns" if for no other reason than to avoid the admission that one has erred. Yet

---

88. Spence, "The Person as Willing Agent," 61–2; Van Kuiken, "Falling Forward," 13.
89. Gunton, *Christ and Creation*, 51; emphasis added. Van Kuiken, "Falling Forward," 13.
90. Van Kuiken, "Falling Forward," 13.
91. Webster, "Gunton and Barth," 28.
92. Gunton, *One, the Three and the Many*, 2–3, 55.
93. Gunton, *Christ and Creation*, 70; cf. *Yesterday and Today*, 15.
94. Jenson, "Decision Tree," 16.

perhaps in regard to Gunton such optimism was not entirely ill-founded. He had changed course before, most notably in regard to his pneumatology, after accepting the critique of others.[95] In his later years Gunton had even begun to read his work in draft form to students, in order to benefit from their constructive criticism.

It is also possible, of course, that Gunton would have maintained his views in the face of the critiques highlighted above. Many of the charges were familiar to him, and his work displays a fairly consistent treatment of the Trinity, creation, and the supposed influence of Augustine upon these doctrines. Yet while we are left to wonder how Gunton's unfinished dogmatic theology would have dealt with such charges, we are now prepared to render an important conclusion.

Conclusion

In light of the above critiques, we may conclude that Gunton's theological project is deserving of some further evaluation. In illustrating this, we have highlighted concerns of Trinitarian projectionism, historical distortion, and an improper relation between Christ and creation. Yet to evaluate these charges individually would take us well beyond the scope of a single monograph. With this in mind, the following chapters will continue to focus on a particular facet of Gunton's theology: his reading of Augustine and the "Augustinian" tradition as it pertains to the doctrine of the Trinity and the doctrine of creation.

Toward this end, we may now survey the broad outline of the present book. While chapter 1 provided an introduction to Gunton's claims on the Trinity, creation, and the legacy of Augustine, the present chapter has shown how these arguments have been profoundly challenged. In light of this, chapter 3 will evaluate

---

95. See again the previous citation from Gunton, *Christ and Creation*, 11.

Gunton's specific charge of a monistic imbalance in Augustine's doctrine of the Trinity, while chapter 4 will turn to the doctrine of creation, and to Gunton's claim that Augustine evidenced a damaging dualism in his view of matter, time, and triune mediation. Chapters 5 and 6 will evaluate how these supposed errors were appropriated by Augustine's medieval successors, while chapter 7 will trace Augustine's influence upon the Reformation era. Then, in chapter 8, we will turn to evaluate Gunton's argument regarding Augustine's influence upon the dawn of modern thought, especially in the person of René Descartes. Finally, in chapters 9 and 10, we will return to a time before Augustine, in order to evaluate Gunton's claim that the bishop of Hippo squandered key advances in the work of Irenaeus and the Cappadocian fathers. In all of this, the overarching goal will be to evaluate not only the legacy of Saint Augustine (on the Trinity and creation), but also that of Colin Gunton as it pertains specifically to the Augustinian inheritance.

3

Gunton and Augustine's God: The Question of Monistic Imbalance in Augustine's Trinitarianism

For some, it may seem almost oxymoronic to accuse Augustine of a monistic view of God. After all, he did devote over two decades to the detailed composition of *De Trinitate*, a work which even Gunton ranked "among the glories of Western theology."[1] Despite this, Gunton's charge was that a tendency toward monism in Augustine's doctrine of God was linked to a damaging dualism in his doctrine of creation. The purpose of this chapter is to evaluate the first half of this claim. Our question is this: To what extent was Gunton justified in alleging that key elements of Augustine's thought lend themselves to a monistic construal of the Trinity?

After some preliminary ground clearing, we will begin by exploring Gunton's argument regarding the origin of a monistic

1. Gunton, *The Promise of Trinitarian Theology* (London: T&T Clark, 1991), 31.

imbalance in Augustine's handling of divine simplicity. Second, we will test this allegation through an examination of Augustine's treatment of the particularity of triune persons. Finally, we will engage in a fresh reading of *De Trinitate*, in order to highlight certain strengths and weaknesses in Gunton's argument. In the end, this chapter will attempt to modify both the claims of Gunton and those of his most dismissive critics. In so doing, we will argue that while Augustine does acquit himself of Gunton's most sweeping critiques, this reality must also be weighed against some potentially problematic facets of Augustine's Trinitarian methodology.

Most notably, we will come to see a viable connection between Augustine's so-called inward turn and the dualistic repercussions that this move would have in time. Thus while Gunton was indeed unfair to Saint Augustine, we will see that his thesis regarding the *Augustinian legacy* (that is, the selective appropriation of Augustine's thought by key figures within the subsequent tradition) remains viable in certain limited respects. Before moving to the evidence, however, we must first deal with a potential problem.

Dismembering Augustine

In the words of Isidore of Seville (c. 560–636), "Whoever claims to have read the whole of Augustine's works must be a liar."[2] As Possidius, Augustine's first biographer, would state, "There is so much that he dictated and published" that "scarcely anyone" could read it all.[3] To this day, over five million words remain extant.[4] In light of this, it is impossible in a chapter of this length to give a comprehensive handling of Augustine's Trinitarian theology. Thus

---

2. Isidore of Seville, *Carmina* [Ascripta]. See Migne, PL, 83.1109.
3. Possidius, *Vita*, 18. Cited in James J. O'Donnell, *Augustine: A New Biography* (New York: Harper, 2005), 135.
4. O'Donnell, *Augustine: A New Biography*, 5.

Gunton's work, and indeed the present book, leaves itself open to the charge of presenting an insufficiently contextualized reading of Augustine's thought. Bits and pieces must be selected, and this process leaves Augustine (in the phrase of Michel René Barnes) somewhat "dismembered."[5]

This is not a charge we seek to deny entirely. Still, it is one that can be somewhat neutralized. This is a study, first and foremost, on the work of Colin Gunton, and as we have seen, Gunton's goal was never to present a full-orbed handling of Augustine's thought. For Gunton, Augustine's *legacy* was the chief concern. As Holmes remarks, "For [Gunton] 'history' meant something: it was a series of lessons in how beliefs propagate and distort, how a wrong emphasis that enters the tradition grows and evolves to produce serious consequences centuries later."[6] In light of this, our intention will be to focus on Augustine's legacy, and to ask whether certain influential aspects of his theology may have lent themselves to a monistic (mis)interpretation. This approach, while limited, seems reasonable, by virtue of one of Augustine's recent defenders. As Barnes notes, "In point of fact there may have never been a 'contextualised' reading of Augustine. . . . Indeed, in bits and pieces sometimes seems to be the only way that Augustine's trinitarian theology has been read. The medievals who read him, read him in that way. The moderns who read him have continued the practice."[7] With this in mind, we will proceed *not* to give a comprehensive handling of Augustine's doctrine of God, but to evaluate Gunton's specific claims in light of recent scholarship.

---

5. Michel Barnes, "Rereading Augustine's Theology of the Trinity," in *The Trinity: An Interdisciplinary Symposium on the Trinity*, ed. Stephen T. Davis, Daniel Kendall, and Gerald O'Collins (Oxford: Oxford University Press, 1999), 147.
6. Holmes, in introduction to Colin Gunton, *Revelation and Reason*, ed. P. H. Brazier (London: T&T Clark, 2008), 7.
7. Barnes, "Rereading Augustine," 147.

Framing Gunton's Charge

For Gunton, the danger in Augustine was not that he was "propounding straightforward versions of the various heresies to which he [was] near." Rather, Gunton's claim was that Augustine ultimately lacked "the conceptual equipment to avoid a final collapse into something like [these errors]."[8] In Gunton's view, the cause of this collapse was at once historical and philosophical in nature. As he argued,

> In the fifth century, the dogmatic shape of Christianity was more or less formed. What was apparently required was the defence of certain doctrines of the creed against their philosophical opponents, and it is this which dominates Augustine's approach. To a certain extent, he receives the doctrine from the tradition. But he receives it in such a way that certain problems remain for him. In *every case*, they centre on his continuing adherence to platonic ways of thought, and in every case mean that certain points are problematic for him.[9]

For Gunton, Augustine rightly set out to defend the Christian faith from its intellectual opponents,[10] yet he often did so with the unfortunate weaponry of Platonism.[11] Thus while certain heresies were indeed dethroned (whether Manichaean or Pelagian in nature), this victory was allegedly tainted by the problematic acceptance of certain philosophical assumptions, which contributed to future problems. We turn now to the first of these philosophical concepts.

---

8. Gunton, *Promise of Trinitarian Theology*, 55. Gunton was here referring to the danger of a monistic (and modalistic) view of God.
9. Gunton, *The Triune Creator: A Historical and Systematic Study* (Grand Rapids: Eerdmans, 1998), 74. Emphasis added.
10. See Gunton, *Promise of Trinitarian Theology*, 34; cf. *Act and Being: Towards a Theology of the Divine Attributes* (London: SCM Press, 2002), 135.
11. See Gunton, *The One, the Three and the Many: God, Creation and the Culture of Modernity* (Cambridge: Cambridge University Press, 1993), 84.

Augustine and Divine Simplicity

At the core of Gunton's critique against Augustine's doctrine of the Trinity lay the issue of divine simplicity. As proof of this, Gunton wrote the following, in an unpublished draft of his planned dogmatic theology: "Augustine's chief weakness is that he asked the wrong question . . . about how to reconcile the absolute simplicity of God with the apparent plurality of the persons, rather than [seeking] a concept of divine unity on the basis of the economy."[12] Before evaluating this claim, we must first begin with an explication of precisely what the doctrine of divine simplicity entails.

For Augustine, as well as others, the doctrine of simplicity meant that a perfect God must be entirely devoid of any ontological complexity or composition.[13] A simple God cannot have "parts" because such parts would be ontologically prior to his being, thus rendering him vulnerable to corruptibility and change. In Augustine's doctrine of simplicity, God's existence is his essence; God *is* what he is said to have, or he is not God.[14] In light of this, it soon becomes obvious that one's understanding of divine simplicity will be deeply connected to one's understanding of what it means for God to be triune.[15] What, though, was Gunton's more specific charge against Augustine's treatment of this issue?

---

12. Colin Gunton, *A Christian Dogmatic Theology*, vol. 1, *The Triune God: A Doctrine of the Trinity as Though Jesus Makes a Difference*, 2003, unpublished typescript, chapter 5. Cited in Robert Jenson, "A Decision Tree of Colin Gunton's Thinking," in *The Theology of Colin Gunton*, ed. Lincoln Harvey (London: T&T Clark, 2010), 10.
13. See James E. Dolezal, *God without Parts: Divine Simplicity and the Metaphysics of God's Absoluteness* (Eugene: Wipf and Stock, 2011), 31.
14. See Augustine, *Trin.* 5.10.11, 7.1.2, 15.5.7; *Civ.* 8.6, 11.10; cf. Lewis Ayres, *Nicaea and Its Legacy*, 380.
15. See Stephen R. Holmes, "'Something Much too Plain to Say': Towards a Defence of the Doctrine of Divine Simplicity," *Neue Zeitschrift für Systematische Theologie und Religionsphilosophie* 43 (2001): 137–54.

A Certain Kind of Simple: Gunton's Case against Augustine

While the entire notion of divine simplicity has been rejected by many modern theologians,[16] the problem for Gunton centered not on Augustine's affirmation of the concept,[17] but in his supposed misappropriation of it.[18] In Gunton's view, the problem was that Augustine absolutized divine simplicity in such a way that the particularity of triune persons was imperiled, and the Christian God was distanced from the economy of salvation.[19] The path to this conclusion spans the breadth of Gunton's career, and in tracing it we see what appears to be a progression from an earlier, and more sweeping condemnation of simplicity, to a later and more precise critique.

In his 1975 doctoral thesis, Gunton took aim at the so-called classical concept of God.[20] By this, he meant the "system in which an account of the attributes of God is developed in at least relative independence of biblical revelation."[21] While Gunton then saw Aquinas as the Christian source of this theology, he would soon locate its more substantial roots in Augustine.[22] In so doing, he found unlikely allies in the form of Karl Barth and Charles Hartshorne. As

---

16. Ibid., 137–38.
17. As Holmes notes, Augustine was preceded in his affirmation of divine simplicity by some of Gunton's heroes: Athanasius, Basil (at least in the traditional ascription of *Ep. 8*), Gregory Nazianzen and Gregory Nyssen. Ibid., 147–48.
18. See Gunton's affirmation of simplicity (rightly conceived), and his citation of Holmes's paper in *Act and Being*, 32, 122-3.
19. See again Jenson's quotation from Gunton's unfinished dogmatic theology. Jenson, "Decision Tree," 10; cf. Gunton, *Act and Being*, 122.
20. Gunton, *Becoming and Being: The Doctrine of God in Charles Hartshorne and Karl Barth*, new ed. (London: SCM, 2001), 1–7.
21. Ibid., 243. This reference, although indicative of Gunton's thesis (first published in 1978 as *Becoming and Being*), is taken from the new epilogue to the work, written by Gunton in 2001. In his thesis, Gunton saw the classical concept as typified by (1) *supernaturalism*: the preference to speak of God in negative opposition to the natural world; (2) *timelessness*, in some correspondence to Plato's timeless forms; and (3) the *hierarchal ordering of reality*, which constructs a chain of being through which certain entities are improperly marginalized (2–3).
22. Ibid., 229–38. For confirmation, see Gunton's epilogue to the 2001 reprinting.

Gunton argued, both men critiqued the "classical concept" with its supposedly Platonic underpinnings, yet in Barth especially, Gunton found a stern reaction to divine simplicity. As Gunton wrote, "If unity is construed as simplicity, and that is understood in the classical sense of absence of composition, then [citing Barth] 'the simple is an utterly unmoved being, remote from this world altogether.'"[23] While Gunton later qualified this charge,[24] we see here an early indicator of his later complaint against Augustine. If simplicity was conceived *numerically*, then the concept allegedly resulted in either a de facto monism, or an impossible mathematical contortion by which "three" must be made to equal "one."[25] In either case, Gunton saw the exercise as inserting a kind of ugly broad ditch between God and his creation.

To evidence this supposed problem in Augustine, we may highlight a passage that, though not cited by Gunton, is somewhat illustrative of his intended point. Here, in a tractate on John, Augustine struggles with those texts that seem to reference the Father speaking, as if he had a body. This was a recurring issue for Augustine, and one that led him to a kind of world-denying self-talk. In this, Augustine adjures himself to "take away all bodily things. See simplicity, if you are simple. But how will you be simple? If you do not entangle yourself [in the world], you will be simple."[26]

While too much should not be inferred from an isolated passage, one can easily see how such language might be taken to present, in Barth's words, "the Simple as . . . a being, remote from this world altogether."[27] After all, as one might ask, Why, when Augustine

---

23. Ibid., 203. Citing Barth, *CD*, 2/1, 449.
24. See Gunton, *Act and Being*, 32, 122–3.
25. Gunton, *Promise of Trinitarian Theology*, 31.
26. Augustine, *Jo. ev. tr.* 23.8 (likely written sometime after 408 AD). Cited in Ayres, *Augustine and the Trinity* (Cambridge: Cambridge University Press, 2010), 93.
27. Barth, *CD* 2/1. Cited in Gunton, *Becoming and Being*, 203.

wants to conceive of the divine, does he not turn his gaze to Christ, "the image of the invisible God" (Col. 1:15), and "the exact representation of his being" (Heb. 1:3)? Why must he set aside "all bodily things" if the Word became flesh? For Gunton, such statements came to illustrate the victory of sophistry over Scripture, and the movement toward a monistic view of God and a dualistic view of the material creation.[28] Yet lest we move too quickly, we must now attempt to understand the potential value of Augustine's doctrine of divine simplicity.

Simplicity and Augustine's Inward Turn

In the *Confessions*, Augustine pinpoints a particular difficulty in his many attempts to contemplate the divine. In reflecting upon his past dalliances with Manichaeism and the works of Aristotle, he writes that "I tried to conceive you also, my God, wonderfully simple and immutable, as if you too were a subject of which magnitude and beauty are attributes."[29] Likewise, in *De Trinitate*, the logic of this problem assumes a clear progression.

First, Augustine deeply desired an understanding of the God that Scripture claimed that he would one day "see."[30] As he wrote, "That sight alone [the beatific vision] . . . is our chief good."[31] Yet Scripture also claimed that "God is spirit" (John 4:24) and thus for Augustine, his *natura* or *substantia* or *esse* "cannot be seen corporally."[32] Therefore, the problem was that when the younger Augustine

---

28. See Gunton, *One, the Three and the Many*, 23. As Jenson notes, it was "the incompatibility of this doctrine with the biblical portrayal of God that never ceased to agitate Gunton." Jenson, "Decision Tree," 10.
29. Augustine, *Conf.* 4.16.29. This citation is from the Henry Chadwick translation (Oxford: Oxford University Press, 1991), 69. Subsequent citations from this version unless otherwise noted. Italics mine.
30. Ps. 27:4; 1 Cor. 13:12; 1 John 3:2; Matt. 5:8. Augustine cites all these passages in *Trin.* 1.13.31.
31. Augustine, *Trin.* 1.13.31.
32. Ibid., 2.18.35.

thought of the divine, his tendency was to picture something material, divisible, and thus imperfect. This thought was by necessity an idolatrous one. When speaking of this tendency within his early life, Augustine wrote that "I had my back to the light and my face towards the things which are illumined."[33] What then was the solution?

As Augustine noted, he received some help by virtue of Platonic thought.[34] For the Neoplatonic philosopher Plotinus (c. 204–270 AD), the answer to such material conceptions of ultimate reality was the *simplicity* of the totally transcendent "One." In this paradigm, the One was like a light source that spread in the darkness through a series of emanations, the chief of which resulted in the construction of the *nous*. For Plotinus, although humans cannot glimpse this ultimate reality corporally, they can be enlightened through the conduit of the immaterial "mind."[35] Once purified by the heavenly *eros*, the human *nous* may be set free from the beguilement of the body in order to attain a mystical union with the One.[36] In all of this, the potential parallels between Plotinian and Augustinian simplicity have been much debated.[37]

Augustine read Plotinus as at least one part of the famous *platonicorum libros* mentioned in *Confessions* 7.[38] And by Augustine's own admission this reading helped to bring about a decisive moment in his theological journey. As he wrote, "By the Platonic books I was

---

33. Augustine, *Conf.* 4.16.30.
34. See *Conf.* 7. We will return to this text momentarily.
35. See Plotinus, *The Enneads*, trans. Stephen MacKenna, ed. John Dillon (London: Penguin Books, 1991).
36. This description is that of J. N. D. Kelly, *Early Christian Doctrines*, 5th ed. (New York: Harper, 1978), 19–20.
37. For a helpful survey of the voluminous literature on Augustine's Platonism, see Robert Crouse, "'Paucis Mutatis Verbis': St. Augustine's Platonism," in *Augustine and his Critics*, ed. Robert Dodaro and George Lawless (New York: Routledge, 2000). We will return to this discussion in ch. 4 when we examine Augustine's doctrine of creation.
38. See ibid., 37.

admonished to return into myself. With you [God] as my guide I entered into my innermost citadel."[39] For many scholars, including Lewis Ayres,[40] this shift is spoken of as Augustine's "inward turn."[41] Once *in*, it was by the grammar of simplicity that Augustine heard afresh the words of the Christian God: "I am who I am" (Exod. 3:14).[42] This resonated. Here, Augustine thought, was a God whose existence *is* his essence. Here was simplicity in the covenant name of *Yahweh*.

Like Plotinus, Augustine was enthralled with light. And like Plotinus, the rational mind would become for him a kind of touch point for ultimate reality. Thus while Augustine was clear that a total comprehension of God remains impossible, he could also assert that "God belongs to the mind," just as "material bodies belong to the eyes."[43] In Augustine's view, the mind (*mens*) comprised the highest part of the immaterial human soul (*animus*), and as such it may become the primary locus for examining the image of God.[44] While such Neoplatonic parallels within Augustine's work are widely noted,[45] the question still remains: Do they really damn Augustine's conception of divine simplicity to a monistic imbalance? After all, Augustine was an avowed *Trinitarian*. How then do simplicity and divine triunity coexist within his thought?

---

39. Augustine, *Conf.* 7.10.16.
40. See Ayres, *Augustine and the Trinity*, 138.
41. For an introduction to this subject, see Philip Cary's entry on "Interiority," in *Augustine through the Ages: An Encyclopedia*, ed. Allan Fitzgerald (Grand Rapids: Eerdmans, 1999), 454.
42. Augustine, *Conf.* 7.10.16.
43. Augustine, *Sermon* 117.5 (*Ad mentum Deus perinet, inteligendus est; ad oculos corpus, videndum est*). Cited in David Bradshaw, "Augustine the Metaphysician," in *Orthodox Readings of Augustine*, ed. G.E. Demacopoulos and A. Papanikolaou (Crestwood, NY: St. Vladimir's Seminary Press, 2008), 245.
44. See Wayne Hankey, "Mind," in Fitzgerald, *Augustine through the Ages*, 563–67. For Augustine's so-called psychic analogies, see books 9, 10, and 12 of *De Trinitate*. As Augustine states there, "Man was not made in the image of God according to the shape of his body, but according to his rational mind" (*Trin.* 12.7.12).
45. See Crouse's survey of the prior scholarship in "St. Augustine's Platonism," 37–50.

In Defense of Divine Simplicity

While acknowledging the Plotinian roots of divine simplicity within Augustine, Lewis Ayres argues that Augustine utilized this Platonic tool to do precisely the opposite of what Gunton claims. For Ayres, the "grammar of simplicity" did not *bring down* the theology of Nicea, it gave it "wings."[46] His argument is that Augustine's use of simplicity was not numerical, as Gunton claimed;[47] it did not reduce the Three to an amorphous One, or turn the Trinity into a mathematical problem. Instead, for Ayres, Augustine's use of simplicity was "substantial" in that it provided a coherent framework for affirming the consubstantial nature of the Father and the Son. As Ayres states,

> The grammar of simplicity means that we must say that for God the Father to generate another, a "Son," both the generator and the generated must be Wisdom and God "in themselves": the grammar of simplicity allows us to say truly that "the Father has given the Son to have life in himself" (Jn. 5:26). Thus, Augustine is using simplicity as a tool for exploring the unity and multiplicity that the principles of Nicene trinitarian belief commend, and by this we see that a simple being may generate another who is also co-equal and simple.[48]

As Ayres argues, for Augustine (as with many other pro-Nicene theologians), the doctrine of divine simplicity was used to lend some philosophic credibility to the Christian *credo*. Thus while Augustine did not "think his way to God," by virtue of "the Platonic books," he did come to see the gracious hand of God in his journey from Plotinus to the gospel. As Augustine writes in his *Confessions*, "I

---

46. See Lewis Ayres, "Giving Wings to Nicaea: Reconceiving Augustine's Earliest Trinitarian Theology," *Augustinian Studies* 38, no. 1 (2007): 21–40. See also Ayres, "Fundamental Grammar," in Fitzgerald, *Augustine through the Ages*. While Ayres does not mention Gunton in the above passages, he is critiquing Gunton's conclusions.
47. See again Gunton's words as cited above in Jenson, "Decision Tree," 10.
48. Ayres, "Fundamental Grammar," 65.

seized the sacred writings of your Spirit and especially the apostle Paul. . . . I began reading and found that all the truth I had read in the Platonists was stated here together with the commendation of your grace."[49] For Augustine, God used the truth from the Platonists (divine simplicity) as a stepping-stone to the grace and truth to be found only in Christ. Thus, when simplicity was coupled with a corollary emphasis upon the *irreducibility* of the Father, Son, and Holy Spirit,[50] Ayres argues that the Platonic grammar gave "wings" to Nicea. It did so by showing that while our understanding of the triune God will always be incomplete, it is not irrational.[51] If God is simple, then all three persons may possess full divinity, without being three gods.

Judging the Effects of Divine Simplicity: A Way Forward

We come then to an impasse. On the one side, Gunton and a chorus of modern theologians see divine simplicity as an imposition of an alien metaphysic upon the God of Scripture. For Barth, the concept was exalted to "[an] idol . . . devouring everything concrete,"[52] and for Alvin Plantinga, a simple God must either be nonrelational or nonpersonal.[53] Yet on the other side are scores of premodern Christians, who, while avowedly Trinitarian, apparently had no trouble with divine simplicity. Thus, as Stephen Holmes writes: "If the problems of reconciling the concept of simplicity with the triune God of Scripture are as obvious as we have been led to think in

---

49. Augustine, *Conf.* 7.21.27.
50. We will explore Augustine's handling of the irreducibility of the three members of the Trinity in a later portion of this chapter.
51. By *rational* we of course do not mean the rationality of the Enlightenment, but rather the widespread acceptance of certain Neoplatonic presuppositions (for instance, regarding simplicity) at the time Augustine was writing.
52. Barth, *CD* 2/1, 329. Cited in Holmes, "Something Much Too Plain to Say," 137.
53. Alvin Plantinga, *Does God Have a Nature?* (Milwaukee: Marquette University Press, 1980), 42, 53. Cited in Holmes, "Something Much Too Plain to Say," 139.

recent years, someone in this tradition should have noticed, and the apparent fact that nobody did suggests that the modern problems are a result of a misunderstanding of the tradition."[54] While delivering this paper in Gunton's presence, Holmes argued that we wrongly assume a monistic (and Platonic) ontology in our forebears when we ought to assume a "personal" (and Trinitarian) one. Thus for early Christian thinkers like Augustine, to say that God is *simple* meant "(amongst other things) that his nature, his *personal* nature, is basic and unchanging."[55] When applied to the incarnation, this ontological simplicity meant only "that the personal character displayed by the man Jesus Christ is an accurate revelation of the personal character of God—an important point, but hardly an original or difficult one."[56] In all of this, Gunton could admit that Holmes made an intriguing case for a Trinitarian affirmation of divine simplicity.[57]

Yet is this "personal ontology" really presupposed *consistently* throughout Augustine's work? Having now explored an initial facet of Gunton's argument, we are at last prepared to set forth an approach that must be carried forward: as Gunton would ultimately acknowledge, the fact that Augustine used simplicity to articulate the divine unity is not by itself the proof of a monistic drift.[58] The proof, if there is any, must be seen by tracing how divine simplicity distorted (or perhaps clarified) other aspects of Augustine's theology. How did divine simplicity color Augustine's handling of creation, mediation, incarnation, and the doctrine of the Holy Spirit?

---

54. Holmes, "Something Much Too Plain to Say," 140.
55. Ibid., 147.
56. Ibid.
57. Gunton, *Act and Being*, 122-23. For a rebuttal to Holmes's argument, see R. T. Mullins, "Simply Impossible: A Case against Divine Simplicity," in *The Journal of Reformed Theology*, 7 (2013): 181–203.
58. As Gunton stated, while "it has become fashionable to deny the doctrine of divine simplicity ... this will not do if we wish to hold on to a doctrine of the unity and coherence of the divine being." *Act and Being*, 32.

To determine the veracity of Gunton's charge against Augustine's usage of divine simplicity, we must examine these other elements of Augustine's thought. In doing so himself, Gunton came to believe that Augustine's grammar did, in the words of Ayres, "give wings to Nicaea." Yet in Gunton's view, those wings served to carry Augustine's God up and away from the divine economy. To examine this charge, we turn now to the question at the heart of Gunton's case: How did Augustine safeguard the biblical distinctness of the Father, Son, and Holy Spirit?

Triune Persons and Particularity

Gunton's claim was that Augustine's concern for divine simplicity had led him to obscure the "particularity" of triune persons.[59] As evidence, Gunton often turned to Augustine's professed confusion over the Cappadocian distinction between *ousia* and *hypostasis*.[60] In the passage below, it is instructive to note that Augustine made this statement immediately after an affirmation of divine simplicity. As we have seen, Gunton did not see this as a mere coincidence. As Augustine wrote,

> [For God] it is not one thing to be, and another to be great, but to Him it is the same thing to be as to be great [hence, divine simplicity];[61] therefore, as we do not say three essences . . . I say one essence and one greatness. I say essence, which in Greek is called *ousia*, and which we call more usually substance. They indeed use also the word *hypostasis*; but they intend to put a difference, I know not what, between *ousia* and

---

59. See Gunton, *Promise of Trinitarian Theology*, xxiv, 43, 73; *Act and Being*, 134. As seen in ch. 1, Gunton defined "particularity" (or substantiality) as the relative independence that is the product of mutually constitutive relations. See *One, the Three and the Many*, ch. 7. For a book-length treatment of this concept in Gunton, see David Höhne, *Spirit and Sonship: Colin Gunton's Theology of Particularity and the Holy Spirit* (Burlington, VT: Ashgate, 2010).
60. See Augustine, *Trin.* 5.8, 9; cf. 7.4.7.
61. While this bracketed insertion is my own, the words *wholly* and *completely* are inserted by Shedd.

hypostasis. . . . Yet, when the question is asked, What three? Human language labors altogether under great poverty of speech. The answer, however, is given three "persons" [*personae*], not that it might be [completely] spoken, but that it might not be left [wholly] unspoken.[62]

For Gunton, the translator's insertion of the bracketed terms *completely* and *wholly* represents an attempt to place in Augustine's mouth what he ought to have said.[63] What he did say was, in Gunton's view, more problematic.[64] For Gunton, Augustine's inability to grasp this distinction as anything more than a linguistic device raised questions about his ability to affirm the full personhood of the Son and Holy Spirit. Thus the question of a monistic imbalance was again in play.[65]

Yet Gunton's thesis has again been challenged. In reference to the above passage from *De Trinitate*, Green asks if Augustine may not be interpreted more charitably: "Is it possible that Augustine feels little use in quibbling over the exact term, as long as the same concept is affirmed?"[66] Indeed Gunton does appear to make much of an isolated passage when more charitable interpretations have been offered. As some have argued, Augustine's statement may prove little more than what O'Donnell calls his "pathetic" grasp of Greek.[67] Or, more likely, the apparent confusion (whether real or feigned) may reflect only

---

62. Augustine, *Trin.* 5.8, 9.
63. Gunton, *Promise of Trinitarian Theology*, 40.
64. In his translation of *Trin.*, Shedd expressed surprise over Augustine's inability to grasp the Greek distinction, noting "it would seem as if his only moderate acquaintance with the Greek language would have been more than compensated by his profound trinitarian knowledge," 92n7.
65. See Gunton, *Promise of Trinitarian Theology*, 39–40.
66. Green, "The Protomodern Augustine? Colin Gunton and the Failure of Augustine," *International Journal of Systematic Theology* 9, no. 3 (July, 2009): 334n26.
67. O'Donnell, *Augustine: A New Biography*, 126. In contrast to this view, it has been argued that Augustine's knowledge of Greek (at least by the time he wrote *Trin.*) was actually rather good. See Gerald Bonner, *St Augustine of Hippo: Life and Controversies* (Norwich: The Canterbury Press, 1986), 394–95. Cited in Holmes, *The Quest for the Trinity: The Doctrine of God in Scripture, History, and Modernity* (Downers Grove, IL: IVP Academic), 131.

that Augustine had come to reject the usefulness of genus/species terminology for describing the Trinity.[68] In any case, it remains true that the distinction between *ousia* and *hypostasis* had even recently remained a matter of some debate within the Greek-speaking East.[69] The larger question then, is whether Augustine actually does affirm the same concept as the unnamed "Greeks" to whom he refers.[70]

In answer to this question, the critics of Gunton's argument point out the various instances in which Augustine affirms the irreducibility of the Father, Son, and Holy Spirit. In a passage from an early work, *De fide et symbolo* (AD 393), Augustine writes, "This Trinity is one God. Not that Father, Son and Spirit are identically the same. But Father is Father, the Son is Son and the Holy Spirit is Holy Spirit."[71] This is, of course, a kind of distinction. But is it enough to guard against a monistic imbalance? In the oft-cited patristic saying that the only difference of attribute between the Father and the Son is that the Father is the Father and Son is the Son, Gunton saw signs that that "the divine attributes [were] considered almost exclusively with respect to the doctrine of the one God . . . leaving the particular persons to languish in a kind of limbo."[72] For Gunton, *particularity* demanded more than a mere assertion that the Father is the Father and the Son is the Son. As John Webster summarizes, Gunton's notion of particularity demanded that we take seriously the biblical

---

68. See Richard Cross, "'Quid Tres?' On What Precisely Augustine Professes Not to Understand in *De Trinitate* 5 and 7," in *Harvard Theological Review* 100, no. 2 (2007): 215–32.
69. We will return to this issue in ch. 10 as we explore the Cappadocian treatments of the Trinity.
70. With regard to which Greek sources Augustine read prior to completing *De Trinitate*, Richard Cross cites the work of Irénée Chevalier, who claims that Augustine had access to pertinent sections of Gregory of Nazianzus and Didymus the Blind, and perhaps Basil of Caesarea and Epiphanius of Salamis. It is less clear, however, whether he had in fact read Gregory of Nyssa. See Irénée Chevalier, *Saint Augustin et la pensée grecque. Les relations trinitaires*, Collectanea Friburgensia 24 (Fribourg: Librairie de l'Université, 1940), 98. Cited in Cross, "Quid Tres," 229. See also Joseph T. Lienhard, "Augustine of Hippo, Basil of Caesarea, and Gregory Nazianzen," in Demacopoulos and Papanikolaou, *Orthodox Readings of Augustine*, 81–99.
71. Augustine, *f. et symb.* 9.6. Cited in Ayres, "Fundamental Grammar," 59.
72. Gunton, *Act and Being*, 134.

account of God's "distinct, though related, modes of action in relation to the creation."⁷³ Does Augustine do this?

In a more promising passage (*Epistle* 120, AD 410), Augustine seems to explicitly rebut the suspicion (set forth by Gunton) that his theology presents "an unknown substance *supporting* the three persons."⁷⁴ In opposition to this notion, Augustine asserts that "the divinity which they [the Father, Son and Spirit] have in common, is not a sort of fourth person, but the Godhead is ineffably and inseparably a Trinity," and "the essence is nothing else than the Trinity itself."⁷⁵ Here, at least, it appears that Gunton's allegation of a substance behind the persons is overtly rejected. Yet what other evidence does Gunton find for Augustine's supposed overemphasis upon divine oneness?

One before Three?: Gunton and De Régnon's Paradigm

Following Karl Rahner (1904–1984), Gunton believed that an additional indicator of Augustine's monistic drift could be seen in the way subsequent theologians chose to divide their doctrine of God into two parts (*De Deo Uno* and *De Deo Trino*), while giving a supposed primacy to God's oneness.⁷⁶ Indeed, at one point, a part of this thesis was even affirmed by some of Augustine's supporters. In his 1963 translator's introduction to *De Trinitate*, Stephen McKenna wrote,

> The very plan that [Augustine] follows differs from that of the Greeks. They begin by affirming their belief in the Father, Son and the Holy

---

73. John Webster, "Systematic Theology after Barth: Jüngel, Jenson and Gunton," in *The Modern Theologians: An Introduction to Christian Theology since 1918*, ed. David Ford and Rachel Muers (Oxford: Blackwell, 2005), 260.
74. Gunton, *Promise of Trinitarian Theology*, 43; cf. 74. Italics original. See also *Act and Being*, 134–5.
75. Augustine, *Ep.* 120.3.13, 17. Cited in Ayres, "Fundamental Grammar," 62.
76. Gunton, *Promise of Trinitarian Theology*, 31. See Karl Rahner, *The Trinity*, ed. and trans. Joseph Donceel (London: Burns and Oates, 1970), 17.

> Spirit according to the Scriptures. . . . But to Augustine it seemed better to begin with the unity of the divine nature, since this is a truth which is demonstrated by reason. . . . The logic of this arrangement is today commonly recognized, and in the text-books of dogma the treatise *De Deo Uno* precedes that of *De Deo Trino*.[77]

For Gunton, this sentiment was important, first, because it presented an approving consensus regarding the order and logic of Augustine's Trinitarianism, and second, because it illustrated what he saw as an imbalance in favor of oneness and *reason* over Trinity and *revelation*.[78] The supposed result, as Gunton argued, was that after Augustine, God's unity was both proven and prioritized through an appeal to philosophical constructs (for instance, divine simplicity), while the importance of salvation history was minimized.[79]

Yet once again, Gunton's claim has been challenged. As we have seen,[80] it is now widely questioned as to whether it is even possible to present the Trinitarian methodologies of Augustine and the Cappadocians as easily defined and polar positions. As Barnes argues, "Belief in the existence of this Greek/Latin paradigm [Greeks giving priority to the three persons, and Augustine granting priority to the one substance] is a unique property of modern trinitarian theology," derived "from a book written about 100 years ago, namely Theodore de Régnon's studies on the Trinity."[81] Ironically, as Holmes notes, "the original deployment of the paradigm was an attempt to criticize the Cappadocian theology and laud Augustine as the crown of the patristic development."[82] Yet for Barnes and others, the twentieth-

---

77. Stephen McKenna, "Introduction" to *Saint Augustine: The Trinity*. (Washington, DC: Catholic University of America Press, 1963). Both Rahner and Gunton cite this reference. See Gunton, *Promise of Trinitarian Theology*, 32.
78. Cf. Gunton, *Revelation and Reason*, ch. 5.
79. Gunton, *Promise of Trinitarian Theology*, 32.
80. See again ch. 2.
81. Barnes, "Augustine in Contemporary Trinitarian Theology," *Theological Studies* 56 (1995): 238; Theodore de Régnon, S.J., *Études de théologie positive sur la Sainte Trinité*, four vols. in three (Paris: Victor Retaux, 1892, 1998).

century tendency to merely accept de Régnon's idealized categories has led Augustine's critics to misrepresent his theology as the monistic counterpart to Cappadocian Trinitarianism.[83] In sum, the tides have shifted in patristic scholarship, and the validity de Régnon's so-called paradigm is now increasingly in doubt.[84] Did Gunton ever recognize this?

In his final published work, Gunton did acknowledge that his idealized schema regarding the purported starting points of "Greek" and "Latin" Trinitarianism was indeed an "oversimplification."[85] Thus it remains possible that his planned dogmatic theology would have tempered certain prior statements. In fairness, however, it also remains to be seen if Barnes and others can succeed in pinning even the broadest notion of an East/West distinction on the work of a nineteenth-century historian.[86] As illustrated by the background to the great Arian debates, some in the West had long suspected the more Origenist East of tritheism, while many in the East had suspected the West of a version of Sabellianism. Thus, as Khaled Anatolios notes, "the notion of an East/West theological divide in the fourth-century debates was sometimes articulated during these very debates."[87]

---

82. Holmes, *Quest for the Trinity*, 130.
83. Barnes, "Augustine in Contemporary Trinitarian Theology," 238. While Barnes does not name Gunton here, it is clear that Gunton's view of Augustine falls within the spectrum that includes the likes of de Régnon, Harnack, Rahner, Jenson, Zizioulas, and LaCugna.
84. For further confirmation from an Orthodox perspective, see John Behr, "Response to Ayres: The Legacies of Nicaea, East and West," in *Harvard Theological Review* 100, no. 2 (2007): 145–46.
85. "The real difference . . . tends not to be in the starting point but in the way in which the oneness and threeness of God are weighted in relation to one another." Gunton, *Father, Son, and Holy Spirit: Toward a Fully Trinitarian Theology* (London: T&T Clark, 2003), 43.
86. See Kristin Hennessy, "An Answer to de Régnon's Accusers: Why We Should Not Speak of 'His' Paradigm," in *Harvard Theological Review* 100, no. 2 (April, 2007): 179–97. As Hennessy argues, the simplistic Greek/Latin Paradigm, while faulty, is not that of de Régnon.
87. Khaled Anatolios, *Retrieving Nicaea: The Development and Meaning of Trinitarian Doctrine* (Grand Rapids: Baker, 2011), 20n19. As proof, Anatolios points to Hilary's *On the Synods*. Likewise, as J. N. D. Kelly suggests, Augustine's Trinity has long been accused (rightly or wrongly) of

In the end, however, Gunton's critics seem right to note that he overreached when claiming Augustine as the inspiration for those subsequent theologians who would choose to order and divide their doctrine of God into (1) *De Deo Uno* and (2) *De Deo Trino*. As we will see momentarily, *De Trinitate* is hardly arranged according to these firmly delineated categories. Thus while later chapters must revisit this critique as it pertains to Augustine's supposed inheritors, we must conclude for now that this also is one of Gunton's allegations that needs to be tempered. It is an assertion without substantial argumentation, and thus it deserves to be challenged.

The Undivided Nature of Divine Action

The next of Gunton's charges was that Augustine's emphasis on the inseparable nature of divine action failed to establish an adequate distinction between the economic roles of the Father, Son and Spirit. As Gunton put it, certain "problems with the theology of the church run in parallel with some of the chief weaknesses of Augustine's theology of the Trinity. . . . If all divine actions are actions of the one God, so that the actions of the Trinity towards the world are undivided in an absolute sense, the persons are irrelevant for thought, and a kind of monism results."[88] As the statement indicates, Gunton's qualm was not with the notion that "the actions of the Trinity outwards are undivided" (*opera Trinitatis ad extra sunt indivisa*). Indeed, as he stated, "no objection can be taken to this principle if it means that everything that God does he does in the unity of his being."[89] Rather Gunton's critique centered on the alleged absolutizing of this principle. As he wrote: "If [this dictum] is so stressed, as it tends

---

"obliterat[ing] the several roles of the three Persons." *Early Christian Doctrines*, 272–73. Thanks to Thomas A. Noble for pointing out this insight.
88. Gunton, *Promise of Trinitarian Theology*, 57.
89. Ibid., 4.

to be in Augustine, that the distinctiveness and particularity of the actions of the Son and Spirit in the economy are overridden, the doctrine of the Trinity is divorced from its basis in history and made an irrelevance."[90] Where though is the evidence for this error?

One potential indicator of this deficiency within Augustine's thought may be seen in his earliest treatment of the Trinity (*Epistle* 11).[91] Here, in response to a question about the particular actions of the Son, Augustine asserts that the biblical manner of distinguishing between the acts of the divine three is merely a semblance, and an accommodation to the weakness of our fallen minds: "Wherefore, although in all things the Divine Persons act perfectly in common, and without possibility of separation, nevertheless their operations behooved to be exhibited in such a way as to be distinguished from each other, on account of the weakness which is in us, who have fallen from unity into variety."[92] In validation of Gunton's concern, it is hard to see how such language does not at least *obscure* the particularity of triune persons. If the distinct modes of divine action are presented merely as concessions to our "weakness," then the link between the immanent and economic Trinity would seem to be imperiled, and our confidence in the knowability of God would be dealt a significant blow. In Gunton's view, this tendency in Augustine would even help sow the seeds of a dualistic and skeptical (read: Kantian) epistemology.[93]

The problem with Gunton's charge is that there are other passages in Augustine (indeed there are *always* other passages in Augustine!), which go on to affirm the distinct actions of particular persons within the Godhead. In *Sermon* 52, Augustine asserts that it was of course

---

90. Gunton, *Promise of Trinitarian Theology*, 198.
91. So says Barnes, "Rereading Augustine," 154.
92. Augustine, *Ep.* 11.4 (c. 389 AD). For more context on the letter, see Ayres, *Augustine and the Trinity*, 59.
93. Gunton, *Promise of Trinitarian Theology*, 30–31; *One, the Three and the Many*, 86, 202–3.

the Son and not the Father who suffered, and that in such instances "you have the persons *quite distinct*, and their working inseparable."[94] Likewise, in the opening of *De Trinitate*, Augustine asserts that it was not the three that descended upon Jesus in the Jordan "but the Spirit alone," just as it was not the three that spoke from heaven, "but the Father alone." Nevertheless, as Augustine states, the persons are inseparable and they "work inseparably" (*inseparabiliter operunt*).[95]

How then should we view this potential tension in Augustine's thought? Lewis Ayres provides an answer. For Ayres, the places in which Augustine affirms the particularity of the divine three often come at the beginning of a discourse. At such points, Augustine is merely affirming the rule of faith as seen within the pro-Nicene tradition. At the opening of a work, Augustine often deals with the biblical text as "unadorned" with philosophical (and more specifically, Platonic) accouterments.[96] Such adornments come later, and for Augustine they serve to aid the reader's understanding.[97] This approach then follows not only a certain style of Latin rhetoric, but also Augustine's dictum that "unless you believe, you will not understand."[98]

The real question, however, is whether such philosophical "adornments" ultimately create more problems than they solve. Here *both* Gunton and Augustine may stand in need of some correction. As with divine simplicity, Augustine saw an appeal to indivisible divine action as a way of safeguarding the equality of the Father

---

94. Augustine, *Hom.* 52.14. Cited in Ayres, *Augustine and the Trinity*, 111. Emphasis mine.
95. Augustine, *Trin.* 1.4.7. Cited in Ayres, *Augustine and the Trinity*, 96.
96. This notion continues to refute the idea that Augustine somehow "began" with the one substance of God. As Ormerod notes in his critique of Gunton, Augustine's "starting point" in *De Trinitate* is actually "Scripture and Church teaching." Ormerod, "Augustine and the Trinity: Whose Crisis?" in *Pacifica* 16, Feb., 2003, 20.
97. See Ayres, *Augustine and the Trinity*, 95–117.
98. As we have seen, Gunton affirmed this dictum as a kind of proto-Polanyian approach to theological epistemology. See *Enlightenment and Alienation: An Essay towards a Trinitarian Theology* (Grand Rapids: Eerdmans, 1985), 3, 51, 131.

and the Son against some Arian opponents.[99] Thus, in his rush to judgment, Gunton often failed to acknowledge both (1) the pro-Nicene intentions behind Augustine's argument, and (2) the other passages in which Augustine affirms the particularity of triune persons. In light of this, Gunton's critics are again right to say that he was unfair to Augustine.

Yet examples like that of *Epistle* 11 must also be noted. At such points, there does seem to be a tension in Augustine's thought. By explaining this, Ayres gains a partial acquittal for Augustine himself, while also tacitly affirming that the passages are ripe for misconstrual. In such cases, the tension between the biblical affirmation and the philosophical extrapolation suggests that the beauty of the Trinity may be more visible *without* the philosophical adornment. As Ayres shows, such finery served a pro-Nicene purpose, yet as the Platonic paradigm was replaced by others, it is at least possible that the adornment came to veil, rather than reveal a vision of the triune God.[100] In such instances, Augustine's emphasis on the undivided nature of divine action may have come to unwittingly marginalize the particularity of triune persons.

The Spirit as the "Link of Love"

A final charge against Augustine's handling of triune particularity involves the doctrine of the Holy Spirit. In Gunton's view, Augustine's identification of the Spirit as the "bond of love" (*vinculum amoris*)[101] between the Father and the Son was both insightful and

---

99. As noted previously (ch. 1), while these later "Arians" may not have overtly traced their theological ancestry to Arius himself, a certain continuity of theology remains in their various Homoian Christologies. For further context on the use of the Arian label, see Behr, *The Nicene Faith*, part 1 (Crestwood, NY: St. Vladimir's Seminary Press, 2004), 26.
100. We will return to this discussion in ch. 6 as we look at Ockham and Augustine's medieval legacy.
101. See Augustine, *Trin.* 6.5.

inadequate. The strength of this conception was said to reside in the recognition that the Holy Spirit is in some sense the perfecting agent of community, even within the Godhead.[102]

The inadequacy of the "link of love" analogy stemmed, in Gunton's view, from the alleged fact that Augustine failed to make the outward or eschatological move so that the Holy Spirit was seen also as the perfecting agent within history.[103] In this way, the *link of love* analogy, while accurate, was also incomplete in that it tended, in Gunton's view, to "turn the deity into an eternal inward turning circle rather than a being from eternity directed outwards to the other."[104] In response to this perception, Gunton's reaction was strong:

> God is no lonely monad or self-absorbed tyrant, but one whose orientation to the other is intrinsic to his eternal being as God. God's work "outward" is an expression of what he is eternally. The Spirit, we might say, is the motor of that divine movement outwards, just as the Son is its focus and model (*eikōn*). Augustine called the Spirit the bond of love between the Father and the Son, but this is in danger of leading us to think of God as a kind of self-enclosed circle.[105]

As we will now see, this is perhaps the weakest of Gunton's allegations against Augustine's thought.

In all of this, Gunton's case often proceeds by way of assertion rather than argument. A rare exception to this trend is found in *The Promise of Trinitarian Theology.* Here we find several citations, all from *De Trinitate*, that illustrate Augustine's identification of the Spirit as both "Gift" and "Love."[106] What is not clear from such

---

102. See Gunton, *Promise of Trinitarian Theology*, 49; *Father, Son, and Holy Spirit*, 73, 86; *Christian Faith*, 186.
103. See Gunton, "God the Holy Spirit: Augustine and his Successors," in *Theology through the Theologians: Selected Essays 1972–1995* (Edinburgh: T&T Clark, 1996), 105–128.
104. Gunton, *Christian Faith*, 186. Gunton's inward-turning circle analogy is borrowed from Karl Rahner, *The Trinity*, 18. See also Gunton, *Father, Son, and Holy Spirit*, 73.
105. Gunton, *Father, Son, and Holy Spirit*, 86.

references, however, is how such language presents the Trinity as "a self-enclosed circle." As Gunton noted, Augustine did grant the Spirit the outward function of uniting the individual soul to God, yet even this was seen as insufficient. For Gunton, the deficiency could be witnessed in the way Augustine allegedly showed little interest in God's pneumatological action *in time*. As Gunton wrote,

> By attributing to the Spirit the kind of love that he does, Augustine thus attracts attention away from the economy of salvation . . . [and] he obscures the specific hypostatic uniqueness of the Holy Spirit. Because . . . he has an inadequate conception of love as love for the other as other, he is unable to conceive true otherness in the Trinity, another feature which can be seen to be a function of too strong an emphasis on the unity of God.[107]

Here again the critique returns to Augustine's supposedly deficient grasp of the particularity of the divine persons. Yet to evaluate Augustine's pneumatology, we must look beyond the few passages that Gunton cites.

In *De Civitate Dei*, for instance, we find several instances in which Augustine affirms a distinctly "outward moving" doctrine of the Holy Spirit. Here he speaks of the Spirit as both the goodness (*bonitas*) and the holiness (*sanctitas*) of the Father and the Son. Such titles are then connected to the creation narratives, of which Augustine asks three questions: (1) Who made this? (2) by what means?, and (3) for what purpose? Based on the divine sight that the creation was "good" (*bonitas*), Augustine identifies the Spirit as an answer to all these questions.[108] In light of this logic (however dubious the

---

106. Augustine, *Trin.* 15.31,29; and 15.27, 29, 31 respectively.
107. Gunton, *Promise of Trinitarian Theology*, 51.
108. Augustine, *Civ.* 11.24: "And by the words, 'God saw that it was good,' it is sufficiently intimated that God made what was made not from any necessity, nor for the sake of supplying any want, but solely from His own goodness. . . . And if we are right in understanding; that this goodness is the Holy Spirit, then the whole Trinity is revealed to us in the creation."

exegesis by our modern standards) Ayres notes that we have a clear example of Augustine referencing the Holy Spirit as both an active agent in creation, and the *End* toward which it is aimed.[109] At this point, one might ask how Augustine's pneumatology is demonstrably different from one of Gunton's theological heroes: Basil of Caesarea. It was Basil, who (much to Gunton's delight)[110] referred to the Spirit as the *Perfecting Cause* of the divine economy.[111] Yet here in the aforementioned passages from *De Civitate Dei*, we find Augustine doing something very similar. Thus, if Gunton had only read Augustine more thoroughly, he might have actually found some further patristic support for his "outward moving" doctrine of the Holy Spirit.

To evidence a further problem with Gunton's case, we now turn to his most sweeping allegation. In a new epilogue to the published version of his doctoral thesis, Gunton claimed that "the Achilles' heel of all Western theology is Augustine's failure to make the Spirit a person. . . . Augustine's understanding of the Spirit as the bond of love between the Father and the Son effectively rendered him an impersonal link closing the gap, so to speak, between those two who are effectively the persons of the Godhead."[112] The charge is as bold as it is unsubstantiated. Contrary to Gunton's assertion, Augustine does not limit the Spirit's role to that of linking the Father and the Son in eternity. This is a famous image from *De Trinitate*, but as we have seen already, Augustine likewise viewed the Spirit as being active within history. In creation the Spirit is the Goodness

---

109. See Ayres, *Augustine and the Trinity*, 255.
110. For just one example of Gunton's use of Basil as an antidote to Augustine, see Gunton, *Father, Son, and Holy Spirit*, 45–7, 81–6.
111. Basil of Caesarea, *On the Holy Spirit*, 15.36, 38. Cited in Gunton, *Father, Son, and Holy Spirit*, 81.
112. Gunton, *Becoming and Being*, 238. Here again, Basil is cited as the solution so ignominiously ignored by the West.

(*bonitas*) from which the Father makes all things,[113] in redemption the Spirit is the Gift that distinguishes "sons" and connects them to God,[114] in ecclesiology the Spirit is the Bringer of Oneness,[115] and in eschatology the Spirit is the origin and blessedness of the coming city of God.[116] Augustine's exegesis, and his commitment to the pro-Nicene tradition led him to affirm *all* of these realities.

In light of such evidence, a final question now presents itself: Is there anything significant to be affirmed in Gunton's argument regarding Augustine's supposed monistic imbalance? To answer this, we must allow for a final detour in order to demonstrate the basic argument of this chapter. Thus far, our response to Gunton's argument has been almost entirely negative. In the ensuing section, however, we will deal with the importance of *De Trinitate*, and in so doing, we will attempt to indicate that while Gunton's allegation of a monistic imbalance is indeed unfair to Augustine, his concerns regarding the selective appropriation of Augustine's work remains more viable once it has been properly qualified.

Once More, *De Trinitate*

In the above discussion, a certain pattern has emerged. First, we find Gunton making bold assertions about the disastrous deficiencies in Augustine's treatment of the Trinity. As he argued, Augustine's Neoplatonism led to a monistic imbalance that served to distance the triune God from the economy of salvation. Next, this charge was "supported" by some isolated passages, pulled often from *De Trinitate*.

---

113. Augustine, *Civ.* 11.24.
114. This is the whole point of identifying the Spirit as God's Gift/Love. As Augustine states, "There is no gift more excellent than this [Love/Holy Spirit]. It alone distinguishes the sons of the eternal kingdom and the sons of eternal perdition." *Trin.* 15.18–19. See also Augustine's frequent use of Rom. 5:5.
115. See Augustine, *Jo. ev. tr.* 39 where Augustine identifies the Spirit as that which "makes many souls one soul and many hearts one heart." Cited in Ayres, *Augustine and the Trinity*, 257.
116. Augustine, *Civ.* 11.24.

Finally, Gunton's case was closed by tracing the alleged results of these errors through Augustine's theological descendants.[117]

In response to this method, Gunton's critics have rightly decried both the sweeping nature of his claims, and his failure to acknowledge other passages (often outside of *De Trinitate*)[118] that may be seen to acquit Augustine of monistic errors. With respect to the first half of this rebuttal, we have seen that Gunton's critics have good reason to object. With regard to the second half, however, it would seem that a rather uncontroversial reality must now be considered: *De Trinitate* is Augustine's most enduring contribution to Trinitarian thought. Indeed, as Gunton noted, the work remains "among the glories of Western theology."[119] Thus when the discussion turns from Augustine to his legacy, the enduring status of *De Trinitate* becomes even more important. With this in mind, we now turn to consider an emerging consensus on what Michel Barnes refers to as the "genre" of this masterpiece.

The Lost Polemic: Rethinking the Genre Of *De Trinitate*

In his trenchant defense of Augustine, Barnes makes a lengthy argument that significant portions of *De Trinitate* should be seen in the context of an anti-Arian polemic.[120] As evidence, Barnes notes how Augustine prefaces his discussion of Christ with reference to those "who have affirmed that our Lord Jesus Christ is not God,

---

117. See ch. 3 in Gunton, *Promise of Trinitarian Theology*; cf. *Triune Creator*, 73–86.
118. See Drecoll's polite critique of Ayres on the basis that his extensive defense of Augustine's Trinitarianism "nearly ignored" the latter books of *De Trinitate*. Volker Henning Drecoll, review of *Augustine and the Trinity*, by Lewis Ayres, *Scottish Journal of Theology* 66, no. 1 (Feb. 2013): 88–98.
119. Gunton, *Promise of Trinitarian Theology*, 31.
120. Barnes, "Augustine in Contemporary Trinitarian Theology," 246–50. Also, "The Arians of Book V, and the Genre of *De Trinitate*," *Journal of Theological Studies* 44 (1993): 185–95; and "Exegesis and Polemic in Augustine's *De Trinitate* I," *Augustinian Studies* 30 (1999): 43–59. While Barnes does not mention Gunton, his work is picked up by Bradley Green toward that end. See Green, "The Protomodern Augustine," 338.

or is not true God, or is not with the Father the one and only God."[121] In addition, Barnes also shows that Augustine chooses to deal specifically with those biblical passages most often used by certain Arian opponents. To refute such errors, Augustine responds naturally with a polemical emphasis upon the divine unity, utilizing the extensive exegetical and Platonic weaponry at his disposal.[122]

Unfortunately, as Barnes argues, the polemic nature of Augustine's masterpiece was soon downplayed. In time, *De Trinitate* came to be seen primarily as an irenic and exploratory work.[123] Thus Basil Studer could comment that while nonpolemical works were relatively rare in the patristic period, "a few may be named" and "above all" Augustine's *De Trinitate*."[124] For Barnes, this misconception led modern critics to falsely assume a monistic (and eternalizing) tendency in Augustine's thought where there was merely a polemic counterbalance to Arian errors.[125]

While Barnes makes his case in order to defend Augustine, it is important to note that the same argument could be utilized to show how *De Trinitate* may have contributed to a subsequent imbalance amongst some of Augustine's inheritors. Polemics, after all, are meant to swing the pendulum of public opinion in the desired direction, yet if history is any indicator, such pendulums are sometimes difficult to stop. If Barnes is correct (and Green assumes he is)[126] then it seems at least possible that *De Trinitate's* polemic emphases may have

---

121. Augustine, *Trin.* 1.9.
122. Barnes, "Augustine in Contemporary Trinitarian Theology," 247.
123. For further explication of this phenomenon, see Roland Kany, "'Fidei Contemnentes Initium': On Certain Positions Opposed by Augustine in *De Trinitate*", in *Studia Patristica* 27, ed. E. A. Livingstone (Leuven: Peeters Press, 1993), 327.
124. Basil Studer, *History of Theology*, 1: *The Patristic Period*, ed. A. Berardino and B. Studer, trans. M. J. O'Connell (Collegeville, MN: Liturgical Press, 1997), 8. According to Barnes, Studer has since backed off from this statement. See Barnes, "Exegesis and Polemic," 59n40.
125. While Gunton goes mostly unnamed among these modern critics, his sort of thinking is clearly under attack. Green goes on to utilize Barnes's work in his critique of Gunton. See Green, "The Protomodern Augustine," 338.
126. Ibid.

had some unintended consequences among Augustine's theological descendants. This possibility, however, has not been greatly explored in the previous evaluations of Gunton's claims; thus, the coming chapters must evaluate this possibility.[127]

Having now addressed one of the polemical intents within *De Trinitate*, we must now highlight what Gunton thought to be one of its most problematic facets, the search for triune "analogies" (or more aptly, "similitudes")[128] within the inward world of the individual human psyche.

Through the Looking Glass: The Basis for Augustine's "Inward Turn"

In Book 8 of *De Trinitate*, Augustine announces a transition in his manner of exploring the mystery of trinitarian theology. As he puts it, he will now begin to "discuss in a more inward manner" the things that have already been covered.[129] This signals a shift from the Trinity as affirmed in Scripture and tradition, and toward some possible triune similitudes within the human self. What follows in the latter books of *De Trinitate* are the well-known explorations of various triads that are meant to form imperfect echoes of divine triunity. Most famously, Augustine sets forth the triads of (1) *lover, beloved, love*;[130] (2) *mind, love, knowledge*;[131] and (3) *memory, understanding, will*.[132] The potential faults of such similitudes are also well rehearsed. On the spectrum of tritheism versus monism, the so-called psychic analogies would seem to tilt decidedly toward the latter. After all, if

---

127. See chs. 5–6.
128. As Ayres notes, "Augustine avoids the term *analogia* in favour of a number of terms that indicate a much looser set of likenesses (*similitudines*)." Ayres, *Augustine and the Trinity*, 288.
129. Augustine, *Trin.* 8.1.
130. *Trin.* 8.
131. *Trin.* 9.
132. *Trin.* 10.

taken at face value, such entities as memory, understanding, and will are but the faculties of a single person.[133]

In Gunton's view, such inward "speculation" turned the Trinity into a "theological irrelevance" in which the divine three cease to be *persons*, and thus cease to address how triune relatedness can be brought to bear on human relatedness.[134] Before delving into such critiques, however, we must first begin with a rather different question: What led Augustine to such internal triads in the first place? Why search for a trace of the Trinity within the individual human being? For Augustine, the answer lay with the *imago Dei*.

While Augustine once believed that Adam was fashioned in the image and likeness of the Son,[135] he would later change his mind on this issue.[136] For the more mature Augustine, the second plural of Gen. 1:26 ("Let us make mankind in *our* image") proved that "man was made to the image, not of the Father alone or of the Son alone or of the Holy Spirit alone, but of the Trinity itself."[137] With this crucial point established, Augustine naturally turned to ask which part of the human being should be seen as the *imago Trinitatis*. In his view, the only suitable candidate was the rational mind.[138] As Augustine asked, "From what likeness or comparison of known things can we believe, in order that we may love God, whom we do not yet know?"[139]

---

133. So says Shedd in his introduction to *Trin.*, *Nicene and Post-Nicene Fathers*, trans. Arthur Haddan, revised and annotated by W. G. T. Shedd, series 1, vol. 3 (New York: Cosimo Classics, 1887, 2007), 9.
134. Colin Gunton, "Trinity, Ontology and Anthropology: Towards a Renewal of the Doctrine of the *Imago Dei*," in *Persons, Divine and Human*, ed. Christoph Schwöbel and Colin Gunton (Edinburgh: T&T Clark, 1991), 47.
135. See Augustine, *Gn. litt. imp.* 16.57–8 (c. 393–94 AD).
136. The shift had already occurred by the writing of *Conf.* 13.22.32 (c. 397–401 AD).
137. Augustine states this in a later amendment to *Gn. litt. imp.* 16.61 (c. 426–27 AD).
138. To be sure, Augustine was hardly the first to speak of the mind (or soul) as the location of the divine image. As Ayres notes, many prominent pro-Nicenes of the period (including Athanasius, Nyssen, and Nazianzen) would speak similarly of the mind (or soul) as the location of the *imago Dei*. See Ayres, *Nicaea and Its Legacy*, 326.
139. Augustine, *Trin.* 8.5.8.

At this point, any reference to material analogies had already been rejected on the previously surveyed grounds of God's simplicity. So Augustine turned *within*, with the acknowledgment that "not only most true reason but also the authority of the apostle himself declares, man was not made in the image of God according to the shape of his body, but according to his rational mind."[140] This statement must be dissected. In regard to "most true reason," it seems likely that Augustine was referring both to a Platonic preference for mind over matter, and to a more basic observation. As he later notes, "A mind without the eyes of the flesh is still human, but the eyes of the flesh without a mind are bestial."[141] This, we might agree, seems "reasonable," yet as Gunton would be quick to note, it is not itself a justification for associating the mind *alone* with the *imago Dei*.[142] What then of Augustine's other appeal, to the "authority of the apostle"?

Augustine was referring, as he often was, to Paul. But where does Paul equate the human mind with the *imago Dei*? The texts immediately cited are references to "putting on the new man" (Col. 3:9–10) by which one is to be "renewed in the spirit of your mind . . . which is created after God" (Eph. 4:23–24).[143] While modern scholars might question Augustine's exegesis at this point, the fact remains that the basis for his understanding of the *imago Dei* was not (in his own opinion) purely the product of Platonic reason; it was something that he claimed to find in Scripture. As O'Donnell perhaps overstates it, "Whenever Augustine is saying something that moderns find troubling, the best first resort for an interpreter is to look closely

---

140. *Trin.* 12.7.12.
141. *Trin.* 14.14.19.
142. See Gunton, "Trinity, Ontology and Anthropology," 47–9.
143. *Trin.* 12.7.12. The scriptural quotations are those of Augustine, as translated by Shedd.

to see what Scripture he has in mind and how it more or less forces him to say what he says."[144]

This attention to Scripture becomes more apparent when we turn to what is arguably the most important biblical passage in *De Trinitate:* 1 Corinthians 13. The text is referenced more than twenty times in the work, and it can be seen to provide an exegetical impetus for Augustine's plunge into the looking glass.[145] The passage is about *love*, and as Augustine states, "thou dost see the Trinity if thou seest love."[146] By using the imagery of someone looking into a mirror, the apostle asserts that while we see now "in a mirror, dimly, . . . then we will see face to face" (13:12, NRSV). For Augustine, such imagery was an invitation to see in the looking glass, an imperfect reflection of the triune God.[147] It was an invitation not from "the Platonists," but from Paul, to look into the mirror, to "know thyself" and to find in that enigma the *vestigia trinitatis*.[148] And so Augustine looked; he saw himself, and plunged in.

Such passages are instructive not only because they show how Augustine's inward turn was shaped by Scripture, but also because they illustrate how this turn was redirected toward the goal of outward love. As Augustine states in the section that contains his similitude of lover, beloved, love: "Let no one say, I do not know what I love. Let him love his brother, and he will love the same love" (that is, God).[149] Given Gunton's claims, the question must be asked: Does this triad really tilt toward inwardness, individualism, and a monistic view of God? Surely not. In pointing to *love* as a

---

144. O'Donnell, *Augustine: A New Biography*, 292.
145. See the scriptural index in Shedd's translation, 559.
146. *Trin.* 8.8.12.
147. Thus the passage accords with his reading of Gen. 1.26. See *Trin.* 7.6.12; *Gn. litt. imp.* 16.61; *Conf.* 13.22.
148. For Augustine's explanation of *enigma* as "an obscure allegory," see *Trin.* 15.8–9.
149. *Trin.* 8.8.

picture of the Trinity, Augustine draws upon what is perhaps the most relational (and "social") concept of all.[150] Thus as Bradley Green argues, we should not view the sacred triads as *merely* the result of so much Neoplatonic navel gazing. There is a Platonic background here, but there is also an outward and relational focus that Augustine found within the Christian Scriptures. As Augustine would proclaim, "This trinity of the mind is not therefore the image of God because it remembers, understands, and loves itself; but because it can also remember, understand, and love Him by whom it was made."[151]

For his own part, Gunton seemed largely blind to (or perhaps uninterested in) this reality. Thus his appraisals of Augustine's Trinitarian analogies lack both context and fairness. Yet to stop here would be to miss a crucial point. For Gunton, the question was not whether Augustine could devise (in his inward turn) an acceptable marriage of Platonic and Pauline concepts. For Gunton, the real question was whether this imperfect union would do damage, as it was appropriated by the subsequent tradition.[152] With this in mind, we now turn to some potential dangers in Augustine's so-called psychic analogies.

Some Dangers in Augustine's Mental Triads

For Gunton, Augustine's identification of the *imago Dei* with the individual rational mind would have disastrous consequences in time. As he argued, it would go on to contribute to the conception of a partially divinized *nous* pushing around a mechanical body.[153] Here the human mind would become, in Ryle's words, "the ghost in the

---

150. Thanks to Thomas A. Noble for pointing this out in conversation. See also Michael Hanby, *Augustine and Modernity* (New York: Routledge, 2003), 14.
151. Augustine, *Trin.* 14.12.15.
152. See again Holmes's comments in *Revelation and Reason*, 8.
153. Gunton, *Revelation and Reason*, 42–43. Gunton here cites Edward Craig, *The Mind of God and the Works of Man* (Oxford: Oxford University Press, 1987).

machine."[154] As Gunton argued, Augustine's depiction of God as a kind of "super mind" would also result in an individualistic or monistic imbalance, wherein I am like God in terms of my rational mind.[155]

The problem, in Gunton's view, was that such inward faculties (whatever they are) are not *persons*, and as such, they do not *act* in the world of space and time. Beyond this, Gunton's claim was that such intellectualism would lead to later individualism, regardless of Augustine's intent. As he wrote, "The crucial analogy for Augustine is between the inner structure of the human mind and the inner being of God, because it is in the former that the latter is made known, this side of eternity at any rate, more really than in the 'outer' economy of grace."[156] Such sweeping statements have raised questions. For instance, what of Augustine's frequent caveat that these so-called mental analogies were imperfect and limited in value? Gunton would have none of this. For him, the fact that such triads mirrored the *internal* life of the *individual* hinted at a later problem that could not be whisked away by an admission that all analogies are inadequate: "Whatever he says, Augustine is not merely producing analogies. . . . He is in fact developing a doctrine of God, with the stress on the unity."[157]

What then of Augustine's biblical justification for his plunge into the looking glass? In response to this, Gunton's claim was that an appeal to Scripture is not synonymous with an emphasis upon the divine economy. The economy was, in Gunton's thought, a way of talking about divine action within salvation history;[158] thus while

---

154. See Gunton citing Ryle in "Trinity, Ontology and Anthropology," 47. We will deal in the next chapter with the veracity of this allegation as it pertains to Augustine's doctrine of creation.
155. Gunton, *Promise of Trinitarian Theology*, 44n17. Gunton here credits Schwöbel with this suggestion.
156. Ibid., 45.
157. Ibid., in reference to book 10 of *Trin.*

Scripture *presents* this economy, Scripture may be misread. This was precisely what Gunton believed to have happened in Augustine. Given this charge, one might expect large portions of Gunton's work to be involved in a kind of exegetical rehabilitation of the biblical material. Oddly, this was not the case. As Höhne notes, "[John] Webster is correct in criticising Gunton's theology for a lack of exegetical description. Considering that Gunton felt free to rebuke Augustine for a lack of Scriptural support for his understanding of the Trinity, it is only appropriate that Gunton's work receive the same scrutiny."[159] Perhaps this weakness stems partly from a distinction in discipline; Gunton was not a biblical scholar by trade. Yet whatever the reason, the fact remains that Gunton's arguments might have been strengthened by a more lengthy treatment of the exegetical description that he so frequently found lacking in others.

Thus the question remains: If Gunton had taken more time to evaluate the biblical justification for his charge against Augustine, would his claim have been supported? As Augustine notes, Ephesians does speak of the mind as being renewed by God. Likewise, the biblical writer also sees this renewal as being connected to the putting on of the new *anthropon*, created in God's likeness (Eph. 4:24). Yet for the author of Ephesians, this notion led not to a subsequent dissection of the human *nous*, but to a new way of seeing particular humans (Jews and Gentiles no less!) as having been made *one* in the body of the Messiah.[160] Put simply, in the New Testament Jesus is the true *imago Dei*.[161] Thus in Ephesians and elsewhere the opening into the

---

158. See especially P. H. Brazier's explanatory notes on the subject in Gunton, *Revelation and Reason*, 29.
159. Höhne, *Spirit and Sonship*, 14; cf. Webster, "Systematic Theology after Barth," 262. Contrast this with Gunton's acknowledgement that "all faithful Christian theology must be . . . an interpretation of the scriptures." *Christ and Creation*, 11.
160. See esp. Eph. 4:1-6.
161. See, for example 2 Cor. 4:4; Col. 1:15–20; Heb. 1:1–3; Rom. 8:29; 1 Cor. 15:49. For a survey of the New Testament material, see Stanley Grenz, "The Social God and the Relational

triune mystery is not the immaterial human mind, but the scarred and resurrected *body* of the incarnate Christ.[162]

At points Augustine seems aware of this. In book four of *De Trinitate*, he cites Jesus' high-priestly prayer (John 17:21–22) in order to articulate how the Many become One through the Mediator. Thus, we even find here an emphasis upon ecclesial communion as a reflection of the triune life: "As the Father and Son are one, not only in equality of substance, but also in will, *so those also may be one*, between whom God the Son is mediator, not only in that they are of the same nature, but also through the same union of love."[163] In response to this passage, one might be tempted to say that we have here something that approaches what would eventually be seen as a kind of social Trinitarianism, founded upon Christ's words in John 17. Gunton never cites this passage, and his critics rightly use such omissions to highlight a biased reading of Augustine.[164]

Yet here again the potential problem lies not merely in Gunton's reading, but in the novel elements and disproportionate emphases within Augustine's own work. By focusing the vast majority of his argument upon the immaterial mind as the *imago Trinitatis*, Augustine signals a shift away from what we will come to see as the Irenaean viewpoint that the whole human was created after the image (or pattern) of the incarnate Christ.[165] While this shift does not mean that Augustine's doctrine of the Trinity was decidedly monistic, it does raise questions about how his inward turn would be appropriated

---

Self: Toward a Trinitarian Theology of the *Imago Dei*," in *Trinitarian Soundings in Systematic Theology*, ed. Paul L. Metzger (London: T&T Clark, 2005). Like Gunton, Grenz critiques the "Augustinian inward turn" for ultimately overshadowing this New Testament treatment of the *imago Dei* (96).

162. See, for instance, N. T. Wright, *Justification: God's Plan and Paul's Vision* (Downers Grove, IL: IVP Academic, 2009), 171–75.
163. Augustine, *Trin.* 4.9. Italics mine.
164. See Green, "The Protomodern Augustine," 335–41.
165. For support, see Mary T. Clark, "Image Doctrine," in Fitzgerald, *Augustine through the Ages*, 440–41. We will return to Irenaeus in ch. 9.

by later thinkers. As Barth asked, "Do we not have in this idea of the *vestigium trinitatis* an ancient Trojan horse which one day . . . was unsuspectingly allowed entry into the theological Ilium, and in whose belly . . . we can hear a threatening clank?"[166] As Christopher Beeley has likewise noted in critique of Ayres's near-total exoneration of Augustine: the "exegetical choices in the latter passages [of *De Trinitate*] often run counter to the plain(er) sense of the biblical text."[167] By this time, the philosophical adornment may have partly veiled the potential radiance of the biblical affirmation.

The same is true in Augustine's rather problematic reading of 1 Corinthians 13. Here again, he seems to see in his looking glass *not* a "whole person" reflecting dimly the perfect image of Christ, but rather the internal workings of an immaterial mind reflecting dimly the "three-in-oneness" of the Trinity. As we have seen, the reason for this exegetical move resides partly in Augustine's understanding of the plurals in Gen.1:26 ("Let us make mankind in *our* image"). Yet for Gunton, the answer could also be traced to Augustine's abiding suspicion of material and temporal being.

Thus we may rightly view the immaterial mental triads within the latter books of *De Trinitate,* as the "hinge points" between Gunton's charge of a monistic imbalance within Augustine's Trinitarianism, and his subsequent claim of a dualistic imbalance within Augustine's treatment of material being. With this suggestion now noted, we are at last prepared to turn to the second facet of Gunton's case against Augustine: the alleged dualism in his doctrine of creation. Before doing this, however, we must first gather the strands from the present chapter.

---

166. Barth, *CD* 1/1, 335–36.
167. Christopher Beeley, review of *Augustine and the Trinity*, by Lewis Ayres, *Scottish Journal of Theology*, 66, no. 1 (Feb. 2013): 99–100. Likewise, Volker Henning Drecoll has critiqued Ayres's failure to adequately acknowledge the Platonic influence upon Augustine's Trinitarianism. See Drecoll, review of *Augustine and the Trinity*, 89.

Conclusions

Our goal in this chapter has been to examine Gunton's claims regarding the purported monistic imbalance in Augustine's Trinitarianism. In so doing, we have sided frequently with Gunton's critics, who have rightly noted that his arguments were lacking both in context and in fairness. Yet while Augustine often acquits himself of Gunton's monistic allegations, such passages must also be weighed against some potentially problematic emphases within his theology—most notably his focus upon finding a trace of the Trinity within the rational mind of the individual human. This argument has been illustrated in a number of respects.

First, in examining divine simplicity as the supposed "chief weakness" of Augustine's thought, we came to agree with Holmes that the presence of this concept is not itself an indicator of monistic drift. Yet in affirming this, we saw also that Gunton had good reason to ask whether simplicity did not contribute to potential problems for Augustine's treatment of creation. Indeed it was, in part, the logic of simplicity which compelled Augustine to "take away all bodily things" and to look within himself in order to encounter the triune image of God.[168] In the end, the precise character of simplicity in Augustine must be judged by how adequately Augustine was able to treat the second focus of this chapter, the particularity of the Father, Son, and Holy Spirit.

Second, with regard to Augustine's treatment of the particularity of triune persons, we began by noting several faults in Gunton's argument. As we found, Gunton's accusation about the order and logic of Augustine's Trinitarianism uncritically accepted the conclusions of the so-called de Régnon paradigm without bothering to provide compelling evidence for his argument. Next, we noted

---

168. Augustine, *Jo. ev. tr.* 23.8.

that Augustine's frequent emphasis on the undivided nature of divine action was in fact accompanied by a corollary on the irreducibility of the Father, Son and Spirit. And finally, with respect to Augustine's pneumatology, we saw that, contrary to Gunton's assertion, Augustine did in fact speak of the Spirit in ways that went far beyond the intratrinitarian "link of love." In all of this, Gunton's monistic allegations proved unfounded.

Yet despite these frequent acquittals of Augustine, the third and final portion of this chapter brought forth some evidence for taking Gunton more seriously with regard to certain aspects of Augustine's legacy. In our examination of *De Trinitate*, we found what recent scholars have seen to be a polemical emphasis upon the unity of God. Thus while Augustine had good reason for his stress upon the unity of the immanent Trinity (that is, to refute some Arian opponents), Barnes's argument regarding the forgotten nature of this polemic may lend a measure of viability to Gunton's claim about Augustine's intellectual descendants. Future chapters must evaluate this possibility.

More importantly, by virtue of his plunge into the looking glass, in order to find a sort of "trinity" within, it also remains viable (though not yet proven) to claim that Augustine unwittingly contributed to certain imbalances within the subsequent tradition: namely, a bent toward inwardness and intellectualism. Thus while Gunton was often unfair to Augustine regarding the near monism/modalism in his doctrine of the Trinity, we will come to see that this "inward turn" did contribute to *some* of the subsequent developments decried by Gunton. Yet to elucidate this claim, we must turn from Augustine's treatment of the Trinity to his doctrine of creation.

4

Gunton and Augustine's World: The Question of Dualism in Augustine's Doctrine of Creation

In Gunton's words, "the most fundamental ontological question of all is that concerning the nature of the world in which we live. What kind of world is it?"[1] What status should we ascribe to such things as time, matter, and human physicality? As Gunton argued, the way the modern West would come to think about such questions stood in troubling relation to Augustine of Hippo. Thus his overarching claim was that a monistic imbalance in Augustine's doctrine of God was linked to a damaging dualism in his doctrine of creation.[2] The purpose of this chapter is to evaluate the second half of this allegation. Our question is this: To what extent was Gunton justified in alleging

---

1. Gunton, *The Promise of Trinitarian Theology* (London: T&T Clark, 1991), 53.
2. See ch. 1.

that key elements of Augustine's thought represent a damaging and unbiblical dualism?

In terms of organization, we will address Gunton's critiques as they pertain to the subjects of (1) *matter,* (2) *time* and (3) *mediation.* In the end, the claim of this chapter remains similar to that of the previous one. In what follows, we will argue that while Gunton failed to present a fair and comprehensive reading of Augustine, it remains viable to contend that certain aspects of Augustine's doctrine of creation do present a problematic tension between mind and matter, Christ and creation, time and eternity. Thus while Augustine's dualism was indeed "limited,"[3] it remains reasonable to examine (as we shall do in chapters 5 through 8) whether this limitation actually made Augustine's imbalances more *transferable* to the subsequent tradition. This was Gunton's claim.[4] Yet before turning to the evidence, we must first begin with a matter of conceptual clarification.

Defining *Dualism*

As N. T. Wright has noted, the term *dualism* has come to denote such a variety of theological and philosophical positions that it is in danger of losing its meaning.[5] So what did Gunton mean when he

---

3. As claimed by Bradley G. Green, *Colin Gunton and the Failure of Augustine: The Theology of Colin Gunton in Light of Augustine* (Eugene, OR: Pickwick, 2011), 89, 96, 174.
4. See Gunton, *The Triune Creator: A Historical and Systematic Study* (Grand Rapids: Eerdmans, 1998), 76. For Gunton, the "controlled" nature of Augustine's dualism enabled it to avoid an outright condemnation.
5. N. T. Wright, *The New Testament and the People of God* (Minneapolis: Fortress, 1992), 252–53. Wright sets out ten different ways in which the language of dualism (or "duality") is frequently employed. On the one hand, Gunton would be happy to affirm what Wright refers to as the "theological/cosmological duality" (the "differentiation" between Creator and creation; see Gunton, *Yesterday and Today: A Study of Continuities of Christology* [Grand Rapids: Eerdmans, 1983], 86). Likewise, Gunton could also affirm a certain version of what Wright refers to as the "anthropological duality" (that there is some "distinction" between the body and the soul of the human person). As Gunton claimed, "Scripture is clear that the body is a subordinate part of the person, to be subjected to control of the spirit. But it is not an ontological dualism:

leveled this charge against Augustine's doctrine of creation? Broadly speaking, Gunton defined such dualism as "an assumption that the divine and the human are *opposing* realms."⁶ Yet with regard to Augustine, this error was seen to be more subtle. As Gunton stated, "Mainstream Christianity has always held that God is other than the world, but because he is its Creator, has denied that the two are related in a negative way. . . . Dualism denies such an interaction either explicitly or by conceiving the two in such a way that it becomes impossible consistently to relate them."⁷ It was this latter and more subtle tendency—the alleged inability to relate *consistently* the Creator and the creation—that Gunton found so troublesome within Augustine.⁸

Once again, this error was traced ("in every case") to Augustine's "continuing adherence to platonic ways of thought."⁹ As we will see, there were crucial differences between Augustine and the various non-Christian "Platonic" treatments of material and temporal being.¹⁰ Yet while noting this,¹¹ Gunton's claim was that there remained a "dualistic or Platonizing doctrine" in Augustine's thought.¹² As he put it, "With the platonists, he found it difficult to

---

body and spirit alike are created" (Gunton, *Triune Creator*, 211). What Gunton objected to in Augustine was a broadly Platonic dualism that would minimize the full being and goodness of God's material and temporal creation (see Gunton, *Promise of Trinitarian Theology*, 33).

6. Gunton, *The Christian Faith: An Introduction to Christian Doctrine* (Oxford: Blackwell, 2002), 87. Italics in original. Cf. Gunton, *Act and Being: Towards a Theology of the Divine Attributes* (London: SCM Press, 2002), 13.
7. Gunton, *Yesterday and Today*, 86.
8. See especially Gunton, *Triune Creator*, 73–86.
9. Ibid., 74.
10. For some helpful introductions, see Frederick Van Fleteren, "Plato, Platonism," in *Augustine through the Ages: An Encyclopedia*, ed. Allan Fitzgerald (Grand Rapids: Eerdmans, 1999), 651-54; Anne-Marie Bowery, "Plotinus," in ibid., 654–57; Crouse, "*Paucis mutatis verbis*," in *Augustine and his Critics*, ed. Robert Dodaro and George Lawless (New York: Routledge, 2000), 37–50.
11. See, for instance, the acknowledgement that Augustine "distinguishes creation from emanation for *christological* reasons." Gunton, *Triune Creator*, 75. Italics original.
12. Gunton, *The One, the Three and the Many: God, Creation and the Culture of Modernity* (Cambridge: Cambridge University Press, 1993), 2–3; cf. 55.

believe that the material and sensible realm could either be truly real or the object or the vehicle of knowledge."[13] Thus, in the end, the charge was that this specific form of dualism would cause abiding problems for Augustine's view of matter, time, and triune mediation. With this allegation now clarified, we turn next to evaluate the validity of Gunton's argument as it pertains to matter.[14]

Matter

In the prior chapter, we argued that the so-called mental analogies of *De Trinitate* can be seen as "hinge points" between Gunton's charge of monistic imbalance in Augustine's doctrine of God and that of dualism in his doctrine of creation. Gunton's claim was that by seeking the *imago Trinitatis* within the *immaterial* human mind, Augustine wrongfully elevated both (1) divine oneness and (2) the superiority of the immaterial realm. Having noted this, we concluded the previous chapter by noting some results of Augustine's trinitarian ruminations.[15]

As we saw, it was in accordance with Paul, and not merely Plotinus, that Augustine looked in the mirror (1 Corinthians 13) to find an imperfect reflection of his God. Yet the trouble emerged when Augustine perceived in his looking glass, not a *whole person* reflecting dimly the perfect image of Christ (Col. 1:15), but rather the internal workings of an immaterial mind reflecting dimly the three-in-oneness of the Trinity. This apparent preference for "mind" over matter therefore leads us now to examine the allegation that Augustine failed to value adequately the material realm.

---

13. Gunton, *Promise of Trinitarian Theology*, 33.
14. A helpful survey of Augustine's view of "matter" (*materia*) can be found in Frederick Van Fleteren, "Matter," in Fitzgerald, *Augustine through the Ages*, 547–49.
15. See again the conclusion to ch. 3.

The Earth as "Close to Being Nothing"

Gunton's first piece of evidence against Augustine's treatment of material creation lay in a critique of what is likely Augustine's most famous work: the *Confessions*. Here Gunton made much of the fact that in handling Gen. 1:1, Augustine opted to speak of the earth *not* as "very good," but as "close to being nothing." As Augustine wrote, "Out of nothing you made heaven and earth, two entities, one close to you, the other close to being nothing; the one to which only you are superior, the other to which what is inferior is nothingness."[16] Gunton recoiled from such language,[17] and went on to state that, "For Augustine, the world is sometimes affirmed as good . . . [and] sometimes denigrated as 'next to nothing' because he still thinks in terms of a Neoplatonist hierarchy of being."[18]

Yet Gunton's charge, as understandable as it may appear, glosses over an important distinction in the passage which he cites. In *Confessions* 12.7, when Augustine speaks of the "earth," he is not referencing the material world of trees and mountains, but rather the invisible and formless matter that God purportedly used to shape the present world.[19] As Augustine states, "You made this *next-to-nothing* [primordial/formless matter] out of nothing, and from it you made great things at which the sons of men wonder."[20] With reference to these "great things" which elicit human wonder, Augustine shows that his treatment of the "earth" of Gen. 1:1 is not as blatantly dualistic as it may appear.[21]

---

16. Augustine, *Conf.* 12.7.
17. See again Gunton, *Triune Creator*, 78.
18. Colin Gunton, *The Doctrine of Creation: Essays in Dogmatics, History and Philosophy* (Edinburgh: T&T Clark, 1997), 5.
19. Augustine, *Conf.* 12.8–9, 12.
20. *Conf.* 12.8. Italics mine.
21. Green acknowledges this point in a footnote, *Gunton and Failure of Augustine*, 39n38.

Here, as elsewhere, it seems that Gunton has presented a somewhat slanted reading of a rather nuanced text. Thus again, the claim of Webster is looming: "When [Gunton's] theology does not persuade, it is usually because he does not pause sufficiently long over exegetical or historical description."[22] Yet in fairness to Gunton, we should also note that Augustine is still speaking of a kind of matter in *Confessions* 12.7, and as Gunton would likely argue, it is still this primordial matter that is juxtaposed with the superiority of the ethereal heavens. What then should we make of this?

In further defense of Augustine, Scott Dunham argues that when referencing the earth as "close to nothing," Augustine is commenting not on the *value* of matter, but rather on its *origin* and *end* apart from God's providence.[23] Dunham argues that by reading the Scriptures, Augustine came to say that it is only in God that we live, move, and have our being (Acts 17:28).[24] Thus for Augustine it seemed logical that *apart* from God's upholding the created order would invariably dissolve into nothingness. In this sense, the earth may be seen as close to being nothing.[25] Given this logic, Dunham sees Augustine's statement as merely an affirmation of divine providence.

Yet here again, Augustine's defender may be missing something. If *Confessions* 12.7 is merely about the necessity of God's upholding, then why is it only the "earth" that is near nothingness? Why not the heavens too? Are they not also on the cusp of nonbeing apart from God's upholding? In such questions we see signs that this critique of

---

22. John Webster, "Systematic Theology after Barth: Jüngel, Jenson and Gunton," in *The Modern Theologians: An Introduction to Christian Theology since 1918*, ed. David Ford and Rachel Muers (Oxford: Blackwell, 2005), 262.
23. A. Dunham, *The Trinity and Creation in Augustine: An Ecological Analysis* (SUNY: Albany, NY, 2008), 107.
24. *Gn. litt.* 4.12.23. As pointed out by Dunham, *Trinity and Creation in Augustine*, 88, 106.
25. Dunham, *Trinity and Creation in Augustine*, 105.

Gunton, while partly accurate, may also fail to "pause sufficiently" in its analysis.[26]

In conclusion to this first debate, we must therefore adopt a mediating position. On the one hand, Augustine clearly does not mean what Gunton implies by his use of "earth" in *Confessions* 12.7. Thus the passage does not represent a blatant devaluing of the present world. Yet on the other hand, the text still presents problems for a fully positive view of material creation. Augustine is still speaking of materiality in *Confessions* 12.7, and in so doing he does treat the "earth" and the "heavens" in an unduly oppositional (that is, dualistic) fashion. Thus we must agree with Gunton that Augustine's way of *contrasting* the heavenly and earthly realms in this passage introduces a duality that goes beyond the general pattern of the Scriptures. In the Bible, both "heaven and earth" are often bound together in their potential transience apart from God's upholding. Thus Jesus states that both entities will "pass away" even while his word endures.[27] With this in mind, we turn now to Gunton's next critique.

Augustine's Two-Part Creation

For Gunton, a further sign of Augustine's Platonic "distrust [of] the material realm"[28] could be seen in his tendency to speak of a two-part creation, first, of ethereal forms and second, of material things. In reaction to this tendency, Gunton wrote the following:

> Creation is one and not dual. In a number of places in Augustine, the Genesis account is taken as indicating a double creation, first of the Platonic or "intellectual" world, second of the material world made in imitation of the (created) eternal forms. The effect of the dual interpretation has led to the depotentiating of the Bible's affirmation of

---

26. The opening paragraph of Dunham's dissertation contains a critique of Gunton, *One, the Three and the Many*. See Dunham, *Trinity and Creation*, 2.
27. Matt. 24:23. See also Matt. 5:18; Rev. 21:1.
28. Gunton, *Triune Creator*, 74.

the goodness of the whole world, in favour of a hierarchy favouring the immaterial.[29]

Here again the charge was that Augustine devalued the goodness of created matter. Yet with no footnote to guide us, we must ask to which "places in Augustine" Gunton was referring.

By one count, Augustine wrote no fewer than six commentaries on creation.[30] Indeed it was a subject that continued to challenge both his intellect and his faith. And as we have noted, Gunton was right to say that Augustine made a distinction between the *heavens* and the *earth* of Gen 1:1. Thus it is uncontroversial to claim that Augustine advocated a form of "double creation."[31] Likewise, there is also a consensus that this dual creation was partly the result of Platonic influence.[32] The *Confessions* especially are littered with allusions to Plotinus, and it seems natural that Augustine would put philosophy to use in service of the gospel.[33] The question then is *not* whether Augustine (1) propounds a "dual creation," or (2) makes selective use of Platonic thought. These realities are uncontested. The real question is whether Gunton was right to say that the result of these moves was a devaluing of materiality.[34] And at this point, it may depend on *which Augustine* one consults. We begin with the bishop

---

29. Gunton, *One, the Three and the Many*, 2.
30. Roland Teske lists the following: (1) *On Genesis, Against the Manichees* (AD 389); (2) *Unfinished Literal Commentary* (AD 393); (3) *Confessions*, books 11–13 (AD 397–98); (4) *Literal Commentary* (AD 401–15); (5) *City of God*, books 11–12 (AD 413–26); (6) *Against the Adversaries of the Law and the Prophets* (AD 419–21). Teske, *Paradoxes of Time in Saint Augustine* (Milwaukee: Marquette University Press, 1996), 67n25.
31. See Augustine, *Conf.* 11.7.9; 13.33.48; *Gn. litt.* 1.15.29; 1.18.36; 4.2.6. While referencing dual creation, Augustine is also quick to point out that both aspects (spiritual and material) are created simultaneously.
32. Although this "Platonic" influence may have come from Christian sources, such as Ambrose. See Rowan Williams, "Creation," in Fitzgerald, *Augustine through the Ages*, 251–54.
33. As Étienne Gilson states, "It is the Christian Creator Augustine adores but the creation he thinks of . . . bears the marks of Plotinus's metaphysics," *Christian Philosophy of Saint Augustine*, trans. L. Lynch (New York: Random House, 1960), 200–1.
34. Gunton, *One, the Three and the Many*, 2.

Gunton often ignores: the "mature Augustine," as loosely defined by his writings after 400 AD.[35]

Matter in the Mature Augustine

In his later work especially, Augustine is *emphatic* about the goodness of the whole created world. Yet while Gunton could sometimes acknowledge this,[36] it remained something to be quickly dismissed: yes, of course Augustine must affirm this, but "[He] does not really believe it."[37] When one actually reads Augustine's later works, however, this sweeping dismissal becomes more difficult to accept. In *De Civitate Dei* especially, Augustine glories in the value of materiality, even stating that "there was no other cause of the world's creation than that good things should be made by a good God."[38]

Likewise, whereas Augustine once believed that resurrected bodies would have no flesh,[39] the more mature Augustine longs for a very *material* resurrection: "To obtain blessedness . . . we need not be rid of every kind of body, but only the corruptible, irksome, painful, dying body. . . . Hence [the resurrection bodies] will be spiritual not because they cease to be bodies, but because they will be sustained by a quickening Spirit."[40] With regard to the composition of our current bodies, John Rist suggests that the mature Augustine developed an anthropology that was more holistic than that of his early writings. While Augustine once spoke of a sharp divide between body and soul

---

35. While AD 400 does not mark an firm division in Augustine's thought, Philip Cary illustrates how the date helps make a general distinction between Augustine's more philosophical early works, and his middle and later periods of anti-Donatist and anti-Pelagian writing. See Philip Cary, *Augustine's Invention of the Inner Self: The Legacy of a Christian Platonist* (Oxford: Oxford University Press, 2000), ch. 3.
36. See Gunton, *Yesterday and Today*, 109.
37. Gunton, *Promise of Trinitarian Theology*, 37.
38. Augustine, *Civ.* 11.23.
39. Augustine, *f. et symb.* 10.24.
40. Augustine, *Civ.* 13.17, 22.

("man is merely a soul *using* a body")[41] after AD 400 he would begin to speak of the "blending," or "miraculous combination" of both.[42] Thus, in a remarkable statement, Augustine proclaims, "I do not want my flesh to be removed from me forever, as if it were something alien to me, but that it be healed, a whole with me."[43] At this point, Gunton could not have said it better himself.

Augustine's movement on materiality can once again be seen as a progression from Plotinus to Paul. In this transition, texts like Eph. 5:29 ("No one hates his own flesh") proved formative.[44] As Rist concludes, "It is clear that as soon as Augustine began to give serious consideration to the dogma of the Resurrection of the body, he found good reasons to conclude that, although the Platonists were right to insist on the subordination of the body to the demands of the soul, they were wrong, and even begin to look 'Manichaean,' when they wish to be rid of the body so far as possible."[45] Gunton largely ignored *this* Augustine, and it is yet another example of a highly biased reading. Yet in acknowledging this, we must now return to a point already made: as we have seen, Gunton's chief concern was never with Augustine himself, but with his *legacy* (that is, his effect upon the subsequent tradition).[46] And at this point there is an early work that exerts an enormous and unquestionable influence.

---

41. Augustine, *Mor.* 1.27, 52.
42. See Augustine, *An. et or.* 30.59; *Ep.* 137.3.11; *Gn. litt.* 3.16.25; *Civ.* 22.24. Cited in John Rist, *Augustine: Ancient Thought Baptized* (Cambridge: University Press, 1994), 99, 101.
43. *Sermon* 30.4. Cited in Rist, *Ancient Thought Baptized*, 92.
44. See the usage in *Doctr. chr.* 1.24.25 and in the sermons on 1 John. Cited in Rist, *Ancient Thought Baptized*, 109; cf. Margaret Miles, *Augustine on the Body* (Eugene, OR: Wipf & Stock, 1979), 61.
45. Rist, *Ancient Thought Baptized*, 109–10.
46. The interest here, as always, was upon what Augustine would "bequeath . . . to the West." Gunton, *Promise of Trinitarian Theology*, 2.

Matter in the *Confessions*

The *Confessions* ranks among the masterpieces of Western literature. With the focus upon the inward world of its author, it has even been dubbed by some as the first "modern" work.[47] Yet in the strictest sense, the *Confessions* is not a modern masterpiece. With an accepted date of 397–401, O'Donnell argues that the book is "the last product of Augustine's youth and the first work of his maturity."[48] This is a crucial statement because in some ways the *Confessions* may be seen to straddle the divide of Augustine's transition toward a more positive view of material goodness. Thus our question is as follows: Does the *Confessions* (as "the last product of Augustine's youth") present us with the kind of material dualism decried by Gunton?

In answer to this query, Augustine specialist John Rist makes a provocative assertion: "The *Confessions* may be the latest major work of Augustine in which he thought that we are souls *fallen into* rather than with a body."[49] That such a notion can be seriously entertained by such a respected scholar of Augustine is of great importance to our study. If a book as influential as the *Confessions* connects embodiment to the fall, then Gunton's allegation regarding Augustine's legacy gains a measure of support.

To be fair, it is never explicitly argued in the *Confessions* that we are souls fallen into bodies. Yet the implications are sometimes strong.[50] There are multiple allusions to the idea that our souls "flowed

---

47. So says Frederick Van Fleteren, "Confessions," in Fitzgerald, *Augustine through the Ages*, 227.
48. James J. O'Donnell, *Augustine: Confessions*, vol. 1 (Oxford: Clarendon Press, 1992), 1.
49. Rist, *Ancient Thought Baptized*, 112. Italics in original. Roland Teske presents a similar view to that of Rist: "Even as late as the *Confessions*, there is language which implies the fall of the soul." Teske, "Augustine's Theory of Soul," in *The Cambridge Companion to Augustine*, ed. Eleonore Stump and Norman Kretzmann (Cambridge: Cambridge University Press, 2001), 121.
50. Perhaps the most extensive explication of this thesis exists in the Augustine scholarship of Robert J. O'Connell. For an introduction to O'Connell's work, see Ronnie J. Rombs, *Saint Augustine and the Fall of the Soul: Beyond O'Connell and his Critics* (Washington, DC: CUA Press, 2006).

downward" from the "Heaven of Heavens" into the world of matter and time.[51] Based on this, Augustine states that "we [know] there is a home to which we may return because we *fell* from it."[52] Similarly, Augustine goes on to state that it was from the immaterial heavens that souls "leapt down into times." And as the context illustrates, this is not an event to be celebrated.[53]

We will return to this discussion as we explore Gunton's charge of temporal dualism, yet with regard to *matter* a further tension centers on the relationship between mutability and being. A case in point appears in book 13 of the *Confessions*. Here Augustine states that while all creation is somehow good, "formless spiritual being is *superior* to formed body," even as "formless physical entities are better than no existence at all."[54] Here we see what Gunton referred to as a "hierarchy of being,"[55] and while Augustine's view of matter was much improved in later works, this ontic hierarchy remained.

Augustine's Hierarchy of Being

In *De Civitate Dei,* Augustine wrote that "in the scale of value extending from things earthly to things heavenly, from things visible to things invisible, there are some good things which are better than others."[56] Gunton bristled at this notion. For him, such assertions

---

51. Augustine, *Conf.* 4.31; 12.12–15; 13.9. Cited in R. J. O'Connell, "Peter Brown on the Soul's Fall," *Augustinian Studies* 24 (1993): 109.
52. *Conf.* 4.31. Italics added.
53. *Conf.* 11.39. As O'Connell argues, Augustine here implies that prior to this leap, the soul was outside of time, and hence at home in God's own eternity (cf. *Conf.* 4.31). R. J. O'Connell, *Images of Conversion in Saint Augustine's Confessions* (New York: Fordham University Press, 1996), 249.
54. *Conf.* 13.2. Italics mine. Cf. *Conf.* 12.28.38.
55. Gunton, *Triune Creator*, 78; cf. Gunton, *A Brief Theology of Revelation*, the 1993 Warfield Lectures (Edinburgh: T&T Clark, 1995), 45. This connects to Gunton's early critique of the hierarchal ordering of reality in *Becoming and Being: The Doctrine of God in Charles Hartshorne and Karl Barth*, new ed. (London: SCM, 2001), 3–4.
56. Augustine, *Civ.* 11.22.

ran contrary to the idea that there are no degrees of being in God's good world, only Creator and creation.[57] To say otherwise was to impose a Neoplatonic hierarchy upon on the Scriptures, and to call into question the full being of that which fell lower on Augustine's ontic ladder.[58] Here the lower rungs were clearly reserved for visible matter. Thus as Gunton put it, while "everything is 'very good' [for Augustine], some things are definitely 'less good' than others."[59] As we have seen already,[60] there is truth in this evaluation, and as Gilson states, "Augustine is here heir to all the difficulties inherent in the Platonic view of matter conceived as quasi non-being."[61]

Yet again we must not go too far. As should be obvious, an ontic hierarchy is not the same as a full-fledged Platonic dualism. Thus to say that Augustine sometimes eschewed materiality is *not* to confirm with Harnack that the whole apparatus of early theology was an imposition of a false metaphysic upon the gospel.[62] In his more measured moments, Gunton would not go all the way with Harnack here.[63] It is clear that Augustine remained a deeply Christian thinker. Yet at the same time, there are aspects of his thought, especially in the influential pages of the *Confessions*, that served to undermine the status of material creation. As O'Donnell states, "Augustine is reluctant to go as far as the Platonists in thinking that any contact with a body was itself polluting, but he often uses . . . language that points in that direction, and he never fully rejects the style. He certainly shares with them throughout a preference for a perfect un-

---

57. Gunton, *Triune Creator*, 71–72, 79. As Gunton notes, this does not deny the special place of humanity as bearers of the divine image.
58. Ibid., 33.
59. Ibid., 78.
60. See again, *Conf.* 12.28; 13.2.
61. Gilson, *Christian Philosophy of Saint Augustine*, 204.
62. See Adolf Von Harnack, *History of Dogma*, ed. and trans. Neil Buchanan (London: Williams and Norgate, 1897), cited in Gunton, *Promise of Trinitarian Theology*, 57.
63. Ibid., 60, 104, 107.

world over this imperfect one, for the unseen over the seen."[64] As Gunton claimed, there is a hierarchy of being at work in Augustine, and it sometimes served to undermine the full goodness of materiality.

In light of this, a crucial point must now be made. In Gunton's view, Augustine's dualism was actually "more dangerous" (that is, more *enduring*) because it was "controlled" enough to avoid the condemnations reserved for men like Origen and Marcion.[65] Because this was Gunton's claim, it is simply *not* possible enough to exonerate Augustine (and his legacy) merely on the grounds that his dualism was "limited."[66] For Gunton, this limitation was precisely what made Augustine's imbalance more dangerous, in that it made it more transferable to the subsequent tradition. Thus while we must await the future chapters to address Augustine's *afterlife*, we may conclude for now that some of Gunton's concerns regarding material dualism remain viable, despite the oversimplifications that sometimes surrounded them. With this said, we turn now to Augustine's handling of *time*.

Time

With regard to temporality, Gunton's emphasis upon the divine economy stressed a God who "takes his time" in perfecting the project of creation.[67] In this way, "the eternal" was "conceived as a time-embracing and not a time-denying reality."[68] Yet in Augustine, Gunton saw a dualism that pitted the temporal against the eternal so that "to be in time is . . . to be in a sphere . . . finally lacking in

---

64. O'Donnell, *Augustine: A New Biography*, 82.
65. See Gunton, *Triune Creator*, 76.
66. Pace Green, *Gunton and Failure of Augustine*, 89, 96, 174.
67. See ch. 1; cf. Gunton, *One, the Three and the Many*, 80–81; *Triune Creator*, 83–84.
68. Gunton, *Yesterday and Today*, 130.

reality."[69] The result, in Gunton's view, was troubling: "Ever since Augustine, Western theology has operated with a conceptuality in which the otherness of time and eternity has been strongly accentuated."[70] Here again we find a sweeping charge, and here again we ask for evidence.

Instantaneous Creation

Gunton's allegation rested partly on Augustine's decision to view creation as an *instantaneous* act.[71] On the one hand, this may seem rather confusing, given our prior acknowledgment that Augustine also believed in a "two-stage" creation. After all, how can creation occur instantaneously while also consisting of two parts? Augustine's answer was that the differentiation is not one of temporal order but one of *source*. God made the ordered world out of formless matter, yet any appearance of a temporal succession merely illustrates the limitation of human language to convey things that happen simultaneously. For Augustine, the language of "days" in Genesis 1 caused problems for his view of God. After all, if God spoke the world into being through his *coeternal* Word,[72] then how could this Word be distended over time? In pondering this, Augustine reached a firm conclusion: God made all things simultaneously.[73]

In this, Gunton saw an inability to acknowledge God's "self-limitation" in time as an expression (rather than a negation) of his sovereignty.[74] Once again, the problem was seen to reside in Augustine's Platonic presuppositions. As Gunton wrote,

---

69. Ibid., 109. Italics in original.
70. Ibid., 28. See also Gunton, *Becoming and Being*, 2–3.
71. See Augustine, *Gen. Litt.* 1.15.
72. Augustine, *Gn. litt*, 1.9.15.
73. Ibid., 1.15.29; 1.18.36; 4.2.6; 4.33.52–54; 5.3.5; 5.11.27; 5.17.35; 5.23.44–46; cf. *Conf.* 11.7.9.
74. Gunton, *Triune Creator*, 16.

> [Augustine's] concern [as opposed to that of Irenaeus] is not . . . with affirming the worldly, but with solving the philosophical puzzle of how the temporal and changing can derive from the timeless and unchanging. In sum, Augustine tends to conclude that because creation is the act of the timeless God, then all God's acts must be timeless. The outcome for him is that God's act of creation is understood to be instantaneous. . . . However, if the divine creation of all things is simultaneous, it is difficult to take the order of time and space seriously as the good creation of God. Symptomatic is Augustine's tendency to hold that the fact that activities and events take time is a sign of their fallenness, making a gnostic equation of materiality and fallenness dangerously close.[75]

Here we see the supposed connection between Augustine's *temporal* and *material* dualism. Yet the charge is so sweeping that one wonders if the various components can hold up to scrutiny.

The first problem lies in Gunton's construal of Augustine's motivation. Here Augustine's view of instantaneous creation is seen as the result of a rather abstract philosophical game (a "puzzle").[76] This contention is unfair. For Augustine, a crucial impetus for his view of instantaneous creation was not philosophical speculation, but theological crisis. His first great religious experience was with the Manichees, and it was a likely taunt of theirs that he was attempting to counter with his view of simultaneous creation. As Teske notes, "Just as [Augustine] was unable to answer the Manichaean question, 'Where does evil come from?' without the concept of God as a non-bodily substance . . . so he could not solve the other Manichaean question, 'What was God doing before he made heaven and earth?' without the concept of God as a non-temporal being."[77] For Augustine, the way to defend his flock from Manichaen heresy was to conceive of God as timeless, and creation as an instantaneous

---

75. Ibid., 83.
76. Ibid.
77. Teske, *Paradoxes of Time in Saint Augustine*, 15–16.

act. This is not to say, however, that Augustine's conclusion is an altogether happy one; still, it does explain the pastoral intent behind his position. Gunton never notes this point, and in this oversight, he ends up accusing Augustine of the very thing he was trying to refute, a lingering Manichaeism.[78]

Second, in yet another modification to Gunton's charge, it should be noted that Augustine found some "biblical" support for his conclusion on instantaneous creation. Littered throughout his works on Genesis are references to Sir. 18:1: "He who lives forever created all things simultaneously."[79] For Augustine, this passage clearly carried the weight of divine inspiration, and thus it must be reconciled with Genesis. As Augustine states, "They are both true ... because they were both written under the inspiration of the one Spirit of Truth."[80] For later readers, with a different understanding of the canon, it is crucial to note what Augustine saw to be the biblical basis for his view. Once again, Gunton's treatment ignores this reality in an attempt to emphasize Augustine's Platonism.[81] To be sure, the Platonic influence is there as well, yet before turning to this topic, we must first examine what Gunton saw as a second sign of temporal dualism.

Time as a *Distension* of the Mind

In the *Confessions*, Augustine famously remarks that he knows well what time is, until someone asks him to explain it.[82] Over sixteen-hundred years later, in an age of post-Einsteinian physics, the remark is still relatable. For Augustine, however, the sentiment is an echo

---

78. "He can never fully distinguish the temporal from the fallen. The Manichee never quite disappears." Gunton, *One, the Three and the Many*, 82.
79. See, for instance, Augustine, *Gn. litt.* 4.33.52.
80. Ibid., 4.34.53.
81. See Gunton, *One, the Three and the Many*, 83–4.
82. Augustine, *Conf.* 11.14.17.

of Plotinus,[83] and it leads to an inquiry into the ontology of time. Augustine's question is this: What "being" does the temporal possess given that the *future* (the "not yet") continually collapses into the *past* (the "no longer") through an indefinable and ever-disappearing *present*? The context for the question is again the story of creation, and Augustine's investigation leads him to a tentative conclusion: "I have come to think that time is simply a distension [*distentio*]. But of what? . . . It would be surprising if it is not that of the mind itself."[84]

As we have seen already,[85] Gunton drew a bold line from here to Kant and the modern notion that temporal realities are but projections of the mind.[86] Later chapters must address this rather sweeping historical trajectory, yet for now we focus on Augustine himself. For Gunton, the problem with viewing time as *distentio* lies in the way it may be seen to equate temporality with fallenness. If time is *essentially* fallen (that is, fallen in its very essence) then redemption takes the form of an eschatological escape.[87] The result, in Gunton's view, was again an opposition that wrongfully pitted time against eternity. Yet was Gunton's reading fair?

In Augustine's defense, it bears noting that *Confessions* 11.26 is far from a confident attack on temporal goodness. On one level it is not an argument at all, but a prayer. Augustine lays his ignorance before God and pleads for wisdom.[88] And when at last he comes upon

---

83. Plotinus, *Enneads* 3.7.1.1–13. Cited in Teske, *Paradoxes of Time*, 22n78.
84. Augustine, *Conf.* 11.26.33.
85. Ch. 1.
86. See Gunton, *Yesterday and Today*, 110. As Genevieve Lloyd has likewise noted, "The shift that Augustine has made [in *Conf.* 11] is from seeing consciousness as in time to seeing time as in consciousness. It is a shift we will see undone and remade throughout the subsequent philosophical tradition." Lloyd, "Augustine and the 'Problem' of Time," in *The Augustinian Tradition*, ed. Gareth Matthews (Berkeley: University of California Press, 1999), 56. Lloyd also draws comparisons to Kant at this point (60).
87. Gunton, *One, the Three and the Many*, 81–85; cf. *Triune Creator*, 221.
88. "My mind is on fire to solve this very intricate enigma. Do not shut the door, Lord my God. Good Father, through Christ I beg you, do not shut the door on my longing to understand these things which are both familiar and obscure." Augustine, *Conf.* 11.22.28.

what seems the only explanation (time as a *distentio animi*), even this is offered up with reticence. Thus even Gunton could acknowledge Augustine's cautiousness as a partial virtue.[89] As scholars have long noted, the prayerful attitude of the *Confessions* has a tendency to draw the reader in and lower the defenses. As Brown puts it, Augustine's claims are "all the more unanswerable for being addressed not to a human audience, but to God."[90] Because of this, the reader gains the sense that he or she is merely listening in as Augustine "gossips" with the divine.[91] Yet as O'Donnell argues, this effect can have problematic consequences if it keeps us from questioning both Augustine's motives and his conclusions.[92] In particular, we may be tempted to overlook the possibility that some of the answers to Augustine's prayers lead in dualistic and unbiblical directions.

On this point, Roland Teske arrives at a conclusion similar to that of Gunton. On the subject of time he notes that while Augustine petitions the Christian God, his answer comes more directly from Plotinus.[93] Plotinus also spoke of time as a distension (διάστασις), yet the Greek term carries a more neutral connotation of "extension," while Augustine's Latin (*distentio*) suggests a tension, spasm, or distortion.[94] The more negative meaning fits Augustine's common usage,[95] as seen elsewhere when he asks whether "diverse pleasures do not *distend* [rack; pull apart] the human heart."[96] All this leads Teske

---

89. Gunton, *Yesterday and Today*, 109.
90. Peter Brown, *Augustine of Hippo: A Biography*, 2nd ed. (Berkeley: University of California Press, 2000), 156.
91. See Dodds's famous claim that "Plotinus never gossiped with the One as Augustine gossips in the *Confessions*." E. R. Dodds, "Augustine's Confessions: A Study of Spiritual Maladjustment," *Hibbert Journal* 26 (1927–28): 471. Cited in Brown, *Augustine of Hippo*, 160.
92. James J. O'Donnell, "Augustine's Unconfessions," in *Augustine and Postmodernism: Confessions and Circumfession*, ed. John Caputo and Michael Scanlon (Bloomington, IN: Indiana University Press, 2005), 212–19.
93. Teske, *Pardoxes of Time*, 29, 32.
94. Ibid., 86n109.
95. So Gerard O'Daly, *Augustine's Philosophy of Mind* (London: Duckworth, 1987), 153.
96. Teske, *Paradoxes of Time*, 28. Citing Augustine, *Conf.* 8.10.24.

to a familiar conclusion. As he states of the *Confessions*, "Our being in time, it seems, is a penalty for sin. . . . [And] since our presence in time is the penalty of our fall, Augustine sees the purpose of Christ's coming as to set us free from time."[97] Such an indictment from a noted Augustine specialist lends credibility to Gunton's critique.[98] Yet the idea of an escape from time can only be properly evaluated through an examination of Augustine's doctrine of last things.

The End of Time

For Gunton, Augustine's eschatology also showed forth certain problems. His logic was straightforward: if the value of matter is lessened in a hierarchical chain of being, and if existence in time is, at points, connected with the fall, then the solution is an eschatology of escape to a timeless and spiritual realm. Thus Gunton claimed that Augustine's eschatology was "essentially dualistic" because it tended to "require a choice between this world and the next, rather than seeking a realization of the next in the materiality of the present."[99] Is this accurate?

As Teske shows, there are passages that seem to support the charge of an eschatological escapism within Augustine. Nearly a decade after writing the *Confessions*, Augustine could still state that "[Christ] came to set us free from time."[100] Yet this hardly captures the totality of his thought. In *The Literal Meaning of Genesis* (written between 401 and 415 AD), Augustine writes beautifully of how God uses time to bring

---

97. Teske, *Paradoxes of Time,*, 30-31. Teske here cites Augustine, *Jo. ev. tr.* 31.5; see also *Sermon* 340.5.
98. Likewise, as Lloyd notes of the *Confessions*, Augustine "gradually learns to turn away from the physical world to the world of consciousness as the story of his religious conversion. His turning away from the physical world to contemplate himself begins the process of turning toward God." Lloyd, "Augustine and the 'Problem' of Time," 56.
99. Gunton, *Promise of Trinitarian Theology*, 50. Emphasis mine; cf. Gunton, *Intellect and Action: Elucidations on Christian Theology and the Life of Faith* (Edinburgh: T&T Clark, 2001), 140.
100. Augustine, *Jo. ev. tr.* 31.5 (c. AD 406-7); cf. *Sermon* 340.5. Cited in Teske, *Paradoxes of Time*, 31.

forth his glorious ends. As he states, "Some things, you see, abide by soaring over all the whole rolling wheel of time ... while other things do so according to the limits of their time, and thus it is through things giving way to and taking the place of one another that the beautiful tapestry of the ages is woven."[101] Gunton is grossly unfair to *this* Augustine.

The unfairness resurfaces when Gunton accuses Augustine of confusing the garden of Eden with a paradise, and the eschaton with a mere "return to the perfection which ... existed before the fall."[102] There is a grain of truth in this, but only that. As a recent convert, Augustine clearly saw future redemption as a return to the original (and disembodied) paradisaic state.[103] Likewise, the mature Augustine could speak of both Eden and heaven as "Paradise."[104] Yet what Gunton never notes is that in fifth-century Latin Bibles, this term (*paradisus*) was not merely a theological assessment, but a *proper name* for the garden in Gen. 2:8. Thus in opening his Bible, Augustine would have read that "God planted *Paradise* in the east; in Eden."[105] Upon seeing this same term used of heaven in the New Testament (perhaps most notably in Luke 23:43), an eschatological association would be natural. After all, one can hardly fault Augustine for what his Bible said.

In further rebuttal to Gunton's charge, *De Civitate Dei* makes it clear that the end will *not* be a mere return to the beginning. As proof of this, Augustine writes that "whereas that first man ... had no certainty of his future," we will one day "share ... the endless

---

101. Augustine, *Gn. litt.* 1.8.14.
102. Gunton, *Triune Creator*, 11.
103. See Augustine, *Gn. adv. man.* (c. AD 388/90).
104. Augustine, *Gn. litt.* 8.1.1.
105. See Edmund Hill's note on Augustine's usage of the term in *Gn. litt.* 5.7.21. From *On Genesis*, trans. Edmund Hill, The Works of Saint Augustine; A Translation for the 21st Century, part 1, vol. 13 (Hyde Park, NY: New City Press, 2002), 286.

enjoyment of God."[106] For Augustine, this eternal and unthreatened felicity makes our final state *more* blessed than the first.[107] Given this, it is inaccurate to reduce Augustine's eschatology to a mere return. Yet while Gunton's charge is lacking at this point, his case is somewhat strengthened when we turn to another aspect of Augustine's doctrine of last things.

One of Augustine's more famous eschatological innovations involved his reinterpretation of Christian millenarianism.[108] Previously, men like Irenaeus could approvingly cite the teaching of Papias, who proclaimed a very material and earthly climax to Christian history. At that time "each vine will have a thousand branches . . . and . . . each cluster ten thousand grapes."[109] This was an expectation of a kingdom truly come *on earth*.[110] Yet even before Augustine, such hopes of terrestrial abundance were being challenged. For Origen, the wine to be wrung from such grapes was that of divine wisdom, and the bread, the "Bread of Life."[111] In Augustine's view, this brand of allegorical exegesis seemed preferable for a variety of reasons. For one, it could be used to quell the North African penchant for worldly wine and feasting at the shrines of their beloved martyrs. At such times Augustine's congregants would gather not merely to honor the dead, but to anticipate the life of the millennium, and as Augustine tells us, get splendidly drunk![112]

---

106. Augustine, *Civ.* 11.22.
107. See Harry Maier, "The End of the City and the City without End: The *City of God* as Revelation," *Augustinian Studies* 30, no. 2 (1999): 153–64.
108. By *millenarianism* we mean broadly, with Paula Fredriksen, "The belief that the redemption brought by the End . . . will be collective, historical, and earthly (as opposed to heavenly or exclusively spiritual): [Here] the idea of a thousand-year period . . . is less essential to its import than is its focus on the earth and human history as the ultimate arena of redemption." Paula Fredriksen, "Apocalypse and Redemption in Early Christianity: From John of Patmos to Augustine of Hippo," *Vigiliae Christianae* 45 (1991): 168n3.
109. Irenaeus, *AH*, 5.33.3.
110. Fredriksen, "Apocalypse and Redemption," 156.
111. Origen, *De Principiis* 2.11.2–3. Cited in Frederiksen, "Apocalypse and Redemption," 154.
112. See Augustine, *Ep.* 78.3. Note also the reference to "carnal banquets" in *Civ.* 20.7.

Beyond this, a more spiritualized millennium also resonated at a time when the future of Rome (the once-vaunted holy city) was increasingly in doubt.

In contrast to the earthly *millenarii*, De Civitate Dei set forth a rival eschatology. Here the first resurrection (of Revelation 20) was "of the soul," while the earthly reign of Christ was presently ongoing, and the thousand years were to be taken figuratively.[113] As we have seen, this did not negate Augustine's mature belief in a bodily resurrection, but it did affect the status of creation. As Fredriksen summarizes, for Augustine "this raised . . . body will not dwell on a transformed earth. In nonchalant defiance of the scientific thinking of his day, Augustine insists that these corporeal bodies will dwell in the heavens: the Kingdom of God will *not* come on earth."[114] In fairness, Augustine did affirm the biblical account of a new heaven and a new earth.[115] Yet whatever this meant (and he was not certain) it did not change the fact that the final abode of our bodies was to be in the *heavens*.[116] As Leo Ferrari concludes, "For Augustine the terrestrial realm was a world from which to escape."[117]

Indicative of this problem was Augustine's severely strained interpretation of the term *creation* within Rom. 8:19–23. While Paul states that the created order "will be liberated from its bondage to decay," Augustine identified this "creation" *not* with the material world, but with the individual human being.[118] This again reveals Augustine's problematic tendency with regard to the status of material and temporal being. In light of such evidence, it seems that Gunton was right to allege that Augustine's view of the end had

---

113. Augustine, *Civ.* 20.7.10.
114. Frederiksen, "Apocalypse and Redemption," 166.
115. Augustine, *Civ.* 20.16 (Rev. 21:1).
116. *Civ.* 22.4, 11; cf. 13.18.
117. Leo Ferrari, "Augustine's Cosmography," *Augustinian Studies* 27, no. 2 (1996): 176.
118. Augustine, *Exp. Prop. Rm.* 53.4 (AD 395/96).

committed itself to some remarkable exegetical contortions in order to downplay the reality of a material habitation in the age to come.[119]

In summation, our exploration of time has led us to acknowledge the complexity of Augustine's various statements. On the one hand, Gunton sometimes assumed too much from isolated passages deprived of context. Yet as we have also seen, there are elements in Augustine's treatment of temporality that evidence a problematic dualism. Thus in his more nuanced moments, Gunton was right to say that Augustine's view of time was not flatly wrong, but "bewilderingly many-sided,"[120] and his contributions on creation "so various that it is difficult to know which of them to stress."[121] Based on our assessment, this conclusion is essentially fair.

What was not fair, however, is that despite the good and bad of Augustine's many-sided doctrine, Gunton chose to focus almost solely on the negative. The reason for this emphasis stemmed, in part, from what Gunton saw to be a final consequence of Augustine's limited dualism: if one could not think rightly about being *in time* and being *in matter*, then one was bound to think wrongly about the most central of Christian doctrines: the incarnation. Thus we turn at last to the question of dualism in Augustine's handling of creation and triune mediation.

Mediation

As we have seen, Gunton viewed triune mediation as the crucial concept in articulating how God can act *within*, while remaining *distinct from* the created order.[122] Within this paradigm there was an emphasis upon the Spirit-enabled humanity of Jesus. For Gunton,

---

119. Gunton, *Promise of Trinitarian Theology*, 50.
120. Gunton, *Yesterday and Today*, 109.
121. Gunton, *Triune Creator*, 73.
122. See ch. 1.

it was Christ's connection to creation that qualified him to be our great high priest.[123] Yet in Augustine, Gunton believed that the sole mediatorship of the *incarnate* Christ had been impinged upon by other (nonphysical) forces: most notably (1) the angels, (2) the monistic *will* of God, (3) the *Logos asarkos* (the unfleshed Word), and (4) the immaterial human soul.[124] In this supposed preference for nonbodily mediation, Gunton again saw a deficiency in Augustine's doctrine of creation.

Augustine and Angelic Mediation

For Gunton, one sign of this "anti-incarnational" dualism was to be seen in Augustine's handling of the Old Testament theophanies. His charge was that by viewing the theophanies as the work of angels, Augustine revealed that he did not have the "conceptual equipment" to develop a theology that was "genuinely incarnational."[125] As Gunton wrote, "There are signs that [Augustine] is rather embarrassed by too close an involvement of God in matter. . . . The prefiguring of the Son in the Old Testament is not by means of the Word, but by angels; God is not *substantially* involved. . . . The angels tend in Augustine to take the place of the Word as the mediators of God's relation with the world."[126]

Before evaluating Gunton's charge, it may help to clarify the two questions that lie at the center of any theophany debate: (1) "Who?" and (2) "How?"[127] The first question asks, Who exactly (which person?) was revealed to the likes of Moses and Elijah on Sinai and

---

123. Thus Gunton: "The Father sends the Spirit to form a body for his Son out of the only material available to hand: the soiled flesh of the created order which he comes to redeem." *Triune Creator*, 223.
124. See the prior survey of these claims in ch. 1.
125. Gunton, *Promise of Trinitarian Theology*, 34.
126. Ibid., 34–35; cf. 172–73. Gunton sees similar problems with the prominence of angels in Augustine, *Civ.* 11–12.

Horeb?[128] The second question asks, How is God made visible in these instances, given that none can see [his] face and live (Exod. 33:20)? Prior to Augustine, it was common to answer the first question by way of the *Logos*.[129] Here it was the Son who, on account of his future manifestation in the flesh, appeared also in the Old Testament theophanies.[130]

Augustine changed this trend. As he argued, the question was unanswerable. For Augustine, any or all of the divine persons could be revealed in the theophanies.[131] The justification for this was to be found in an answer to the second question ("How?"). Here Augustine concluded that while the theophanies were manifestations of God, they were worked through created entities (*per creatura*), and more specifically, by the angels: "If I am asked, in what manner either words or sensible forms and appearances were wrought before the incarnation of the Word of God . . . I reply that God wrought those things by the angels."[132] In light of this, we see that Gunton was correct to say that Augustine represents a change in the tradition. Yet is it fair to say that this change was rooted in an "anti-incarnational Platonism"?[133]

In response to Gunton's claim, Barnes contends that Augustine adopted his position largely to head off Arian opponents who viewed the theophanic visibility of the *Logos* as proof that the Son could not be fully divine.[134] In the face of this heresy, Barnes explains that Augustine found himself in a difficult position. On the one hand, the

---

127. This approach is that of John Panteleimon Manoussakis, "Theophany and Indication: Reconciling Augustinian and Palamite Aesthetics," in *Modern Theology* 26, no. 1 (January, 2010): 77.
128. See Exod. 3, 19, 33; 1 Kgs 19.
129. So Irenaeus, Justin Martyr, Tertullian, Hilary, and Ambrose. See Manoussakis, "Theophany," 78.
130. See Manoussakis, "Theophany," 77–78.
131. See Augustine, *Trin.* 2.18.35.
132. *Trin.* 4.31.
133. Gunton, *Promise of Trinitarian Theology*, 34.

traditional position (theophany as "Christophany") had been helpful to combat the heresy of modalism. Yet on the other hand, this same view also left the church open to an Arian polemic.[135] After all, if the Son was seen, how could he be fully divine, for God was said to be "invisible" (1 Tim. 6:16)? To combat this question, Barnes explains that Augustine took a daring approach: *He accepted the premise of the Arians that divinity cannot be seen.*[136] Thus Augustine viewed the theophanies as revelations of God by virtue of the angels. For Barnes, however, this shift was motivated not by a semignostic view of matter, but by a pro-Nicene desire to defend the divinity and equality of each member of the Trinity.[137]

What does this mean for Gunton's charge? As Barnes implies, Gunton failed to note the pro-Nicene intentions behind Augustine's innovation. Gunton's concern (as was often the case) was with "Platonic dualism," and thus he did not fully expound the degree to which Augustine was merely finding tools to defend the creedal tradition. Yet here again, the matter is not wholly settled. In modification of both Barnes *and* Gunton, the real problem in Augustine's treatment of the theophanies does not reside in the fact that he connected them to the angels,[138] but in the way he was willing to accept the Homoian premise regarding the necessity of divine

---

134. Michel René Barnes, "The Visible Christ and the Invisible Trinity: Mt. 5.8 in Augustine's Trinitarian Theology of 400," in *Modern Theology* 19, no. 3 (July 2003): 329–55. Barnes critiques Gunton's claim specifically, 348n4.
135. According to Barnes, Augustine found himself between the Scylla of Modalism and the Charybdis of the Arians. Ibid., 341.
136. This judgment, however striking, is that of Barnes himself: "Augustine does not dispute their [the Arians] fundamental presupposition, namely, that divinity is invisible and anything visible is not divine." Ibid., 353n59.
137. Ibid., 331, 341.
138. The use of *angel* for the Son is common in patristic writings on the theophanies, its roots being in the biblical accounts that speak the "Angel of the Lord." Thus Augustine's innovation lies in disconnecting the angelic referent from the distinctive person of the Son. See Kari Kloos, *Preparing for the Vision of God: Augustine's Interpretation of the Biblical Theophany Narratives* (Ann Arbor, MI: UMI Dissertation Publishing, 2003), 24.

invisibility, even in the person of the incarnate Christ.[139] In one sense, Augustine was correct. As one may conclude from the Gospels, there was nothing in the visible appearance of Jesus to prove that he was God.[140] Yet at points Augustine goes beyond this fact and claims that nothing *visible* or *material* must be taken for God. As he puts it: "We reject everything that is material. Even in the world of spirit, nothing changeable must be taken for God."[141] Herein lies the danger, for this position may be seen to create tensions for a robust theology of the incarnation.

It bears noting that there were other options at Augustine's disposal for resolving the tension of those passages that assert divine invisibility. One might identify the invisible person with the Father, while maintaining that the Son was seen and affirmed in the flesh, not merely as a servant, but as Lord and God (John 20:28).[142] By this move one might hold together the Father's invisibility with triune equality, while at the same time avoiding a dualistic tendency to downgrade that which is visible (most notably, the incarnate Christ). Yet Augustine did not choose this path. Perhaps his decision should be traced to a belief that this approach would not quell the Arian critique. Perhaps he was right. Yet in countering one heresy, Augustine may be seen to further an "opposition" (what Gunton called a dualism)[143] between invisible divinity and visible matter.

---

139. Thus Gunton was right to say that Augustine's position on the theophanies is connected to his appropriation of the incarnation. For Augustine, the divinity of Christ remained unseen, as he appeared only in the form of a servant. See *Trin.*, book 1. Cf. Barnes, "The Visible Christ," 329–40.
140. A possible exception to this claim can be seen in the transfiguration (Matt. 17:1–9; Mark 9:2–8; Luke 9:28–36; 2 Pet. 1:16–18). See again Manoussakis, "Theophany."
141. Augustine, *Trin.* 8.2.3. Cited by Gunton in *Promise of Trinitarian Theology*, 38n11; cf. *Trin.* 2.6–9. Augustine's argument here is in marked contrast to that of Irenaeus, who stated that "He [although] beyond comprehension, and boundless and invisible, rendered himself visible . . . that he might vivify those who receive and behold him through faith. For as his greatness is past finding out, so also his goodness is beyond expression" *AH*, 4.20.
142. For variations of this view, see Irenaeus, *AH*, 4.20.1–4; Justin Martyr, *Dialogue with Trypho*, 56; Novation, *De Trinitate*, 11; Hilary, *De Trinitate*, 4.25.

In this important nuance, the claim of this chapter again shows forth: in modification of Gunton's charge, Augustine's treatment of the angels should be framed in the context of a pro-Nicene polemic. Yet in deference to Gunton, Augustine's *way* of defending the tradition can be seen to further a dualistic imbalance in which the immaterial and invisible trumps that which may be seen. Thus again, we find a kernel of truth in Gunton's somewhat uncontextualized critique.

Mediation and the (Allegedly) "Monistic" Will of God

The next charge against Augustine's view of triune mediation pertains to his supposed appeal to an arbitrary and monistic will of God.[144] At this point, Gunton's contention was that while an account of creation by virtue of God's "two hands" placed God in a positive relation with the created order, an account of creation that appeals primarily to an omnipotent divine will keeps the Son and Spirit at a distance. As Gunton put it,

> Because in. . . [Augustine's] theology, the mediation by Christ and the Spirit . . . play too limited a role . . . it comes to be that the theme of love becomes subordinate to that of will. If not in Augustine, certainly in those who learned from him, creation becomes very much the product of pure, unmotivated and therefore arbitrary will, a will that operates equally arbitrarily in the theology of double predestination that became after him so much a mark of the Western tradition.[145]

In short, Gunton would come to believe that "Augustine's stress on God's willing of the world [left] little reason except sheer will."[146]

---

143. Gunton, *Yesterday and Today*, 86.
144. See Green, *Gunton and the Failure of Augustine*, 175.
145. Gunton, *One, the Three and the Many*, 120–21.
146. Gunton, *Triune Creator*, 76.

In response to this charge, it seems fair to say that Augustine was, as Gunton claimed, "a theologian of the will."[147] As such, Augustine identified "the will of God [as] the first and highest cause of all bodily appearances and motions."[148] Yet in his critique of Gunton, Green rejects the notion that Augustine's emphasis upon the divine will implies a deficient grasp of mediation. As he states, "Gunton's criticism . . . appears to fail to take into consideration Augustine's clear affirmation . . . that God creates out of his goodness."[149] To illustrate this, Green supplies a catena of citations to affirm that "on Augustine's own terms, God creates because he *wills* . . . to do what is loving, good, etc."[150] In the *Confessions,* Augustine states that "your creation has its being from the fullness of your goodness."[151] Likewise, in *De Civitate Dei*, he writes that the best cause for God to create is simply "that good might be created by the good God."[152]

In all this, Green is right to note Augustine's emphasis upon the *goodness* of God's creative will.[153] Indeed, for Augustine, there was an inextricable connection between God's willing and his loving. This is shown most tellingly by the fact that *will* and *love* are used interchangeably as the third qualities in one of Augustine's sacred triads. As Augustine states, "And these two, the begetter and the begotten, are coupled together by love, as by a third, which is nothing else than will, seeking or holding fast the enjoyment of something. We held, therefore, that a trinity of the mind is to be intimated also by these three terms, memory, intelligence, will."[154] Beyond this, we have already noted Augustine's appeal to the link of

---

147. Ibid.
148. Augustine, *Trin.* 3.4.9.
149. Green, *Gunton and the Failure of Augustine*, 176.
150. Ibid., 175. Emphasis in original.
151. Augustine, *Conf.* 13.2.2.
152. Augustine, *Civ.* 11.21. Cited in Green, *Gunton and the Failure of Augustine*, 175.
153. See again ch. 3.
154. Augustine, *Trin.* 14.6.8. Cf. *Trin.* 14.7.10.

love (the Holy Spirit) as an active agent in creation.[155] All this merely confirms Green's analysis that, in Augustine, the will of God was not detached from the concept of divine love.[156]

Yet in revisiting Gunton's above quotation, we see that this is not the full extent of his critique. Once again, his ultimate charge had more to do with Augustine's legacy. Thus the caveat in Gunton's comment: "*If not in Augustine*, certainly in those who learned from him, creation becomes very much the product of . . . [an] arbitrary will."[157] Here Gunton seemed to acknowledge the possibility that in Augustine himself, the divine will was not entirely detached from its trinitarian and teleological moorings. Yet why saddle Augustine with the blame for errors not fully his own? Can a good tree produce bad fruit? A full answer to such questions must await our examination of Augustine's afterlife,[158] yet for now, we must acknowledge that Augustine's treatment of the divine will did *not* evidence a clear devaluing of created goodness, or a deemphasis of mediation by the Son and Spirit.

The *Logos Asarkos* and the Ministry Of Jesus

Gunton's next charge against Augustine's notion of triune mediation had to do with a supposed preference to derive an understanding of the Son from the *Logos asarkos* (the "unfleshed Word") rather than the incarnate Christ. As we have seen, Gunton bemoaned this so-called docetic tendency within many orthodox Christologies.[159] His contention was that if the full humanity of Christ is deemphasized, so too is the relation between Creator and creation.[160] As Gunton wrote,

---

155. See Augustine, *Civ.* 11.24.
156. See also Marianne Djuth, "Will as Love," in Fitzgerald, *Augustine Through the Ages*, 883ff.
157. Gunton, *One, the Three and the Many*, 120. Emphasis added.
158. See esp. chs. 6 and 7, and our treatment of both Ockham and Calvin.
159. Gunton, *Christ and Creation*, the Didsbury Lectures, 1990 (Eugene, OR: Wipf and Stock, 2005), 70; cf. *Yesterday and Today*, 70.

> Augustine's interpretation of the Son largely in terms of Word ... is surely one of the reasons why the attributes of the Son are so heavily drawn from his eternal being rather than his action as incarnate. In some ways this is understandable and inevitable, coming as it does at a time when the chief need was to defend the full and eternal divinity of the Son. ... [Yet] we need to identify the divine person by means of his human being if we are to avoid positing a *logos asarkos* who is in some way conceived independently of the human Jesus. Divinity is discussed in the absence of the human story, which is precisely where we should expect to find *what kind of divine person* we are encountering.[161]

Before evaluating this passage, we should first note its uniqueness. Here we see a rare instance in which Gunton offered a somewhat charitable explanation for *why* Augustine took the position that he did. First, he acknowledged that Augustine's emphasis upon the *Logos* was somewhat "inevitable" in the face of the Arian heresies that he was battling. Beyond this, Gunton would also go on to acknowledge the degree to which Augustine's focus upon the *Logos* was merely following the lead of a Latin predecessor, Hilary of Poitiers.[162]

These two acknowledgments—first of polemical intent and second of continuity with the preceding Latin pro-Nicene tradition—are important because they provide a slice of historical context that Gunton's critics rightly find absent within much of his Augustinian narrative.[163] Thus we see that by the end of his career,[164] Gunton (1) was at least aware of the valid motives behind Augustine's position, and (2) that these valid motives were *not* his chief concern. Once

---

160. As Gunton admitted, this tendency was not absolute in Augustine, thus he praised Augustine's sacramental theology for "teaching that, as visible words, the 'sacraments' depend upon the *word* which Jesus is." *Christian Faith*, 130. Emphasis added.
161. Gunton, *Act and Being*, 135–36. Emphasis in original.
162. Ibid. Augustine acknowledged the work of Hilary in *Trin.* 6.10.11.
163. The failure to note Augustine's polemical motives is pointed out most notably by Michel René Barnes. In a complementary fashion, Lewis Ayres notes the need to recognize Augustine's continuity with the preceding Latin and pro-Nicene tradition. As we noted in ch. 2, Green draws heavily upon both sources.
164. *Act and Being* was published in 2002.

again, Gunton's chief concern was with Augustine's legacy. His argument was that Augustine's preference for the *Logos*, however understandable in light of Arian opposition, was damaging in that it helped to further an abiding dualism between time and eternity, seen and unseen, matter and spirit. Yet is this fair?

Having already surveyed Augustine's treatment of matter, we now focus more specifically on the *material person* of Jesus. As we saw in chapter 2, Bradley Green has challenged Gunton's allegation on the basis of the cross. Green's argument is that while Augustine did stress the *Logos* in order to refute those who questioned the Son's equality, Augustine *also* stressed the flesh-and-blood atonement in order to shame those who would balk at the physicality of the God-Man. Thus Gunton allegedly failed to recognize the extent to which an "earthy, bloody cross" was indispensible for Augustine. As Green puts it, "If [Augustine] is trying to show that the only way to God is through a crucified, bloody, physical man, then Augustine seems to have a rather high view of this material, created world."[165]

Green's argument is partly right. One indicator of this can be glimpsed in a striking passage from *De Trinitate,* which deserves to be quoted at length.

> There are many . . . things in the incarnation of Christ, displeasing as it is to the proud, that are to be observed. . . . One of them is that it has been demonstrated to man what place he has in the things which God has created; since human nature could so be joined to God, that one person could be made of two substances . . . so that those proud malignant spirits [demons] do not therefore dare to place themselves above man because they have not flesh. . . . Man learns also how far he has gone away from God . . . when he returns through such a Mediator, who both as God assists men by His divinity, and as man agrees with men by His weakness. . . . Nay, wherein could the reward of obedience itself be

---

165. Green, "The Protomodern Augustine? Colin Gunton and the Failure of Augustine," *International Journal of Systematic Theology* 9, no. 3 (July, 2009): 338; cf. 186.

better shown, than in the flesh of so great a Mediator, which rose again to eternal life?[166]

Here Augustine openly taunts both proud men (Platonic dualists) and proud spirits (demonic forces) with the crucified and risen *flesh* of the Mediator.[167] Thus the passage ripples with unbridled celebration of the incarnation.

Yet there is also a sense in which Green's argument actually concedes a key element of Gunton's charge. As we have seen, Gunton's claim was *not* that Augustine somehow rejected the incarnation or the cross (who would claim this?). Rather, Gunton's allegation was that Augustine's Christology was *imbalanced* in that "the doctrine of the divinity of Christ [as seen in the *Logos*] is more important . . . than that of the humanity."[168] It was this more subtle tendency that Gunton saw as bequeathing problems to the later tradition, and ironically, it is this tendency that Green himself affirms when he states that, for Augustine, "the pre-existent Christ is more central."[169] As in *De Trinitate*, Augustine's need to prove the equality and eternality of the Father and the Son led him to focus upon the *Logos asarkos*, and to derive attributes from the preexistent and *immaterial* Son. This does not mean that the cross was unimportant, but it does indicate, by Green's own admission, that an imbalance may be seen in the way Augustine draws upon the humanity of Jesus. Thus Gunton is partially justified in his concern that Augustine's

---

166. *Trin.* 13.17.22.
167. After AD 411, Augustine came to speak more clearly of the unity of the divine and the human in Christ. Thus in *Ep.* 137.2, he states, "As the soul makes use of the body in a single person to form a man, so God makes use of man in a single Person to form Christ. In the former person there is a mingling of soul and body; in the latter Person there is a mingling of God and man." Cited in Miles, *Augustine on the Body*, 94.
168. Gunton, *Promise of Trinitarian Theology*, 34.
169. Green, *Gunton and the Failure of Augustine*, 177.

Christology may have gone on to contribute to subsequent dualistic imbalances in the work of others.

In further support of Gunton's critique, we must now probe deeper into Augustine's stress upon the *Logos asarkos*. As Cary suggests, this focus in Augustine's thought should also be traced to the problematic Christian Platonism of his so-called inward turn.[170] To illustrate this crucial point, we now look to the mediatorial role of the human *soul* in one of Augustine's most enduring works.

Mediation and the Human Soul

As Peter Brown suggests, "The *Confessions* are a manifesto of the inner world."[171] Herein, a central question pertained to where one may turn when looking for divine truth. Augustine's answer was to turn within himself, for as he stated: "You [God] were *within* me and I was in the external world and sought you there."[172] Suggestive of God's inner presence for Augustine were passages like Eph. 3:17 where Christ's dwelling place was connected to the human "heart." For someone recently immersed in the "Platonic books," the identification of Paul's "heart" with the Platonist "soul" would be a natural one.[173]

The soul, for Augustine (with the rational mind as its highest component), occupied a kind of middle position between the immutable God and physical bodies.[174] As such, the soul possessed a capacity for divine indwelling (*capax Dei*).[175] Yet as Cary suggests, this equation of Paul's "heart" and the Platonist "soul" also raises an important question: "What part of Christ . . . will be found in

---

170. Cary, *Augustine's Invention of the Inner Self*.
171. Brown, *Augustine*, 162. Italics mine.
172. Augustine, *Conf.* 10.27.38. Emphasis added.
173. See Cary, *Augustine's Invention of the Inner Self*, 50.
174. See Roland Teske on the "Soul," in Fitzgerald, *Augustine through the Ages*, 807–12.
175. See Augustine, *Trin.* 14.4.6; 8.1.

our hearts? The *body* of Christ cannot be [there]. . . . Hence what remains is his divinity, not his humanity."[176] Thus, as Cary puts it, "[Augustine's] inward turn is not a turn away from Christ, but it is a turn away from Christ's flesh."[177] This was Gunton's fear.

In fairness to Augustine, it is important to note with Green that any access to the God within (via the soul) is made possible only by the outward work of the incarnate Christ. Indeed, the cross is indispensible.[178] Yet now that this atoning work has happened, the *Confessions* does stress the mediatorial significance of the immaterial human soul as the inward space where God is to be found. And while Augustine's later thinking would temper his earlier Neoplatonic enthusiasm,[179] these words from the *Confessions* were never retracted. On the contrary, as Peter Brown observes, when Augustine did take time to present a dry catalogue of his prior works within the *Retractationes,* the *Confessions* would elicit what is perhaps the only moment of genuine pathos within the entire work: "As for me," Augustine wrote, "they still move me, when I read them now, as they moved me when I first wrote them."[180]

In his final years Augustine would take to circulating copies of his autobiography to spiritual seekers, while appealing to it as his most popular work.[181] In the Middle Ages, when much of Augustine was known piecemeal and passed on through *Sentences,* like those of Peter Lombard, the *Confessions* may have been, at times, the only work of Augustine that was readily accessible in a completed form.[182]

---

176. Cary, *Augustine's Invention of the Inner Self,* 50.
177. Ibid., 60.
178. Thus Green: "Rather than an unmediated platonic remembrance or illumination, we come to a true knowledge of God through what God has done in this world," *Gunton and the Failure of Augustine,* 183.
179. See especially Augustine, *Civ.,* books 8–10.
180. Augustine, *Retract.* 2.32. Cited in Brown, *Augustine,* 158.
181. See Augustine, *Ep.* 231.6; Brown, *Augustine,* 408.
182. Thanks to Stephen R. Holmes for passing on this insight to me in my doctoral Viva.

The popularity of the work remains today, for while students may find more recent works of medieval theology to be quite foreign to modern sensibilities, the *Confessions* remain remarkably accessible. As O'Donnell remarks, the reason for this is that "even if [Augustine's] theology did not prevail, his psychology persists."[183] In answer to the question of where one finds God, or truth, or happiness, the modern mind would often concur with the *Confessions*: one looks *within*.[184]

For Gunton, this shift was not to be celebrated, for as the immaterial and internal world was elevated, the humanity of Christ, and the goodness of the outward world, must be also deemphasized. This was not Augustine's goal, yet as Cary argues, the influential pages of the *Confessions* may be seen to tilt in this direction: "Because of Augustine's immense prestige and influence in Western Christianity, an inward turn remains a permanent possibility for orthodox piety in the West. . . . From medieval mysticism to contemporary theologies of religious experience, the West has conceived of the God within the self."[185] The viability of this historical assessment is the subject of the next four chapters. For now, however, the present argument has dealt merely with Augustine's own treatment of the created order.

Conclusion

Our basic argument has maintained that while Gunton was unfair to Augustine, it remains true that certain elements in Augustine's treatment of creation may be seen to present a dualistic opposition between time and eternity, mind and matter, Christ and creation. This case has been confirmed in the following respects.

---

183. O'Donnell, *Augustine: Confessions*, 327.
184. One example of this may be seen in the often un-Augustinian *Confessions of* Jean-Jeacques Rousseau.
185. Cary, *Augustine's Invention of the Inner Self*, 60.

(1) With regard to *material dualism*, we once again agreed with Gunton's critics that he often presented an insufficiently contextualized reading of Augustine's thought.[186] Likewise, he failed to account for the maturation of Augustine's thought throughout his life. Yet in deference to Gunton's claims on matter, we noted also the problematic nature of Augustine's so-called hierarchy of being. In this hierarchy, the full goodness of matter did appear to be undermined, despite claims to the contrary. Thus, while Augustine's resulting dualism was "limited," it is *not* sufficient to conclude that this does away with Gunton's charge.[187] On the contrary, for Gunton it was precisely the limited nature of Augustine's dualism which allowed it to be passed on to future generations. This claim remains partly viable and we must return to it in later chapters.

(2) With respect to *temporal dualism*, we noted a similar ambiguity in Augustine's various statements. First, Gunton was wrong to allege that Augustine's position on instantaneous creation was merely the result of Platonic presuppositions. As we witnessed, Augustine's thinking was also deeply influenced by the Bible he read, albeit a somewhat different Bible than that of modern Protestants.[188] In further contrast to Gunton, we also noted Augustine's caution, and his ability to write movingly of how God uses time to bring forth his glory. In all of this, Gunton's allegations were unfair. Yet on the other hand, the charge of temporal dualism was partially supported by other factors. In the *Confessions* especially we found an assessment that came close to seeing temporality as a penalty for the fall. Thus, when coupled with Augustine's world-denying eschatology, such

---

186. See Augustine *Conf.* 12.7.
187. Pace Green, *Gunton and Failure of Augustine*, 89, 96, 174. While Green does not claim that the limited nature of Augustine's dualism completely discredits Gunton's charge, he does fail to note the fact that Gunton saw this "limitation" as precisely the thing that made Augustine's imbalance so dangerous. See again Gunton, *Triune Creator*, 76.
188. See Sir. 18:1: "He who lives forever created all things simultaneously."

emphases, from such an influential work, reveal that it remains viable to contend that Augustine's view of temporal being, while by no means heretical, may have contributed to similar imbalances within the subsequent tradition.

(3) Finally, in turning to the subject of *mediation* we noted again the partial validity and frequent exaggeration of Gunton's case. In contrast with Gunton, we saw that Augustine's use of the angels and the *Logos asarkos* did not mean that the Son's divinity was discussed "in the absence of the human story."[189] Yet while Augustine gloried in the flesh-and-blood atonement,[190] there remained an imbalance within his Christology that may be seen to tilt toward dualism. First, and crucially, by accepting the premise of the Arians on divine invisibility, Augustine can be seen to downgrade the status of that which may be seen (most notably, the *incarnate* God-man). Second, by giving priority to the *Logos asarkos* when addressing the Son's attributes, Augustine can be seen to deemphasize the humanity of Christ. And third, by granting an almost mediatorial significance to the immaterial human soul (especially in *Confessions*) Augustine gave short shrift to the outward and material realm of salvation history as the place where God is to be encountered.

In all of this, we found a grain of truth in Gunton's exaggerated charges against Augustine's doctrine of creation. Yet at this point there remains another question to be asked: Is it really likely that these *limited* deficiencies in Augustine actually had a profound influence upon the subsequent tradition? We turn next to address this question.

---

189. Gunton, *Act and Being*, 135.
190. See again Augustine, *Trin.* 13.17.22.

5

Gunton and Augustine's Medieval Afterlife (Part One)

Augustine's "afterlife" began in August of the year 430. He died, perhaps appropriately, surrounded by the books that he had written.[1] Yet as Gunton argued, Augustine's legacy involves not only what he wrote, but also those who read him. In claiming this, Gunton traced a bold line from Augustine to some of the most influential and problematic tendencies in Western thought.[2] Because this was Gunton's argument, it soon becomes obvious that any comprehensive attempt to evaluate Gunton's charges must also examine the *appropriation* of Augustine by his intellectual descendants. Such is the task of the next few chapters.

Yet herein lies a problem: the history of Augustine's massive influence is voluminous, and an unbounded survey would far exceed

---

1. See Peter Brown, *Augustine of Hippo: A Biography*, 2nd ed. (Berkeley: University of California Press, 2000), 436.
2. See ch. 1.

the limits of a single book. Quite simply, if one were to engage in a full-fledged interaction with both primary and secondary source literature of even a handful of medieval "Augustinians," then the study would quite quickly balloon into a multivolume opus. Thus we must narrow the scope of our investigation. To do so, we will enlist the work of a noted church historian, both to synthesize the glut of historical data, and to help evaluate the viability of Gunton's Augustinian narrative. Yet which historian should be chosen? While himself noting that a comprehensive account of Augustine's legacy still demands to be written, James J. O'Donnell argues that the "best guide" to Augustine's "afterlife" can be seen in Jaroslav Pelikan's "magisterial" history of Christian doctrine.[3]

Others concur with this evaluation. In the view of Mark Noll, Pelikan was (before his death in 2006), "perhaps the foremost living student of church history,"[4] and as Robert Wilken claimed, "he had the largest vision" of any recent church historian.[5] With regard to Augustine's medieval legacy in particular, Colin Morris claimed that Pelikan was particularly qualified "to show how the influence of St Augustine reached to almost every area of medieval thought and how the Augustinian tradition was assimilated, modified and supplemented."[6] With such evaluations in mind, the current chapter, and the one that follows it, will seek to evaluate Augustine's medieval legacy by using Pelikan's *Christian Tradition* (*CT*) as a kind of "primary arbiter" between Gunton and his critics.[7] This is not to

---

3. O'Donnell, *Augustine: A New Biography*, 336.
4. Mark A. Noll, "The Doctrine Doctor," in *Christianity Today*, Sept. 10, 1990, 17–18.
5. Robert Louis Wilken, "Jaroslav Pelikan, Doctor Ecclesiae," in *First Things*, Aug. 2006, 22.
6. Colin Morris, review of *The Christian Tradition: A History of the Development of Doctrine*, vol. 3, *The Growth of Medieval Theology (600–1300)*, by Jaroslav Pelikan, *Journal of Ecclesiastical History* 31, no. 3 (July 1980): 346–47.
7. Jaroslav Pelikan, *The Christian Tradition: A History of the Development of Doctrine*, 5 vols. (Chicago: University of Chicago Press, 1971–85). Hereafter, *CT*, with reference to volume and page number.

say, however, that Pelikan will be our only arbiter. At key points in this journey, we will also drill down more deeply into the work of particular medieval thinkers, while also noting the contributions of more recent specialists who have something to add regarding the way Augustine's influence was appropriated. By doing this, we will seek to avoid the perception that Pelikan has been made determinative on every point, while also benefitting from his immense historical scholarship.

In terms of organization, we will begin by laying the necessary groundwork. First, before delving into the work of various medieval "Augustinians," we must briefly address the very *plausibility* that one man could exert such a profound influence upon the subsequent tradition. Next, we will divide the medieval era itself into three periods: (1) *Early* (c. AD 500–1000), (2) *High* (AD 1000–c. 1300) and (3) *Late* (AD 1300–c. 1500). In order to shorten an already lengthy chapter, the key figures from the Late Middle Ages will be dealt with in the subsequent chapter, along with our conclusions from the medieval era as a whole. While such broad divisions are purely heuristic, the goal in each period will be to trace Augustine's influence in the areas critiqued by Gunton.

The broader argument will be as follows: As we have seen before, Gunton was often unfair to Augustine, and this unfairness was sometimes extended to Augustine's supposed intellectual inheritors. Yet in the view of Pelikan and other specialists, it remains viable to contend that *isolated elements* in Augustine (most notably his "inward turn") were at times appropriated in such a way as to further the kinds of imbalances alleged by Gunton. In turning to Augustine's afterlife, however, an additional caveat is now required: to appropriate the thought of another is invariably *to alter* it in terms of content, emphasis, or application.[8] Thus we will also note the ways in which the line from Hippo Regius to the medieval or modern world is not nearly as direct as Gunton claimed.

Evaluating the Scope of Augustine's Influence

Before this broader thesis can be proven, however, a more basic question must first be answered. Is it plausible that this one man could exert such a profound impact on the subsequent tradition? As Gunton argued, Augustine was indisputably the "dominating" influence with regard to the theology of the Middle Ages.[9] Yet how does this judgment measure up to the analysis of others? In many regards, Pelikan confirms Gunton's sentiment regarding the size (though not always the *shape*) of Augustine's influence. Thus in a rephrasing of Whitehead's famous epigram, Pelikan states that Western church history could often be written as a series of "footnotes to Augustine."[10] As he puts it, "Almost anywhere one touches the history of early Christian doctrine, Augustine is there either as a synthesizer or as a creator or as both. . . . There is probably no Christian theologian . . . whose . . . influence can match his."[11] And when writing more specifically of the medieval era, Pelikan states that "since the apostles, no figure . . . has so dominated a millennium . . . as Augustine did."[12]

Such sweeping statements are a relative rarity in Pelikan's cautious history, yet the analysis is confirmed by others. As Holmes notes, "Augustine, by any estimation, towers like a colossus over Western theology."[13] And as Green states, "Augustine sowed the seeds of

---

8. As the Latin (*appropriare*) suggests, to *appropriate* is "to make one's own."
9. Gunton, *The Triune Creator: A Historical and Systematic Study* (Grand Rapids: Eerdmans, 1998), 97.
10. Pelikan, *CT*, 1:330; cf. 2:4.
11. *CT*, 1:293–94, 1:292.
12. *CT*, 3:viii.
13. Holmes, *The Quest for the Trinity: The Doctrine of God in Scripture, History, and Modernity* (Downers Grove, IL: IVP Academic), 129.

virtually the entire Western theological edifice.... Gunton is surely accurate in affirming the magnitude and significance of Augustine's place in the history of Western thought."[14] Given this agreement, we may now move beyond the generalizations regarding the scope of Augustine's impact, and inquire more precisely as to what this impact was.

As we will see, few (if any) of the figures surveyed below will demonstrate a slavish replication of Augustine on every point. As Stephen Menn suggests, "The history of Augustinianism is the history of the many revivals of Augustine by different thinkers, who have each discovered some aspect of Augustine's thought, and seen in it a way to answer the philosophical and theological challenges of their own times."[15] In light of this, we must inquire as to what extent Gunton's claims remain viable regarding the influence of Augustine throughout the Middle Ages. For the sake of space, it will be impossible to deal with every influential theologian of the period. Thus while our selections render the present study vulnerable to certain critiques (perhaps of historical bias, or insufficient contextualization), we will attempt to mitigate such concerns by allowing the work of Pelikan and others to complement that of Gunton and his critics. We begin with two men who, in the years soon after Augustine's death, would help to bridge the gap between the ancient and medieval eras.

The Early Middle Ages

For the figure known as Boethius (c. 480–524/26), Augustine's use of Greek philosophy gave permission to further the connection between biblical revelation and Hellenistic reason, while for the pontiff known

---

14. Bradley Green, "Augustine," in *Shapers of Christian Orthodoxy*, ed. Bradley Green (Downers Grove, IL: IVP, 2010), 235.
15. Stephen Menn, *Descartes and Augustine* (Cambridge: Cambridge University Press, 1998), ix.

as Gregory the Great (c. 540–604), Augustine's doctrinal schema would be used to forge something of a theological consensus within a fragmenting Christendom. Despite their differences, both men would appropriate Augustine in ways that would come to typify the Early Middle Ages. Thus while Boethius and Gregory stand at the onset of the period in question, Pelikan notes that their appropriation of Augustine served to "frame the theology of the subsequent centuries."[16] Yet to what extent are these two figures truly *Augustinian*?

Boethius and the Legacy of Augustine

Anicius Manlius Serverinus Boethius bore many titles in his short life. He was a senator, a consul, and a political prisoner. Yet while much of his story falls beyond the scope of our study, certain details are necessary to lend context to Gunton's Augustinian argument. As a Roman patrician, Boethius worked to bolster relations with the Greek-speaking East. He translated parts of Aristotle into the Latin tongue,[17] and in so doing, he sought to show the relative "harmony" between Plato and his famous pupil.[18]

As a Christian, one of Boethius's goals was to mobilize Greek philosophy in defense of Catholic dogma.[19] Thus he penned polemics on the Trinity and Christ, which though "thoroughly orthodox,"[20] were designed to push the bounds of revelation and reason.[21] In the end, he would run afoul of an Arian emperor (Theodoric the Great), and while "languishing in prison for treason and presumably for his fidelity to trinitarian orthodoxy," Boethius would pen what has been

---

16. *CT*, 1:349.
17. *CT*, 1:349.
18. See Boethius, *Commentary on Aristotle's "On Interpretation,"* 2. Cited in Pelikan, *CT*, 1:42.
19. *CT*, 1:42.
20. *CT*, 1:349.
21. So says Pelikan, *CT*, 1:44.

called "the noblest literary work of the final period of antiquity," the *Consolation of Philosophy*.[22]

The *Consolation* played a key role in medieval literature and devotion. Manuscripts were widely distributed, and it was translated by the likes of King Alfred, Chaucer, and perhaps even Queen Elizabeth I. The work also provided comfort to Dante Alighieri in his bereavement over Beatrice.[23] In its form, the *Consolation* was a dialogue with philosophy personified. As such, it dealt with the problem of evil, human freedom, and fate. Yet as Pelikan notes, the controversy consists in this: "On the basis of content alone, there seems reason to doubt . . . that the *Consolation* was written by a Christian theologian."[24] In the words of one scholar, "There is not a trace of anything specifically Christian or Biblical in the entire work."[25] Hence for Pelikan, "Boethius' *Consolation of Philosophy* only dramatizes a more general problem. The victory of orthodox Christian doctrine over classical thought was to some extent a Pyrrhic victory, for the theology that triumphed over Greek philosophy has continued to be shaped ever since by the language and the thought of classical metaphysics."[26] For Pelikan, this problem was seen in the way Boethius chose to cope with his impending demise. As he put it, "In his hour of utmost need," when facing torture and eventual death, this Christian thinker seemingly "found solace more in natural reason than in the Christian revelation."[27] Yet how does this connect to Gunton's narrative?

While sharing Pelikan's concern over Boethius's elevation of Greek reason,[28] Gunton went further in linking this imbalance to

---

22. *CT*, 1:43.
23. Ibid.
24. Ibid.
25. Edward K. Rand, *Founders of the Middle Ages* (Cambridge, MA: Harvard Press, 1929), 178.
26. *CT*, 1:44.
27. Ibid.

Augustine's influence. On creation, Gunton's claim was that Boethius's "dualism of reason and faith"[29] furthered Augustine's tendency to allow Greek philosophy to "displace theology as the basis of the doctrine."[30] On the Trinity, his charge was that Boethius shared Augustine's failure to understand "personhood" within a truly relational matrix. As Gunton noted, Boethius defined the *person* as "an individual substance of a rational nature."[31] In this, Gunton sensed Augustine's tilt toward (1) intellectualism and (2) individualism.[32] Thus for Gunton, Boethius became, in some ways, the missing link between the Platonism of Augustine and the Aristotelian methodology of Aquinas.[33] Despite their differences, Gunton claimed that both schemas evidenced a dualism in the doctrine of creation and a monistic imbalance in the doctrine of God.[34] Thus in Gunton's words, "Boethius was the last of the ancients and the first of the 'Medievalists.'"[35]

What should be said to such charges? First, there is no question that Boethius drew heavily, and at points, almost exclusively upon Augustine's writings. In this vein, Chadwick describes him as "deeply Augustinian,"[36] while Holmes notes that his theological reading seems to have been confined almost exclusively to Augustine.[37] On

---

28. See Gunton, *Revelation and Reason*, ed. P. H. Brazier (London: T&T Clark, 2008), 111: "Boethius' *Consolation of Philosophy* is an important work even though it is non-Christian."
29. Gunton, *Triune Creator*, 99.
30. Ibid.; cf. Gunton, *Revelation and Reason*, 110–12.
31. Boethius, *Contra Eutychem*, 3, 4–5. Gunton notes this definition in *The Promise of Trinitarian Theology* (London: T&T Clark, 1991), 92.
32. Gunton, *Promise of Trinitarian Theology*, 92; cf. *The One, the Three and the Many: God, Creation and the Culture of Modernity* (Cambridge: Cambridge University Press, 1993), 52.
33. See Gunton, *Triune Creator*, 99.
34. For more on this, see our treatment of Aquinas later in this chapter.
35. Gunton, *Revelation and Reason*, 110.
36. Henry Chadwick, *Boethius: The Consolations of Music, Logic Theology, and Philosophy* (Oxford: Clarendon Press, 1981). Likewise, Bowery notes the "considerable influence [from Augustine] with respect to philosophical and theological issues." Anne-Marie Bowery, "Boethius," in *Augustine through the Ages: An Encyclopedia*, ed. Allan Fitzgerald (Grand Rapids: Eerdmans, 1999), 108.

the Trinity, David Bradshaw notes the "striking" fact that while Boethius's "facility in Greek could have opened for him the entire world of patristic theology," his own work (*On the Trinity*) mentions *only* Augustine. Indeed, as he puts it, "There is little sign either here or elsewhere that [Boethius] read *any* of the other Church Fathers."[38]

Second, both Pelikan and others also confirm the validity of viewing Boethius as a crucial bridge between Augustine and the subsequent medieval tradition. On the subjects of Christ and the Trinity, Pelikan states that Boethius's work would "be the basis of commentaries for a millennium,"[39] while John Marenbon notes that within the Middle Ages, "only Aristotle and Augustine had so great a direct influence over so wide a range of intellectual life."[40]

So far so good for Gunton's Augustinian narrative. Yet in moving past Boethius's debt to Augustine, and his unquestionable influence upon the later tradition, it now becomes necessary to ask whether one should affirm any of Gunton's claims regarding the Augustinian origins of supposed Boethian imbalances. What, for instance, of Gunton's particular claim that Augustine's use of Hellenistic philosophy was taken up by Boethius to further an alleged "dualism of reason and faith"?[41]

On this point, Pelikan gives a slight nod of support. In particular, he cites Boethius's belief that his philosophical speculation on the Trinity was merely bringing to fruition "the seeds of *reason* from . . . the blessed Augustine."[42] Thus, according to Boethius himself, it was Augustine's use of Greek philosophy that provided the theological

---

37. Holmes, *Quest for the Trinity*, 141.
38. David Bradshaw, "The *Opuscula sacra*: Boethius and Theology," in *The Cambridge Companion to Boethius*, ed. John Marenbon (Cambridge: Cambridge University Press, 2009), 209.
39. *CT*, 1:349.
40. John Marenbon, *Boethius* (Oxford: Oxford University Press, 2003), 164.
41. Gunton, *Triune Creator*, 99.
42. Boethius, *On the Trinity*. Cited in *CT*, 1:350. Italics mine.

sanction for his own appeal to Aristotelian and Platonic wisdom. In complementary fashion, Chadwick argues that even the apparently secular and purely philosophical tenor of the *Consolation* was partly inspired by Boethius's reading of Augustine's early works of Christian Platonism. As he puts it, "There is nothing in the Platonic themes admitted to the *Consolation* which one cannot also find accepted in the philosophical dialogues and the *Confessions* of the young Augustine."[43]

More importantly, Pelikan also notes what he sees to be a viable connection between the Augustine-inspired theology of Boethius, and the modern search for (as Kant would term it) a "religion within the boundaries of reason alone."[44] Thus in the final volume of his *Christian Tradition*, Pelikan cites the likelihood that Boethius, along with others,[45] contributed to a culture in which "logic and metaphysics were being preferred to the catechism, philosophical ethics to Christian ethics, and the Hellenization of Christianity to a faithful exposition of . . . Scripture."[46] In all of this, Pelikan acknowledges that certain problematic tendencies in Augustine, with respect to Greek philosophy especially,[47] were amplified by Boethius, before being passed to later thinkers.

---

43. Chadwick, *Boethius*, 249.
44. *CT*, 5:107; cf. Gunton, *Revelation and Reason*, 111. On this point, see also the claims of Pierre Courcelle, *La Consolation de Philosophie dans la tradition littéraire* (Paris: Études Augustiniennes, 1967), 337–44. Cited in Marenbon, *Boethius*, 156.
45. Perhaps the bookend to the Boethian use of Augustine in the Early Middle Ages can be seen in the theology of John Scotus Erigena (c. 815–c. 877). As Pelikan notes, both appealed to Augustine in support of rampant philosophical speculation, and both introduced the Latin West to the work of an influential Greek thinker. While Boethius translated parts of Aristotle, Erigena made available the work of Pseudo-Dionysius. *CT*, 3:100.
46. *CT*, 5:106.
47. As Pelikan states, "It is quite another question whether [Augustine's] doctrine of the Creator was determined in its fundamental content by the Christocentric perspective which Augustine espoused in principle. When he came to speak of the divine essence, it was usually defined in relation to absoluteness and impassibility rather than on the basis of the active involvement of God in creation and redemption." *CT*, 1:296.

Yet if one is avoid the error of seeing every influence of "classical philosophy" as a corrupting one, then it becomes important to ask what theological imbalances should be linked to the philosophical borrowings of both Boethius and Augustine. On this point, David Bradshaw joins Pelikan in lending some credence to Gunton's Trinitarian concerns. In his recent overview of Boethius's *Opuscula sacra*, Bradshaw suggests that the allegation of a monistic imbalance may well be justified in certain respects. After all, it was on the Trinity in particular that Boethius desired to develop "the seeds of reason" sown by Augustine,[48] and on this subject, Bradshaw notes the "troublesome" fact that Boethius "has so little to say about the 'otherness of [the] persons.'"[49] In some instances, "Boethius seems to treat God as a single person,"[50] and, in Bradshaw's view, such imbalances "derive in part from Boethius's desire to treat theological issues using a purely philosophical method, and in part from his exclusive reliance on Augustine as a theological authority."[51]

In Augustine's defense, both Pelikan and Bradshaw note that what Boethius bequeathed to the medieval scholastics was indeed a "*reinterpreted* Augustinism."[52] Thus while Boethius may have built on certain tendencies in Augustine, it would be unfair to blame Augustine for every feature of the ultimate construction. As Bradshaw notes, Boethius failed to appropriate sufficiently Augustine's attention to Scripture, his apophatic tendencies, and his more thorough recognition of the limitations of human language.[53] Likewise, Pelikan illustrates that, at certain points, the Boethian legacy stands distinct from that of Augustine. One example comes in

---

48. Boethius, *On the Trinity*, 5. Cited in Bradshaw, "Boethius and Theology," 109.
49. Bradshaw, "Boethius and Theology," 112.
50. Ibid., 121.
51. Ibid., 125.
52. *CT*, 1:350. Emphasis mine.
53. Bradshaw, "Boethius and Theology," 115.

reference to a passage from Peter Abelard (1079–1142). Here, when speaking of the Trinity in ways that Pelikan believed "imperil[ed] the distinction of persons,"[54] Abelard traces key parts of his doctrine *not* to Augustine, but to that which "was handed down to us by Boethius alone."[55] Thus while Pelikan acknowledges certain Augustinian "parallels" in the Hellenistic imbalances of later thinkers,[56] he is more careful in distinguishing the "sins of the father" from those of Augustine's theological descendants.

Perhaps one reason for this more charitable reading of Augustine was that, unlike Gunton, Pelikan spent time chronicling other aspects of Augustine's early legacy, as can be seen in his treatment of such figures as Gregory the Great.

Gregory the Great and the Legacy of Augustine

Pelikan referred to Gregory as the "last of the church fathers and first of the popes."[57] Among his many achievements, Gregory represented a turning point in the power of the papacy, fostered missionary endeavors to Britain, and helped to solidify beliefs on such issues as purgatory and the sacrifice of the Mass.[58] Yet our concern is to highlight how Gregory typifies a second branch among Augustine's early inheritors. While Boethius appealed to Augustine's use of Greek philosophy, Gregory drew upon Augustine as a resource in forging a Catholic consensus amid a fragmenting Christendom. Thus, as one biographer wrote of Gregory's relation to Augustine, there has "never been an author who owed more to the writings of another."[59]

---

54. *CT*, 3:265.
55. Peter Abelard, *Christian Theology*, 1.52. Cited in *CT*, 3:265.
56. *CT*, 3:266. At this point, Pelikan also references the work of Gilbert de La Porrée (c. 1075–1154).
57. *CT*, 1:349.
58. See *CT*, 1:353.
59. Frederick H. Dudden, cited in *CT*, 1:350.

In his many treatments of Augustine's afterlife, Gunton never focused on the work of Gregory. Perhaps one reason for this omission is that many of Gregory's contributions have been seen to reside in areas other than the doctrines of the Trinity and creation.[60] Yet Gregory's inclusion here is important for at least two reasons. First, it allows us to acknowledge aspects of Augustine's influence that were overlooked in Gunton's narrative. And second, it again reveals a tendency among Augustine's interpreters to mute, amplify, or otherwise alter certain aspects of his thought. Thus, as Reinhold Seeberg wrote of Gregory, "Almost everything in him has its roots in Augustine, and yet almost nothing is genuinely Augustinian."[61]

What specifically is meant by Seeberg's comment? As Pelikan notes, while Gregory drew heavily upon Augustine, he also worked to *soften* his statements on divine predestination and the status of the human will. Gregory's goal was, in part, to shield Augustine from the charges that his thought was tainted by a fatalistic Hellenism.[62] Thus for Pelikan, this modification (which began prior to Gregory)[63] would ultimately help to ensure that Augustine was forever "spared ... the fate of Origen."[64] For one of Gunton's critics, however, it was this very *alteration* to Augustine that would ultimately contribute to the sort of "modern self" decried by Gunton.[65] Thus we come now to an instance in which we must move beyond Pelikan in order to engage with a more recent criticism.

---

60. See, for example, Charles Kannengiesser's focus upon Gregory's ecclesial, social, and ethical contributions. "Boethius, Cassiodorus, Gregory the Great," in *The Medieval Theologians: An Introduction to Theology in the Medieval Period*, ed. G.R. Evans (Malden, MA: Blackwell, 2001), 24–36.
61. Reinhold Seeberg, cited in *CT*, 1:350.
62. *CT*, 1:319-20.
63. Ibid. More on this anon.
64. *CT*, 1:351. As Pelikan himself indicates (*CT*, 1:338), it may be doubted as to whether Augustine was ever in serious danger of Origen's fate. Still, the fact remains that after Gregory it would be much more difficult for the medieval church to seriously question aspects of Augustine's thought.
65. See Hanby, *Augustine and Modernity* (New York: Routledge, 2003), 132–33.

Hanby's Challenge to Gunton's Augustinian Narrative

Like Gunton, Michael Hanby has linked certain notions of Cartesian inwardness and autonomy to a "de-trinitization of God" and a faulty view of his creation.[66] Yet unlike Gunton, Hanby's work denies that *any* of these errors can be found in Augustine himself. For him, the mistakes emerged only later with some of Augustine's earliest interpreters: John Cassian (c. 360–435), Faustus of Riez (c. 405–495), and especially Gregory the Great. In such figures, the attempt to soften Augustine's views on predestination purportedly led to the adoption of Stoic (that is, "semi-Pelagian") conclusions on the abiding freedom of the human will.[67] With Gregory, Hanby contends that this error was "codified" in "a conception of the will primarily as a faculty of 'choice' locked in a successive relationship to grace."[68] As he puts it, "The Augustinianism . . . institutionalized in the Christendom of Gregory the Great, was one therefore implicitly reliant upon the metaphysical underpinnings of a pagan virtue which it had been Augustine's great achievement to refute."[69] For Hanby, the full effects of Gregory's modifications to Augustine took years to germinate, in part, because the communal setting of medieval monasticism would delay the individualistic consequences of such changes. Thus, as Hanby claims, "the full realization of this logic would have to wait until the seventeenth century and the philosophy of René Descartes."[70]

---

66. Ibid., 135.
67. Ibid., 127. Hanby explains his case as follows: "The primary analogue for displaying *voluntas* in Augustine's theology . . . is not the relation of cause to effect [as it is in Gregory], but rather of lover to beloved. This analogy assumes further that the beauty and intelligibility of the beloved is already *in* the lover. . . . To become a voluntarist, Augustine must be relieved of his trinitarianism and his Platonism, a feat that has been achieved more than once by opponents and apologists alike. The result is always an *election* that is more Pelagian than Augustinian and a god who looks like Pelagian man writ large," 118.
68. Ibid., 127. Here Hanby cites Gregory's *Moral Discourses on Job*, 35:14.28.
69. Hanby, *Augustine and Modernity*, 133.
70. Ibid.

The Importance of *De Libero Arbitrio:* A Response to Hanby

How should we respond to Hanby's argument? While a treatment of Descartes must await another chapter, some other points may now be noted. On the one hand, Hanby's attention to Gregory (and his aforementioned predecessors) supports our claim that Augustine's heirs, at times, adapted his work in such a way as to further problems that cannot be blamed (at least not fully) on Augustine himself. Yet as we have attempted to show at length in the previous two chapters, the dogged refusal to trace *any* of these later imbalances (on the treatment of the Trinity and creation) to actual tensions in Augustine is not altogether convincing.[71]

With regard to the status of the human will, it bears noting that the early Augustine wrote an entire treatise on this subject (*De Libero Arbitrio*).[72] And in this work his views sound strikingly similar to those Hanby attributes to Gregory's corrupting influence.[73] In *De Libero Arbitrio*, Augustine actually affirmed (to Pelagius's great delight!) that "nothing is so much within our power as the will itself."[74] To be sure, he would eventually speak differently on this subject,[75] yet while Augustine clearly changed his views on human freedom, the *Retractationes* would stubbornly refuse to acknowledge that a genuine shift had taken place from *De Libero Arbitrio*.[76] Thus as O'Donnell argues,

---

71. See again the conclusions of chs. 3 and 4. In Wayne Hankey's view, Hanby's allegiance to the "Radical Orthodoxy" of John Milbank prevents him from noting the full extent of Platonic influence upon Augustine's theology. See Wayne J. Hankey, "Philosophical Religion and the Neoplatonic Turn to the Subject," in *Deconstructing Radical Orthodoxy: Postmodern Theology, Rhetoric and Truth*, ed. Wayne Hankey and Douglas Hedley (Burlington, VT: Ashgate, 2005), 23.
72. c. AD 387–395. Subsequent citations taken from the English translation by Thomas Williams, *On Free Choice of the Will* (Indianapolis, IN: Hacket, 1993).
73. See Augustine, *Lib. arb.* 3.12; 3.16.
74. Augustine, *Retr.* 1.9.2, in reference to *Lib. arb.* 1.12.
75. For the mature Augustine, as relayed by Peter Brown, "Men choose because they love . . . [thus] freedom can only be the culmination of a process of healing." *Augustine of Hippo*, 375–76.

The ideas of *Free Choice of the Will* were brought forth by an Augustine who had not yet settled on his distinctive reading of Paul, and thus on his ideas of grace and predestination. In the *Reconsiderations*, Augustine wants to make it seem as if the ideas that Pelagius is missing were simply irrelevant to the narrow topic of the early book. Few readers not already committed to finding Augustine in the right on every possible point have been persuaded by this.⁷⁷

On this topic, it seems that Hanby is in the scholarly minority. Because this "unretracted" tension exists within Augustine's own corpus, it remained possible for men like Gregory to cite Augustine as a defender of the abiding "free choice" of the human will. Given this, it would seem that Hanby's total exoneration of Augustine's influence is problematic. In short, it depends on which Augustine one is reading.

In time, Pelikan will add further corroboration to this analysis by linking certain aspects of Descartes's *cogito* to "its undeniable ancestry in Augustine."⁷⁸ Thus while Gunton went too far in blaming Augustine for the failures of his progeny, Hanby errs in the opposite direction. In the end, we will come to see that the "all-or-nothing" approach of both histories stands in need of revision. Yet for now, we return to Pelikan, Gregory, and another feature of Augustine's early legacy.

In addition to softening Augustine's statements on the status of the human will, Gregory also *solidified* other notions that Augustine set forth only cautiously. Whereas purgatory was proposed tentatively by Augustine,⁷⁹ Gregory set forth the doctrine as "something that

---

76. In another portion of *Retract.* (not dealing with the content of *Lib. arb.*) Augustine admits that "I invested much labor on behalf of the free choice of the human will, but the grace of God triumphed." Cited in David J. Marshall, "John Calvin," in Fitzgerald, *Augustine through the Ages*, 118.
77. O'Donnell, *Augustine: A New Biography*, 318.
78. *CT*, 3:306. See ch. 8.
79. See *CT*, 3:32–33. For Augustine's treatment of the issue, see *Civ.* 21.13, 21.24.

has to be believed."[80] Here a certain irony exists. In his afterlife, Augustine would at times be cited as the *proof* of ideas that he himself had seen as still *unproven*. Gregory is indicative of this phenomenon, and for him, the practice often served to bolster the authority of the Holy See. Thus as Pelikan notes, this aspect of Augustine's afterlife may be typified by a statement that would become a favorite within Roman Christendom: "For my part," Augustine once declared, "I should not believe the gospel except as moved by the authority of the catholic church."[81]

Already by the sixth century, Augustine had become a crucial part of this authority. As Pelikan states, "It was principally Augustine, either directly or indirectly, upon whom the seventh and eighth centuries—as well as the ninth and those that followed—drew for their understanding of church doctrine."[82] Yet for many in the Early Middle Ages, the Augustine they received, was handed down, at least in part, through the likes of Gregory and Boethius.[83] Both men served as hinge points between Augustine and the high medieval era; both drew heavily upon Augustine's writings; both altered key aspects of his thought while claiming faithfulness to him; and both contributed to what Pelikan calls the "Augustinian synthesis" of early medieval theology. This synthesis involved the pervasive appeal to Augustine for the definitive explication of "the integrity of the catholic tradition."[84]

Yet as Pelikan notes, it would soon become obvious that "simply invoking [Augustine's] name . . . would not suffice as a guarantee of catholicity and of orthodoxy."[85] The Augustinian synthesis would

---

80. Gregory the Great, *Dialogues*, 4.39.
81. Augustine, *c. ep. Man.*, 5. Cited in *CT*, 1:303.
82. *CT*, 3:16.
83. "For all his repetition of Augustine [Gregory the Great] was 'the most widely read of the Western church fathers.'" *CT*, 3:16, citing Adolf Von Harnack.
84. Ibid., 49.
85. Ibid., 50.

need to be "interpreted," and perhaps "transcended."[86] Thus we turn now to another chapter in Augustine's afterlife.

The High Middle Ages

When speaking of theological history, Gunton could often exhibit a "merciless clarity"[87] over what went wrong, and who was to blame. In this vein, the High Middle Ages were seen to evidence a damaging "synthesis of the classical and the Christian," and once again the fault lay often with Augustine.[88] As Holmes relays, Gunton sometimes claimed that Augustine's marriage of "Greek" and "Hebrew" thought resulted in an ironic form of "semi-Pelagianism: whereby we ascend as far as our reason will take us, and then God rewards our efforts with the gift of Revelation." In response to this claim in Gunton's classroom lectures, Holmes writes, "I do not suppose Augustine was any more Pelagian here than in his strictures about salvation. . . . *Fides quaerens intellectum* is characteristically Augustinian, and surely a more adequate picture of the whole scholastic enterprise (Aquinas as well as Anselm) than the one [Gunton] offers."[89]

In light of this critique, the present section turns to evaluate this portion of Gunton's Augustinian narrative. We will begin with a group of medieval thinkers from Anselm to Bonaventure, while moving next to a treatment of perhaps the most important medieval theologian of all: Thomas Aquinas.

---

86. Ibid., 50.
87. So says Holmes, in introduction to *Revelation and Reason*, 5.
88. Gunton, *Triune Creator*, 97–98; cf. *A Brief Theology of Revelation*, the 1993 Warfield Lectures (Edinburgh: T&T Clark, 1995), 42.
89. Holmes, in *Revelation and Reason*, 8. In fairness to both Gunton and Holmes, this quotation pertains to the raw transcripts of Gunton's posthumously published classroom lectures. As we have noted already, it is doubtful whether many professors would be happy to find their off-hand comments committed to print.

From Anselm to Bonaventure

Like Barth before him, Gunton praised the epistemic implications of Anselm's *fides quaerens intellectum*.[90] At times, he could even bring himself to admit (perhaps begrudgingly) that the insight had roots in Augustine's famous dictum, "Unless you believe, you will not understand."[91] Yet for Gunton, the question was not whether one affirmed such notions in principle, but whether one's theology led to their further embodiment in practice.[92] In Gunton's view, Anselm was relatively successful in giving revelation priority over human reason. After all, even his ontological argument "was given as the response to prayer."[93]

Yet between Anselm (c. 1033–1109) and Bonaventure (1221–1274), Gunton believed that the search for rational understanding had come to undermine the very premise of *fides quaerens intellectum*. Behind this was Augustine's alleged baptism of Hellenistic reason, and the identification of the rational mind as the *imago Trinitatis*.[94] As Gunton argued, such moves provided a foothold for "reason" to claim its place as an autonomous source of truth.[95] We

---

90. See Gunton, *The Barth Lectures*, ed. P. H. Brazier (London: T&T Clark, 2007), 53ff.; Barth, *Fides Quaerens Intellectum: Anselm's Proof of the Existence of God in the Context of His Theological Scheme*, trans. I. W. Robertson (London: SCM Press, 1960), 25-26. Gunton notes this passage in *Brief Theology of Revelation*, 12.
91. Gunton, *Barth Lectures*, 64–65. As Pelikan notes, Augustine's dictum could be traced to an early Latin translation of Isa. 7:9. While Augustine knew of Jerome's alternative rendering ("Unless you believe, you will not abide"), he continued to quote the older version to show that faith must precede understanding. See *CT*, 3:258–9. For Anselm's acknowledgement of Augustine's influence, see the preface to his *Monologion*. For an additional acknowledgement of the Augustinian origins of *fides quaerens intellectum*, see G.R. Evans, "Anselm of Canterbury," in Fitzgerald, *Augustine through the Ages*, 24.
92. See Gunton, *Act and Being: Towards a Theology of the Divine Attributes* (London: SCM Press, 2002), 49.
93. Gunton, *Barth Lectures*, 60. One may wonder why Gunton doesn't make more of the same quality in Augustine's *Confessions*.
94. See Augustine, *Trin.* 12.7.12. See again our treatment of this in ch. 3.
95. See also Gunton, *Barth Lectures*, 52.

must now ask how this medieval portion of the argument holds up to closer scrutiny.

Parts of Gunton's medieval narrative are uncontroversial. In the High Middle Ages, Augustine was indisputably the dominating voice from the preceding postbiblical tradition. For Bernard of Clairvaux (1090–1153), the *Confessions* provided the impetus to "turn your minds inward upon yourselves."[96] For Peter Lombard (c. 1100–1160) Augustine was cited more than twice as often as all other church fathers combined.[97] For Richard of Saint Victor (d. 1173), he was raised (almost?) to the place of Scripture, as one "filled with the Spirit of the prophets and apostles."[98] And for Bonaventure he was "the most authentic doctor" among all expositors of the sacred text.[99] As Pelikan states of such men, "For all of them Augustine was 'the greatest philosopher' among Christians," and "his speculations about the 'traces of the Trinity' in the human mind were the outstanding example of faith in search of understanding."[100] Here again we see the great importance of Augustine and his "inward turn."[101]

Yet as Pelikan also notes, many of Augustine's medieval admirers went far beyond him in the realm of theological speculation.[102] Perhaps the clearest example of this exists in the occasional attempts to "prove" the truths of the Trinity by rational means. Thus Hugh

---

96. Bernard of Clairvaux, *Sermons on the Song of Songs*, 3.1.1. Cited in *CT*, 3:304.
97. *CT*, 3:271. With regard to Peter Lombard in particular, one cannot overlook the importance of his *Sentences* as, at times, the primary conduit by which Augustine's thought was passed on to subsequent medieval theologians. Josef Pieper called it "a systematically organized Augustinian breviary," and as Wayne Hankey notes, "Until the late Middle Ages, it was a principal source for the scholastic knowledge of Augustine." Josef Pieper, *Scholasticism: Personalities and Problems of Medieval Philosophy*, trans. R. Winston and C. Winston (London: Faber and Faber, 1961), 98; Wayne J. Hankey, "Reading Augustine through Dionysius: Aquinas's Correction of One Platonism by Another," in *Aquinas the Augustinian*, ed. M. Dauphinais, B. David, and M. Levering (Washington, DC: Catholic University of America Press, 2007), 246.
98. Richard of Saint Victor, *Sermones centum*, 99. Cited in *CT*, 3:223.
99. Bonaventure, *Disputed Questions*, 4. Cited *CT*, 3:271.
100. *CT*, 3:259–60, citing Peter Abelard, *Dialogue between a Philosopher, a Jew, and a Christian*.
101. See again chs. 3–4.
102. *CT*, 3:260.

of Saint Victor (c. 1096–1141) could argue, as Pelikan puts it, that "to some degree the human reason has the power to penetrate to the truth of the Trinity," while Richard, his protégé, would go further, "to the point of proving the doctrine of the *filioque* on the basis of reason alone, without the authority of Scripture or tradition."[103]

In response, it bears noting that even these figures were technically beginning from a place of faith. As Pelikan states of the period, "There were heretics and infidels but agnosticism was non-existent."[104] Despite this fact, such methods did raise, for Pelikan, an important question: "If it was permissible to apply the methods of rational speculation to the mystery of the Trinity . . . what was to prevent someone from beginning with the same rational method but coming to conclusions that did not accord with the orthodox doctrine?" For Gunton, this same logic would reveal the dangerous link between medieval speculation and modern rationalism.

In spite of this possibility, it would be foolish to blame Augustine for this trajectory merely on the basis that his writings were revered. Thus the crucial question is as follows: Can such rational speculations be linked to a *specific* facet of Augustine's own theology? For Pelikan, the key connection resides again in Augustine's "exegesis of the plural in Genesis 1.26, 'Let us make man in our image.'" As he states, "It was a universal patristic consensus . . . that the plural was a reference to the Trinity,"[105] yet Augustine's innovation was to see this as a ground for equating the rational mind with the *imago Trinitatis*.[106] As Pelikan notes, Augustine "almost single-handedly turned Western theology in this direction."[107]

---

103. Ibid., 263. See Hugh of Saint Victor, *Sacraments of the Christian Faith*, 1.3.28; Richard of Saint-Victor, *On the Trinity*, 5.8.
104. *CT*, 3:3.
105. Ibid., 281.
106. Augustine, *Trin.* 9.12.18; 14.19.25. See again ch. 3.
107. *CT*, 3:281. As we will see momentarily, this insight would prove crucial for Aquinas as well.

The danger of this development was that such rational introspection would ultimately contribute to the very modern malady diagnosed by Gunton: reason as an autonomous source of truth. As Pelikan puts it,

> The Augustinian combination of objective and subjective truth led Bonaventure to assert that "when the soul speculates on its triune Principle . . . which makes it the image of God, it is assisted by the lights of knowledge, which perfect and inform it . . . ." Profoundly Augustinian and thoroughly medieval though this theology was in Bonaventure, it was to become something quite different in later centuries. As the natural theology of the scholastics eventually lost its connection with the traditional doctrine out of which it had come, so the experiential theology of Bonaventure and of Augustine was transformed into an autonomous source of truth.[108]

This is a crucial statement. In it Pelikan notes what he sees as the legitimate historical trajectory between (1) Augustine's inward turn, (2) the natural theology of some medieval scholastics, and (3) the modern elevation of reason to the place of revelation. Incidentally, this was also what Barth had in mind when he referred to Augustine's *vestigium Trinitatis* as "an ancient Trojan horse which one day . . . was unsuspectingly allowed entry into the theological Ilium."[109]

Yet in Pelikan's above quotation, the word *transformed* is of great importance. Here he notes the degree to which Augustine is both innocent of modern crimes and partly instrumental in their development. It is this important nuance that is often lacking in both Gunton and his critics.[110] For his own part, Augustine was clear that his inward turn remained a fundamentally doxological action. As he wrote within *De Trinitate*, "This trinity of the mind is not

---

108. *CT*, 3:306, citing Bonaventure, *The Journey of the Mind to God*, 3.6.
109. Barth, CD 1:1, 335–36.
110. See, for instance, Hanby's attempt to pin all blame on the work of Augustine's earliest interpreters.

the image of God because it remembers, understands, and loves itself, but because it can remember, understand and love Him by whom it was made."[111] Likewise Anselm argued that the way for any "rational creature" to express the divine image is by "remembering, understanding, and loving the *Summum Bonum*."[112]

Yet as we saw in our own examination of Augustine's thought, the exegesis behind this inward turn does exhibit certain problems. In turning to his looking glass (1 Cor. 13:12), Augustine seemed to see not a "whole person" reflecting dimly the perfect image of Christ, but rather the internal workings of an immaterial rational mind reflecting dimly the three-in-oneness of the Trinity.[113] This, as we have argued, was problematic. Furthermore, as chapter 4 went on to illustrate, one reason for this conclusion can be traced to an abiding tension in Augustine's treatment of the temporal and material creation.[114] Thus while such "misplayed notes" in Augustine remain a far cry from both (1) modern rationalism, and (2) scholastic speculation, Pelikan reveals how certain figures between Anselm and Bonaventure may have added to the Platonic imbalances in Augustine's own theology.

This, as Holmes describes it, was one of Gunton's central arguments: "Ideas make a difference to each other; one wrong note echoes down through the symphony, affecting every theme in surprising and significant ways."[115] Yet if the Middle Ages are indeed a symphonic movement, then there remains at least one composer who demands a section to himself.

---

111. Augustine, *Trin.* 14.12.15. This translation is that of Hanby, *Augustine and Modernity*, v.
112. Anselm, *Monologion*, 68. Cited in *CT*, 3:260. See also Marilyn McCord Adams, "Romancing the Good: God and the Self according to St. Anselm of Canterbury," in *The Augustinian Tradition*, ed. Gareth Matthews (Berkeley: University of California Press, 1999), 91–109.
113. See again ch. 3. In ch. 9 we will contrast Augustine and Irenaeus on this very point.
114. See, for instance, the treatment of Augustine's hierarchy of being in ch. 4.
115. Holmes, in description of Gunton's way of doing history. *Revelation and Reason*, 8.

Aquinas and Augustine's Afterlife

When dealing with Augustine's medieval heirs, Gunton's focus often turned almost immediately to Thomas Aquinas (1225–1274).[116] As we have seen, in Gunton's own doctoral thesis it was Aquinas alone who was first identified as the archetype of the baneful, "classical concept of God."[117] While the more decisive blame for this phenomenon would soon shift to Augustine,[118] Gunton always maintained Aquinas's role in translating certain Augustinian errors into the context of medieval scholasticism. On this point, his basic charge was that Aquinas's continued reliance on "Greek" thought (albeit in a more Aristotelian form than that of Augustine) led to a monistic imbalance in the doctrine of God and an abiding dualism in the doctrine of creation.

With regard to creation, Gunton's first claim was that Aquinas's *via negativa* continued Augustine's tendency to place God in a kind of "negative opposition" to the created world.[119] "Instead of defining God from revelation," Gunton alleged that Aquinas preferred to define him "as that which the world is not."[120] While affirming the attempt to stress God's otherness,[121] Gunton believed that "the negative way should be rejected absolutely, because it takes the form of an ascent out of the creation to a God who is essentially its opposite

---

116. See, for instance, Gunton, *Triune Creator*, 99.
117. Gunton, *Becoming and Being: The Doctrine of God in Charles Hartshorne and Karl Barth*, new ed. (London: SCM, 2001), 1–6. See again ch. 3. Here, as we explained, "the classical concept" was typified by an emphasis upon (1) *supernaturalism* (the preference to speak of God in negative opposition to the world); (2) *timelessness*, and a (3) *hierarchical ordering of reality*, in which material entities are improperly marginalized. For Gunton, "Aquinas' Five Ways illustrate all these points." *Becoming and Being*, 3.
118. Indeed the shift is fully apparent in Gunton's 1983 publication of *Yesterday and Today: A Study of Continuities of Christology* (Grand Rapids: Eerdmans, 1983).
119. See Gunton, *Act and Being*, 62. Gunton here cites Aquinas's statement: "Wcannot know what God is, but only what he is not." Aquinas, *Summa Theologica*, Ia.2, conclusion.
120. Gunton, *Act and Being*, 53.
121. For the important distinction between "otherness" and "opposition," see *Act and Being*, 20, and *Becoming and Being*, 2–3.

rather than its other-in-relation."[122] Thus, in his view, "negative theology runs the risk . . . of identifying existence with fallenness."[123] In qualification to this charge, Gunton acknowledged that Aquinas did at times make use of God's "positive characteristics."[124] In addition, he would also admit that the *Summa* was "not rightly described as a natural theology," given that Aquinas (like other scholastics) was technically beginning from the place of faith.[125] In the end, however, Gunton maintained that the *via negativa* furthered Augustine's imbalances by constructing a doctrine of God largely from a priori notions of being, rather than drawing upon the biblical account of God's acts in human history.[126]

Gunton's second charge with regard to creation was that Aquinas's dualism was exacerbated by a hierarchical structuring of reality.[127] As in Augustine, Gunton believed that any graded chains of being undermined the "ontological homogeneity" (or universal goodness) of all created things.[128] As evidence of this, Gunton cited Aquinas's statement that "some things are found to be more good, more true, more noble, and so on, and other things less. But such comparative terms describe varying degrees of approximation to a superlative."[129] In all of this, Gunton's critique of Aquinas was similar to that leveled against Augustine. As he put it, "The Platonic forms or Aristotelian and Stoic *rationes* tend to displace Christ as the framework of creation. The effect is to displace something oriented to materiality with something at best ambivalent about it."[130]

---

122. Gunton, *Act and Being*, 154.
123. Ibid., 47.
124. Ibid., 50.
125. Ibid., 49.
126. Ibid., 51–54; cf. Gunton, *Revelation and Reason*, 120–25.
127. See Gunton, *Becoming and Being*, 3; *Triune Creator*, 99.
128. See Gunton, *Triune Creator*, 99.
129. Aquinas, *Summa Theologica*, Ia.2.3. Cited in Gunton, *Act and Being*, 61. Unless otherwise noted, further citations from the *Summa* will be taken from the translation available from New Advent at http://www.newadvent.org/summa.

Yet what should be said in response to Gunton's charges on the doctrine of creation? Here again there are some problems. As even Gunton was aware, the more significant origin of Aquinas's negative theology resided not in Augustine, but in his use of Pseudo-Dionysius the Areopagite (c. fifth century AD).[131] Thus while Augustine did claim that "we know what God is *not* rather than what he is,"[132] the fact remains that the more substantial root of the *via negativa* runs east, through John of Damascus, to Dionysius, and ultimately to certain Origenist facets in the work of some of Gunton's heroes: the Cappadocian Fathers.[133]

Beyond this, Pseudo-Dionysius can also be seen as the more prominent Christian source for Aquinas's hierarchal structuring of reality. As Pelikan affirms, it was upon the Dionysian *Celestial Hierarchy* that Thomas constructed his "hierarchal view of reality as proceeding from the divine goodness in orderly and graded fashion."[134] Thus while Pelikan hints that this hierarchy does indeed evidence a certain material dualism, the fact remains that its origins in Aquinas reside more in the Areopagite than in Augustine.[135] Given this, we must conclude that even if Gunton is seen to be correct in his critique of Aquinas's doctrine of creation (and we have not attempted to make this argument), such supposed "errors" cannot be traced primarily to the influence of Augustine.[136] To put it bluntly, Gunton's narrative is simply wrong at this particular point.

---

130. Gunton, *Triune Creator*, 102.
131. See Gunton, *Act and Being*, 14, 45.
132. *CT*, 4:67, citing Augustine, *en. Ps.* 85:8. Emphasis mine.
133. Ch. 10 will address this flaw in Gunton's contrast between Augustine the Cappadocians.
134. *CT*, 3:293.
135. Ibid., 294. For Pelikan, most of the anathematized ideas of Origen "were far less dangerous to the tradition of catholic orthodoxy than the Crypto-Origenism canonized in the works of Dionysius the Areopagite." Ibid., 1:348.
136. In supplement to Pelikan, see Joseph Wawrykow's comments on Aquinas's "uneven" appropriation of Augustine's influence. "Thomas Aquinas," in Fitzgerald, *Augustine through the Ages*, 830.

What, though, of Aquinas's doctrine of the Trinity? On this subject, Gunton's charge was that Aquinas was "in the tradition of Augustine" because his treatment of creation tended to be "rather monistically conceived."[137] By this, Gunton alleged that Aquinas sometimes spoke of creation as the product of a unitary divine will, rather than the mediated handiwork of the Son and Spirit.[138] In Gunton's view, this God appeared more like Aristotle's "first cause" than the triune Creator of the Bible.

As evidence, Gunton claimed that when dealing with creation in the *Summa*, Aquinas went on for six full articles before mentioning the Trinitarian attributions of the doctrine.[139] And even here, when the Trinity was mentioned, the reference was to Augustine's *vestigia trinitatis* within the human mind. Far from helping, Gunton believed that this selective appropriation of Augustine led to a rather "un-Augustinian" (that is, semi-Pelagian) position on the "unfallenness" of the human intellect.[140] Thus, as Gunton claimed in classroom lectures, "There is a confidence in even unfallen reason for Aquinas. . . . Certain things can be known with certainty apart from Revelation because the mind is to a degree 'unfallen.' . . . The Thomist view is that the will is 'fallen,' you can't do what is right, but the intellect to a degree is unfallen, you can know to a degree what is true."[141] In all of this, the charge was that Aquinas's Aristotelian appropriation of Augustine furthered the dubious "marriage between reason and revelation."[142]

---

137. Gunton, *Triune Creator*, 100; cf. *Promise of Trinitarian Theology*, 31–32; *One, the Three and the Many*, 38–40.
138. See Gunton, *Triune Creator*, 100.
139. Ibid., 100, 121n9. See also Aquinas, *Summa Theologica*, I, q.65.
140. On this, Gunton states that Aquinas has departed from "a more radically Augustinian position." *Revelation and Reason*, 122.
141. Ibid.
142. Gunton, *Brief Theology of Revelation*, 32.

In his time, Gunton was hardly alone in leveling such charges. As Holmes notes, "Thomas was blamed by many in the twentieth-century Trinitarian revival for subordinating the doctrine of the Trinity to a philosophically determined account of God's life."[143] Yet while such charges may have once been common, they have now been roundly criticized by both Pelikan and a host of more recent scholars.[144] For his own part, Pelikan asserts that Aquinas's comments on the Trinity are "unrivalled as precise statements of the Christian faith."[145]

To be sure, it is universally acknowledged that Aquinas's Trinitarian theology drew heavily upon Augustine. As Gilles Emery notes, the debt is particularly apparent in Aquinas's triune interpretation of the image of God.[146] Here, as John O'Callaghan writes, Aquinas followed Augustine in thinking that "the task of understanding the *imago Dei* requires a turning within of the soul to understand itself."[147] Yet while this facet of Augustine's inward turn led other scholastics to great flights of mystical speculation (even to the point of attempting to "prove" the dogma of the Trinity),[148] Aquinas believed that such endeavors "detracted from the faith ... by subjecting it to the ridicule of its despisers."[149] Thus he claimed that

---

143. Holmes, *Quest for the Trinity*, 155. As examples of this allegation, Holmes notes the work of Rahner and Moltmann in particular.
144. For a succinct overview of these twentieth-century charges against Aquinas, as well as the more recent retrieval and rehabilitation of his Trinitarian theology, see the opening of Karen Kilby's article, "Aquinas, the Trinity and the Limits of Understanding," *International Journal of Systematic Theology* 7, no. 4 (Oct., 2005): 414–27.
145. *CT*, 3:279.
146. See Emery, "Trinitarian Theology as Spiritual Exercise in Augustine and Aquinas," in Dauphinais et al, *Aquinas the Augustinian*, 1. See also, *CT*, 3:279; David Cairns, *The Image of God in Man* (New York: Philosophical Library, 1953), 114.
147. John O'Callaghan, "*Imago Dei*: A Test Case for St. Thomas's Augustinianism," in Dauphinais et al., *Aquinas the Augustinian*, 110.
148. *CT*, 3:284.
149. Ibid., 287.

it is "impossible to attain to the knowledge of the Trinity by natural reason."[150]

In all of this, Pelikan argues that even Aquinas's natural theology is rooted in a prior appeal to Scripture, and to such texts as the Vulgate's rendering of Rom. 1:20: "The invisible things of [God] are clearly seen, being understood through the things that have been made." As Pelikan writes, "It was by the authority of revelation that the theologian proceeded to argue even apart from revelation that God could be known from his creation."[151] Beyond this, Aquinas appealed to Exod. 3:14 in order to show that since God's name was *I am*, "any Christian philosopher had to posit 'I am' as his first principle."[152] As we have seen, Augustine also made use of this text.[153] Yet for Pelikan, the primary point was that even Aquinas's appeal to Greek (Aristotelian) reason was rooted in a prior appeal to biblical revelation.[154]

Alongside Pelikan's conclusions on this subject, Gilles Emery has led an increasing number of contemporary scholars in vindicating Aquinas's Trinitarian theology against the sort of charges made by Gunton.[155] Whereas Gunton rather incautiously claimed (in classroom lectures) that Aquinas adapted Augustine's view of reason as the *imago Dei* into a kind of intellectual semi-Pelagianism,[156]

---

150. Aquinas, *Summa Theologica*, 1.32.1.
151. *CT*, 3:289.
152. Aquinas, *Summa Theologica*, 1.2.3. As Pelikan states in summary, "The equation of the God of Abraham, Isaac, and Jacob with the first principle of being permitted the theologian . . . to engage also in the philosophical enterprise of measuring the capacity of reason to establish the truth of the divine being; and in this he was obliged to state a natural theology." *CT*, 3:289.
153. *Conf.* 7.10.16. See again our extended treatment of divine simplicity in ch. 3.
154. *CT*, 3:291.
155. See especially Gilles Emery, *Trinity in Aquinas* (Ypsilanti, MI: Sapientia Press, 2003). Also, Matthew Levering, *Scripture and Metaphysics: Aquinas and the Renewal of Trinitarian Theology* (Oxford: Blackwell, 2004). For a recent treatment of Aquinas's own legacy, and its misrepresentation, see Fergus Kerr, *After Aquinas: Versions of Thomism* (Oxford: Blackwell, 2002). Thanks to Stephen Holmes for pointing me toward the need to incorporate such recent scholarship.
156. See again Gunton, *Revelation and Reason*, 122.

Emery argues that Aquinas actually follows Augustine in "a very clear rejection of all rationalism."[157] As Aquinas clearly states, "The analogy from our intellect does not establish anything about God conclusively because it is not in the same sense that we speak of intellect in God and in us. And that is why Augustine says that it is by faith that one arrives at knowledge but not vice versa."[158] In commenting upon such passages, Emery notes that "Thomas refers explicitly to Augustine in order to mark out the *limits* of the study of the image of God in Trinitarian theology. . . . It is faith that seeks understanding, and not understanding that precedes faith."[159]

With regard to such "limits" in our human understanding of God, Karen Kilby has recently argued that Thomas's Trinitarian theology is praiseworthy precisely *because*, unlike so many twentieth-century systematicians, he often refuses the temptation to go too far in attempting to explain and apply the inner workings of the Trinity. When dealing with the notion of processions within God and the presentation of "subsistent relations," Kilby posits that what we find in Thomas is actually the opposite of an unbridled rationalism. This is so because, at several points, "Thomas can be read as deliberately saying things that are unexplained and unexplainable."[160] He is sometimes reticent and apophatic in his handling of the inner workings of the Godhead, realizing correctly that "it might be a virtue rather than a weakness of trinitarian theology to leave certain things radically, and very clearly, unexplained."[161] With regard to the Trinity, Thomas is, as Timothy Smith puts it, "not so much probing the mystery as protecting it."[162] While the details of this admittedly

---

157. Emery, "Trinitarian Theology as Spiritual Exercise," 18.
158. Aquinas, *Summa Theologica*, I, q. 32, a. I, ad 2. See Emery, "Trinitarian Theology as Spiritual Exercise," 23.
159. Emery, "Trinitarian Theology as Spiritual Exercise," 23. Italics mine.
160. Kilby, "Aquinas, Limits of Understanding," 415.
161. Ibid., 419.

dense and somewhat disputed reading of Thomas's theology may be left for specialists,[163] the point with Kilby's work, as well as that of Emery, is that Aquinas (like Augustine before him) was careful to grant priority to revelation over human reason.

As we have seen, Gunton did not dispute this fact entirely.[164] Yet neither was he terribly interested in it. For him, the fact that Aquinas technically belonged in the tradition of *fides quaerens intellectum* did not change the reality that tethering the gospel to a given paradigm of Greek philosophy would reap profound consequences in time. As he put it, "When Plato and Aristotle were dethroned, so was Christ."[165] Yet to test the merits of this claim, we must turn to another chapter, and to the increasingly selective reading of Augustine that would take place within the Late Middle Ages.

Conclusion

While broad conclusions regarding Augustine's medieval legacy must await the following chapter, our treatment of the early and high Middle Ages is now complete. As we have seen, the character of Augustine's influence in this period was varied. In Boethius, Augustine's early and more Platonic works would provide the motivation to expand the speculative use of classical reason, even while Augustine himself would likely not have approved of Boethius's often scanty attention to the Scriptures. In Gregory, it was also the early Augustine whose "unretracted" positive statements about the freedom of the human will would result in an appropriation

---

162. Timothy Smith, *Thomas Aquinas' Trinitarian Theology: A Study in Theological Method* (Washington, DC: Catholic University of America Press, 2003), 157. Cited in Kilby, "Aquinas, Limits of Understanding," 422.
163. Kilby is here critiquing the work of Matthew Levering for failing to account adequately for the apophatic implications of Thomas's Trinitarian theology. For a window into this debate, see Levering, *Scripture and Metaphysics*, 58ff.
164. Gunton, *Act and Being*, 51.
165. Gunton, *Brief Theology of Revelation*, 46.

of Augustine that stood at odds with his later writings. In both cases we have noted an important insight. When evaluating the charges leveled against Augustine, it matters greatly *which Augustine* one is reading. The late Augustine is far less vulnerable to Gunton's claims than the early one; yet it was not always the late Augustine that was most inspiring to certain medieval thinkers.

In the line of thinkers from Anselm to Bonaventure, Augustine's inward turn provided the speculative motivation to view the rational mind as the *vestigium trinitatis*. Yet while this was sometimes problematic, we saw that such thinkers went far beyond Augustine in terms of theological speculation. With regard to Aquinas in particular, we found that Gunton's case received far less support. As Pelikan showed, some elements in Thomas that Gunton deemed to be problematic should in fact be traced more to Pseudo-Dionysius, while, as Emery and others have noted, other aspects of Aquinas's thought (specifically his Trinitarian theology and his use of classical philosophy) were far less problematic that Gunton claimed. In all of this, we have begun to see the diversity of uses to which Augustine's massive writings would be put throughout the medieval era. This is a theme that will be amplified as we now transition to the latter Middle Ages.

6

Gunton and Augustine's Medieval Afterlife (Part Two)

For Gunton, the Late Middle Ages brought a challenge to aspects of the Augustinian inheritance. Whereas Augustine (and later Aquinas) had forged an alleged synthesis between revelation and reason, Gunton argued that this "system broke down in the late Middle Ages through its own inadequacies."[1] Yet this did not mean that Augustine was any less revered in the period. As Pelikan notes, he remained "the recognized Master of all,"[2] and thus, "No important doctrinal issue in the fourteenth and fifteenth centuries . . . was unaffected by the study of Augustine, and on many issues his influence was decisive."[3]

In Gunton's own account of the Late Middle Ages, he focused largely upon the work of two key figures: John Duns Scotus (c.

---

1. Colin Gunton, *Revelation and Reason*, ed. P. H. Brazier (London: T&T Clark, 2008), 108.
2. *CT*, 4:17. Citing Daniel Callus, *The Condemnation of St Thomas at Oxford*, 2nd ed. (London: 1955).
3. *CT*, 4:22.

1265–1308) and William of Ockham (c. 1285–1348). In their own ways, both men would signal a growing dissatisfaction with the philosophical presuppositions of both Augustine and Aquinas. As Gunton put it, "In the high Middle Ages . . . it can be said that the framework for culture was provided more by Aristotelian-Platonic formalities than by a theology of creation." Thus Guton went on to argue that "one of the reasons for the rejection by Scotus and Ockham of their philosophical past was that they rejected the enterprise of basing Christian thought on pagan philosophy."[4]

While both Scotus and Ockham lived at the onset of the era in question, it is because of their importance (both to Gunton and to Western philosophy as a whole) that our survey must begin with their respective appropriations of Augustine's thought. Beyond this, our use of Pelikan will also lead us to a third and often-neglected figure within Augustine's afterlife: Francesco Petrarch (1304–1374). As we will see, Petrarch's reading of Augustine's early works, and especially the *Confesssions*, would attempt to "claim him as a resource for Christian humanism."[5]

In the end, we will come to see that while Gunton's narrative on Scotus and Ockham stands in need of revision, his case might have been strengthened had he paid more attention to the likes of Petrarch and the humanist appropriation of Augustine's earlier and more philosophical treatises.

John Duns Scotus and the Legacy of Augustine

According to tradition, John Duns Scotus was born in the very year that marked the death of both Aquinas and Bonaventure (1274). The tradition is a false one. Yet as Pelikan notes, "The intuition . . .

---

4. Gunton, *A Brief Theology of Revelation*, the 1993 Warfield Lectures (Edinburgh: T&T Clark, 1995), 55.
5. *CT*, 4:20.

regarding [Scotus's] place in late medieval theology is correct."[6] As he argues, Scotus crafted the "most formidable" alternative to the Thomist "species of Augustinianism."[7] In this system, the *via negativa* was rejected, and emphasis was placed upon the divine *will* as Scotus set out to defend the freedom of God in executing the plan of salvation.[8] Much could be written in summation of this project, yet our focus is more narrowly upon Augustine's legacy. Thus we turn now to note why Gunton saw Scotus as a welcome turning point in Augustine's afterlife.

For Gunton, there was much in Scotus to admire. A first example pertained to his notion of the so-called "univocity" of created being.[9] The point of this concept was *not* that all created things are essentially the same,[10] but rather that the use of ontic hierarchies should be rejected.[11] As we have seen, it was this hierarchical schema that Gunton decried in both Augustine and others. Yet in Scotus there was a supposed alternative. Here the *haecceitas*, or "this-ness" of particular entities was stressed, rather than the correspondence to Hellenistic universals, or *rationes*.[12] Thus as Gunton put it, "When we say that something *is* we are simply ascribing existence to it and not placing it on a scale of being."[13] For Gunton, this shift was to be lauded because such hierarchies invariably favored the immaterial and the eternal over that which exists in time and matter.[14] When

---

6. Ibid., 13.
7. Ibid.
8. See esp. ibid., 27–33. Also, M. J. Inwood, "Duns Scotus," in *The Oxford Companion to Philosophy*, ed. Ted Honderich (Oxford: Oxford University Press, 1995), 208–9.
9. See Duns Scotus, *Oxford Commentary on the Sentences*, I, 3, 2, no. 5. Cited in Frederick Copleston, *A History of Philosophy*, vol. 2, book 1 (Garden City, NY: Image Books, 1985), 502.
10. See Gunton's clarification of "ontological homogeneity" in *The Triune Creator: A Historical and Systematic Study* (Grand Rapids: Eerdmans, 1998), 119.
11. Gunton, *Brief Theology of Revelation*, 52–3; *Triune Creator*, 119–20; *Act and Being: Towards a Theology of the Divine Attributes* (London: SCM Press, 2002), 69, 85, 146.
12. Gunton, *Triune Creator*, 118–19.
13. Ibid.
14. See again ch. 4.

this happened, the full goodness of God's creation was seen to be imperiled; therefore, Gunton came to see Scotus's notion of the univocity of being as a safeguard against such errors.

Secondly, Gunton also praised Scotus for what he saw as an incarnational orientation in his doctrine of creation. As Scotus famously argued in opposition to Aquinas, there would have been an incarnation even apart from human sin.[15] For Gunton, this allowed for the reality that the creature was, from the beginning, "ordained to God *through Christ*."[16] Here Gunton's second affirmation connected to the first. As he put it, "Scotus was the first major figure to object to the idea that the forms existed in the mind of God";[17] thus, "any mediation between God and the world derives not from the Platonic forms or their Aristotelian equivalents, but from Christology."[18] Behind this praise, there lay a clear critique of both Augustine and Aquinas.

Yet what should we say in response to Gunton's narrative as it pertains to Scotus and Augustine? As Holmes notes, Gunton is surely correct in noting that the forms (or *rationes*) had proved "resilient" in the tradition from Augustine to Aquinas. In such figures, they remained useful after a relocation to the mind of God.[19] For Gunton, Scotus was right to challenge this notion because the eternality of "entities other than God" (even within the divine mind) might serve to undermine the very doctrine of creation *ex nihilo*.[20] Yet in response to this assertion, Holmes sets forth a crucial question: Why must these forms or ideas be seen as "entities other than God?"[21] After all, "this

---

15. Duns Scotus, *Paris Commentary on the Sentences*, 3.7.4.4. Cited in *CT*, 4:27.
16. Gunton, *Triune Creator*, 121n9. Emphasis his.
17. Gunton, *Revelation and Reason*, 117.
18. Gunton, *Triune Creator*, 120.
19. See Holmes, "'Something Much too Plain to Say': Towards a Defence of the Doctrine of Divine Simplicity," *Neue Zeitschrift für Systematische Theologie und Religionsphilosophie* 43 (2001): 152.
20. Gunton, *Triune Creator*, 78n29.
21. Holmes, "Something Much Too Plain to Say," 152.

entire tradition . . . held to the doctrine of divine simplicity, and if these entities exist in God's mind then they are . . . simply God."[22] Indeed Aquinas makes this very point by appealing to none other than Augustine![23]

Holmes's point has merit. But what does it mean for Gunton's broader thesis? As evidenced by chapter 4, this claim does not change the fact that Augustine's ontic hierarchy did (at times) undermine the full goodness of created being. Nor does it change the reality that Augustine's dualism may have been all the more enduring by being limited in certain key respects.[24] Yet Holmes does reveal an apparent problem in Gunton's argument regarding Augustine's supposed tilt toward (1) monism in the doctrine of God, and (2) dualism in the doctrine of creation. If, as Gunton claims, Augustine absolutized the doctrine of divine simplicity (resulting in a monistic imbalance),[25] then it seems altogether unlikely that he would *simultaneously* allow for "entities other than God" to take up residence within the divine mind. At this point, Gunton's two theses are ill-suited for one another. Thus while Gunton is justified in critiquing Augustine's hierarchy of being, his praise for Scotus may actually reveal a further weakness in his argument. Having acknowledged this, we now move on to the next stage in Gunton's late medieval narrative.

While praising Scotus for the above reasons, Gunton was more ambivalent about a second feature of his thought: the return to a more Augustinian emphasis upon the divine *will*. As Pelikan notes, with Scotus there was "a shift of emphasis from the primacy of intellect (as expounded by Thomas Aquinas) to the primacy of will (as maintained by Augustine and Bonaventure)."[26] For Gunton, this

22. Ibid.
23. See the *sed contra* of the *Summa Theologica*, I.a 15.2. The appeal is to Augustine's *div. qu.*, 46.
24. See again ch. 4.
25. See again ch. 3.
26. *CT*, 4:62–63; cf. ibid. 28–30.

shift would ultimately help to pave the way for the next figure to be surveyed here. As Gunton put it, "The weakness of Scotus' account of particularity [that is, his use of *haecceitas*]—apart from its obscurity is shown by the fact that it was succeeded not by a strengthening of its case, but rather by Ockham's non-relational nominalism."[27] Because this claim has more to do with Ockham than it does with Scotus, we must now turn to evaluate William's importance to Augustine's late medieval legacy.

William of Ockham and Augustine's Legacy

For Gunton, William of Ockham formed a crucial link between the medieval appropriation of Augustine and the perils of modernity. As he argued,

> In Ockham . . . there are three features whose combination proved explosive. First is the . . . view that only particulars exist. Second is the denial of the way of relating them that had been inherited from Plato and Aristotle. Third is the non-christological and non-pneumatological—that is to say, arbitrary and ambiguous—concept of the will. . . . If there are no universals, then only the will of God is able to hold things together.[28]

While much could be said of these assertions, our concern is limited to the supposed link between Ockham and Augustine. At first, the connection seems tenuous. After all, if Ockham "destroyed" key aspects of the "Augustinian synthesis,"[29] then he appears to bring a *reversal* and not an *appropriation* of Augustine's influence. With regard to the appeal to so-called universals, this is certainly true. Yet here

---

27. Gunton, *The One, the Three and the Many: God, Creation and the Culture of Modernity* (Cambridge: Cambridge University Press, 1993), 198–99.
28. Ibid., 57–58.
29. Gunton, *Brief Theology of Revelation*, 47. This supposed synthesis pertains to the fusion of biblical revelation and Greek reason (especially the appeal universal forms or *rationes*). See again Pelikan's use of this phrase in *CT*, 3:49.

again the crucial point resides in Ockham's elevation of the will. As Gunton wrote of Ockham, "If there are no universals, then only the will of God is able [to] hold things together. But it is a divine will of a very distinctive kind. The link between the particulars of our experience is made by a God essentially conceived after the image of the individual rational will so prominent in theological anthropology after Augustine."[30] Here again we arrive at a familiar argument. In Gunton's view, Ockham followed Augustine in explaining reality through an appeal to an apparently *arbitrary* and *monistic* will of God.[31] Thus as Gunton argued, modernity arose when the "arbitrary will of the Ockhamist deity [was] metamorphosed into the arbitrary will of the human agent."[32]

On Augustine's concept of the divine will, we have seen already the faults in Gunton's argument.[33] While Gunton claimed that Augustine's treatment of creation left "little reason except sheer will,"[34] we have seen that for Augustine, God's willing was also intimately connected to his *loving*.[35] Beyond this, we have also seen that Augustine's use of "will" within his sacred triads evidenced an attempt to place the divine *voluntas* within a Trinitarian matrix. Here the will of God was intimately connected with the *love* of God, as evidenced by the fact that Augustine could use the two terms

---

30. Gunton, *One, the Three and the Many*, 58; cf. *Brief Theology of Revelation*, 47. Here Gunton states that Ockham "destroyed the old link [between reason and revelation], but had nothing to put in its place but mere authority."
31. See ch. 1.
32. Gunton, *Brief Theology of Revelation*, 48. Here Gunton utilized the work of Blumenberg and Buckley. Hans Blumenberg, *The Legitimacy of the Modern Age*, trans. R. M. Wallace (Cambridge, MA: MIT Press, 1983); Michael Buckley, *At the Origins of Modern Atheism* (New Haven, CT: Yale University Press, 1987). Both works are again cited in *One, the Three and the Many*, 57–58.
33. See ch. 4.
34. Gunton, *Triune Creator*, 76.
35. See Bradley G. Green, *Colin Gunton and the Failure of Augustine: The Theology of Colin Gunton in Light of Augustine* (Eugene, OR: Pickwick, 2011), 175; also, Augustine, *Conf.* 13.2.2; *Civ.* 11.21.

(*will* and *love*) interchangeably within his sacred triads.[36] Given this, we have found that a more careful and comprehensive reading of Augustine often exonerates him of Gunton's charge. Yet not every reading of Augustine was careful or comprehensive. Thus we return to Ockham's appropriation of Augustine's legacy.

Like anyone, Ockham was a person of his time. And as Pelikan notes, the late medieval discussions of God's will often centered not on (1) the divine love that lay behind creation, but on (2) the divine predestination that lay behind the salvation (and damnation?) of particular individuals.[37] Of special concern was God's double predestination, which "Augustine had quite overtly asserted . . . in his *Enchiridion* and elsewhere."[38] Thus we arrive at a second ground for Gunton's claim that, after Augustine, "the theme of [divine] love becomes subordinate to that of will."[39] In Augustine's later embrace of double predestination, Gunton charged that the "fundamental" orientation of eschatology was seen as "tilting hellwards."[40] This was evidenced in Augustine's attempt to "explain away"[41] the apparent meaning of Paul's claim that God "wants all people to be saved" (1 Tim. 2:4).[42] A fuller treatment of this subject must await our treatment of the Augustinianism of men like Calvin,[43] yet for now, we limit ourselves to Ockham and Augustine's late medieval legacy.

---

36. Augustine, *Trin.* 14.6.8; 14.7.10.
37. *CT*, 4:28. As Pelikan here notes of the period, "The doctrine of predestination became a test case of Augustinianism."
38. *CT*, 4:31. See Augustine, *Ench.* 26.100.
39. Gunton, *One, the Three and the Many*, 120.
40. Gunton, *Christ and Creation*, the Didsbury Lectures, 1990 (Eugene, OR: Wipf and Stock, 2005), 95.
41. Peter Brown, *Augustine of Hippo: A Biography*, 2nd ed. (Berkeley: University of California Press, 2000), 404.
42. See Augustine, *Corrept.* 14. Gunton seems to have 1 Tim. 2:4 in mind when critiquing the "Augustinian conception" of double predestination. *Christ and Creation*, 95. See also Mathijs Lamberigts, "Predestination," in *Augustine through the Ages*, 679.
43. See ch. 7.

For Ockham, and others like him, the focus on predestination did not mean that the liberty of the postlapsarian human will should be rejected. As Pelikan asserts of the period, "The freedom of the will was axiomatic, in spite of the antinomy between it and the divine will. . . . It was no less axiomatic for the 'Augustinians.'"[44] Yet for Ockham, the antinomy of this axiom was, at times, exacerbated. As Pelikan states, William's "combination of predestination with voluntarism . . . managed to appear simultaneously deterministic and Pelagian."[45] Here we perhaps see the flowering of what Hanby noted with regard to Gregory and Augustine's early legacy.[46]

Throughout the Middle Ages, as Pelikan put it, "what was embarrassing about [the mature Augustine] on predestination was his clarity."[47] Thus the proliferation of quotes from a Pseudo-Augustine, attempting to carve out more space for the inherent freedom of the human will.[48] In addition, as we have seen already, there were the unretracted words from such earlier works as *De Libero Arbitrio*, in which Augustine placed much more confidence in the freedom of the human will. In Ockham, Pelikan notes the fusion of these various "Augustines" (early and late; pseudo and genuine), which explains the claim that in William there was a strange mixture of divine determinism and "Pelagian" anthropology.[49]

In all of this, Gunton seems justified in saying that "the scene is . . . set for a contest of wills."[50] Pelagian humanity could not abide with a deterministic God. And in this looming contest we see a partial root of two future developments: (1) Reformation anthropology and

---

44. *CT*, 4:33. In context, this statement is meant to apply to such men as Scotus, Ockham, Wycliffe, and Hus.
45. *CT*, 4:35.
46. See again our view of Hanby and the Gregorian appropriation of Augustine.
47. *CT*, 3:81.
48. See ibid., 89, 276 for the abiding medieval influence of Pseudo-Augustine.
49. See again ibid., 4:35.
50. Gunton, *One, the Three and the Many*, 58.

(2) modernist rebellion.[51] Yet as with Scotus, the connection between Ockham's voluntarism and the mature Augustine is a tenuous one. Here again we see the need for Gunton to be more precise in his usage of the adjective *Augustinian*. As Schwöbel notes, Gunton sometimes used the word merely as a "red [flag] indicating difficulties and problems in the Western tradition." Yet if Pelikan is right to assert of the period that "everyone was an 'Augustinian,'" then the term begins to lose its usefulness in identifying which ideas are genuinely traceable to Augustine himself.[52] Despite the overall weakness of Gunton's argument with regard to the selective Augustinianism of Scotus and Ockham, there is perhaps another area where Gunton's medieval case might have been more plausible, if he had taken time to examine it.

Francesco Petrarch and Augustine's Legacy

As Pelikan notes, the use of the *Confessions* would ebb and flow throughout the centuries.[53] In the Late Middle Ages, the classic work would again became "the object of increased literary attention and the foundation for a theology of experience."[54] Thus while schoolmen plumbed the depths of doctrine through *De Trinitate*, other members of the Italian Renaissance went searching "for an Augustine who could once again inspire and legitimate a synthesis of Christianity with classical thought."[55] As Pelikan states, "One of the two faces of humanism was its preoccupation with Augustine."[56] And at the fore of this new movement stood the figure known as Petrarch.

---

51. We will return to this subject in the next chapter.
52. See Schwöbel, "The Shape of Colin Gunton's Theology: On the Way Towards a Fully Trinitarian Theology," in *The Theology of Colin Gunton*, 207n59.
53. See *CT*, 3:304.
54. Ibid., 4:21.
55. Ibid., 19–20.
56. Ibid., 20.

Often dubbed the "father of humanism," Francesco Petrarch was an Italian poet, diplomat, and scholar. While crowned as poet laureate in Rome for his Latin work *Africa*, he is best known today for his later love poetry, written in Italian to a woman he called Laura. Regarding these verses, Germain Greer notes that "for more than six centuries these poems . . . provided a model of love poetry in all the European languages."[57] While we will return to Petrarch's view of earthly love in a moment, our primary focus will be upon another book: Petrarch's *My Secret* (or, *My Secret Book*), written in approximately 1347. This fascinating and influential work consists of three dialogues between the author and the "ghost" of Augustine.

As Pelikan claims, the work's true character remains a matter of debate. For some, *My Secret* is "an expression of the 'modern desire for pleasure and . . . earthly happiness,'" while for others, it is "a sincere document from the beginning of Petrarch's conversion."[58] In truth, the book is likely something of both, yet as Pelikan puts it, one thing is clear: "*My Secret* is part of an effort to disengage Augustine from the scholasticism that claimed him as a founder and to claim him as a resource for Christian humanism. This Augustine was preeminently the Augustine of the *Confessions*."[59] Here Augustine's early and positive statements on Plato and Cicero provided Petrarch with a justification to reexamine such thinkers,[60] even while the inward turn of the *Confessions* provided him with the ground for a renewed theology of subjective experience.[61] Yet because Petrarch was not

---

57. Germain Greer, in the foreword to a recent publication of Petrarch, *My Secret Book*, trans. J. G. Nichols (London: Hesperus Press, 2002), x. Subsequent quotations from *My Secret* will be from this translation unless otherwise noted.
58. *CT*, 4:20. Citing Giulio Auguso Levi, "Pensiero classic e pensiero cristiano nel 'Secretum' e nella 'Familiari' del Petrarca," *Atene e Roma* 35 (1933): 65–66.
59. *CT*, 4:20.
60. See Petrarch, *My Secret*, 24; cf. Augustine, *Conf.* 3.4.7; 8.7.17.
61. *CT*, 4:21; cf. Carol Quillen, "Renaissance Humanism," in Fitzgerald, *Augustine through the Ages*, 717–18.

a theologian, Augustine's influence upon him has been largely overlooked by both Gunton and the broader theological tradition. Thus while Pelikan has given us a clue as to his appropriation of Augustine's legacy, we will now delve more deeply into this fictitious dialogue between the father of Italian humanism and the ghost of Augustine.

The "Augustine" of *My Secret*

My Secret opens with a despondent Petrarch, weighed down by the cares of this world and "wide awake with anxiety." In the midst of his depression, he looks up to see a beautiful woman descending toward him. The woman is Truth, and it is she who introduces Petrarch to another visitor. As Petrarch tells us, "I had no need to ask his name: his priestly manner, his modest countenance, his serious gaze, his sober step, the combination of his African clothing and (once he began to speak) his Roman eloquence—all made it clear that this was the glorious St Augustine."[62] As Lady Truth reveals, the reason for Augustine's presence is that mortal ears "will give a fairer hearing to a human voice." Yet lest we view his words as fallible, the woman quickly reassures us that all Augustine says has come from her.[63]

The dialogue begins with a contested claim made by Augustine: "Whoever wishes to discard his unhappiness, provided he wishes it really and truly, cannot fail to have his desire." Petrarch recoils from such a notion, for as he argues, "There are innumerable things that we ardently desire," and "which nevertheless no effort … ever will win."[64] In response, Augustine reassures Petrarch that he once felt similarly. With this we return to the familiar fig tree of the *Confessions*, under which Augustine wept with bitter tears.[65] This

---

62. Petrarch, *My Secret*, 4.
63. Ibid., 4–5.
64. Ibid., 7.

work is obviously dear to Petrarch, for as he puts it, "Whenever I read your *Confessions* . . . I have the impression that I am reading not of someone else's but of my own wanderings."[66]

Indeed there are several points at which the experiences of Petrarch and Augustine mirror one another. As young men, both were brilliant and ambitious rhetoricians, conflictingly enamored with philosophy, grandeur, and (periodically) with chastity. Likewise, with regard to the latter, both men would pray "not yet."[67] Like the young Augustine, Petrarch was disgusted by his inability to refrain from "sins of the flesh," and like Augustine, Petrarch would father an illegitimate son, whose early death would cause him great pain. Yet *unlike* the real Augustine, Petrarch seems never to have gained the upper hand against his amorous longings, for which the subsequent poetic tradition has been profoundly grateful.[68]

On the subject of romantic love, Augustine's ghost chides Petrarch for his long infatuation with the woman Laura.[69] While there is no evidence that Petrarch and Laura were ever physically intimate (indeed the already married woman seems to have rebuffed what was perhaps Petrarch's only actual advance),[70] Augustine scolds the poet for his continued fixation upon her. As Augustine admits, his wisdom on such matters "comes from experience,"[71] yet it seems that Petrarch's infatuation with Laura goes well beyond Augustine's admittedly strong attachment to the mother of his own child. As evidence, Augustine's ghost seems flabbergasted as he reminds Petrarch that "not satisfied with seeing in the flesh the woman [Laura] . . . you had her portrait painted by a famous artist so that you could

---

65. Ibid., 12–13; cf. Augustine, *Conf.* 8.12.
66. Ibid., 13.
67. See ibid., 41; cf. Augustine, *Conf.* 8.7.
68. See Greer's comments in her foreword to *My Secret*, ix.
69. Much of the third dialogue in *My Secret* is taken up with this theme.
70. Ibid., 66.
71. Ibid., 69.

carry it about with you and always have a reason to weep."[72] Then comes what is perhaps the most genuinely Augustinian argument in the entire work. As Augustine puts it, "She has distracted you from the love of the Creator to love of one of His creatures."[73] Indeed, "the worst effect of love is to make us forget God and forget ourselves."[74]

Augustine's supposed solution to such earthly longings (whether for Laura or for poetic glory) is a simple one: "Think of death!"[75] As he states, "This thought will . . . teach you to despise mortal things and will show you the other direction which your life should take."[76] If Petrarch can do this, Augustine is certain that he will abandon both his vain literary endeavors and his romantic attachments. With this argument now made (apparently to Petrarch's satisfaction), Augustine's parting words are startling: "Save yourself," and do *not* say "your will is impotent."[77]

The Ghost and the Reality: The Authenticity of Petrarch's "Augustine"

With this encounter briefly outlined, we must now ask what likeness Petrarch's "ghost" of Augustine bears to the actual man from Hippo Regius. On the one hand, the "Augustine" of *My Secret* unquestionably evidences some of the theological imbalances decried by Gunton. By continually alluding to "the sacred words of the philosophers"[78] and almost *entirely* ignoring the sacred words of Scripture, Petrarch's Augustine clearly elevates classical wisdom over biblical revelation. As with the real Augustine, salvation comes

---

72. Ibid., 68.
73. Ibid., 63.
74. Ibid., 69.
75. Ibid., 78.
76. Ibid., 92.
77. Ibid., 92–93.
78. Ibid., 8.

through the command of *tolle lege* ("take up and read!"), yet for Petrarch, the required reading is that of non-Christian poets and philosophers, whereas for Augustine it was the book of Romans.[79] Oddly, the only reference to "the apostle" in *My Secret* is a misidentified allusion to Wis. 9:15, which speaks of the soul being "weighed down by the perishable body."[80]

This brings us to another problem: As with the younger Augustine,[81] there is an abiding dualism throughout *My Secret* that can be seen to denigrate the goodness of human physicality. As Petrarch has Augustine state, "Just as I do not deny that your soul was nobly formed in heaven, so you should have no doubt that, as a result of contact with this body which clothes it, it has *since degenerated*."[82] The proof of this bodily filth is to be found, not in an appeal to Scripture, but in reading Virgil, who speaks of the noble soul being "weighed down" and "imprisoned" by "guilty mortal bodies."[83]

Apart from the classical authors themselves, Petrarch traces another supposed justification for this view of the body to Augustine's early work *De Vera Religione*, which was written just prior to his ordination in AD 390.[84] Petrarch had acquired a copy of this work in 1335, and he was delighted to discover its Ciceronian character.[85] It was also in this early work that Augustine spoke most warmly of Platonism, even going so far as to say that "if Plato [and the other great philosophers] were to come to life again and find the churches full and the temples empty," they would be delighted, and "with the change of a few words and sentiments, they would become Christians."[86] In time,

---

79. See Augustine, *Conf.* 8.12.29.
80. Ibid., 24.
81. See ch. 4.
82. Petrarch, *My Secret*, 23. Italics mine.
83. Ibid., 23.
84. Ibid., 24. See Frederick Van Fleteren, "*Vera religione*," in Fitzgerald, *Augustine through the Ages*, 864.
85. See Greer, "Foreword," vii.

Augustine's enthusiasm for such philosophers would dampen, yet as Van Fleteren notes, *De Vera Religione* is the last work in his corpus in which Neoplatonism has such a pervasive influence.[87] It is no surprise that this is the Augustine loved by Petrarch.

A careful reading of *De Vera Religione* reveals that the work does display a certain dualism with regard to human physicality and sexuality. Yet at the same time, Augustine also makes some positive use of Platonism in order to counter the extreme denigration of created being within the Manichaeans.[88] As Augustine writes, "Matter participates in something belonging to the ideal world . . . [thus] to ask who created matter is to ask for him who is supreme in the ideal world."[89]

In this way, the work has what Gunton rightly referred to as a kind of double-mindedness on human physicality.[90] As evidence, the Augustine of *De Vera Religione* also goes on to boast that while Plato failed in getting young people to reject marital relations, Christianity has succeeded: "That thousands of young men and maidens contemn marriage and live in chastity causes no one surprise. Plato might have suggested that, but he so dreaded the perverse opinion of his times that he is said to have given in to nature and declared incontinence to be no sin."[91] This same attitude can be seen in the rather dualistic advice given centuries later to Petrarch.

Finally, in reading *My Secret*, we come to the ironic fact that the ghost of Augustine appears to have converted to a form of Pelagianism. Here the human will is not bound, but free, and as the

---

86. Augustine, *Vera rel.*, 4.6–7. Subsequent citations of this work are from *Augustine: Earlier Writings*, trans. John Burleigh (Philadelphia: Westminster Press, 1953).
87. Van Fleteren, "*Vera religione*," 864.
88. See Augustine, *Retrac.* 1.13.
89. Augustine, *Vera rel.* 11.21.
90. Gunton, *One, the Three and the Many,* 53n17.
91. Augustine, *Vera rel.* 4.5.

phantasmal Augustine makes clear throughout the first dialogue, the only necessity for happiness and moral transformation is to try harder, think of death, and of course read lots of Cicero. As this Augustine puts it, "Anyone who [truly] tries to achieve [happiness] is able to achieve it."[92] Do not say "your will is impotent."[93]

The mature and genuine Augustine could never say such things. Thus Michael Hanby is partly right to say that the "Augustinianism" of later centuries was "implicitly reliant upon the metaphysical underpinnings of a pagan virtue which it had been Augustine's great achievement to refute."[94] But Hanby is also partly wrong. He is wrong because men like Petrarch were not reading the mature and vehemently anti-Pelagian Augustine. Petrarch was reading Augustine's earlier and more philosophical works, written before he had come to formulate his distinctive views on Paul and grace and sin. Thus, as a much older Augustine would admit of this earlier period, "I labored hard in defense of the free choice of the human will; but the grace of God conquered."[95]

De Libero Arbitrio was composed during this early period (c. 387–395), and as Pelagius was delighted to point out, this Augustine had actually celebrated the fact that "it is up to our will whether we lack such a great and true good [that is, virtue]. For what is so much in the power of the will as the will itself?"[96] In light of this, it is fascinating that, like Petrarch's *My Secret*, Augustine's *De Libero Arbitrio* was also composed as a three part philosophical dialogue

---

92. Ibid., 6.
93. Ibid., 93.
94. Hanby, *Augustine and Modernity* (New York: Routledge, 2003), 133.
95. Augustine, *Retrac.* 2.1.27. It is interesting to note again that when speaking specifically of *Lib. arb.* in *Retrac.*, Augustine wants to make it out as if his readers have simply *misunderstood* his early works. Once again, as O'Donnell states, "Few readers not already committed to finding Augustine in the right on every possible point have been persuaded by this." *Augustine: A New Biography*, 318.
96. Augustine, *Lib. arb.*, 1.12; see our treatment of this same subject in ch. 5.

between Augustine and a friend. Likewise, just as the "ghost" of Augustine would attempt to convince Petrarch that "no one can . . . be made unhappy except by his own fault,"[97] so too the real Augustine (of *De Libero Arbitrio*) would attempt to convince Evodius that "it is by the will that human beings achieve a happy life."[98] Indeed, at certain points, one almost gathers that Petrarch was patterning his own dialogue on the original questions and answers given in book 1 of *De Libero Arbitrio*. After all, both works begin with the same questions posed to Augustine about whether happiness is a product of the will.

Concluding Thoughts on Petrarch and Augustine

What then should we make of Petrarch's "Augustinian" pedigree? In the end, the arguments made by the younger Augustine, and the ones made by his supposed "ghost" *are not identical*. Even in his earlier works, Augustine was far more attuned to Scripture, and far less dependent upon the classical Greek and Latin writers. Still, Petrarch's "ghost" is similar enough to the fourth-century Augustine to highlight another key contention of the present book: As seen in previous chapters, parts of Gunton's narrative are bolstered if and when the *Confessions*, and other earlier works of Augustine, are granted a certain priority.[99] In these works, Augustine's limited but still problematic dualism, his optimism regarding human free will, and his decision to look inward in order to encounter truth are far more pervasive.

While Gunton never dealt with Petrarch, his claim was that the modern shift toward voluntarism and inward introspection were partly a result of Augustine's influence. As we have seen, a more

---

97. Petrarch, *My Secret*, 9.
98. Augustine, *Lib. arb.*, 1.14.
99. See esp. ch. 4.

fully contextualized reading of Augustine largely acquits him of such modern errors. Yet as Barnes noted, there has likely "never been a 'contextualised' reading of Augustine." Indeed: "bits and pieces" have always been selected.[100] Thus with Petrarch, Pelikan notes a move to appropriate some other "pieces" of Augustine's massive influence: "From Petrarch's treatment of the authority of Augustine it is clear that 'more important to him than the strict letter of Augustinian orthodoxy was the paradigmatic quality of the Saint's own experience of wandering, ambivalence, psychic division and ultimate resolution.'"[101] Derrida was not the first to sound these depths. Thus again we find a justification for Cary's prior comments: "Because of Augustine's . . . influence in Western Christianity, an inward turn remains a permanent possibility for orthodox piety in the West."[102] This is so, because, as O'Donnell states, "even if [Augustine's] theology did not prevail, his psychology persists."[103]

With Petrarch, Pelikan notes that "the exploration of subjectivity was a constituent part of the Augustinian tradition."[104] As with Bernard and Bonaventure, the entreaty to "turn your minds inward upon yourselves," was to some extent the product of Augustine's influence.[105] While Gregory of Nyssa would speak of the soul as the "mirror" of the infinite,[106] and while many would connect the *imago Dei* with the rationality of the mind,[107] Augustine alone would

---

100. Michel Barnes, "Rereading Augustine's Theology of the Trinity," in *The Trinity: An Interdisciplinary Symposium on the Trinity*, ed. Stephen T. Davis, Daniel Kendall, and Gerald O'Collins (Oxford: Oxford University Press, 1999), 147.
101. *CT*, 4:21. Citing Charles Trinkaus, "Erasmus, Augustine, and the Nominalists," in *Archiv für Reformationsgeschichte* 66 (1976): 14.
102. Philip Cary, *Augustine's Invention of the Inner Self: The Legacy of a Christian Platonist* (Oxford: Oxford University Press, 2000), 60. See again ch. 4.
103. O'Donnell, *Augustine: A New Biography*, 327.
104. *CT*, 3:304.
105. Ibid.
106. For a careful study of this similarity between Nyssan and Augustine, see David Bentley Hart, "The Mirror of the Infinite: Gregory of Nyssa on the *Vestigia Trinitatis*," in *Modern Theology* 18, no. 4 (Oct., 2002): 541–56.

commend this inward plunge in such striking and alluring ways as to produce an introspective masterpiece like the *Confessions*. This inward turn emerged in Augustine's study of the Trinity, and it affected his treatment of creation.[108] Thus as Pelikan notes in the final sentence of his volume on *The Growth of Medieval Theology*, "the transposition of this experience" would ultimately become a formative influence for the individualistic introspection of such later figures as René Descartes.[109] At this more narrow point, Gunton and Pelikan are in agreement. The implications of this conclusion must await a later chapter, yet for now we turn to summarize the conclusions from the Middle Ages as a whole.

Conclusions from the Middle Ages

Our goal in the last two chapters has been to evaluate the viability of Gunton's arguments on Augustine's medieval legacy. As in prior chapters, we have seen that Gunton's history was often reductive and unfair to Augustine. Thus the line from Hippo Regius to the later centuries is not as direct as Gunton often supposed. Still, in view of Pelikan's history and our own reading of the source material, it remains viable to claim that certain isolated elements in Augustine were, at times, appropriated in such a way as to further the kinds of tensions alleged by Gunton. This argument has been demonstrated in the following respects:

(1) Early Middle Ages. At the onset of the medieval era, we noted the emergence of two strands within the Augustinian tradition. First, in the speculative philosophy of Boethius we found a partial justification of Gunton's thesis. As Boethius attempted to bring to

---

107. Ch. 7 will note this tendency in some of Gunton's heroes, Irenaeus and the Cappadocian fathers.
108. See again chs. 3 and 4
109. *CT*, 3:307.

fruition "the seeds of *reason* from the blessed Augustine,"[110] this philosophical appropriation was seen by both Pelikan and others as contributing to a culture that preferred "the Hellenization of Christianity to the faithful exposition of . . . Scripture."[111] In this regard, it remains viable to claim that Boethius furthered an imbalance in Augustine's own thought, while at the same time taking Greek philosophy much *further* than the mature Augustine would have allowed.

For Gregory the Great, it was "Augustine the bishop" and not "Augustine the philosopher" who mattered most. Yet while Gregory appealed constantly to his hero, he also altered certain aspects of his thought. Thus it could be said that "almost everything in him [had] its roots in Augustine, and yet almost nothing [was] genuinely Augustinian."[112] By softening certain unpalatable elements in Augustine (most notably on predestination and the status the will), Gregory helped to protect the reputation of his predecessor.[113] Still, the preference for the Augustine of *De Libero Arbitrio* also created space for an individualistic voluntarism that both Hanby and Gunton saw behind later modern and medieval errors. While Gregory was a "less than genuine" Augustinian, we found that even his alterations helped to cement Augustine's place as the most reverenced theologian in the years to follow.

(2) High Middle Ages. In the high medieval period we began our survey with a train of thinkers from Anselm to Bonaventure. For these figures, Augustine's "speculations about the 'traces of the Trinity' in the human mind were the outstanding example of faith in search of understanding."[114] In the growth of scholastic speculation,

---

110. Ibid., 1:350, citing Boethius, *On the Trinity*, prologue. Emphasis mine.
111. *CT*, 5:106.
112. Ibid., 1:350, citing Seeberg.
113. *CT*, 1:351; cf. ibid., 338.
114. Ibid., 3:259–60.

Pelikan confirmed a part of Gunton's narrative regarding the unintended consequences of Augustine's focus upon the rational mind as the *imago Trinitatis*. As he put it, "the experiential theology of Bonaventure and of Augustine," would eventually be "transformed into an autonomous source of truth."[115] This judgment, while more nuanced than that of Gunton, did support one component of his Augustinian narrative.

On Aquinas, however, Gunton's case was more doubtful. While Gunton found in Aquinas an Aristotelian translation of Augustine's errors, Pelikan and a host of more contemporary Aquinas specialists, including Gilles Emery, showed no signs of affirming this analysis. On creation, the more prominent roots of Aquinas's *via negativa* and his hierarchical structuring of reality were linked more to such figures as Pseudo-Dionysius than to Augustine. Likewise, on the Trinity, we found that Aquinas tempered the speculations of others, and grounded even his so-called natural theology in the biblical text.

(3) Late Middle Ages. In the present chapter, we began with an emerging challenge to the theology of Augustine and Aquinas. In Scotus and Ockham, the Augustinian appeal to Platonic or Aristotelian universals was questioned, even as another aspect of Augustine's theology was revived. In both figures, an emphasis was again laid on the concept of the will, in both its divine and human attributions. Yet while Gunton blamed Augustine for the emergence of a "monistic" and "arbitrary" concept of the divine will, our research again found problems with this view. As we saw, Augustine's treatment of God's will was often tethered to a Trinitarian conception of God's *love* for his creation. Thus again, Gunton's charges proved unfair.

---

115. Ibid., 3:306.

Despite such faults in Gunton's narrative, our treatment of Petrarch uncovered one area where his argument might have been bolstered, if he had taken time to explore it. In the humanist appropriation of Augustine's "inward turn,"[116] Pelikan cited the connection between such early works as the *Confessions*, and the patterns of individual introspection that would pave the way for aspects of the modern ethos. Our own analysis confirmed this point. As with others, Petrarch's use of Augustine was both creative and selective. In this way, he also was a "less than genuine" Augustinian. Yet here again, we found a limited justification of our prior claim: *parts of Gunton's critique are bolstered if and when Augustine's earlier works, and more specifically the Confessions, are granted a certain priority by later readers.* To test this claim, however, we must turn now to the next chapter of Augustine's afterlife: the Reformation.

---

116. See again our definition of this phrase in ch. 3.

7

Gunton and Augustine's Reformation Afterlife

For Pelikan, the Reformation could be partially characterized as a dispute "between two ways of reading Augustine."[1] It was, in B. B. Warfield's estimation, "the ultimate triumph of Augustine's doctrine of grace over Augustine's doctrine of the church."[2] While such statements contain an obvious amount of oversimplification, none would deny the incredible influence of Augustine upon such figures as Martin Luther and John Calvin. As we will note, both men took their stands, not only on the principle of *sola scriptura*, but also upon a reading of the Scriptures that was partly drawn from the ruins of Hippo Regius. Thus as we prepare to examine Gunton's claims regarding Augustine's *modern* legacy, we must first deal with that period (the Reformation) that may be seen to reside somewhat ambiguously between the medieval and modern epochs.

1. *CT*, 4:8–9.
2. B. B. Warfield, *Calvin and Augustine* (Philadelphia, 1956), 322.

In terms of method, the work of Pelikan will again serve as a frequent arbiter between Gunton and his critics. We will begin with Augustine's influence upon Martin Luther, while moving next to Calvin and the Reformed tradition. As in the previous chapter, this survey of Augustine's Reformation "inheritors" must remain selective. Without question, the Protestant Reformation was much larger than Luther, Calvin, and their immediate descendants. Yet, for sake of space, our choice of representatives will again be guided by a decision to respond primarily to Gunton's particular allegations. As before, we will make no attempt to offer a full critique of Gunton's views on Luther, Calvin, or any other Reformation figure. Instead, our study will be limited to an evaluation of Gunton's particular claims regarding Augustine's influence upon these thinkers.

In the end, the argument of this chapter will continue to note the ways in which Gunton's case was often lacking both in nuance and in fairness. One reason will connect to a theme already mentioned in the prior chapters. Because Luther and Calvin were often drawing upon Augustine's more mature writings, we will find them to be less prone to the kind of early "Augustinian" imbalances that might be noted in the work of Boethius, Petrarch, or even (later) René Descartes.[3] Yet again, if there is a kernel of truth to be uncovered in Gunton's overblown critiques, it will reside the selective appropriation of Augustine's so-called inward turn. Before this point can be explained, however, we must turn first to Luther and his unique appropriation of Augustine's legacy.

Luther and Augustine's Legacy

When writing of Martin Luther (1483–1546), Pelikan argued that "not since Augustine had the spiritual odyssey of one man [so

---

3. We will deal with Descartes in the subsequent chapter.

coincided] with the spiritual exigency of Western Christendom."[4] Augustine's importance to Luther is by now "proverbial,"[5] for as Pelikan put it, "The presupposition for [Luther's] doctrine of justification was a vigorous reassertion of Augustinian anthropology." For his own part, "Luther identified Pelagianism as the one perennial heresy of Christian history,"[6] and thus "accused the scholastics of treating Augustine's doctrine of 'grace alone' as an exaggeration."[7] As Luther himself argued, "Augustine has to this day not been accepted by the church of Rome."[8] In contrast to such statements, Luther also critiqued Augustine for "having said so little about faith."[9] Yet in general, his theology marked a retrieval of Augustine's teachings on grace and human sinfulness. For most students of church history, such facts are likely well rehearsed. Yet what were Gunton's specific claims regarding Luther's appropriation of Augustine's influence? We begin with the positives.

Gunton's Praise of Luther

Gunton often praised Luther for rejecting certain aspects of Augustine's thought. As he put it, the Reformer was "contemptuous of Augustine's mystical interpretation of [Genesis 1–5]," and of the view that God created all things instantaneously.[10] Gunton also praised Luther for denying "Augustine's neoplatonising view that matter is almost nothing."[11] Here the Reformer claimed to "disagree entirely" with Augustine's argument.[12] One reason for this

---

4. *CT*, 4:127.
5. So says Philip Krey, "Martin Luther," in *Augustine through the Ages: An Encyclopedia*, ed. Allan Fitzgerald (Grand Rapids: Eerdmans, 1999), 518.
6. *CT*, 4:139.
7. Ibid., 140–41.
8. Luther, *Lectures on the First Epistle of John*, 4.15. Cited in *CT*, 4:141.
9. *CT*, 4:141. See Luther, *Lectures on the First Epistle of John*, 5.4.
10. Gunton, *The Triune Creator: A Historical and Systematic Study* (Grand Rapids: Eerdmans, 1998), 148n2; cf. Luther, *Lectures on Genesis chapters 1–5*, ed. J. Pelikan (St. Louis: Concordia, 1958), 9.

disagreement lay in Luther's views on human reason and the Bible's revelation. For Luther, Greek Reason (especially in its scholastic and Aristotelian manifestations) had become "the devil's bride," and "that pretty whore" who seduces the church.[13] Here again, Gunton's view of Luther was a positive one. As he wrote, Luther "always [spoke] about creation in terms of the Trinity,"[14] and in his view this resulted in a correction to Augustine's supposed errors. As Gunton wrote, "Whereas relation to God is for Augustine very much a direct relation between God and the soul, for Luther it is 'a relation mediated in an authentically worldly way.' . . . Thus is Luther able to affirm what is central to a Christian theology of creation, that creation is to be understood not only as God's address *to* but also *through* the creature."[15] Here again Gunton's view of Luther was affirming, yet he would also critique the Reformer for some other appropriations of Augustine's thought.

As we will see, Gunton's criticism of Luther may be subdivided under the headings of (1) *individualism*, (2) *embodiment*, and (3) *justification*. In each of these areas, Gunton noted what he saw as the "Augustinian" origins of certain Reformation imbalances.[16]

Individualism

For Gunton, Luther's positive contributions must be balanced against a creeping individualism that resulted from his influence. Beneath

---

11. Gunton, *Triune Creator*, 148. See again ch. 4 for our mixed review of Augustine's statement that the *earth* of Gen. 1:1 is "close to being nothing" (Augustine, *Conf.* 12.7).
12. Luther, *Lectures on Genesis*, 5. Cited in Gunton, *Triune Creator*, 148.
13. Gunton, *Revelation and Reason*, ed. P. H. Brazier (London: T&T Clark, 2008), 126. Citing "Martin Luther's Last Sermon in Wittenberg, Second Sunday in Epiphany, 17 January 1546."
14. Gunton, *Triune Creator*, 148. Citing Regin Prenter, *Spiritus Creator: Luther's Concept of the Holy Spirit* (Philadelphia: Muhlenberg, 1953), 192.
15. Gunton, *Triune Creator*, 149n8. Citing Oswald Bayer's *Schöpfung als Anrede* (Tübingen: J.C.B. Mohr, Paul Siebeck, 1990), 95.
16. See Gunton, *The Promise of Trinitarian Theology* (Edinburgh: T&T Clark, 1991), 122–23 for Gunton's own enumeration of these three subjects.

this, Gunton sensed an imbalance in the Reformer's view of Christian liberty. As Luther argued in his famous treatise on *The Freedom of a Christian*, "A Christian is a perfectly free lord of all, subject to none . . . [and] a perfectly dutiful servant of all, subject to all."[17] While praising this insight in some regards, Gunton's complaint was that Luther overemphasized the *inner freedom* to be found when the *individual* is confronted with the gospel. As he wrote, "With Luther, very little attention was paid to the way freedom might be conceived to take shape in community."[18] Thus the problem was a tilt toward individualism. Yet how does this connect to Augustine?

For Gunton, Luther's individualistic imbalance could be partly traced to Augustine's alleged neglect of the Spirit's *outward* work to grant freedom in and through community.[19] Once again, the claim was that Augustine tended to "reduce the Spirit to a . . . link between Father and Son—and therefore to . . . a repetition of the single-person deity of the Western tradition."[20] Once done, this pneumatological error allegedly became the "Achilles' heel of all Western theology."[21]

We have met this claim already. As seen in chapter 3, the fatal problem with Gunton's pneumatological critique is that Augustine simply did *not* reduce the Spirit to a mere link between the Father and the Son. As Augustine argued, this same Spirit was also active in the divine economy. In creation, the Spirit was the Goodness (*bonitas*) from which the Father makes all things.[22] In redemption, the Spirit was the Gift that distinguishes "sons" and connects them to God.[23] In

---

17. Martin Luther, "The Freedom of a Christian," in *Martin Luther's Basic Theological Writings*, ed. Timothy F. Lull (Minneapolis: Augsburg Fortress, 1989), 596. Gunton references this passage in *Promise of Trinitarian Theology*, 118.
18. Gunton, *Promise of Trinitarian Theology*, 122. Emphasis added.
19. Ibid., 136. See also our prior treatment of this in ch. 3.
20. Ibid., 134.
21. Gunton, *Becoming and Being: The Doctrine of God in Charles Hartshorne and Karl Barth*, 2nd ed. (London: SCM Press, 2001), 238 (2001 epilogue).
22. Augustine, *Civ.* 11.24.

eschatology, the Spirit was the origin and blessedness of the coming city of God.²⁴ And in the church, the Spirit is the Bringer of oneness who constitutes biblical community.²⁵ Augustine's pneumatology affirmed *all* of these realities; thus, we have seen Gunton's claim to be ill-founded at this particular point.²⁶

This is not to say, of course, that Gunton was necessarily wrong about the individualistic repercussions of the Reformation. It remains possible, for instance, to contend that the principle of *sola scriptura* may have unintentionally contributed to a subsequent modern elevation of private (that is, individual) judgment.²⁷ Yet while this argument remains plausible, its viability lies beyond the scope of this book,²⁸ and it is certainly wrong to blame Augustine's pneumatology for such developments. As Pelikan notes, the "most succinct, and rhetorically effective" defense of catholic *tradition* (over and against the notion of *sola scriptura*) was taken from Augustine: "For my part, I should not believe the gospel except as moved by the authority of the catholic church."²⁹

Embodiment

Gunton's subsequent claim against Luther's appropriation of Augustine involved the relation between freedom, community, and the notion of *embodiment*. As he argued, both Luther and Calvin tended to "lose sight" of a central reality. In Gunton's words,

---

23. See especially Augustine, *Trin.* 15.18–9: "There is no gift more excellent than this [Love/Holy Spirit]. It alone distinguishes the sons of the eternal kingdom and the sons of eternal perdition."
24. Augustine, *Civ.* 11.24.
25. See *Jo. ev. tr.* 39 where Augustine identifies the Spirit as that which "makes many souls one soul and many hearts one heart." Cited in Lewis Ayres, *Augustine and the Trinity* (Cambridge: Cambridge University Press, 2010), 257.
26. See again ch. 3.
27. See Pelikan's treatment of this in *CT*, 5:85.
28. As argued, for instance, by Brad S. Gregory, *The Unintended Reformation: How a Religious Revolution Secularized Society* (Cambridge, MA: Harvard University Press, 2012), ch. 2.
29. *CT*, 4:263. Citing Augustine, *c. ep. Man.*, 5.

We are related to one another through the medium of our bodies. In this respect, there is . . . a tendency to *spiritualising* to be found in both of the Reformers, and that is why the questions must inevitably appear to be different in the times after the Enlightenment. Is there not something lacking in the Reformation legacy—deriving perhaps from Augustine's Platonism—which later led to the feeling that an important element, particularly that concerning the material and social dimensions of human living, had been omitted?[30]

The style is classic Gunton. Here in the span of just two sentences we are asked to trace the results of so-called Platonic errors through Augustine, to the Reformers, and on to the post-Enlightenment world. Yet in sketching this grand narrative, Gunton offers no evidence to support his charge. Instead, we have only a rather vague supposition that Luther's "spiritualizing" of human freedom was derived "perhaps" from Augustine's Platonism. And this, it seems, is a rather large *perhaps*.

On the surface, with his famous rejection of celibacy and medieval asceticism, Martin Luther would appear to typify a distinctly positive approach to human embodiment. In addition, as Heiko Oberman points out, it was precisely Augustine's Neoplatonism that Luther found troubling at points: "As a nominalist Luther began making a conscious distinction between knowledge of the world and faith in God. . . . Thus not even Augustine, *especially Augustine the neo-Platonist*, could become the new infallible authority."[31] So what was Gunton getting at in his claim that Augustine's Platonism may have negatively affected Luther's treatment of embodiment?

---

30. Gunton, *Promise of Trinitarian Theology*, 122. Emphasis added. Gunton here admits that his critique of Luther (and the Reformation Tradition) is drawn, in part, from a Lutheran theologian: Robert Jenson.
31. Oberman, *Luther: Man between God and the Devil*, trans. Eileen Walisser-Schwarzbart (New Haven: Yale University Press, 1989), 160–61. Emphasis mine.

To be sure, Gunton was hardly ignorant of Luther's nominalism.[32] As he acknowledged, the Reformer "was essentially taught by the Ockhamists," which provided yet another impetus for his aversion to certain forms of Greek philosophy. Likewise, Gunton was not claiming that Luther somehow disdained the physical and material aspects of human being.[33] Gunton's charge was that both Luther and Calvin followed Augustine by placing "too much stress on our spiritual natures—where 'spiritual' tends to mean 'inward' rather than 'in relation to God the Holy Spirit'."[34] Here again, the claim was that Luther was influenced by Augustine's preoccupation with the inner realm, and thus he evidenced a tendency to "spiritualize" by speaking of liberty primarily in context of the *internal* world of the individual.

To bolster his charge, Gunton again cited Luther's treatise on *The Freedom of a Christian*. As the text reveals, Luther does speak of liberty in the context of the "inner man," while discussing servitude "according to the bodily nature."[35] As Gunton admitted (with Jüngel), this did not mean that Luther's inner freedom had nothing to do with outward or social realities. Indeed, it may be argued that Luther's view of Christian liberty was actually *completed* by its direction toward the neighbor.[36] Yet for Gunton this was not

---

32. Gunton, *Revelation and Reason*, 126. See again our treatment of Ockham in ch. 6.
33. See again the previously cited quotation from Gunton, *Triune Creator*, 149n8.
34. Gunton, *Promise of Trinitarian Theology*, 122.
35. See Luther, *The Freedom of a Christian*, 596: "Man has a twofold nature, a spiritual and a bodily one. According to the spiritual nature, which men refer to as the soul, he is called a spiritual, inner, or new man. According to the bodily nature, which men refer to as flesh, he is called a carnal, outward, or old man. . . . Because of the this diversity of nature the Scriptures assert contradictory things [liberty/slavery] concerning the same man" (596).
    The turning point in Luther's treatise (from inner to outer; freedom to servitude) can be seen here: "Let this suffice concerning the inner man, his liberty, and the source of his liberty, the righteousness of faith. . . . Now let us turn to the second part, the outer man. . . . This is the place to assert that which was said above, namely, that a Christian is the servant of all and made subject to all" (610).
36. Gunton, *Promise of Trinitarian Theology*, 119. Here Gunton again acknowledges the argument of Eberhard Jüngel, *Zur Freiheit eines Christenmenschen. Eine Erinnerung an Luthers Schrift* (München: Christian Kaiser, 1987), 108.

sufficient. As he argued, Luther's Augustinian emphasis upon the inward and "spiritual" realm would contribute to certain modern maladies: namely, a "false spiritualising of reality" and an "individualistic conception of the person."[37] Yet to evidence this, Gunton turned at last to the central doctrine of Luther's theology: justification by faith.

Justification

For Gunton, Luther's Augustinianism ultimately resulted in an overemphasis upon the inner freedom to be attained through the *justification* of the individual. As Pelikan put it, "Luther's 'discovery' of justification . . . took place in the struggle of his own conscience." His question was, How can I find a God who is gracious to me?[38] The breakthrough came from reading Paul: "The righteous will live by faith" (Rom. 1:17, NIV).[39] Yet in this process, Luther also found some confirmation in the writings of Augustine. As he recounted,

> I hated St. Paul with all my heart when I read: "the righteousness of God is revealed in the Gospel." But afterward, when I saw how it went on . . .: "The just shall live by faith," and also consulted St. Augustine on the passage, then I became glad, for I learned and saw that the righteousness of God is His mercy through which he regards us and keeps us just. Thus I was comforted.[40]

With Augustine's perceived support for his position, Luther's understanding of justification would become the doctrine by which

---

37. Gunton, *Promise of Trinitarian Theology*, 123.
38. *CT*, 4:138.
39. Ibid.
40. Martin Luther, *Werke: Kritische Gesamtausgabe, Tischreden* [Table talk], vol. 4 (Weimar, 1912–21), no. 4007; 73, 15–24; Sept. 12, 1538. Cited and translated by Oberman, *Luther*, 153.

the church either stands or falls.⁴¹ Yet in the face of this emphasis, Gunton raised a further objection. As he put it,

> [Luther's] conception of justification, dominated as it was by features of his personal experience as well as by the Western church's Augustinian heritage, led to the neglect of some of the features we have seen to be important. The meaning of the justice of God . . . came to be too closely tied to individual sin and forgiveness, too loosely to the cosmic and social dimensions. . . . The chief point, however, is not to apportion blame for the development so much as to realise what has happened since then. The increasingly subjective turn of the modern mind has meant that treatments of the human plight and its healing have taken an increasingly inward and individualistic direction, as the thought of two modern heirs of Luther, Kierkegaard and Bultmann, demonstrates clearly.⁴²

With regard to Augustine's afterlife, this statement is perhaps a fairer one.⁴³ As Gunton wrote, "The chief point . . . is not to apportion blame," but rather to recognize how the combination of certain theological emphases (Augustine's inward turn and Luther's critique of church tradition) may have unintentionally combined in such a way as to contribute to a subsequent modern propensity for inwardness, individualism, and subjectivity.⁴⁴ At this more narrow point, Pelikan's history is more open to Gunton's narrative.

As Pelikan argues, the church's modern elevation of the individual's inward world was shaped, in part, by the "understanding

---

41. As Pelikan notes, this would be equally true for Calvin and his immediate successors: "The seventeenth-century Reformed followers of John Calvin knew that they disagreed with the followers of Luther on many questions, but they recognized that *all* of them agreed on this doctrine." *CT*, 4:138–9.
42. Gunton, *The Actuality of Atonement: A Study of Metaphor, Rationality, and the Christian Tradition* (Grand Rapids, MI: Eerdmans, 1989), 101.
43. As Gunton notes, Luther sometimes emphasized the cosmic and social dimensions of redemption. See *Triune Creator*, 226; *Promise of Trinitarian Theology*, 119.
44. To be clear, this is not to say that Luther was somehow a "modern" thinker. As Oberman points out, "For Luther reformation was the beginning not of modern times but of the Last Days," *Luther*, 266.

of Christian faith and experience as a phenomenon based on the relation between 'God and the soul, the soul and God.'"[45] The latter quotation was taken from Augustine's *Soliloquies,* in which a younger Augustine claimed that the *only* things worth knowing were (1) the nature of an immaterial God, and (2) the nature of one's internal soul. As we have seen, the statement should not be taken as comprehensive summation of Augustine's mature theology, yet as O'Donnell argues, these two themes did "remain the poles of Augustine's thought . . . throughout his writings."[46] As he puts it,

> In all the books and sermons and letters we have of Augustine, a consistent pattern emerges. The fundamental human relationship is the solitary individual's relationship with his god. . . . Over and over the small and large distances that separate people from one another persist and usually grow larger for Augustine as he intensifies the divine connection, until he ends there, alone with his god, alone.[47]

The fairness of this statement may be doubted, yet as the Reformation prioritized "Augustine's doctrine of grace over Augustine's doctrine of the church,"[48] Pelikan notes how this selective appropriation of Augustine may have *unwittingly* contributed to the growth of modern inwardness and individualism. Augustine would have hated this, yet in this more nuanced respect, Gunton's claim remains viable.

Summing Up: Luther and Augustine

What then may we conclude regarding Gunton's view of Luther and Augustine's modern legacy? First, as we have seen, it is misguided to claim that Augustine's pneumatology somehow lies behind the incipient *individualism* of both Luther and the modern West. Second,

---

45. *CT*, 5:289. Citing Augustine, *Soliloq.* 1.2.7.
46. O'Donnell, *Augustine: A New Biography*, 290.
47. Ibid., 317.
48. *CT*, 4:9. Citing Warfield, *Calvin and Augustine*, 322.

on the subject of *embodiment*, it would seem that Gunton's suppositions regarding Luther's "Augustinian" and "Platonic" errors lack the evidence that is necessary to support his claims. Yet in spite of these deficiencies, Pelikan does reveal a *potential* connection between Augustine's "inward turn"[49] and the so-called introspective conscience of both Luther and the West.[50] Thus while our examination has not attempted to fully settle this ongoing debate, it may be said that Pelikan's history has helped us to separate the more or less *viable* components in Gunton's narrative.

Calvin and Augustine's Legacy

In turning to John Calvin (1509–1564), Gunton's claims were similar to those connected to the work of Luther. As a self-consciously "Reformed theologian,"[51] Gunton recalled with fondness the evaluation of a one-time teacher, the late G. V. Bennett: "Calvin is the greatest theologian of the West, Augustine not excepted, by virtue of the thoroughly trinitarian structure of his thinking."[52] On the Trinity, Gunton praised Calvin for his pneumatological emphases,[53] for "moving toward a relational concept of the persons in God,"[54] and for articulating a position similar to Basil on the particular roles accorded to the Father, Son and Spirit.[55] Likewise, on creation, Gunton credited Calvin for helping to recover the doctrine

---

49. See ch. 3.
50. See Krister Stendahl, "The Apostle Paul and the Introspective Conscience of the West," in *The Harvard Theological Review* 56, no. 3 (July, 1963): 199–215.
51. Robert Jenson, "A Decision Tree of Colin Gunton's Thinking," in *The Theology of Colin Gunton*, 15.
52. Gunton, *Father, Son, and Holy Spirit: Toward a Fully Trinitarian Theology* (London: T&T Clark, 2003), 7. Gunton here cites (from memory) the spoken words of Bennett.
53. See Gunton, *Promise of Trinitarian Theology*, 146. Gunton was especially fond of Calvin's statement that "it is the Spirit who, everywhere diffused, sustains all things, causes them to grow, and quickens them in heaven and in earth." John Calvin, *Institutes of the Christian Religion*, ed. J. T. McNeill, trans. F. L. Battles (Philadelphia: Westminster Press, 1960), 1. xiii, 14.
54. Ibid., 94.

from its medieval captivity,[56] for rejecting ontic hierarchies within created being, and for continuing to shift away from more Aristotelian notions of causality.[57]

Yet as with Luther, Gunton also critiqued Calvin for his appropriation of Augustine.[58] In what follows, we will evaluate this criticism as it pertains again to a supposed monistic imbalance in the doctrine of the Trinity, and a limited (but still problematic) dualism in the doctrine of creation.

Calvin and Augustine's (Allegedly) "Monistic" Will of God

For Gunton, the "notorious flaws" in Calvin showed forth in those moments when he failed to think in a sufficiently Trinitarian manner.[59] In such moments, Gunton again sensed that a seemingly monistic, arbitrary, and "necessitarian" will of God was granted priority over the triune love of God for his creation.[60] Thus again, Gunton heard echoes of Augustine in one of Calvin's most controversial doctrines: the notion of double predestination.[61] As he put it, "The place where the worst influence of Calvin's theology is often discerned is in the fact that he appears, like Augustine before him, to have placed the divine double decree of election and reprobation prior to the revelation of God's gracious and saving action in Christ."[62] In Gunton's view, "We meet here more of a

---

55. "To the Father is attributed the beginning of activity, and the fountain and well-spring of all things; to the Son, wisdom, counsel and the ordered disposition of all things; but to the Spirit is assigned the powers and efficacy of that activity." Calvin, *Institutes*, 1. xiii, 18. As cited in Gunton, *Father, Son, and Holy Spirit*, 81; cf. *Promise of Trinitarian Theology*, xxvii.
56. Gunton, *Promise of Trinitarian Theology*, 153.
57. See Gunton, *Triune Creator*, 153.
58. Thus Calvin's own legacy on the Trinity and creation was seen to be "somewhat ambiguous." Ibid., 150.
59. Gunton, *Father, Son, and Holy Spirit*, 7–8.
60. See Gunton, *Triune Creator*, 151.
61. See especially Gunton's chapter on "Election and Ecclesiology," in *Intellect and Action: Elucidations on Christian Theology and the Life of Faith* (Edinburgh: T&T Clark, 2001), 139–55.

theology of will than of love, more of an omnipotent *monocausal* God than of the one who works through his two hands, the Son and the Spirit."[63] In this way, Calvin's Augustinian treatment of double predestination was seen to evidence a Trinitarian deficiency.

To grasp the full nature of Gunton's charge, it may help to understand his own position on the subjects of election and predestination. As Gunton stated in his classroom lectures, the Bible speaks of election primarily as God's calling "to perform a particular task or function on earth."[64] Here "God does not simply elect one group rather than another; he elects one group for the sake of and on behalf of the others."[65] Yet with Augustine (and his heirs) this emphasis was allegedly altered. As Gunton claimed of much of the Western theological tradition, "The question now raised is not: what is Israel's calling and mission in the world? The question now is: who is going to get there [to heaven] and how? The answer for Augustine and his successors is that most people are damned, most are aiming for destruction; God's grace and mercy is shown in that he calls a few."[66] For Gunton, this "negative"[67] view of election was unacceptable because the "eschatological directedness" of humankind was seen as "tilting hellwards."[68] In contrast, Gunton followed Barth

62. Gunton, *Act and Being: Towards a Theology of the Divine Attributes* (London: SCM Press, 2002), 86. In the very next sentence, Gunton goes on to admit that although this charge is not entirely fair, it does speak to Calvin's effect upon the subsequent tradition.
63. Gunton, *Triune Creator*, 153. Emphasis mine. Cf. Gunton, *The One, the Three and the Many: God, Creation and the Culture of Modernity* (Cambridge: Cambridge University Press, 1993), 121: "If not in Augustine, *certainly in those who learned from him*, creation becomes very much the product of pure, unmotivated and therefore arbitrary will, a will that operates equally arbitrarily in the theology of double predestination that became after him so much a mark of the Western tradition," italics mine.
64. Gunton, *The Barth Lectures*, ed. P. H. Brazier (London: T&T Clark, 2007), 111.
65. Gunton, *The Christian Faith: An Introduction to Christian Doctrine* (Oxford: Blackwell, 2002), 164; cf. *Intellect and Action*, 140.
66. Gunton, *Barth Lectures*, 111.
67. Ibid., 112.
68. Gunton, *Christ and Creation*, the Didsbury Lectures, 1990 (Eugene, OR: Wipf and Stock, 2005), 95.

in seeking to reconfigure radically the traditional Augustinian and Calvinistic treatments of election.

For Gunton, "God has chosen the human race, all of it, in Christ, to come into loving relationship with its creator."[69] Yet despite the commonalities with Barth, Gunton also sought to improve upon Barth's doctrine by placing more of an emphasis upon the Spirit's role to bring this election to fruition.[70] As he put it, "Jesus does indeed do something for the whole human race; but the perfecting of that complete work continues to depend on its realization in time by the work of the Spirit. . . . Reconciliation is thus universal in intent, but not yet fully realized."[71] In spite of such apparently universalistic tendencies, Gunton did leave open "the small possibility owed to human freedom that some will finally turn their back on [God's love] and choose rejection."[72] Yet on this point, he refused to offer a definitive conclusion.[73] For Gunton, this view of election was more *Trinitarian* in that it avoided a "mono-causal" conception of the divine will.[74] In its place, he embraced what he called "the mysterious combination of divine determination and human free-will."[75]

Now that we have briefly outlined both the *critical* and *constructive* features of Gunton's treatment of election (in response to Augustine and Calvin especially), what must we say in response? To be clear, this book makes no attempt to adjudicate all of the biblical and theological questions regarding election and predestination. Likewise, as stated previously, this chapter is not an attempt to

---

69. Gunton, *Christian Faith*, 66.
70. See ibid., 67. For Gunton, this emphasis on the temporal role of the Spirit was in contrast to Barth's overly "eternalised" conception of election in which "the Spirit contributes nothing structurally," *Christ and Creation*, 95; cf. *Intellect and Action*, 147.
71. Gunton, *Christian Faith*, 163–64.
72. Ibid., 67; cf. 164: "We cannot rule out the possibility that some may finally exclude themselves from the kingdom."
73. See Gunton, *Intellect and Action*, 140.
74. See Gunton, *Act and Being*, 86.
75. Gunton, *Christ and Creation*, 88.

evaluate Gunton's overall treatment of Calvin or the Reformed tradition. Our concern is only with the Trinitarian critique that Gunton leveled against Augustine's Reformation legacy. Thus our question is as follows: What should be made of Gunton's claim that the Augustinian (and Calvinistic) treatment of double predestination led to a *monocausal* (that is, "monistic") misconstrual of the divine will? We begin with that which is universally agreed upon.

As with Luther, Augustine's importance to Calvin is unquestioned. As Marshall notes, "Aside from the authors of the New Testament no Christian writer enjoyed a position of authority over the mind of Calvin even remotely comparable to that of St. Augustine."[76] Indeed, by one account, it was in reading Augustine (*De spiritu et littera*) that Calvin had first decided to enlist in the cause of Reformation.[77] On predestination, Calvin could state that "Augustine is so completely of our persuasion, that if I should have to make written profession, it would be quite enough to present a composition made up entirely of excerpts from his writings."[78] Likewise, when the topic turned to reprobation, Calvin also drew upon Augustine's thought. As Pelikan states, the "language of Augustine about 'the damnation of those whom [God] had justly predestined to punishment . . .' came to Calvin's aid in his argument . . . that the only possible doctrine of predestination was a doctrine of double predestination."[79] Here and elsewhere, Calvin cited Augustine's axiom that the will of God is the "necessity" and "cause" of all things.[80] Thus Gunton is surely right to cite Calvin's Augustinian pedigree on this topic.

---

76. David J. Marshall, "John Calvin," in Fitzgerald, *Augustine through the Ages*, 117–18.
77. Ibid.
78. John Calvin, *Aeterna Dei praedestinatione*, in the *Corpus Reformatorum* (Halle: C. A. Schwetschke and Son, 1859), 8:266. Cited in Marshall, "John Calvin," 116.
79. *CT*, 4:224; citing Augustine, *Enchir.* 26.100.
80. *CT*, 4:221; citing Calvin, *Inst.* 3.23.2, 8; Augustine *Gn. litt.* 6.15.26.

Yet while Gunton is hardly the first to find fault with this aspect of the Augustinian tradition,[81] it would also seem that his Trinitarian critique (that is, that such predestinarian viewpoints are rooted in a monistic view of God) leaves crucial questions unanswered. For Augustine (and Luther and Calvin) the central questions of predestination were *exegetical* in nature. Does the Bible teach it? Yet while Gunton emphasized that "all faithful Christian theology must be . . . an interpretation of the scriptures,"[82] his own work again demonstrated a surprising "lack of exegetical description" at this point.[83] Thus while Gunton critiqued Calvin's "Augustinian" and "mono-causal" treatment of predestination, he also failed to grapple extensively (at least in print) with those texts that both Augustine and Calvin believed to support their doctrines. Indeed many of the previously cited comments on "election in the scriptures" come not from Gunton's academic publications, but from the posthumously published transcripts of his classroom lectures.[84]

In noting this, we do not mean to imply that Gunton was entirely wrong in his critique of Augustine's predestinarian legacy. In the words of Pelikan, "The fearful symmetry of salvation and reprobation in the doctrine of double predestination could easily lead its critics, and sometimes its exponents as well, to construct from it a system in which the eternal will of God, as contained in his decrees, became an all-encompassing (and all-explaining) first and only cause."[85] Still, as

---

81. Indeed the Remonstrants, in the preface of their *Confession*, would also object to the exclusive canonization of "this one man Augustine." See *CT*, 4:225.
82. Gunton, *Christ and Creation*, 11.
83. This phrase is that of David Höhne, *Spirit and Sonship: Colin Gunton's Theology of Particularity and the Holy Spirit* (Burlington, VT: Ashgate, 2010), 14; Webster argues similarly in "Systematic Theology after Barth: Jüngel, Jenson and Gunton," in *The Modern Theologians: An Introduction to Christian Theology since 1918*, ed. David Ford and Rachel Muers, 3rd ed. (Oxford: Blackwell, 2005), 262. See our prior acknowledgement of this issue in ch. 3.
84. See Gunton, *Barth Lectures*, 110–11. Here, before launching into a critique of Calvin and Augustine, Gunton devotes two paragraphs to election in the Scriptures. Yet even here, he never engages with such classic texts as Rom. 9:19–23.

stated previously, a full treatment of this topic lies beyond the scope of our investigation.

The contention with regard to Gunton is merely this: by evaluating this complex doctrine primarily through the lens of the Trinity, Gunton failed to follow his own advice on the necessity of thoroughgoing exegesis.[86] Thus the monistic charge remains *insufficient* by itself, given its lack of biblical argumentation, and indeed Gunton's own treatment of election leaves him open to many of the same questions to be leveled against the work of Barth.[87] In fairness, it remains possible that Gunton's planned dogmatic theology would have bolstered and clarified his position on this subject, yet without this work (at least in its completed form), we can only note the insufficiency of Gunton's existing argumentation.

Calvin and Augustine's Dualism

There is, however, another facet to Gunton's argument regarding Calvin's "Augustinianism." In his view, Calvin appropriated not only a monistic imbalance from Augustine's treatment of God's will, but also a deficiency in his handling of material creation. As with Luther, Gunton's claim was that in speaking of the human person, Calvin often made a distinction between the "inner" and "outer" realms, while relegating the discussion of freedom to the nontemporal (that is, "spiritual") jurisdiction.[88] As Calvin put it,

> There is a twofold government in man: one aspect is spiritual, whereby the conscience is instructed in piety, the second is political, whereby

---

85. *CT*, 4:232.
86. The above comments (and those of *Christ and Creation*, 11) should not be taken to imply that Gunton was uncritical toward elements within the biblical narrative. As he wrote, "The writers [of Scripture] were human beings whose particularities and weaknesses—among other things—marked all that they had to say." Gunton, *Christ and Creation*, 14.
87. See, for example, G. C. Berkouwer, *The Triumph of Grace in the Theology of Karl Barth: An Introduction and Critical Appraisal* (London: Paternoster, 1956).
88. Gunton, *Promise of Trinitarian Theology*, 121.

> man is educated for the duties of humanity and citizenship.... These are usually called the 'spiritual' and 'temporal' jurisdictions ... by which is meant that the former sort of government pertains to the life of the soul, while the latter has to do with the concerns of the present life. ... Now these two, as we have divided them, must always be examined separately; and while one is being considered, we must call away and turn aside the mind from thinking about the other.[89]

For Gunton, this way of dividing the human person betrayed a "serious theological weakness," and once again, the practice was linked to "the West's Augustinian heritage."[90] As Gunton wrote,

> What seems to have happened is that the Reformers drew upon aspects of Augustinian thought to equip them to face the urgent need of the day ... the contemporary tendency to Pelagianism. While it would be unjust to expect them to have solved all the accompanying problems, we can with benefit of hindsight see that other dimensions of their Augustinianism bequeathed serious problems for future generations.[91]

As seen previously, this alleged tendency to overemphasize the inward realm of the individual was linked to Augustine's Platonism, and thus the failure was seen as an abiding weakness in the treatment of embodiment. For Gunton, this meant a tendency toward "dualism," "other-worldliness," and a "false eternalising of the gospel."[92] Parts of this critique have been addressed already.[93] Thus our current task is merely to inquire about the relation between Calvin and Augustine's limited Platonic dualism.

---

89. Calvin, *Inst.* 3.19.15. As cited in Gunton, *Promise of Trinitarian Theology*, 121.
90. Gunton, *Promise of Trinitarian Theology*, 121. Elsewhere, Gunton would state that "much, if not all, hangs on the meaning of that term ... 'spiritual' ... [and] as so often in Calvin, there is a Platonic undertow which tends to contrast between the spiritual and the material." *Intellect and Action*, 88–89.
91. Gunton, *Promise of Trinitarian Theology*, 121–22.
92. Ibid., 136.
93. See especially our rejection of Gunton's thesis regarding the implications of Augustine's pneumatology.

While Pelikan offers little commentary on the subject, Gunton is by no means the first to find Platonic commonalities in the thought of Calvin and Augustine. For Barth, Calvin was "from a philosophical point of view," a "classical Platonist."[94] And as Boisset notes, "If Augustine is the theologian to whom Calvin refers most frequently, Plato is the philosopher most often cited and nearly always with favour."[95] Likewise, in Marshall's words,

> When speaking of the most central issues in Christian theology, Calvin will not scruple to go well beyond the language of Scripture and borrow his expressions from the purest idiom of Plato. In one striking case he [asks]: . . .if heaven is our homeland, what is our life on earth other than passage through a foreign country, and insofar as the earth is anathema to us because of sin, what is it other than our very exile and banishment? . . . If freedom is being delivered from this body, what is the body other than a prison?[96]

Such passages appear to illustrate what Gunton saw to be an occasional devaluing of human embodiment. Yet as Gunton himself noted, Calvin's views were more complex than this. As he argued, Calvin sometimes shifted between "a Platonic dualism of the person and the view that the whole person, spiritual and material, is the locus of the image of God."[97]

For Gunton, this vacillation was indicative of the "double-mind of the West" (that is, the tendency to fluctuate between what Gunton somewhat simplistically referred to as Hebraic and Hellenistic views on human physicality).[98] In truth, Calvin himself seemed to

---

94. Barth, *CD* 1/2, 728; cf. *CD*, 3/2 where Barth critiques Calvin's "platonic" handling of anthropology.
95. Jean Boisset, *Sagesse et Sainteté dans la Pensée de Jean Calvin* (Paris: Université de France, 1959), 284, 221. Cited in Charles Partee, *Calvin and Classical Philosophy* (Louisville: Westminster John Knox, 2006), 111.
96. Marshall, "John Calvin," 119; citing Calvin, *Inst.* 3.9.4. Indeed, this was not only occasion in which Calvin would refer to the body as a prison. See *Inst.* 3.6.5. Calvin here quotes from Plato's *Phaedo*.
97. Gunton, *One, the Three and the Many*, 53n17.

recognize, and indeed lament, an occasional double-mindedness in his treatment of embodiment. At one point he even expressed public regret for his tendency to speak "grossly" of the body. As Bouwsma recounts, Calvin "apologized to his congregation for implying that it [that is, the body] might be intrinsically corrupt. 'Our bodies,' he emphasized, 'are in their essence, good creations of God.'"[99] Yet while Gunton may be correct to note a certain double-mindedness in Calvin,[100] it seems *absurd* that this tendency is really "all a function" of the "Augustinian heritage."[101] As we have seen, Calvin read Plato as well as Augustine; thus one could also trace the supposed appearances of Platonic dualism to such works as the *Phaedo*.[102] Here again Gunton employed the *Augustinian* adjective in a rather careless fashion. Thus as Schwöbel indicates, the word has begun to function merely as "red flag" that indicates "problems in the Western tradition."[103]

The actual relation between Calvin and Augustine was more complex.[104] In his *Institutes*, Calvin went well beyond Augustine to claim that the divine image is discernible in every part of human being, "even in the body itself."[105] Yet in other instances, Calvin followed Augustine in asserting that "the mind . . . is [God's] true image."[106] At one point, Calvin chastised Augustine for being "excessively addicted to the philosophy of Plato,"[107] while elsewhere,

---

98. Ibid.
99. See Calvin, *Serm.* no. 58 on Job. Cited in William J. Bouwsma, *John Calvin: A Sixteenth Century Portrait* (New York: Oxford University Press, 1988), 134.
100. Once again, the veracity of this charge is not the primary concern of this chapter.
101. Gunton, *Promise of Trinitarian Theology*, 121.
102. See Partee, *Calvin and Classical Philosophy*, 111n28.
103. See Schwöbel, "Shape of Gunton's Theology: On the Way Towards a Fully Trinitarian Theology," in Harvey, *Theology of Colin Gunton*, 207n59.
104. As Bouwsma notes, "Calvin's age was utterly eclectic." Thus a simplistic identification of his influences seems "unlikely to yield major returns," *John Calvin*, 2–3.
105. Calvin, *Inst.* 1.15.3.
106. Calvin, *Com. Acts* 17.22. For further context on this discussion, see Bouwsma, *Calvin*, 79.
107. Calvin, *Com. John* 1.3, trans. William Pringle (Grand Rapids: CCEL, 1847), 18.

when discussing creation and the nature of evil, Marshall notes that "Calvin's position is much closer to Plato's than to Augustine's."[108] For Augustine, the full goodness of God's creation required that evil is not a reality *in se*, but only a privation of good (*malum est privatio boni*).[109] Calvin rejected this contention.[110] Thus it is only in the light of this complex relationship that we are prepared to render some conclusions regarding the validity of Gunton's charges.

Summing Up: Calvin and Augustine

First, there are moments in which both Calvin and Augustine seem to reveal a similar weakness on the subject of embodiment. As we have seen, Calvin himself would admit as much with regard to himself. Second, both Calvin and Augustine made genuine strides to overcome this limited dualism in order to embrace a more positive treatment of embodiment. Yet third, while Gunton may be right to note an abiding double-mindedness in the Western treatment of physicality, he was surely wrong to attribute "all" of this to the "Augustinian heritage."[111] Such language, even if typological, serves to damage Gunton's credibility. It does so by tethering a viable historical insight (the so-called double-mindedness of the West on the subject of embodiment) to an oversimplified origination. And with that we must move to sum up our treatment of Augustine and the Reformation era.

---

108. Marshall, "John Calvin," in 119.
109. See Augustine, *Conf.* 7.12; *nat. b.* 1.
110. See Calvin, *De aeterna Dei praedestinatione*, in *Corpus Reformatorum*, 8:353. Cited in Marshall, "John Calvin," 119.
111. Gunton, *Promise of Trinitarian Theology*, 121.

Beyond Luther and Calvin

In the preceding sections, we examined Gunton's arguments regarding Augustine's influence upon both Luther and Calvin. Yet it should go without saying that Augustine's "Reformation legacy" is far larger than these two men. Thus while some in the period would draw upon Augustine's doctrine of grace to counter an allegedly resurgent Pelagianism, others would read Augustine very differently.

For opponents of Luther and Calvin, Augustine "had contended not only against Pelagius but also against the Manicheans, to whom the Protestant denial of free will . . . was manifesting a strong family resemblance."[112] Beyond this, Augustine's anti-Donatist polemics were used to show Protestant "schismatics" that "there was no graver sin than sectarianism."[113] After all, the real Augustine "made unity the fundamental attribute of the church."[114] On the subject of justification, the Council of Trent (1545–1563) would respond to Luther's *sola fide* with the contention that "love was more central to the Augustinian system than faith."[115] And when the conversation turned again to the nature of the sacraments, Augustine's "haphazard"[116] statements would be used by virtually every side in this ongoing debate.[117] In short, Luther and Calvin were hardly the only "Augustinians" of their day.

Yet while there were diverse appropriations of Augustine's legacy throughout the sixteenth century (and beyond), our concern has been to respond to Gunton's *specific charges*, and for Gunton himself, the "Reformation chapter" in Augustine's afterlife was focused almost exclusively on the work Luther and Calvin. In his mind, these men

---

112. *CT*, 4:259; cited in reference to both Erasmus and Henry VIII.
113. Ibid., 274.
114. Ibid., 84.
115. Ibid., 253. These words are those of Pelikan.
116. The word is that of Calvin, *Replies to Joachim Westphal*, 3. Cited in *CT*, 4:196.
117. *CT*, 4:196.

occupied the "borderlands" between Augustine's medieval and early modern inheritors.[118]

Conclusions

With regard to the Reformation era, Gunton's claim was that Augustine's *monistic* imbalance in the doctrine of the Trinity led to individualistic consequences, a misunderstanding of biblical community, and a focus of the "mono-causal" will of God. Beyond this, Gunton also claimed that Augustine's Platonic *dualism* (while "controlled" enough to avoid an outright condemnation)[119] also contributed to a "double-mindedness" in the Western treatment of materiality. In response, our verdict was as follows: in his link between Augustine and the dawn of modern thought, Gunton's *Reformation argument* was often lacking both in nuance and in fairness. Indeed, at certain points, it was simply false.

On Luther, Gunton was wrong to claim that Augustine's pneumatology lacked an emphasis upon the Spirit's outward role in bringing freedom in and through community. Likewise, on the subject of *embodiment*, Gunton's claims regarding Luther's "Augustinian" errors were lacking both in specificity and in evidence. Thus again his case proceeded by way of assertion rather than argumentation. Despite such weaknesses, Pelikan did reveal a *potential* connection between Augustine's inward focus (as seen in the *Confessions*),[120] and the so-called introspective conscience of both Luther and the West.

On Calvin, Gunton's Augustinian narrative received similarly mixed reviews. As we saw, there were moments in which both Calvin and Augustine did evidence a *dualistic* tendency on the subject

---

118. Gunton, *Promise of Trinitarian Theology*, 146.
119. Gunton, *Triune Creator*, 76.
120. See again our treatment of this in ch. 3.

of embodiment. Yet despite this tension, both made genuine strides to embrace a more positive (and biblical) treatment of human physicality. Thus while Gunton may be right to note an abiding "double-mindedness" in the Western treatment of embodiment, he was surely wrong to attribute "all" of this to the "Augustinian heritage."[121] Such language (even if typological in nature) serves to damage Gunton's credibility by tethering a viable historical insight to an oversimplified origination. Yet if the Reformation chapter in Augustine's afterlife produced a more thoroughly negative assessment of Gunton's case, we will find a more sustainable component of his narrative as we turn to the final stop in our journey toward the dawn of modern thought.

---

121. Gunton, *Promise of Trinitarian Theology*, 121.

8

Gunton and Augustine's Modern Afterlife

In the opening sentence of *The One, the Three and the Many*, Gunton quoted the words of William Morris: "Modernism began and continues, wherever civilisation began and continues to deny Christ."[1] The statement is a frank one. Yet while others might point to Descartes or the Enlightenment as the geneses of "modernism," Gunton sought to draw attention to the theological origins of this phenomenon.[2] In particular, as we have seen, he often blamed deficiencies within the "Augustinian" inheritance for contributing to later problems. In the previous chapter, we sought to evaluate this charge as it pertained to Augustine's Reformation legacy. In the present one, we will examine Gunton's narrative regarding Augustine's influence upon the dawn of modern thought.

1. Gunton, *The One, the Three and the Many: God, Creation and the Culture of Modernity* (Cambridge: Cambridge University Press, 1993),, 1. Gunton cited Morris's words from Peter Fuller, *Theoria: Art, and the Absence of Grace* (London: Chatto & Windus, 1988), 139. The italics are those of Fuller.
2. So says Green, "The Protomodern Augustine? Colin Gunton and the Failure of Augustine," *International Journal of Systematic Theology* 9, no. 3 (July, 2009): 336; cf. Gunton, *One, the Three and the Many*, 1.

Once again, the work of Pelikan will provide some guidance, yet because this part of Gunton's narrative centers on the Augustinian influence upon René Descartes, we will not rely as heavily upon Pelikan's more narrowly *doctrinal* history.[3] Instead, we will engage with other specialists, as well as primary sources, in order to evaluate the charges at hand. Yet before such charges can be outlined, we must first begin by framing what is meant by the dawning of the modern ethos.

While various disciplines emphasize a variety of turning points between the medieval and modern eras, Bruce McCormack notes that "philosophers quite rightly begin their story with Cartesian rationalism."[4] In this vein, Gunton drew primarily upon philosophical and theological categories when stating that modernity arose "when the basis of rationality [was] displaced from divine to human agency."[5] In his view, this was a catastrophic shift.[6] Yet as we have noted, one of the distinct aspects of Gunton's modern genealogy was the claim that significant blame for this transition should be laid at the door of "Christian apologists," who inadvertently helped to pave the way for modern atheism.[7] One of these so-called apologists was the father of modern philosophy: René Descartes.

Augustine and Descartes

"*Cogito ergo sum* is perhaps the most famous sentence in all philosophy." As Gareth Matthews notes, the dictum "sounds

---

3. See *CT*, 5:6 for Pelikan's clarification that his is primarily a "doctrinal" (and not a political or philosophical) history.
4. Bruce McCormack, *Mapping Modern Theology: A Thematic and Historical Introduction*, ed. Kelly M. Kapic and Bruce L. McCormack (Grand Rapids, MI: Baker Academic, 2012), 2.
5. Gunton, *A Brief Theology of Revelation*, the 1993 Warfield Lectures (Edinburgh: T&T Clark, 1995), 48.
6. See again the opening sentence from Gunton, *One, the Three and the Many*, 1.
7. Gunton, *Revelation and Reason*, ed. P. H. Brazier (London: T&T Clark, 2008), 135; cf. *The Promise of Trinitarian Theology* (Edinburgh: T&T Clark, 1991), 30–31.

peculiarly modern."[8] Thus it bears reminding that René Descartes (1596–1650) was born into the bloody aftermath of religious Reformation. As Brad Gregory argues, it was in part the deadlocked doctrinal controversies of the Reformation that compelled Descartes to articulate universal truths based on reason alone, without reference to authority or tradition. In this regard, the idea of *sola ratio* would be called upon to succeed where the appeal to *sola scriptura* had failed to produce anything approaching a consensus.[9]

Descartes was trained by Jesuits, at the best school of the day, the college of La Flèche. It was here that he likely first encountered the writings of Augustine, in their original language.[10] Latin was required at the school and the mere usage of Descartes's native French could subject the boys to harsh punishment.[11] Despite such strict training, there is evidence that Descartes developed a deep affection for his Jesuit educators, as attested by the fact that he could later refer to one of them as "my second father."[12] Such early bonds were important to Descartes, for in the estimation of one biographer he maintained an "unswerving faithfulness" to his religious roots, perhaps even to the point of serving as a spy for Catholic interests against his native country.[13]

In his own way, Gunton also emphasized Descartes's religious background. As he argued, "It is completely anachronistic" to treat the father of modern philosophy as a freethinker who was attempting to loose the masses "from the shackles of religion."[14] Instead,

---

8. Gareth Matthews, *Thought's Ego in Augustine and Descartes* (Ithaca, NY: Cornell University Press, 1992), 11.
9. Brad S. Gregory, *The Unintended Reformation: How a Religious Revolution Secularized Society* (Cambridge, MA: Harvard University Press, 2012), 379, cf. 185.
10. See Matthews, *Thought's Ego*, 13.
11. See A. C. Grayling, *Descartes: The Life and Times of a Genius* (New York: Walker, 2005), 25.
12. Descartes, letter of February 9, 1645, cited in Grayling, *Descartes*, 22.
13. See Grayling, *Descartes*, 24.
14. Gunton, *Revelation and Reason*, 133.

Descartes remained, for Gunton, "a Catholic philosopher" who only "inadvertently" helped to undermine the Christian faith.[15] Despite these good intentions, Gunton believed that this undermining happened through the Cartesian elevation of (1) pervasive doubt as the road to certainty,[16] (2) mechanistic dualism as the view of God's creation,[17] and (3) individualistic reason as the inward path to truth.[18] On the whole, this view is shared by Pelikan, who writes that "although the piety of Descartes undoubtedly stood in the catholic tradition, the Cartesian method of philosophy by introspection did not stand or fall with the truth-claims of Christian faith, but increasingly compelled such truth-claims to justify themselves, if they could, by its canons."[19] In this sense, it seems uncontroversial to view Descartes as a crucial figure on the road to the kind of "modernism" defined by Gunton.[20] Yet a further question must now be answered: How did Gunton link the damage of Cartesian thought to Saint Augustine?

Gunton on the "Augustinianism" of René Descartes

For Gunton, the crucial link between Augustine and Descartes was to be found again in the influential implications of Augustine's inward turn.[21] As Gunton argued,

> Reliable, eternal knowledge . . . is possible for Descartes only by the pure concepts of the mind. Where Plato turned outward to eternity, Descartes turned inward to the mind. Only one more step was needed

---

15. Ibid., 134.
16. See Gunton, *Enlightenment and Alienation: An Essay Towards a Trinitarian Theology* (Grand Rapids: Eerdmans, 1985), 11.
17. Gunton, *The Triune Creator: A Historical and Systematic Study* (Grand Rapids: Eerdmans, 1998), 126–27.
18. See especially Gunton, *Enlightenment and Alienation*, 16–21.
19. *CT*, 3:307; cf. *CT*, 5:viii.
20. See again Gunton's definition of the modern shift toward independent human reason. Gunton, *Brief Theology of Revelation*, 48.
21. See, for instance, Gunton, *Revelation and Reason*, 42.

for Kant to deny the link Descartes made between the contents of his mind and the transcendent eternal world. . . . Thus, we might say, Descartes taught Kant to look within. But who taught Descartes? ... Is not the crucial figure of Augustine the one to whom we should look? . . . It can scarcely be denied that the decisive forerunner of the *Meditations'* subjective style of philosophizing is to be found in Augustine's *Confessions*.[22]

Here again, Gunton traced a rather simple line from Plato, to Augustine, to Descartes, and on to full-fledged modernism.

Beyond this, Gunton also claimed that Descartes's *cogito* was itself a restatement of Augustine's prior proof of his existence. In his own early battle with pervasive skepticism, Augustine had similarly dealt with questions of truth, delusion, and sensory perception. And like Descartes, he had countered such doubts by looking inward and asking for a truth that seemed indubitable. We find this argument in two early works that have already figured prominently in our study, *De Libero Arbitrio* and *De Vera Religione*.[23] In addition, we also find another version of the argument in a passage from *De Civitate Dei*. In this text, Augustine's proof of his existence emerges in the midst of his examination of the *imago Trinitatis* within his rational mind.[24]

Here, Augustine asserts that the rational mind's self-knowledge is unquestionable because, unlike other forms of sensory experience, the mind does not know itself "by some bodily sense, as we perceive the things outside of us." For Augustine, the bodily senses may be fooled, for instance, by a "delusive representation of images or phantasms," while the immaterial mind's self-knowledge (and thus its very existence) is beyond question. As Augustine puts it, "I am most certain that I am, and that I know and delight in this. In

---

22. Gunton, *Yesterday and Today: A Study of Continuities of Christology* (Grand Rapids: Eerdmans, 1983), 108–9.
23. Augustine, *Vera rel.* 39; *Lib. arb.* 2.3.
24. Augustine, *Civ.* 11.26.

respect of these truths, I am not at all afraid of the arguments of the Academicians, who say, What if you are deceived? For if I am deceived, I am. For he who is not, cannot be deceived; and if I am deceived, by this same token I am."²⁵ In this passage, we again see two themes that have been important for our study. First, there is the "inward turn" to find a certain trinity within the mental realm of the individual. And second, there is an abiding matter/spirit dualism that privileges the immaterial mind over and against the bodily realm. Beyond this, it is also interesting that in the Marcus Dods translation (used above), Augustine's passage contains a translator's footnote, which points out the similarity between Augustine's argument and the *cogito* of Descartes.

This similarity was not lost on Gunton. As he claimed, Augustine's argument of *fallo ergo sum* (in its various permutations) revealed that Descartes's later dictum was itself "straight out of Augustine."²⁶ Thus long before the solitary Frenchman cogitated in his stove-heated room, Augustine also located the building blocks of certainty by looking inward. This inward focus upon the rational mind was therefore what Gunton had in mind, when, in the context of the classroom, he made the rather brash claim that "Augustine is a 'modern' . . . [for] there is in Augustine this confidence that by looking inwards you will find the divine or the truth."²⁷

While it would be unfair to cite such spontaneous generalizations as a full expression of Gunton's views, he would also trace a similar trajectory in his academic publications. As Gunton argued, "We [moderns] believe that we know ourselves not by observing our relatedness with the other but by some kind of introspection, as a powerful tradition from Plato, through Augustine, Descartes, Kant to

---

25. Ibid.
26. Gunton, *Revelation and Reason*, 42.
27. Ibid., 42–43.

Freud has held."[28] For Gunton, this strand of rational introspection was the "strong though sometimes wavering line" that joined "Augustine and Descartes."[29]

Early Evaluations of Descartes's Relation to Augustine

What should we make of Gunton's argument? As history shows, Gunton was hardly the first to link Augustine and Descartes. In fact, several of Descartes's contemporaries would note that the *cogito* resembled reasoning to be found in Augustine.[30] One of these was a man named Colvius, who wrote to Descartes in order point out the similarity between the *cogito* and the aforementioned passage from *De Civitate Dei*. In response, Descartes would write the following:

> I am obliged to you for drawing my attention to the passage of St. Augustine relevant to my [*cogito ergo sum*]. I went today to the library of this town to read it, and I find that he does really use it to prove the certainty of our existence. He goes on to show that there is a certain likeness of the Trinity in us, in that we exist, we know that we exist, and we love the existence and the knowledge we have. I, on the other hand, use the argument to show that this I which is thinking is an immaterial substance with no bodily element. These are two very different things. In itself it is such a simple and natural thing to infer that one exists from the fact that one is doubting that it could have occurred to any writer. But I am very glad to find myself in agreement with St. Augustine, if only to hush the little minds who have tried to find fault with the principle.[31]

First, in response to this statement, it is important to note that the very distinction that Descartes draws between his insight and that of Augustine (that the thinking "I" is an "immaterial substance") is

---

28. Gunton, *One, the Three and the Many*, 202–3.
29. Gunton, *Yesterday and Today*, 110.
30. Matthews, *Thought's Ego in Augustine and Descartes*, 11.
31. Descartes, letter to Colvius, November, 14, 1640. Cited in Matthews, *Thought's Ego in Descartes and Augustine*, 12.

in fact a further *commonality* between the two men. As we have seen already, one of the stated grounds for Augustine's confidence in the rational mind's self-understanding is that we do not come into contact with such insights "by some bodily sense as we perceive the things outside of us."[32] Indeed, for Augustine, just as much as for Descartes, the rational mind was an incorporeal substance.[33] Thus Descartes's claim to uniqueness at this point is ill-founded.

Second, it is also important to note that that the truthfulness of Descartes's denial that he had previously come in contact with Augustine's argument has now been all but universally dismissed.[34] As Matthews notes, "Both the nature of Descartes's Jesuit education . . . and the strong similarities between passages in Descartes and [Augustine] make such innocence seem quite unlikely."[35] As further evidence, we may cite another of Descartes's contemporaries, a man named Antoine Arnauld (1612–1694). Arnauld drew Descartes's attention to a passage from *De Libero Arbitrio* that bears a striking similarity to a portion of the *Meditations*. Here, both Augustine and Descartes make reference to a great and hypothetical "deceiver," who may fool us on any number of points, except that of our own cognitive existence. As Augustine asserts, this truth remains unquestionable, for "if you did not exist, it would be impossible to be deceived."[36]

Yet if Descartes quite obviously learned from Augustine on such points, then why would he deny the influence? In answer, it seems that Descartes's concern was that his work be seen as a "new

---

32. Augustine, *Civ.* 11.26.
33. See Augustine, *Trin.* 15.12.21; 14.19.26.
34. See especially the meticulous scholarship of Zbigniew Janowski, *Augustinian-Cartesian Index: Texts and Commentary* (South Bend, IN: St. Augustine's Press, 2004). For a survey of the scholarly literature on this question, see Matthews, *Thought's Ego in Augustine and Descartes*, xi.
35. Matthews, *Thought's Ego in Augustine and Descartes*, 13.
36. Augustine, *Lib. arb.*, 2.3. See also Descartes, *Meditation*, 2.

philosophy," and thus, as even Hanby notes, "his project [provided] a vested interest in disavowing traditional authorities."[37] In Descartes's words, "It was necessary, once in the course of my life, to demolish everything and start again."[38] Thus he resolved to set aside tradition, and "to seek no knowledge other than that which could be found in myself or else in the great book of the world."[39] As Descartes put it, "The only way of freeing ourselves from these opinions [of others] is to make the effort . . . to doubt everything which we find to contain even the smallest suspicion of uncertainty."[40] And with this, we find a massive difference between Augustine and Descartes.

As Matthews notes, Augustine has no project like the purely rational reconstruction of human knowledge.[41] In fact, as we have seen, Augustine would come to stake his confidence upon traditional authority: "I would not have believed the gospel except as moved by the authority of the Catholic Church."[42] Thus a comprehensive correspondence with Descartes can be dismissed immediately. Yet long before the origins of "modernity" became a preoccupation for twentieth-century scholars, the *trajectory* between Augustine and Descartes (Gunton's "strong though sometimes wavering line")[43] had already been traced. As one of Descartes's confidants, Marin Mersenne (1588–1648) would put it, "The more learned someone becomes in the teachings of Augustine, the more willingly he will embrace the Cartesian philosophy."[44] Yet if this was argued as early as

---

37. Hanby, *Augustine and Modernity* (New York: Routledge, 2003), 167; cf. Menn, *Descartes and Augustine* (Cambridge University Press, 1998), ix, 10.
38. Descartes, *Meditations*, 1. Cited in Descartes, *Oeuvres*, ed. Charles Adam and Paul Tannery (Paris: J. Vrin, 1964), 7:17. Subsequent citations (*AT*) by volume and page number.
39. Descartes, *Discourse on Method. AT*, 6:1.
40. Descartes, *Principles of First Philosophy. AT*, 8:5.
41. Matthews, *Thought's Ego in Augustine and Descartes*, 61.
42. Augustine, *c. ep. Man.*, 5.
43. Gunton, *Yesterday and Today*, 110.
44. Cited in Menn, *Descartes and Augustine*, 17.

the seventeenth century, then wherein lies the controversy regarding Gunton's link between these thinkers?

Critique of Gunton on Augustine and Descartes

The most extensive critique of Gunton's claims on this subject has again come by way of Michael Hanby. In *Augustine and Modernity*, Hanby devotes nearly three hundred pages to refuting what he calls, the "dominant perspective" that "the modern Cartesian subject . . . originates in Augustine's thought."[45] For Hanby, Gunton's narrative furthers the "reductionist" tendencies of Charles Taylor,[46] who argued that "on the way from Plato to Descartes stands Augustine."[47] In Hanby's view, such statements fail to recognize that the true force behind Descartes's philosophy was not Augustine's neo-Platonic inwardness, but the "stoic voluntarism"[48] that was "institutionalized in the Christendom of Gregory the Great."[49] Parts of Hanby's argument have been dealt with previously,[50] yet for the sake of review, we will briefly survey the ground already covered.

On the one hand, we have noted the significance of Hanby's agreement with Gunton, that certain modern (and Cartesian) notions of inwardness and individual autonomy are the result of a "de-trinitization of God" and a faulty view of his creation.[51] Likewise, we have confirmed that Gunton often exaggerated such errors within Augustine's mature theology especially. In the end, however, we took issue with Hanby's refusal to link *any* of these tendencies toward

---

45. Hanby, *Augustine and Modernity*, i.
46. Ibid., 13.
47. Ibid., 8. Citing Charles Taylor, *Sources of the Self* (Cambridge: Harvard University Press, 1989), 127. For his own part, Gunton affirmed Taylor's work on this subject. See *One, the Three and the Many*, 202–3n36.
48. Ibid., 3.
49. Ibid., 133.
50. See especially chs. 2 and 5.
51. Hanby, *Augustine and Modernity*, 135.

inwardness and material dualism to certain aspects of Augustine's own thought.[52]

As we found, the question often hangs on "which Augustine" one is reading. And while Luther and Calvin mined the *later* (anti-Pelagian) portions of Augustine's corpus, an alternative tradition from Gregory the Great through Francesco Petrarch chose a different focus. This tradition combined certain statements from *De Libero Arbitrio* with the interior focus of the *Confessions* and the latter sections of *De Trinitate*.[53] Thus while this alternative tradition does not present a comprehensive handling of Augustine's mature theology, it does reveal another facet of Augustine's *legacy*. And for Gunton, Augustine's legacy was always the chief concern.

Descartes's Selective Augustinianism

As Pelikan notes, Descartes's *cogito* possessed "an undeniable ancestry in Augustine."[54] Thus, as even Hanby will acknowledge, it is incontestable that "Descartes exhibits a certain 'Augustinianism.' No thinker in the seventeenth century could escape Augustine's enormous shadow." Yet this statement invites the question, "If Descartes is an Augustinian, *what kind* of Augustinian is he?"[55] At this point, the scholarly literature is indeed immense.[56] Despite this, our own examination may be somewhat abbreviated by clarifying what Gunton was *not* claiming.

For Gunton, *what Augustine gave Descartes was not a comprehensive system, but a clue as to where one looks in order to perceive the incontestable truth*.[57] As Augustine wrote, "Do not go outward; return within

---

52. See again the conclusions of chs. 3 and 4.
53. See especially the relevant sections from ch. 5.
54. *CT*, 3:306.
55. Hanby, *Augustine and Modernity*, 137. Emphasis in the original.
56. A helpful survey of the relevant material exists in Menn's *Descartes and Augustine*, 3–17.
57. See again Gunton, *Yesterday and Today*, 110.

yourself. In the inward man dwells truth."⁵⁸ Given this, it is somewhat irrelevant to Gunton's history whether, as Hanby claims, Descartes inherited a decontextualized (or even semi-Pelagian) Augustinianism from his Jesuit roots.⁵⁹ Perhaps he did.⁶⁰ Likewise, it is similarly irrelevant to Gunton whether the "inward turn" of Descartes was identical to that of Augustine. It most certainly was not.⁶¹ Yet for Gunton these were not the key contentions. In Gunton's mind, the crucial question was whether a broadly Neoplatonic imbalance in Augustine (that is, his bent toward inwardness and a partial dualism in the treatment of material creation) influenced more drastic imbalances in the work of Descartes. And on this point, Gunton's argument receives substantial support.

As Stephen Menn asserts, "What Descartes took from Augustine was not, fundamentally, a set of metaphysical theses, but a *discipline* for approaching wisdom . . . [the] discipline that Augustine had himself taken from Plotinus"—the so-called inward turn.⁶² This, as Gunton termed it, was the "strong though sometimes wavering line" that joined Augustine and Descartes.⁶³ As Menn notes, "Descartes, like Plotinus and Augustine, [wanted] to turn the mind's eye from contemplating bodies to contemplating the mind itself, and then

---

58. Augustine, *vera. rel.* 39.72 (c. 390/391).
59. See chapter 4 in Hanby, *Augustine and Modernity*. In response to Hanby's argument, see again Barnes' contention that "in point of fact there may have never been a 'contextualised' reading of Augustine." Indeed his theology was almost always read "in bits and pieces." Michel Barnes, "Rereading Augustine's Theology of the Trinity," in *The Trinity: An Interdisciplinary Symposium on the Trinity*, ed. Stephen T. Davis, Daniel Kendall, and Gerald O'Collins (Oxford: Oxford University Press, 1999) 147.
60. As Grayling notes, Descartes's view on the basic goodness of human nature was both "unorthodox" and positively anti-Augustinian. Grayling, *Descartes*, 187.
61. More on this anon. See Quillen, "Renaissance to the Enlightenment," in *Augustine through the Ages: An Encyclopedia*, ed. Allan Fitzgerald (Grand Rapids: Eerdmans, 1999), 721.
62. Menn, *Descartes and Augustine*, 393. Emphasis in the original.
63. Gunton, *Yesterday and Today*, 110.

to contemplating God."⁶⁴ Thus, as Carol Quillen argues, Descartes found in Augustine a

> method for pursuing [wisdom] that was independent of sense perception. . . . Through his reading of the "Platonists" . . . Augustine learned to posit an incorporeal yet intelligible realm that was both utterly inaccessible to the senses and the locus of the good, which is God. . . . Augustine's distinction between the corporeal and the incorporeal and his conviction that knowledge of God is best sought by turning inward rather than outward find echoes in Descartes' much *starker* dualism.⁶⁵

All this lends weight to Gunton's argument. As we have seen in chapters 3 and 4, the key place at which Gunton's (often-overblown) critique has merit pertains to certain implications of Augustine's inward turn.

As Augustine wrote in his *Confessions*, "I was admonished by the Platonic books to return into myself."⁶⁶ For Augustine, these "Platonists" were providential in preparing him for yet another author: the apostle Paul.⁶⁷ As Augustine wrote, "I seized the sacred writings of your Spirit and especially the apostle Paul . . . and found that all the truth I had read in the Platonists was stated here together with the commendation of your grace."⁶⁸ Thus when Paul spoke of seeing the divine as "but a poor reflection" in the looking glass (1 Corinthians 13), Augustine took this as an invitation to see upon the metaphorical "mirror," an imperfect image of the Trinity.

Yet in turning to this mirror, Augustine's Platonism once again revealed its influence. Instead of seeing a whole person reflecting dimly the image of Christ (Col. 1:15), Augustine saw the internal

---

64. Menn, *Descartes and Augustine*, 399.
65. Carol Quillen, "Renaissance to the Enlightenment," in 720–21. Emphasis mine.
66. Augustine, *Conf.* 7.10.16.
67. See ch. 3.
68. Augustine, *Conf.* 7.21.27.

workings of an immaterial *mind* reflecting dimly the three-in-oneness of the Trinity.[69] This contributed to a number of key developments: (1) the conclusion that the immaterial rational mind was the image of God,[70] (2) the sacred triads as descriptions of the Trinity, and (3) the abiding preference for mind over matter.[71] None of this diminishes the distinctly Christian quality of Augustine's overall theology,[72] yet it does reveal an influential propensity for inwardness and material dualism.[73] It was this propensity that was appropriated by aspects of Cartesian thought. As Pelikan puts it, Descartes's "introspective philosophy [stands] in the apostolic succession of Augustine's Confessions."[74] And as Wayne Hankey argues, "Augustine's Platonism not only confidently borrows from his predecessors . . . but also looks forward to the rigorous reasonings of the mediaevals and of Descartes."[75] "No one who regards Descartes as essential to the construction of the modern self can deny the positive role of Augustine in Descartes's revolution."[76]

In conclusion, both Hanby and Augustine's other defenders are helpful in reiterating that, when his theology is taken whole, Augustine is *not* somehow a "proto-Cartesian" theologian. Nor was he a "proto-modern" thinker,[77] if by this prefix we mean "the first" of those to follow. Gunton's remarks, at times, inferred as much.[78] Thus

---

69. See ch. 3.
70. See Augustine, *Trin.* 12.7.12.
71. See ch. 4.
72. As we have noted, Augustine's perspective on the *imago Trinitatis* was largely motivated by a triune reading of the plurals in Gen. 1:26.
73. See again the conclusions from chs. 3 and 4.
74. Pelikan, in the "Foreword" to Fitzgerald, *Augustine through the Ages*, xiv.
75. Wayne J. Hankey, "Philosophical Religion and the Neoplatonic Turn to the Subject," in *Deconstructing Radical Orthodoxy: Postmodern Theology, Rhetoric and Truth*, ed. Wayne Hankey and Douglas Hedley (Burlington, VT: Ashgate, 2005), 23.
76. Wayne J. Hankey, "Between and Beyond Augustine and Descartes: More Than a Source of the Self," in *Augustinian Studies* 32, no. 1 (2001): 65.
77. So, rightly, Green, "The Protomodern Augustine," 328–41.
78. As when, in context of the classroom, he would state that the *cogito* was itself "straight out of Augustine," and thus "Augustine is a modern." See again Gunton, *Revelation and Reason*, 42–43.

the massive differences between Augustine and Descartes remain important. As Quillen notes,

> For Augustine the turn inward ultimately leads to the recognition of our dependence on God even for knowledge about our selves. Furthermore, without God's grace to redirect our perverted will, we would be incapable of accepting and acting on what we know. . . . Thus for Augustine the turn inward embodied in the *Confessions* signals neither a boundless confidence in the human capacity to know nor a radical subjectivism. This is very different from Descartes' turn inward. . . . For Descartes and his successors, reason provided humans with capacity to master our environment through understanding, and the will was clearly subordinate to it. Ignorance, not perversity, was the problem.[79]

In all of this, the mature Augustine remained far from both Descartes and the brand of modernism decried by Gunton. Yet the "complexity" and "ambiguity" of Augustine's legacy (to use Quillen's words) can be seen in the fact that, while his own thought steers clear of a full-fledged confidence in human reason, a selective reading of Augustine no doubt influenced the Cartesian slide in this direction.[80]

We do not control the way our written thoughts will be appropriated. Thus as Pelikan chronicles, it was "the Augustinian method of introspection" that was (by way of Descartes and others) "transformed into an autonomous source of truth."[81] In this more limited regard, Gunton's link between Augustine and modernity receives a cautious commendation.

Beyond Descartes

Yet what of those who followed on Descartes? Throughout the eighteenth and nineteenth centuries, Augustine's emphasis upon an utterly sovereign God and an intractably sinful people would, at

---

79. Quillen, "Renaissance to the Enlightenment," in 721.
80. Ibid.
81. *CT*, 3:306.

times, be lost almost entirely. As O'Donnell notes, "If moderns agree with anyone, they probably prefer Pelagius."[82] Yet despite this marked difference with regard to basic human goodness and potential, Pelikan illustrates that the importance of the inward turn remained throughout the modern era.

Thus while Immanuel Kant (1724–1804) rejected the rational proof behind Descartes's religion, he retained its inward focus. As Kant put it, "Two things fill the mind with ever new and increasing wonder . . . the starry heaven above and the moral law within me." For Kant, this inner compass became "the essence of true religion."[83] As Pelikan tells it, "The 'moral law within' and the entire range of affections, obligations, and experiences that accompanied it" became a bulwark that remained "even when the supposedly transcendent grounds of faith . . . were subjected to persistent attack."[84]

As John Wesley (1703–1791) stated, "I have sometimes been almost inclined to believe that the wisdom of God has . . . permitted the external evidence of Christianity to be more or less clogged and encumbered for this very end, that men (of reflection especially) might not altogether rest there, but be constrained to *look into themselves* also and attend to the light shining in their hearts."[85]

In a very different way, Friedrich Schleiermacher (1768–1864) would continue the emphasis upon the inward realm of personal experience.[86] As Pelikan notes, the Schleiermachian stress upon the feeling of absolute dependence could be described as an "affectional transposition of doctrine."[87] And while Augustine would have been aghast at some of Schleiermacher's *transpositions*, his inward turn

---

82. O'Donnell, *Augustine: A New Biography*, 276.
83. Immanuel Kant, *Critique of Pure Reason*. Cited in *CT*, 5:118.
84. *CT*, 5:118.
85. John Wesley, *A Plain Account of Genuine Christianity*, 3.4–5. Cited in *CT*, 5:118. Italics added.
86. See *CT*, 5:134–35.
87. *CT*, 5:119.

did provide an inspiration for Schleiermacher's project.[88] Thus, as Michael Scanlon notes, "Augustine was the greatest influence on . . . the father of liberal Protestant theology."[89]

An examination of subsequent modern thinkers could indeed go on and on.[90] Yet the aim of this chapter was *not* to trace Augustine's influence *throughout* modernity, but to evaluate Gunton's narrative regarding Augustine and the "dawn" of modern thought. That task is now accomplished.

Conclusions

Gunton's claim was that certain Augustinian weaknesses contributed to problems within the history of modern Western thought. In particular, he claimed that Augustine's *monistic* imbalance in the doctrine of the Trinity led to individualistic consequences, a misunderstanding of biblical community, and a focus of the "monocausal" will of God. Beyond this, Gunton also claimed that Augustine's Platonic *dualism* (while "controlled" enough to avoid an outright condemnation)[91] would go on to contribute to a "double-mindedness" in the Western treatment of materiality, and a post-Cartesian bent toward inwardness and subjectivity.

In response, our verdict was as follows: In his link between Augustine and the dawn of modern thought, Gunton's case is often lacking both in nuance and in fairness. Indeed, at certain points, it is simply false. Despite these faults, however, one aspect of Gunton's narrative remains more viable. As Pelikan attests, and others confirm, Augustine's "inward turn"—that is, his decision to look inward in

---

88. Thus Pelikan deals with Schleiermacher under a heading that is itself an allusion to Augustine: "God and the Soul." *CT*, 5:130.
89. Michael J. Scanlon, "Modern Theology," in Fitzgerald, *Augustine through the Ages*, 826.
90. For one such study, see Stanley J. Grenz, *The Social God and the Relational Self: A Trinitarian Theology of the Imago Dei* (Louisville: Westminster John Knox Press, 2001), chapters 2–3.
91. Gunton, *Triune Creator*, 76.

order to encounter truth (*Conf.* 7.10)—proved influential in shaping certain modern tendencies. Among these tendencies were propensities toward inwardness, individualism, and a dualistic treatment of material creation. To be fair, many of these tendencies resulted from a rather selective reading of Augustine, yet as we have seen, this selective reading was something Gunton shared with both Augustine's medieval and modern inheritors.[92]

In the selective Augustinianism of René Descartes, we noted a more sustainable component of Gunton's narrative. While Luther and Calvin drew heavily upon Augustine's mature (and often anti-Pelagian) writings, Descartes (like Petrarch before him) drew more from Augustine's earlier and more philosophical treatises. Thus his selective appropriation of these texts proved friendlier to those "modernistic" developments decried by Gunton. Here the relative optimism of *De Libero Arbitrio* was combined with the interiority of the *Confessions* and the latter sections of *De Trinitate*. Thus while Augustine did not provide Descartes with a comprehensive system, he likely did provide an important clue as to where one looks in order to perceive the "indubitable."

As Augustine taught Descartes, one should look within the human self, to the rational and immaterial mind, in order to encounter truth. Here, in the Platonic presuppositions of Augustine's inward turn, we noted the partially Augustinian origins of both the *cogito*, and a subsequent shift toward inwardness and subjectivity. Augustine himself would likely not be fond of such developments; yet this does not change the fact that a selective appropriation of his work would contribute to this evolution. At this more narrow point, we found a cautious corroboration for one element within Gunton's telling of Augustine's afterlife.

---

92. See again Barnes, "Rereading Augustine," 147.

9

Gunton and the Triune Corrective (Part One): Irenaeus as an "Antidote" to Certain Augustinian Imbalances

In the prior chapters we explored the viability of Gunton's arguments regarding aspects of Augustine's legacy. Yet our examination may only be complete by returning to a time *before* Augustine. This is so because, in Gunton's mind, while aspects of Augustine's thought should be seen as "honied poison,"[1] there existed some potential antidotes within the preceding tradition. As Bradley Green notes, "Gunton's favored solution to the problems spawned in Western theology [was] the trinitarian theology of the Cappadocian Fathers and Irenaeus."[2] Thus Gunton's charge was not merely that Augustine

---

1. See ch. 1 for the Barthian origins of this epithet; cf. Gunton, *Father, Son, and Holy Spirit: Toward a Fully Trinitarian Theology* (London: T&T Clark, 2003), 41.
2. Bradley G. Green, *Colin Gunton and the Failure of Augustine: The Theology of Colin Gunton in Light of Augustine* (Eugene, OR: Pickwick, 2011), 7.

contributed to later problems, but also that he *failed to appropriate the achievements of these theologians who preceded him.*

In the next two chapters (9–10), we must ask whether this remains a viable contention. In the present chapter, we will examine Irenaeus and his subversion of various dualisms in the doctrine of creation. Then, in chapter 10, we will turn to the Cappadocian treatments of the doctrine of the Trinity, and to the development of what Gunton viewed as a relational alternative to Augustine's alleged monistic imbalance.[3] In dealing with these figures, the limited parameters of this study should again be noted. Once again, our goal is not to present a comprehensive handling of Irenaeus or the Cappadocian fathers. Instead, we will seek merely to evaluate (1) whether these figures indeed offer consistent correctives to the imbalances decried by Gunton, and (2) whether Augustine can indeed be blamed for not appropriating their work more fully. In the end, our conclusion over the next two chapters will involve a kind of "split decision." While Irenaeus might have provided a helpful counterbalance to certain Augustinian tendencies in the treatment of creation and the *imago Trinitatis*, Gunton's treatment of the Cappadocians (in juxtaposition to Augustine) will be found to be more dubious.

Irenaeus

Gunton viewed Irenaeus (c. AD 140–202) as "the church's greatest theologian of creation."[4] Thus he returned continually to the Irenaean imagery of a God who creates and sustains by his "two hands." As Irenaeus wrote, "It was not angels . . . who made us, nor who formed us . . . nor anyone else, except the Word of the Lord. . . . For God did not stand in need of these [beings] . . . as

---

3. See Gunton, *The Promise of Trinitarian Theology* (Edinburgh: T&T Clark, 1991), 94.
4. Gunton, *The Christian Faith: An Introduction to Christian Doctrine* (Oxford: Blackwell, 2002), 10. See ch. 1.

if He did not possess His own hands ... the Son and the Spirit, by whom and in whom, freely and spontaneously, He made all things."[5] Gunton's references to this metaphor are too numerous to cite, yet he esteemed Irenaeus not merely for a lone analogy. Gunton also praised him for what he saw to be a triune alternative to Augustine's dualism. As Gunton argued, "There is a difference between the doctrine of creation classically conceived, as by Irenaeus, and its increasingly voluntarist and non-trinitarian expression in Augustine and his mediaeval successors."[6] Beyond these "medieval successors," Gunton also claimed that "modernity can be traced to a reaction against a deficient doctrine of creation, in particular one that failed to develop the possibilities within Irenaeus's trinitarian theology."[7] With regard to Augustine, we have addressed these issues under the categories of (1) *matter*, (2) *time*, and (3) *mediation*.[8] Thus we will now evaluate whether Irenaeus actually offers consistent alternatives in these three areas.

Mud and Matter

In chapter 4, we saw that while Gunton was sometimes unfair in his claims against Augustine's doctrine of creation, there was indeed a partial (but abiding) dualism in Augustine's thought. In this dualism, we found that materiality was often relegated to the lower rungs on a ladder of being. In addition, we also argued (in some contrast with Green) that one cannot simply dismiss Gunton's charges merely by acknowledging that Augustine's dualism was of course "limited."[9]

---

5. Irenaeus, *Against the Heresies* [hereafter: *AH*], 4.20.1; cf. 5.1.3.
6. Gunton, *The One, the Three and the Many: God, Creation and the Culture of Modernity* (Cambridge: Cambridge University Press, 1993), 205.
7. Ibid., 151; cf. *The Triune Creator: A Historical and Systematic Study* (Grand Rapids: Eerdmans, 1998), 74.
8. See ch. 4.
9. See Green, *Gunton and Failure of Augustine*, 89, 96, 174.

For Gunton, this limitation was precisely the problem in that it made Augustine's imbalances more transferable to the subsequent tradition.[10] Yet how did Irenaeus handle matter differently?

As Gunton put it, "Irenaeus was a theologian of *crisis*."[11] As such, his emphases were often determined by the heresies of his opponents.[12] While the same could often be said of Augustine, for Irenaeus such heresies involved the scourge of "so-called *gnosis*."[13] As Pelikan notes, this diverse (and purportedly Christian movement) "taught the cosmic redemption of the spirit through knowledge."[14] Thus despite the great variety of gnostic systems, "all included a diagnosis of the cosmological descent of the human spirit into matter and sin."[15] In gnosticism, creation coincided with the fall, while redemption was made possible by "the presence of [a] divine element in the world and in part of humanity."[16] Thus some gnostics counseled converts to "look for [the Supreme God] by taking *yourself* as the starting point . . . you will find him *in* yourself."[17] Here was a kind of gnostic "inward turn," away from matter, and toward the spark of the divine *within* the human mind.

In contrast to such gnostic systems, Irenaeus reveled in the goodness of created matter. In so doing, he emphasized that while humanity was shaped from "mud,"[18] Adam's body was also molded by the very "hands" of God, "the Son and Holy Spirit."[19] This emphasis

10. See again Gunton, *Triune Creator*, 76.
11. Gunton, *The Barth Lectures*, ed. P. H. Brazier (London: T&T Clark, 2007), 29. Emphasis mine.
12. See Denis Minns, *Irenaeus* (London: Chapman, 1994), 79.
13. Thus the extended title to Irenaeus's *magnum opus*: "Unmasking and overthrow of *so-called knowledge*." Emphasis mine. See Eric Osborn, *Irenaeus of Lyons* (Cambridge: Cambridge University Press, 2001), 4. For an introduction to various gnostic theologies, see Robert M. Grant, *Irenaeus of Lyons* (London: Routledge, 1997), chapters 2–3. Gunton's fullest treatment of Gnosticism comes in *Triune Creator*, 47ff.
14. *CT*, 182.
15. Ibid., 87.
16. Ibid., 88.
17. Ibid., 86–87. As relayed by Hippolytus of Rome, *On Heresies*, 8.15.1–2. Emphasis added.
18. Or "clay" (*limum*). See *AH*, 4.20.1.

upon the literal *ground* of human being was also transferred to the Gospels. Thus Irenaeus made much of the fact that Jesus healed by spitting on the earth and making mud (John 9:6).[20] For Irenaeus, this revealed the continuity of creation and redemption.[21] Likewise, Irenaeus also emphasized that eucharistic bread came forth from earthen soil.[22] In all of this, the treatment of materiality was positive, and in all of this one notes a decidedly different tone from that within portions of Augustine's writings.[23]

Materiality and the *Imago Dei*

Irenaeus also differed from Augustine in his treatment of the *imago Dei*. In the Irenaean view, as described by Minns, "when God fashioned the earth-creature from mud he did so after the pattern of the *body* of Christ."[24] Thus, as Steenberg notes, "Irenaeus is clear that humanity is created not in the image of God generally, but in the image of the Son who is known incarnationally."[25] Behind this position stood the various New Testament passages that speak of Christ, or the Son, as "the image" of God (Col. 1:15; 2 Cor. 4:4) to which we must be conformed (1 Cor. 15:49). Thus the basic Irenaean argument regarding the divine image may be summarized as follows: *imago Dei* as *imago Christi*.

As Irenaeus put it, "[God] made man in the image of God; and the image of God is the Son, after whose image man was made: and for

---

19. *AH*, 4. Preface, 4.
20. The spittle here is an allusion to the Spirit, which for Irenaeus was continually compared to the water that moistens the earth and brings forth life and growth. See Osborn, *Irenaeus*, 188; cf. *AH*, 3.17.1–2.
21. See *AH*, 5.15.2. Cited in Minns, *Irenaeus*, 99.
22. See *AH*, 5.2.3.
23. See the conclusions from ch. 4.
24. So says Minns, *Irenaeus*, 60. Emphasis added. Cf. *AH*, 5.16.2. Pelikan reiterates this point, CT, 1:145.
25. M. C. Steenberg, *Of God and Man: Theology as Anthropology from Irenaeus to Athanasius* (London: T&T Clark, 2009), 37.

this cause He appeared in the end of the times that He might show the image (to be) like unto Himself."²⁶ We will return to this theme in our treatment of triune mediation, yet for now we merely note the contrast with Augustine's handling of the *imago Dei* as the *imago Trinitatis*. As Mary Clark notes, "Augustine placed the image in the human soul," while Irenaeus "found the image in the human body, modeled after the flesh of Christ."²⁷ In truth, Irenaeus also connected certain immaterial faculties (such as reason and free will) to the *imago Dei*.²⁸ Thus his goal was not to downplay the importance of such inner capacities, but to integrate them into a more holistic treatment of the divine image. In this way, as Irenaeus argued, the *whole human* was

> moulded after the pattern of the Son. For it is the human being, and not a part of the human being, which, by the hands of the Father (that is, by the Son and the Spirit), comes to be in the likeness of God. Soul and Spirit might be part of the human being, but they cannot constitute the whole of the human being. The perfect human being is a mixture and union of the soul, which receives the Spirit of the Father, mingled with that flesh which is moulded by hand according to the image of God.²⁹

Irenaeus elsewhere confirms this sentiment when he claims that God gave Adam "the outline of his [that is, Christ's] own form,"³⁰ even though "the Word was as yet invisible . . . so that by means of his resemblance to the Son, man might become precious to the Father."³¹

---

26. Irenaeus, *Demonstration of Apostolic Preaching* [hereafter, *Dem.*], trans. A. Robinson (New York: MacMillan, 1920), 22.
27. Mary T. Clark, "Irenaeus," in *Augustine through the Ages: An Encyclopedia*, ed. Allan Fitzgerald (Grand Rapids: Eerdmans, 1999), 457. For Augustine's own treatment of this issue, see *Trin.* 12.7.12 as examined in ch. 3 of this study. See also Stanley J. Grenz, *The Social God and the Relational Self: A Trinitarian Theology of the Imago Dei* (Louisville: Westminster John Knox Press, 2001), 144–48.
28. See *AH*, 4.4.3.
29. Ibid., 5.6.1.
30. Irenaeus, *Dem.* 22.
31. *AH*, 5.16.2.

In all of this, Irenaeus's account of the *imago Dei* stands distinct from almost all other premodern versions of the doctrine.³² It does so by being able to incorporate the body (and not merely the mind or soul) within its scope. Thus as Cairns notes, the "strongly physical emphasis" in Irenaeus remains "one of his most valuable contributions to theological thought."³³ Likewise, as Stanley Grenz points out, this holistic emphasis also fits with certain trends within Old Testament scholarship, where "a new consensus has emerged that concludes that whatever the *imago Dei* may be, it embraces the human person as a whole, encompassing, not separating, the physical and spiritual aspects."³⁴ Thus, as Gerhard von Rad writes, "One will do well to split the physical from the spiritual as little as possible: the whole man is created in God's image."³⁵

The contemporary payoffs of an Irenaeus-inspired image doctrine are also worth considering. After all, if "reason" or "free-will" is not what makes one truly human, then one's *protected status* as an image bearer need not be imperiled in those many instances in which such faculties are not apparent—say in cases of dementia, infirmity, and yes, even in the womb.³⁶ In addition, if "reason" is not the essence of the *imago Dei*, then one need not be surprised if even certain animals (especially primates) are found to display a level of thought that can scarcely be defined as anything other than a kind of rationality.³⁷

---

32. There is a partial exception to this tend in Calvin, who asserts that "even the body itself" shows forth some "sparks" of the divine image. Yet as the presence of the word *even* in the above quotation makes clear, Calvin's position remains some distance from that of Irenaeus. Thus as he goes on to state, "There is no doubt that the *proper* seat of [God's] image is the soul." John Calvin, *Institutes of the Christian Religion*, ed. J. T. McNeill, trans. F. L. Battles (Philadelphia: Westminster Press, 1960), 1.15.3. Italics mine.
33. David Cairns, *The Image of God in Man*, rev. ed. (London: Collins, 1973), 77.
34. Grenz, *The Social God and the Relational Self*, 194.
35. Gerhard von Rad, *Genesis: A Commentary*, trans. John H. Marks, rev. ed. (Philadelphia: Westminster, 1973), 58. Cited in Grenz, *The Social God and the Relational Self*, 194.
36. It is significant that Gen. 9:6 demands an accounting for bloodshed on the specific grounds that humans have been made "in the image of God."
37. See, for instance, Wolfgang Kohler, *The Mentality of Apes* (London: Routledge, 1976).

And finally, in Irenaeus's holistic and reembodied account of image doctrine, Christians need not be concerned if certain older and more Platonic notions of the human soul are being replaced by more recent biblical and scientific understandings.

This last point is particularly relevant with regard to Augustine, for as J.J. O'Donnell bluntly puts it, "Whatever becomes of 'soul' will determine what becomes of Augustine. . . . If his view of the human person and his narrative account of the inner life is supplanted by better science, then all that he has been to centuries of devout and not so devout heirs could crumble very quickly into irrelevance."[38] While O'Donnell's claim may be an exaggeration, it does demonstrate the centrality of Augustine's notion of "the soul" to his entire theological edifice, and especially the *imago Dei*. If, as has been argued, the New Testament use of *psyche* should be more closely aligned with the Hebrew *nephesh* (understood more generally as "life"), then it matters little if the Platonic understanding of the soul as an immaterial entity which rules the body is jettisoned.[39] Likewise, if the *imago Dei* encompasses the human as a whole (just as it is the whole Christ who is the true image of God), then it would seem that Irenaeus's uniquely physical account of image doctrine deserves renewed reflection.

For his own part, Gunton gloried in this incarnational undergirding to Irenaeus's treatment of materiality. As he put it, "The basis of Irenaeus' affirmative attitude to the whole created order is Christological. If God in his Son takes to himself the reality of human flesh, then nothing created, and certainly nothing material, can be downgraded to unreality, semi-reality or treated as fundamentally

---

38. O'Donnell, *Augustine: A New Biography*, 326–27.
39. As N. T. Wright describes a more holistic Pauline anthropology, "*soma* is the whole person seen in terms of public space-time presence, *sarx* is the whole person seen in terms of corruptibility and perhaps rebellion, [and] *psyche* is the whole person seen in terms of, and from the perspective of, what we loosely call the 'inner' life." Wright, *The Resurrection of the Son of God* (Minneapolis: Fortress Press, 2003), 283.

evil."⁴⁰ As Gunton notes, there could be no graded chains of being in the Irenaean ontology,⁴¹ for such a move would simply concede too much to the gnostic heretics.⁴² Matter was created good, thus the material creation itself must be perfected. While the mature Augustine would certainly agree with much of this argument, we have also seen that his continual employment of a chain of being, and his abiding negativity toward certain aspects of material and temporal being, revealed some problematic tensions in his thought. In these regards, some help may be gained by turning to the contrasts to be found within the work of Irenaeus. Likewise, the helpful counterbalance to Augustine will continue as we turn now to examine the materiality of the age to come.

Materiality and the New Millennium

As is perhaps unsurprising, even Irenaeus's millenarian eschatology was tethered to a positive treatment of materiality. As he argued, "Neither the substance nor the essence of the creation will be annihilated."⁴³ Instead, God's kingdom will literally come on earth, at which point "each vine will have a thousand branches [and] each cluster ten thousand grapes."⁴⁴ Some evidence suggests that these statements were suppressed by later copyists who were perhaps embarrassed by the literalism (or was it the materiality?) of Irenaean eschatology.⁴⁵ As we have seen, this is yet another contrast with Augustine.⁴⁶ As Fredrikson notes, despite Augustine's mature belief in

---

40. Gunton, *Triune Creator*, 52.
41. Minns, *Irenaeus*, 33.
42. See Pelikan's comments in *CT*, 1:91.
43. *AH*, 5.36.1.
44. Ibid., 5.33.3.
45. Most medieval manuscripts omit the final chapters of book 5 in *Against the Heresies*. See Minns, *Irenaeus*, 124.
46. See again ch. 4.

the bodily resurrection, he maintained that our "corporeal bodies will dwell in the heavens: the Kingdom of God will *not* come on earth."[47]

For Gunton, these contrasts were to be lamented, *not* because Augustine's statements were straightforwardly heretical,[48] but because they were Christian enough to avoid the condemnations reserved for men like Origen, and yet dualistic enough to contribute to the material double-mindedness of the West.[49] It was therefore with this "double-mindedness" in view that Gunton would claim that Gnosticism "was not only an ancient heresy but remains the alternative to the Christian doctrine of creation in all eras."[50] In a moment we must evaluate the potential tensions within the Irenaean view of matter, yet for now we move again to the subject of temporality.

Time and Telos

For Gunton, Augustine evidenced an influential dualism, not only in his view of matter, but also in his view of *time*.[51] As proof, he appealed to (1) Augustine's belief in instantaneous creation, (2) his statement that time may be a "distension" of the human mind,[52] and (3) an eschatology that looked forward to the end of earthly temporality. In evaluating these charges, we were forced to acknowledge the complexity of Augustine's various statements.[53] Indeed Gunton sometimes claimed too much from isolated passages,[54] yet the fact

---

47. Fredriksen, "Apocalypse and Redemption in Early Christianity: From John of Patmos to Augustine of Hippo," *Vigiliae Christianae* 45 (1991): 166. Italics original.
48. See Gunton, *Triune Creator*, 74.
49. See Gunton, *One, the Three and the Many*, 53n17.
50. Gunton, *Triune Creator*, 227.
51. See ch. 4; cf. Gunton, *Triune Creator*, 83.
52. Augustine, *Conf.* 11.26.33.
53. Here we agreed with Gunton's more cautious statement that Augustine's view of time is not flatly wrong, but "bewilderingly many-sided." *Yesterday and Today: A Study of Continuities of Christology* (Grand Rapids: Eerdmans, 1983), 109.
54. See, for instance, *Conf.* 11.26.33 on time as *distentio*.

remains that Augustine did evidence a certain temporal dualism, as evidenced by Teske's rather striking contention that in the *Confessions*, "being in time, it seems, is a penalty for sin . . . [and] since our presence in time is the penalty of our fall, Augustine sees the purpose of Christ's coming as to set us free from time."[55]

Yet how did Irenaeus offer a superior handling of temporality? In Gunton's view, Irenaeus avoided temporal errors by refusing "a false eternalising of the divine economy."[56] By this, he meant that "no major contrast [was] drawn between the perfection of the timeless eternal and the imperfection of the temporal."[57] Instead, as Gunton argued, Irenaeus conceived of creation as a "project,"[58] with "a movement forward to the perfection of all things." Here "God provides, not for a *spatial* ascent out of the material world, but for a *temporal* movement in and with it, in eschatological perspective."[59] In other words, "The eternal is conceived as a time-embracing and not a time-denying reality." For Gunton, this perspective led him to ask "what might have happened had Augustine analyzed time on [this] basis rather than on the basis of a subjective experience of its fleetingness?"[60]

As one might expect, given the nature of his gnostic opponents, Irenaeus offers a strikingly positive treatment of temporal being.[61] And as Gunton notes, this is made possible at many points through a focus upon the divine *economy* (God's purposeful plan for all redemptive history).[62] Because God is the architect of time, "the

---

55. *Paradoxes of Time in Saint Augustine* (Milwaukee: Marquette University Press, 1996), 30–31.
56. Gunton, *One, the Three and the Many*, 84.
57. Ibid., 80.
58. Gunton, *Triune Creator*, 164. Gunton returns to this word repeatedly.
59. Gunton, *Christian Faith*, 25. Italics in original.
60. Gunton, *Yesterday and Today*, 130.
61. We will illustrate this presently.
62. Οἰκονομία was often rendered as *dispositio* by Irenaeus's Latin translators. As Douglas Farrow notes, one source for this term in Irenaeus is Eph. 1:9–10. Here it states that in Christ, God made known to us "the mystery of his will, according to his purpose, which he set forth in Christ as

change and movement of divine activity . . . give meaning to the story of mankind. They point to God and are seen only through God who moves directly in the world."[63] In this schema, both *time* and *change* may be viewed more positively. As Osborn notes, "they are not to be filtered from the process of knowledge (as Plato wished) for it was within their economies that the mind of God could be learnt."[64] We know God through his works in time, and it is through these redemptive acts that the Creator brings all things to their intended telos. Thus, for Irenaeus, time is linked to teleology.

Given Gunton's critique of Augustine's Neoplatonism, it bears noting that Irenaeus also garnered certain insights from Platonic thought. Shortly after Irenaeus's lifetime, Plotinus also would do battle with the gnostics,[65] and like Irenaeus, he would also critique their proliferation of first principles, and their extreme denigration of the physical world.[66] In similar fashion, Irenaeus also drew upon the Platonic distinction between *being* and *becoming*. As Minns notes, "Irenaeus used this formula to assert that only God *is* while everything else is in a state of coming into being or passing out of it."[67]

The difference between Irenaeus and more dualistic Platonists was what he did with this *becomingness*. In the view of Osborn, "Irenaeus was not conscious of [the] Platonic pattern in his thought [and] his accounts of body, physical world, incarnation and history were opposite to those of Plato."[68] For Irenaeus, mutability in time brought

---

a plan [οἰκονομίαν] for the fullness of time, to unite [or "sum up," ἀνακεφαλαιώσασθαι] all things in him, things in heaven and things on earth" (ESV). See Farrow, "St. Irenaeus of Lyons: The Church and the World," in *Pro Ecclesia* 4 (1995): 339.
63. So says Osborn, *Irenaeus*, 21.
64. Ibid., 94.
65. Ibid., 15–20.
66. See Plotinus, *Enneads*, 2.9.2; 2.9.4. Cited in Osborn, *Irenaeus*, 44.
67. Minns, *Irenaeus*, 34. See his subsequent citation of Plato, *Timaeus*, 27D–28A.
68. Osborn, *Irenaeus*, 16.

the potential that we might be conformed to the very likeness of Christ. Thus, as Donavan describes it, "Through the very process of change the unchanging God draws changeable humanity Godward."[69] As Gunton notes, this can be seen in the somewhat peculiar claim that Adam was first created as a "little one" (or child) so that he might grow into the full stature of Christ.[70] While admitting that this point about the childlike status of Adam and Eve "is not in every way satisfactory," Gunton was still pleased that, in this conception, temporal mutability becomes, not something to be denigrated, but rather a positive component within the divine economy.[71]

As we have seen, Augustine could at times speak similarly about God's use of temporality.[72] As he put it, "It is through things giving way to and taking the place of one another that the beautiful tapestry of the ages is woven."[73] Yet, as we have seen, such statements stand in tension with Augustine's clear *preference* for the immutable and the timeless. The *Confessions* especially come dangerously close to equating time with fallenness,[74] and nearly a decade after writing this work Augustine could still assert that "[Christ] came to set us free from time."[75] On such matters, Minns (like Gunton) draws a contrast between Augustine and Irenaeus. In his words, Augustine was "full of plangent, almost gnostic, lamentation for the fact that, as changing creatures [we] are removed from unchanging Being," whereas Irenaeus, "instead of dwelling on the instability inherent

---

69. Mary Donavan, *One Right Reading? A Guide to Irenaeus*, (Collegeville, MN: The Liturgical Press, 1997), 106.
70. *AH*, 4.38.1. See also Minns, *Irenaeus*, 136. Gunton makes use of this theme in *Triune Creator*, 12.
71. Gunton, *Promise of Trinitarian Theology*, 115–16.
72. See ch. 4.
73. Augustine, *Gn. litt.* 1.8.14.
74. See Augustine's lament that our souls have been plunged "down into times." *Conf.* 11.39.
75. *Jo. ev. tr.* 31.5 (c. 406–7); cf. *Sermon* 340.5. Cited in Teske, *Paradoxes of Time*, 31.

in the condition of Becomingness . . . emphasises the possibility of growth and development."[76]

So far so good for Gunton's reading. Yet in response to all this Irenaean optimism, a further question must be asked: Does Irenaeus take seriously enough the profound effects of sin and fallenness? After all, while passing time may bring us closer to the consummation of the ages, it also shows forth brokenness and entropy. Human bodies grow old and die. Great civilizations, like Rome itself, decline. And at some points the collective sinfulness of humanity may appear to increase with the passing years. Does Irenaeus do justice to such realities? We must return to this question shortly as we explore why some aspects of Irenaeus's thought were not more fully appropriated in the wake of later controversies, yet for now we merely note that this positive view of time and change was made possible for Irenaeus not by the innate possession of human potential, but by the *recapitulative* work of Christ, the second Adam.[77] Thus we turn now to the subject of triune mediation.

Mediation Through the Son and Spirit

For Gunton, *mediation* was the crucial concept in articulating how God can act within, while remaining distinct from, the creation.[78] In Augustine, his charge was that the Spirit-enabled mediatorship of the *incarnate* Christ had been impinged upon by other ("non-physical") mediators: (1) the angels, (2) the monistic will of God, (3) the *Logos asarkos*, and (4) the immaterial human soul. In chapter 4 we examined

---

76. Minns, *Irenaeus*, 69.
77. As Pelikan states, "The language of Irenaeus . . . shows that neither the teachings nor the example of Christ could be isolated from the message of the cross. . . . It was not only by recapitulating each stage of human development that Christ brought salvation, but especially by the obedience of his passion, which on the tree of the cross undid the damage done by the tree of disobedience." *CT*, 1:146; cf. *AH*, 5.1.1; 5.16.3.
78. See ch. 1.

these claims, while noting certain strengths and several weaknesses in Gunton's argument.[79]

In Irenaeus, however, Gunton found what he believed to be an *antidote* to certain maladies of mediation.[80] Once again, the way forward could be seen in the notion that God interacts with the world by virtue of his "two hands"—the Son and Holy Spirit. As Gunton argued, this "apparently crude image" is actually "extremely subtle."[81] Thus, it is "not mere metaphor, but a metaphor that conveys a great and important Christian truth." As Gunton put it,

> All divine action, whether in creation, salvation or final redemption is the action of God the Father; but it is all equally brought about by his two hands, the Son and the Spirit. And these hands do not act separately, like someone holding a baby in one hand and trying to bang in a nail with the other—though I fear that our talk of the Spirit might sometimes suggest that. The Spirit works through the Son, paradigmatically as Jesus' ministry was empowered by the Spirit. All is the unified action of the one God . . . mediated in this twofold way.[82]

As Gunton acknowledged, he was *developing*, and not merely repeating the Irenaean argument.[83] As a second-century thinker, Irenaeus had not been shaped by the debate regarding the *homoousion* and the challenge of the Arians.[84] Thus as Gunton noted, Irenaeus "did not spend time discussing in what sense Father, Son and Spirit are all God, yet together are one God."[85] Yet as Steenberg argues, the Irenaean treatment of the Father, Son and Holy Spirit is "remarkably well developed; and despite dwelling extensively on economic

---

79. See ch. 4.
80. See Gunton, *One, the Three and the Many*, 151, 205; *Triune Creator*, 74.
81. Gunton, *Father, Son, and Holy Spirit*, 10.
82. Ibid., 80.
83. Ibid., 81.
84. See Spence, "The Person as Willing Agent: Classifying Gunton's Christology," in *The Theology of Colin Gunton*, ed. Lincoln Harvey (London: T&T Clark, 2010), 60.
85. Gunton, *Father, Son, and Holy Spirit*, 11.

matters, is nonetheless eternal."[86] As Irenaeus argued, the Father's "hands" are "always" with him, which can be taken to imply that there was never a time when either the Son or Spirit did not exist.[87]

Yet what does Irenaeus's account of mediation look like once we move beyond the initial creation of the heavens and the earth? As Gunton noted, the central concept here within the Irenaean argument is *recapitulation*.[88] While the concept is complex, its viability hinges upon the continuity between Christ and Adam.[89] Following Paul, Irenaeus viewed the human race as one in Adam (Rom. 5:12), who was fashioned after the pattern of the incarnate Christ.[90] Given this solidarity, it was therefore possible for the incarnate Son to take up and redeem the whole of human existence.

As Irenaeus describes it, Christ "took up humanity into himself . . . thus summing up [or, recapitulating] all things in himself."[91] Therefore, just as all were implicated by Adam's sin, so may all be corrected (and indeed perfected) through Christ's obedience. As Irenaeus argued, the transgression of Eden is undone "by the obedience of the tree" (that is, the cross).[92] Despite the difficulty of fully explaining how this recapitulation works, Douglas Farrow notes the biblical connection to the doctrine of *imago Dei* as *imago Christi*: "In Ephesians and Colossians, we hear that God has summed up everything in heaven and earth 'under one head, even Christ,' who

---

86. Steenberg, *Of God and Man*, 16. Gunton makes this same point in *Father, Son, and Holy Spirit*, 70.
87. *AH*, 4.20.1; cf. 3.16.6.
88. Or "summing up." See Gunton, *Father, Son, and Holy Spirit*, 166.
89. See Minns, *Irenaeus*, 88. The importance of this idea can be seen in Irenaeus's concern to show that both Christ and Adam came from "untilled soil" (that is, that both were formed without male intervention). In addition, because Mary was herself a descendent of Adam, Irenaeus argues that the flesh from which Christ was formed was one with Adam's flesh. See Irenaeus, *AH*, 3.21.10; 3.18.7; 3.19.3; 3.22.1; 5.14.2.
90. See *AH*, 5.16.2; *Dem.* 22.
91. *AH*, 3.16.6.
92. Irenaeus, *Dem.* 33. Cited in Steenberg, *Of God and Man*, 44–46.

is 'the *image* of the invisible God, the firstborn over all creation.'"[93] Such logic therefore implies that just as Adam's failure redounds to his offspring, so too does Christ's victory. For as we have seen already, Irenaeus believed that Adam himself was patterned after the yet-to-be-incarnate Messiah, the true head of the human family.

With this framework in mind, Irenaeus makes what is perhaps his most famous statement of recapitulative soteriology:

> Not despising or evading any condition of humanity . . . he came to save all through means of himself—all, I say, who through him are born again to God. . . . He therefore passed through every age, becoming an infant for infants, thus sanctifying infants; a child for children, thus sanctifying those who are of this age. . . . So likewise he was an old man for old men, that he might be a perfect master for all. . . . Then, at last, he came even to death itself, that he might be "the first-born from the dead, that in all things he might have the pre-eminence," the prince of life, existing before all, and going before all.[94]

In response to such statements, it bears noting that the Irenaean focus upon Christ as the true Adam has received an upsurge of recent support in the contemporary discussions of the atonement, both in the realm of both biblical studies,[95] and in systematic theology.[96]

And in all of this, the importance of the Spirit for Irenaeus must not be overlooked. Thus as Farrow states, "Recapitulation . . . is not a solo performance."[97] Just as Irenaeus saw the Spirit as active within the creation of the heavens and the earth (as the "hand" of God), so also is the Spirit essential to Christ's work, not only as the means

---

93. Farrow, "St. Irenaeus of Lyons," 339. Emphasis mine. See also John McHugh, "A Reconsideration of Ephesians 1.10b in the Light of Irenaeus," in *Paul and Paulinism: Essays in Honour of C.K. Barrett*, ed. M. D. Hooker and S. G. Wilson (London: SPCK, 1982), 302–9.
94. *AH*, 2.22.2.
95. See Scot McKnight, *A Community Called Atonement* (Nashville, Abingdon Press, 2007), esp. ch. 13.
96. See Hans Boersma, *Violence, Hospitality, and the Cross: Reappropriating the Atonement Tradition* (Grand Rapids: Baker Academic, 2004), esp. chs. 5 and 8.
97. Farrow, "Irenaeus of Lyons," 345.

by which Jesus is conceived (Matt. 1:18), but also as the one who equips and enables him for messianic ministry.[98] Thus the serpent's temptations are overcome by the help of the "Dove."[99] Likewise, as Irenaeus argues, the point of the incarnation is to "accustom" the Spirit to dwell in human flesh, thereby binding the church together as a body, and rendering her incorruptible.[100] With this end in view, Irenaeus argues that humans are made in the image and likeness of the *Spirit-filled* Christ, for "where the Spirit of the Father is, there is a living man."[101]

As with the Irenaean treatment of matter and time, Gunton praised this recapitulative emphasis that "Jesus is the one who relives the human story in direct inversion of the adamic pattern."[102] Here there was a certain continuity with Nazianzen's claim that "the unassumed is the unhealed,"[103] and in all this, the mediatorial focus in Irenaeus's work remained relentlessly incarnational. Thus various dualisms were again subverted, and here again we note some contrasts with Augustine.

First, while Augustine stressed that theophanies were wrought "through the angels,"[104] Irenaeus located the presence of the *Logos* throughout the Old Testament narratives. It was thus the "Word" who "spoke to Moses face to face,"[105] and "sailed along with Noah."[106] Second, while Augustine wrestled endlessly with Genesis 1–2,[107] Irenaeus often began his treatment of creation with those New

---

98. See *AH*, 3.9.3; 3.17.1.
99. See ibid. 5.19.1.
100. See ibid. 3.17.1–2; 5.9.4; 5.10.2; 5.12.4; 5.20.2.
101. Ibid., 5.9.3.
102. Gunton, *Christ and Creation*, the Didsbury Lectures, 1990 (Eugene, OR: Wipf and Stock, 2005), 30; cf. *Father, Son, and Holy Spirit*, 29.
103. Gregory of Nazianzus, *Ep.* 101; cf. *AH*, 3.18.7; 5.14.2.
104. Augustine, *Trin.* 4.31.
105. *AH*, 4.20.9.
106. See Irenaeus, *Fragment* 53. Gunton cites this passage in *Promise of Trinitarian Theology*, 36.
107. See ch. 4.

Testament passages that stress the role of the Son.[108] Third, while, as even Green admits, "the pre-existent Christ [the *Logos asarkas*] is more central" in Augustine's thought,[109] Irenaeus placed an emphasis upon the Word incarnate in order to counter certain gnostic arguments. Thus again there was a counterbalance to certain Augustinian tendencies, and a rebuke of various dualisms between matter and spirit, time and eternity.

Yet to stop here would be to ignore a crucial question: Why were these Irenaean emphases not more fully appropriated by the likes of Augustine and his theological descendants? Certain reasons have been addressed in prior chapters, yet for now we will focus upon the specific issue of Augustine's reception of Irenaeus's thought.

The Forgotten Irenaeus

We know that Augustine read *Against the Heresies*; he would even cite a Latin version of the text in 421.[110] Yet despite initial acclaim, it also seems that Irenaeus was somewhat overlooked by the subsequent tradition.[111] As Minns notes, when Erasmus eventually republished *Against the Heresies* in 1526, he was delighted to have "restored to light a book that had been virtually *forgotten* for over a thousand years."[112] Why was this? Why was Irenaeus virtually forgotten for so long? An obvious answer is that later heresies were different from the Valentinian Gnosticism denounced by Irenaeus. Thus Augustine

---

108. See *AH*, 1.22.1; 2.2.4. Gunton notes this fact in *Christian Faith*, 14.
109. Green, *Gunton and the Failure of Augustine*, 177.
110. Augustine, *Con. Iul.*, 1.3.5. Here Augustine refutes Julian's charge that he is still a Manichaean. To do so, he aligns himself with various fathers, including Irenaeus. In the passage cited, Irenaeus affirms the necessity of believing in Christ, "who according to the likeness of sinful flesh was lifted up from the earth on the tree" (*AH*, 4.5).
111. As Hans Urs von Balthasar notes, Tertullian, Eusebius, Theodoret, and Epiphanius all showered praise on Irenaeus as indisputably the greatest theologian of his century. See *The Scandal of the Incarnation*, trans. John Saward (San Francisco: Ignatius Press, 1981), 8.
112. So says Minns, *Irenaeus*, viii; cf. 132–34. Emphasis mine.

battled not only Manichaeans (to whom there was a certain gnostic resemblance), but also Arian and Pelagian opponents. And in response to these groups, Irenaeus might be seen as having less to offer.

As we have noted in our examination of *De Trinitate*, one reason for Augustine's emphasis upon the *Logos asarkos* (and the so-called immanent Trinity in general) pertained to his need to subvert the arguments of Arian opponents.[113] Given this, it bears noting that there are statements in Irenaeus which might be viewed as problematic in light of later conflicts. Take for instance the Irenaean claim that the Word "was *made* Jesus Christ" upon his baptism.[114] In response to this, the noted Irenaean scholar Antonio Orbe has asked whether Irenaeus was an "adoptionist."[115] Against this reading, it seems more likely that Irenaeus was merely playing upon the etymology of *Christ* ("anointed one"). Thus when Jesus was anointed by the Spirit in the Jordan, he literally became "the Christ."[116] Despite this explanation, however, one can see how a passage like this might be used by later Homoian thinkers.

Likewise, in the face of Pelagian opposition, Augustine may have seen Irenaeus's relative optimism regarding human progress (not to mention his defense of free will!) as being too weak on the effects of human sinfulness.[117] As Irenaeus wrote, "God made man a free

---

113. See especially Barnes, "Exegesis and Polemic in Augustine's *De Trinitate* I," *Augustinian Studies* 30 (1999): 43–59.
114. Emphasis mine. The passage reads as follows: "Christ did not at that time descend upon Jesus, neither was Christ one and Jesus another; but the Word of God—who is the Savior of all, and the ruler of heaven and earth, who in Jesus, as I have already pointed out, who did also take upon him flesh, and was anointed by the Spirit from the Father—was made Jesus Christ" (*AH*, 3.9.3).
115. Antonio Orbe, "¿San Ireneo Adopcionista? En torno a *adv. haer.* III, 19, 1," in *Gregorianum* 65 (1984): 5–52. For insight into this debate, see Daniel A. Smith, "Irenaeus and the Baptism of Jesus," *Theological Studies* 58 (1997): 618–42.
116. See Kilian McDonnell, "*Quaestio Disputata:* Irenaeus on the Baptism of Jesus, A Rejoinder to Daniel Smith," in *Theological Studies*, 59 (1998): 318.
117. See especially Minns's comparison of the two thinkers on these subjects, 66–70, 135–36.

[agent], possessing his own power" to obey or disobey God.¹¹⁸ In light of this emphasis upon human freedom, even Gunton claimed that Irenaeus "bequeathed problems to the tradition."¹¹⁹ Specifically, Gunton cited those "modernised—and distorted—versions of Irenaeus [specifically of Schleiermacher and Hick] which minimize or suppress the place of sin . . . and produce a rather unqualified affirmation of the world."¹²⁰

For his own part, Irenaeus's emphasis upon the implications of Adam's sin would seem to avoid the more egregious forms of this imbalance. As Minns notes, "Irenaeus would insist as vigorously as Augustine that nothing can be achieved without grace. But he would have been appalled at the thought that God would offer grace to some and withhold it from others."¹²¹ On the former point, Irenaeus affirmed that sin "held sway over the whole man" who was "dragged into slavery and held fast by death." In light of such statements, Irenaeus would certainly agree that apart from Christ, our predicament is helpless.¹²² Yet the fact remains that Irenaeus's polemical emphases lie elsewhere, and thus his arguments rarely center upon the abiding effects of human sinfulness. As Osborn notes, "The perennial appeal of Irenaeus springs" from his "optimism,"¹²³ and for the anti-Pelagian Augustine, such optimism was part of the problem.

Finally, there is what may be the most common reason to set aside the work of Irenaeus. As Osborn puts it, "The reader . . . is confronted by stark problems of incoherence, which provoked the conclusion by two great scholars that the thought of Irenaeus is a

---

118. *AH*, 4.37.1.
119. Gunton, *One, the Three and the Many*, 159.
120. Ibid., 160n6.
121. Minns, *Irenaeus*, 136.
122. *AH*, 3.18.7: "Had it not been God who granted salvation, we could never have possessed it."
123. Osborn, *Irenaeus*, 7.

'jungle' (*Urwald, forêt vierge*)."[124] As Gunton states, his logic "seems to jump all over the place,"[125] and as Pelikan notes, one reason for this stems from the diverse and "sometimes contradictory sources" from which Irenaeus draws.[126] Similarly, Minns notes that Irenaeus occasionally seems like "a polemicist who will pick up any stick to throw at his opponents, heedless of the possibility that it might turn out to be a boomerang."[127] On the subject of human progress and potential, Augustine may have sensed that the *boomerang* was coming back around.

In the end, these three *foci*—(1) the anti-Arian context of *De Trinitate*, (3) the anti-Pelagian context of Augustine's later writings, and (3) the "jungle" of the Irenaean argument—reveal that "Platonic dualism" was not the only reason why Irenaeus's treatment of creation was not more fully appropriated by Augustine and his heirs.

Still, there remains a final question to be explored: Is it possible that Augustine *did* learn from Irenaeus, and that this appropriation (along with a continued reading of the Scriptures) contributed to a more positive position on such things as time and matter? After all, as Augustine noted, "Whoever reads my books in the order they were written in will likely find out how much progress I have made with my writing."[128]

One point of potential influence (or at least convergence between Augustine and Irenaeus) can be seen in Irenaeus's claim that the human being is a "mixture" or "mingling" of body and soul, and that these so-called physical and spiritual parts cannot be set in

---

124. Literally: a "primeval forest." The two scholars were Koch and D'Alès, respectively. As Osborn notes, the former described Irenaeus as "a confused compiler." Osborn, *Irenaeus*, 9n24.
125. Colin Gunton, *Revelation and Reason*, ed. P. H. Brazier (London: T&T Clark, 2008), 29.
126. *CT*, 1:122.
127. Minns, *Irenaeus*, 66.
128. Augustine, *Retr.* prol. 3. The translation is that of James J. O'Donnell, *Augustine: A New Biography*, 318.

opposition.¹²⁹ While Augustine once emphasized the sharp divide between these entities, he would later speak of the "blending," or "miraculous combination" of both.¹³⁰ Thus as we have seen, the mature Augustine could state that "I do not want my flesh to be removed from me forever, as if it were something alien to me, but that it be healed, a whole with me.¹³¹

A second convergence between Augustine and Irenaeus can be seen in reference to the function of the human soul. As seen previously, Gunton critiqued Augustine for treating the rational soul (or *mind*) as a kind of "ghost" within the bodily "machine."¹³² Yet it is interesting that Irenaeus said something similar. For him, "The soul possesses and rules over the body . . . for the body should be compared to an instrument, while the soul possesses the reason of an artist."¹³³ One might compare this sentence with Augustine's early statement that "man is merely a soul using a body."¹³⁴

At such points we again see a similarity between Augustine and Irenaeus. As even Gunton noted, both employed "Greek" weaponry against the respective heresies of their day.¹³⁵ In light of this, the overarching question should not have been whether one's argument was "Hellenistic" in any sense, but whether one was able to avoid certain doctrinal pitfalls from this diverse inheritance. On this point,

---

129. *AH*, 5.6.1.
130. See Augustine, *orig. an.* 30.59; *Ep.* 137.3.11; *Gn. litt.* 3.16.25; *Civ.* 22.24. Cited in Rist, *Ancient Thought Baptized*, 99.
131. *Sermon* 30.4. Cited in John Rist, *Augustine: Ancient Thought Baptized* (Cambridge: Cambridge University Press, 1994), 92.
132. See again ch. 3. Also, Gunton "Trinity, Ontology and Anthropology: Towards a Renewal of the Doctrine of the *Imago Dei*," in *Persons, Divine and Human: King's College Essays in Theological Anthropology*, ed. Christoph Schwöbel and Colin Gunton (Edinburgh: T&T Clark, 1991), 47.
133. *AH*, 2.33.4. Cited in Steenberg, *Of God and Man*, 38.
134. Augustine, *Mor.* 1.27, 52.
135. As Gunton wrote, "All the early theologians are marked by the theology of the Greeks. . . . Irenaeus shares many of the characteristics of Greek theology, including a tendency to conceive of God in terms of intellect." *Act and Being: Towards a Theology of the Divine Attributes* (London: SCM Press, 2002), 78–79.

Holmes admits to "wincing somewhat" at Gunton's occasional characterization that Greek and Hebrew mindsets are fundamentally opposed. In his words, "The day will come when theologians stop believing Von Harnack on this, and it cannot come too soon."[136] With this in mind, we are now prepared to render some conclusions on the use of Irenaeus as an "antidote" to certain Augustinian imbalances.

Conclusions on Augustine and Irenaeus

As is unsurprising, given the nature of his gnostic opponents, Irenaeus offers a firm critique of various dualisms in the doctrine of creation. Thus while his positions are not without their own complexities, Gunton seems justified in contrasting certain Irenaean emphases with the more dualistic aspects of Augustine's legacy.

(1) Matter. Whereas Augustine often relegated materiality to the lower rungs on an ontic ladder, Irenaeus rejected such hierarchies and celebrated the fact that man was shaped from "mud" by the very "hands" of God. Likewise, while Augustine identified the immaterial mind as the *imago Trinitatis*, Irenaeus claimed that the whole human (both body and soul) was shaped in the image and likeness of the incarnate Christ. Finally, while Augustine rejected the view that the eschatological kingdom would truly come on earth, Irenaeus stressed the redemption of the whole created order.

(2) Time. On temporality, Irenaeus also offered a corrective to the Augustinian elevation of the timeless eternal. Whereas Augustine tended to view *mutability* in *time* as a problem, Irenaeus stressed the potentiality within this "becomingness." For him, God's teleological purpose and his recapitulative work in Christ meant that temporal

---

136. Holmes, in introduction to Gunton, *Revelation and Reason*, 8.

change brought not merely the possibility of decay, but also the promise of growth and eventual perfection.

(3) Mediation. Finally, the Irenaean view of triune mediation also stood in distinction to certain Augustinian emphases. This was evidenced not merely in the Irenaean analogy of God's "two hands," but also in his treatment of redemptive history. Thus it was the Son (and not the angels) who was present in Old Testament theophanies, just as it was the incarnate Christ (and not the *Logos asarkos*) who was emphasized within the Irenaean paradigm. Likewise, while it would be unfair to judge Irenaeus's pneumatology by the standards of later centuries, his work remains genuinely Trinitarian while also providing a legitimate launch point for some of Gunton's own insights. In all of this, the appeal to Irenaeus as a corrective to some of Augustine's imbalances was justified.

(4) The forgotten Irenaeus? It is also justified to say that Irenaeus was somewhat forgotten by the subsequent tradition. Yet the reason for this shift involved much more than the supposed "Platonic dualism" of both Augustine and his heirs. With the emergence of Arian and Pelagian opponents, aspects of the Irenaean corpus may have seemed ill-suited for these fights. Thus when added to the "jungle" of the Irenaean argument, such insights lend understanding to why Irenaeus was not more fully appropriated by the likes of Augustine and others. With this in mind, we turn from the subject of creation, to the doctrine of the Trinity.

10

Gunton and the Triune Corrective (Part Two): The Cappadocian Fathers as the "Antidote" to Certain Augustinian Imbalances

If Gunton viewed Irenaeus as a corrective to certain imbalances in Augustine's doctrine of creation, then a supposed remedy to Augustine's deficient doctrine of the Trinity was to be found in the theology of Basil of Caesarea (330–379), Gregory of Nyssa (c. 331–395), and Gregory of Nazianzus (c. 329–390). As Gunton put it, Augustine's account of the Trinity "bequeath[ed] problems to the West, and . . . in solving them some help is to be sought from the Cappadocian Fathers."[1] In particular, the claim was that Augustine "failed to appropriate the ontological achievement of his Eastern

---

1. Gunton, *The Promise of Trinitarian Theology* (Edinburgh: T&T Clark, 1991), 2.

colleagues," and thus "allowed the insidious return of a Hellenism in which being is not communion, but something underlying it."[2]

While the prior chapters have sought to evaluate this claim as it pertains to Augustine and his intellectual descendants, there remains a final (and foundational) question to be asked: Was Gunton right about the "ontological achievement" that Augustine allegedly squandered from his Eastern predecessors? Do the Cappadocian Fathers really offer a praiseworthy alternative to the Trinitarian imbalances decried by Gunton? Or, as some allege, is it true that Gunton misread the Cappadocians, often through dependence upon the work of John Zizioulas?[3]

In answering such questions, the present chapter will provide the second half of the "split decision" mentioned previously.[4] Thus while Irenaeus does provide a helpful counterbalance to certain Augustinian tendencies in the doctrine of creation, Gunton's treatment of the Cappadocians (in juxtaposition to Augustine) will be found to be more dubious. As noted by many, Gunton greatly exaggerated the distinction between "Eastern" and "Western" accounts of the Trinity, and his reading of the Cappadocians was often as selective as was his reading of Augustine.

Despite this critique, however, the present chapter will also elucidate a few ways in which the Cappadocians do stand distinct from Augustine in emphasizing an account of the Trinity that draws some cautious connections between divine and human personhood. Thus while Gunton badly overstates his case, we will also see that the current backlash against any hint of "social Trinitarianism" (or relational ontology) within the Cappadocian corpus may have also

---

2. Ibid., 10–11.
3. See ch. 2.
4. See the opening to ch. 9.

gone too far.[5] Before this argument can be made, however, some preliminary ground clearing is again in order.

Gunton's Reading of "Cappadocian" Trinitarianism

As Lewis Ayres notes, "Some care should be exercised in using the term 'the Cappadocians,'" for despite their many similarities, these three men did have differences."[6] Thus while we will at times refer to them jointly (as Augustine did by calling them "the Greeks"),[7] we must do so while recognizing the limits of this convention. Gunton's claim was that the Cappadocian treatments of the Trinity (and especially that of Basil), allowed for "a new kind of ontology, an ontology of communion."[8]

In particular, through the "desynonimising of *ousia* and *hypostasis*,"[9] the Cappadocians supposedly revealed that "the substance of God, 'God,' has no ontological content, no true being, apart from communion."[10] By quoting Zizioulas here, Gunton again revealed the influence of the Metropolitan of Pergamon upon his work.[11] Yet in his own words, Gunton claimed the following,

> By giving priority to the concept of person in their doctrine of God, they [the Cappadocians] transform at once the meaning of both concepts [*ousia/hypostasis*]. The being of God is not now understood

---

5. For a corroborating argument, see Gijsbert Van Den Brink, "Social Trinitarianism: A Discussion of Some Recent Theological Criticisms," in *International Journal of Systematic Theology* 16, no. 3 (July, 2014): 231–50.
6. Ayres, "The Cappadocians," in *Augustine through the Ages: An Encyclopedia*, ed. Allan Fitzgerald (Grand Rapids: Eerdmans, 1999), 121.
7. Augustine, *Trin.* 5.8, 9.
8. Gunton, *The One, the Three and the Many: God, Creation and the Culture of Modernity* (Cambridge: Cambridge University Press, 1993), 214n4. In stating this, Gunton instructs the reader to see Zizioulas's work in *Being as Communion: Studies in Personhood and the Church* (New York: St. Vladimir's Press, 1985).
9. Gunton, *Promise of Trinitarian Theology*, 10; *One, the Three and the Many*, 191.
10. Gunton, *Promise of Trinitarian Theology*, 9. Citing Zizioulas, *Being as Communion*, 17.
11. See Bradley G. Green, *Colin Gunton and the Failure of Augustine: The Theology of Colin Gunton in Light of Augustine* (Eugene, OR: Pickwick, 2011), 28.

in the way characteristic of Greek metaphysics, but in terms of communion. God *is* "a sort of continuous and indivisible community" says a letter usually attributed to Basil of Caesarea. The writer realises the implications of what he is doing: he is changing the meaning of words and so the way we understand the reality of God. It is, he says, "a new and paradoxical conception of united separation and separated unity." The being of God consists in the community of *hypostaseis* who give and receive reality to and from one another. Another way of putting the matter would be to say that . . . the Cappadocians have brought the concept of the person into the position of logical priority.[12]

In what follows, the above quotation will provide us with a series of claims that must be tested. We begin, however, with the question of authorship.

The Authorship of *Epistle* 38

As seen above, Gunton made particular appeal to Basil's *Epistle* 38 as indicative of the Cappadocian advance toward a relational ontology. Given this, it bears noting that a majority of scholars now suggest that this letter was in fact written by Gregory of Nyssa.[13] On the one hand, this distinction may seem a rather insignificant one; after all, both Basil and Nyssen were "Cappadocian" theologians, and Gunton often referenced their work by this broader designation. Yet the issue gains relevance given that recent scholarship has suggested that Nyssen especially has been misread by members of the twentieth-century "renewal" of Trinitarian theology.

---

12. Gunton, *Promise of Trinitarian Theology*, 94; citing *Ep.* 38. The Italics are those of Gunton. We will return to the Greek text shortly.
13. As Stephen Hildebrand argues, this recent "consensus" is largely due to the analysis of Reinhard Hübner. See Hildebrand, *The Trinitarian Theology of Basil of Caesarea: A Synthesis of Greek Thought and Biblical Truth* (Washington, DC: Catholic University of America Press, 2007), 47. While Gunton was aware of this debate (*Promise of Trinitarian Theology*, 9), he refused to weigh in on it. While the letter is sometimes referred to as *Ad Petrum*, we will continue to cite it as *Ep.* 38 for ease of reference.

In a series of journal articles, Sarah Coakley and a group of other contemporary scholars have taken aim at the conclusions proffered by the likes of Gunton and Zizioulas.[14] At issue is the simplistic distinction between "Eastern" and "Western" trinitarianism, and the question of whether or not the Cappadocians (and Nyssen in particular) may be easily juxtaposed with the likes of Augustine. While these articles raise a number of critiques against the sort of assertions made by Gunton and Zizioulas, we will turn first to the place of *hypostases* within the Cappadocian treatments of the Trinity.

The Priority of Personhood?

In Gunton's view, the Cappadocians would come to see God's being as consisting only "in the community of *hypostaseis* who give and receive their reality to and from one another." Thus, as he put it, they gave a logical "priority to the concept of person in their doctrine of God."[15] Yet in response to claims such as this, Lucian Turcescu argues that such statements "misrepresent Cappadocian theology" by erroneously claiming that they viewed "person as a category [that] is ontologically prior to substance."[16]

For his own part, Zizioulas attempts to avoid this pitfall by claiming that God's nature as communion, "does not mean that the persons have an ontological priority over the one substance of God, but that the one substance of God coincides with the communion of the three persons."[17] Thus for Zizioulas, it is possible to say that the

---

14. See especially Sarah Coakley, ed., *Re-Thinking Gregory of Nyssa* (Oxford: Blackwell, 2003). Chapters from this work will be subsequently cited according to their original appearance in *Modern Theology* 18, no. 2 (Oct., 2002). While Gunton is mentioned only in passing, the critiques are often relevant given his appeal to Zizioulas, whose conclusions are criticized throughout.
15. Gunton, *Promise of Trinitarian Theology*, 94.
16. Lucian Turcescu, "Person Versus Individual, and other Modern Misreadings of Gregory of Nyssa," in *Modern Theology* 18, no. 4 (Oct., 2002): 528, 530.

"concepts of being and person are co-fundamental."[18] Yet what of Gunton's claim?

On the one hand, Gunton is certainly right to claim that the Cappadocians deserve credit for an advance in triune terminology. As G. L. Prestige put it, the distinction between *ousia* and *hypostasis* "was worked out largely by Basil . . . preached by . . . Gregory of Nazianzus, and elaborated by the acute and speculative mind of Gregory of Nyssa."[19] And as Pelikan notes, this move was beneficial in helping "to remove the taint of Sabellianism from the Nicene confession."[20] Yet to say, as Gunton did, that this move gave priority to the *concept* of person likely goes too far. If anything, the Cappadocians may be seen to give a certain (qualified) priority, not to the "concept" of person, but to the *particular person* of the Father.[21] As Coakley argues, "If any *logical* priority is at stake, it must surely be granted to the Father. . . . In this sense Gregory [of Nyssa] 'starts' with this *one* 'person,' as source and cause of the others."[22] In light of this, as even Zizioulas admits, it is problematic to contend that the Cappadocians grant precedence to the "concept" of personhood over the concept of *ousia*.[23]

---

17. Zizioulas, *Being as Communion*, 134. Zizioulas cites Basil's claim in *On the Holy Spirit*, 18: "The unity of God is in the *koinonia tes theotetos*." Cf. Alan Brown, "On the Criticism of *Being as Communion* in Anglophone Orthodox Theology," in *The Theology of John Zizioulas*, ed. Douglas Knight (Burlington, VT: Ashgate, 2007), 35–78.
18. So says Douglas Knight, "Introduction," to Knight, *The Theology of John Zizioulas*, 4. As we shall see, much depends upon whether we are speaking of the *concept* of personhood, or of the particular person of the Father.
19. G. L. Prestige, *God in Patristic Thought* (London: SPCK, 1956), 233.
20. *CT*, 1:220.
21. See Pelikan's affirmation of this reality in ibid., 222–23.
22. Sarah Coakley, "'Persons' in the 'Social' Doctrine of the Trinity: A Critique of Current Analytic Discussion," in *The Trinity: An Interdisciplinary Symposium on the Trinity*, ed. Stephen T. Davis, Daniel Kendall, and Gerald O'Collins (Oxford: Oxford University Press, 1999), 132. Emphasis hers. Coakley names Gunton specifically as one who has bought into this misreading (123n2); cf. Lewis Ayers, "On Not Three People: The Fundamental Themes of Gregory of Nyssa's Trinitarian Theology as Seen in *To Ablabius: On Not Three Gods*," in *Modern Theology* 18, no. 4 (Oct., 2002): 467.

Yet while Gunton may be wrong on this point, he seems right to note that the Cappadocians did sometimes emphasize the *particularity* of triune *hypostases* in ways that differed from Augustine. After all, Augustine was never in danger of needing to pen the work *On Not Three Gods*. Beyond this, the Cappadocian emphasis upon the particularity of the divine persons is seen specifically in Basil's description of the Father as "the original cause," the Son as "the creative cause," and the Spirit as the "perfecting cause" of all that is.[24] On a similar point, Gunton also drew attention to Nyssen's implication that all divine action "begins with the Father, goes through the Son and is completed by the Spirit."[25] Here we see not a priority of "personhood" (as an abstract concept), but a particularity of persons, whose unity is sometimes characterized in terms of *koinonia*.[26] Yet with the introduction of this term we must now note a further question to be posed of Gunton's reading: Does the Cappadocian use of triune *koinonia* ever lend itself to the derivation of certain *relational* implications from the Trinity?

---

23. In other passages, Gunton was more circumspect. In *The One, the Three and the Many*, he approvingly cited the words of Nazianzen: "No sooner do I conceive of the One than I am illumined by the splendour of the Three; no sooner do I distinguish them than I am carried back to the One" (*Theological Oration*, 40.41). In Gunton's view, such words revealed "a dynamic dialectic between the oneness and the three-ness of God of such a kind that the two are both given equal weight in the process of thought." Cited in Gunton, *One, the Three and the Many*, 149.
24. Basil, *On the Holy Spirit*, 15.38; cited in Gunton, *Father, Son, and Holy Spirit: Toward a Fully Trinitarian Theology* (London: T&T Clark, 2003), 114.
25. Gunton, *Father, Son, and Holy Spirit*, 114; in reference to Gregory of Nyssa's *On Not Three God's*. Gunton here cites from *The Trinitarin Controversy*, tr. and ed. William G. Rusch (Philadelphia: Fortress, 1980), 155.
26. See again, *Ep.* 38.4: "In them [Father, Son and Holy Spirit], there is to be seen a sort of continuous and indivisible *community* [χοινωνίαν]." At the same time, it bears noting that this term does not necessarily carry the "personal" connotations of "fellowship." This is evidenced by the fact that Nyssen can use the same term (χοινωνία) to describe the relationship between wine and the vine. See John Behr, *The Nicene Faith*, part 2 (Crestwood, NY: St. Vladimir's Seminary Press, 2004), 421n35, citing Gregory of Nyssa, *Against Eunomius*, 3.1.

Persons Versus Individuals

As seen in chapter 2, one critique of Gunton is that his theology entailed a projection of outside agendas upon the Trinity. As the story goes, a desire to heal certain modern maladies drove Gunton to foist anachronistic "solutions" upon the Cappadocians, while at the same time overplaying the distinction between their thought and that of Augustine.[27] As we have noted, this critique of Gunton's project is part of a much larger reaction against anything which may be broadly dubbed as *social Trinitarianism*.[28]

In response, we noted that Gunton himself was no fan of many so-called social doctrines of the Trinity. In his view, we should be wary of their occasional "tritheist tendencies,"[29] and of the fact that such projects "tread a slippery slope towards mere projection."[30] In addition, as Holmes noted, "Gunton resisted . . . the too-simple move from a 'social doctrine of the Trinity' to human sociality," in part because he desired to avoid Zizioulas's claim that this would require "a strongly Episcopalian ecclesiology."[31] Yet despite these caveats, the question still remains: What was the basis for Gunton's claims regarding the proper implications to be drawn from the Cappadocian treatments of triune and human *koinonia*?

For Gunton, the language of God as a "sort of continuous and indivisible community"[32] allowed for a critique of both individualistic

---

27. See especially Nausner, "The Failure of a Laudable Project: Gunton, the Trinity and Human Self-Understanding," *Scottish Journal of Theology* 62, no. 4 (2009). See ch. 2.
28. See ch. 2; cf. Brown, "Criticism of *Being as Communion*." For a corrective to this blanket dismissal of all forms of "social Trinitarianism," see again the work of Van Den Brink, "Social Trinitarianism."
29. Gunton, *One, the Three and the Many*, 190; cf. *Promise of Trinitarian Theology*, 198.
30. Gunton, *Father, Son, and Holy Spirit*, xiii; cf. *Promise of Trinitarian Theology*, xix.
31. Holmes, "Towards the *Analogia Personae et Relationis*: Developments in Gunton's Trinitarian Thinking," in *The Theology of Colin Gunton*, ed. Lincoln Harvey (London: T&T Clark, 2010), 43.
32. The Greek of *Ep.* 38.4 reads as follows when speaking of the Father, Son and Spirit: τινα δυνεχή χαὶ ἀδιάδπαδτον χοινωίαν ἐν αὐτοῖδθαι. Migne, PG.

and collectivist mentalities. This insight was garnered, in part, from Coleridge, who convinced him that "protologies . . . define all that follows."[33] Likewise, as a part of this project, Gunton often made a clear distinction between "persons" and "individuals."[34] In his words, "To treat the person and the individual as the same thing is to lose both."[35] Particular "persons" are, in Gunton's view, constituted by virtue of perichoretic relationships, whereas "individuals" are defined autonomously, in opposition to the others that surround them. Yet does this distinction ever appear in Cappadocian thought?

As Turcescu argues, the Cappadocians used *person* interchangeably with *individual*.[36] As evidence, he turns to Nyssen, who, in reference to Peter, Paul, and Barnabas, states that "we do not mean anything else but the individual, which is the person" (*atomon oper esti prosopon*). In the same work, Gregory also implies that triune *hypostases* may be identified as "individuals." As he claims, "It is clear that species and individual [*atomon*] are not the same thing, that is, substance is not the same as *hypostasis*."[37] By this parallel construction, it is clear that Nyssen intends for *atomon* and *hypostasis* to act as synonyms. In light of this, Turcescu contends that the distinction between "persons" and "individuals" is derived, not from patristic theology, but from the modern existentialist philosophy of men like John MacMurray and Martin Buber.[38] As he argues, "The

---

33. So says Holmes, "Analogia Personae," 38.
34. On this subject as well, Gunton often expressed his debt to Zizioulas. See Gunton, "Persons and Particularity," in Knight, *The Theology of John Zizioulas*. As Zizioulas puts it, "Individualisation is precisely the fact that accounts for the impossibility of real communion, because it implies distance and hence division instead of difference." John Zizioulas, "Human Capacity and Human Incapacity: A Theological Exploration of Personhood," in *Scottish Journal of Theology* 28, no. 5 (1975): 407.
35. Gunton, *Promise of Trinitarian Theology*, 85. This theme also appears repeatedly in *One, the Three and the Many*.
36. Turcescu, "Person Versus Individual," 533.
37. Gregory of Nyssa, *Ad Graecos*, 23.4–8. Cited in Turcescu, "Person Versus Individual," 534.
38. Turcescu, "Person Versus Individual," 536.

Cappadocian Fathers were not aware of the dangers of individualism," thus a distinction between *person* and *individual* must be "foist[ed]" upon their thought.[39]

In response to Turcescu, one should note that there is at least a potential difference between *projection* and *application*. While the Cappadocians were not developing a triune vocabulary in order to contend with modern Western individualism, this rather obvious reality does not necessarily prohibit one from developing certain Cappadocian insights for later contexts. To assume otherwise, in the argument of Aristotle Papanilolaou, is to impose a restrictive hermeneutic of "patristic fundamentalism" in which evolving contexts and linguistic connotations may not be taken into account.[40] Ironically, this apparent straightjacket of terminological literalism seems remarkably similar to the rigid linguistic hermeneutic rejected by the Cappadocians in their altered use of *hypostasis*. As Papanilolaou puts it, the "attempt to give further expression to the realism of divine-human communion through twentieth-century notions of person is analogous to the [Cappadocian] co-opting of Greek philosophical categories to the same principle."[41] In short, *application* and *projection* need not be synonymous.

In fact, Gunton nowhere claims that the Cappadocians made a firm distinction between "person" (*prosopon/hypostasis*) and "individual" (*atomon*). As Brown argues, such an "isomorphic" use of terminology is simply not required in order to develop certain relational insights from Cappadocian thought.[42] On the contrary, Gunton's appeal rests not upon a Cappadocian distinction between *atomon* and *hypostasis*, but upon their famous distinction between and *ousia* and *hypostasis*.[43]

---

39. Ibid.
40. Aristotle Papanikolaou, "Is John Zizioulas an Existentialist in Disguise? Response to Lucian Turcescu," in *Modern Theology* 20, no. 4 (Oct., 2004): 605.
41. Ibid.
42. Brown, "Criticism of *Being as Communion*," 67.

In this sense, it seems that Turcescu's critique does not necessarily negate the argument of Gunton. Yet while we have clarified what Gunton was not claiming, we have yet to show that his reading represents a *valid* development of certain Cappadocian insights. Thus we must return to the text which Gunton cited most frequently: *Epistle* 38.

Intimations of a "Relational Ontology" in *Epistle* 38

Regardless of authorship, the purpose of *Epistle* 38 is to address the appropriate theological distinction between *ousia* and *hypostasis*.[44] To accomplish this, the writer freely acknowledges the limitations of human language and analogy. As he states, "The communion and the distinction apprehended in Them [the triune *hypostases*] are, in a certain sense, ineffable and inconceivable, the continuity of nature being never rent asunder by the distinction of the *hypostases*, nor the notes of proper distinction confounded in the community of *ousia*."[45] Yet despite this apophatic qualifier, the letter is equally bold in stating that "indeed, even in objects perceptible to the senses, anyone who approaches the subject in a candid and uncontentious spirit, may find similar conditions of things."[46]

In stating this, the claim is that this paradoxical Trinitarian "notion of conjoined separation and separated conjunction" can indeed be glimpsed (albeit imperfectly) beyond the Trinity itself.[47] Thus as Peter Leithart argues, for this writer "Trinitarian theology opened

---

43. See ch. 1; cf. the conclusion to *One, the Three and the Many*.
44. For some historical context on these terms, see Joseph T. Lienhard, "*Ousia* and *Hypostasis:* The Cappadocian Settlement and the Theology of 'One *Hypostasis*,'" in Davis et al, *The Trinity: An Interdisciplinary Symposium*, 99–121.
45. *Ep.* 38.4. Subsequent citations of this letter will be from the NPNF translation unless otherwise noted.
46. *Ep.* 38.4.
47. *Ep.* 38.4. χαιὴν χαὶ παράδοξον διάχρδίν τε δυνημμένην χαὶ διαχεχριμένην δυνάφειαν. Migne, PG.

up a 'new' way of conceiving God's own existence and being, and also a new way of conceiving the 'condition of things.' This certainly sounds as if [he] is offering a tentative, rudimentary trinitarian ontology."[48] Yet if this is true, then *where* should one look for intimations of this "unified separation" and "separated unity"?

Aside from brief references to both a rainbow and a chain,[49] the primary analogy of *Epistle* 38 is that of human persons[50] (such as "Andrew, John, and James," or "Paul, Silvanus, and Timothy").[51] When referencing this so-called three men analogy, Coakley and company are quick to point out that in *Ad Ablabium* (*On Not Three Gods*), it is not Nyssen himself who first proffers this similitude but Ablabius, who mentions it in order to voice the critiques of those who oppose the Cappadocian articulation of the Trinity. The implication, then, is that Gregory is not so much *suggesting* the "three men" analogy as he is responding to its misuse by his opponents.[52]

While Coakley's claim may be true of *Ad Ablabium*, it is definitely not the case in *Epistle 38*. Here it is author himself (presumably Nyssen) who sets forth the so-called three men analogy as a way of explicating the Cappadocian use of *ousia* and *hypostasis*. And while the potential dangers of likening the divine *hypostases* to, say, "Andrew, James, and John" should be obvious, patristic specialist Khaled Anatolios notes that it is Jesus himself who provides the basis for the notion that "human communion [is] to be a certain image of the oneness of the Father and the Son." As Jesus states in his high

---

48. Peter J. Leithart, "Cappadocian Innovations?" Leithart.com, entry posted December 7, 2009, http://www.leithart.com/2009/12/07/cappadocian-innovations/.
49. *Ep.* 38.5 and 38.4 respectively.
50. By *persons* here we mean only to employ the colloquial usage of the term.
51. *Ep.* 38.2–3.
52. See, for instance, Ayres, "On Not Three People," 447–8; Coakley, "Re-Thinking Gregory of Nyssa," 433.

priestly prayer: "I pray . . . that all of them may be one, Father, just as you are in me and I am in you" (John 17:20–21).[53]

It bears noting that the *them* that Jesus speaks of in John 17 include the very persons mentioned by Nyssen in *Epistle* 38. Christ's prayer is that his eventual followers—men like "Paul, Silvanus, and Timothy"—would be "one" just as he and the Father are one. Thus, if anything, Jesus' prayer is striking for its lack of apophatic qualifiers. This does not, of course, provide us with a detailed roadmap for a "triune" ecclesiology,[54] nor does it pull back the veil and provide us with a privileged look into the inner life of God. Such speculations go beyond the text, and Gunton himself would never join the ranks of these more incautious "social Trinitarians." What the passage in John 17 does provide us with is a biblical basis for drawing certain cautious analogical connections between divine and human persons.[55] And *Epistle* 38 continues this trajectory.

In further defense of this so-called three men analogy, the writer of *Epistle* 38 goes on to discuss the opening verses of the book of Job. As he puts it, "When purposing to narrate the events of his life, Job first mentions the common, and says 'a man'; then . . . particularises by adding 'a certain.'"[56] While such a point may sound tenuous to modern exegetes, the distinction is proper, in the view of *Epistle* 38, because there is a limited (yet profound) analogy between that which is common and distinct in humans, and that which is common and distinct within the Trinity. Thus in a striking sentence, the reader is instructed to "transfer, then, to the divine dogmas the same standard of difference which you recognise in the case both of *ousia* and *hypostasis* in human affairs, and you will not go wrong."[57]

53. Anatolios, *Retrieving Nicaea: The Development and Meaning of Trinitarian Doctrine* (Grand Rapids, MI: Baker Academic, 2011), 290.
54. Contra the likes of Moltmann, Volf, and Zizioulas.
55. See again Van Den Brink, "Social Trinitarianism."
56. *Ep.* 38.3.

The claim appears audacious, and with advice like this it is perhaps unsurprising that Nyssen (and the other Cappadocians) would be forced to respond to charges of tritheism. In order to avoid this heresy, the author clarifies his use of the analogy by arguing that even to speak of *many men* (while common) is in fact an "abuse of language." In reality, "There are many who have shared in the nature [of man] . . . but the man in them all is one."[58]

It is noteworthy that Gunton himself made no use of this sort of "Andrew, James, and John" analogy.[59] As he argued, the "danger" of such models is "a form of tritheism which appears to relate the three persons in such a way as to suggest that they have distinct wills. Here lies the importance of the doctrine of *perichoresis*, the inter-animation in relation, of Father, Son and Spirit . . . [thus] all that is done is indeed the act of all three."[60] In this, we see that Gunton's use of the Cappadocians was almost as selective as his use of Augustine. In both cases, key phrases were seized upon and quoted frequently without extensive background. Thus the focus was more dogmatically constructive than historically contextualized. As Holmes notes of Gunton, "the hint from the tradition is taken up and made his own, but the hint is vital in setting his train of thought running."[61]

The strength of Gunton's reading resides in the fact that *Epistle* 38 does offer some enticing hints toward what might be called a

---

57. *Ep.* 38.3.
58. Gregory of Nyssa, *On Not Three Gods* (NPNF). In clarification of Nyssen's trinitarianism, Coakley notes that "Gregory offers many other, mutually corrective, analogies for the Trinity alongside the 'three men' one." See Coakley, "Re-Thinking Gregory of Nyssa," 433.
59. While acknowledging the inherent difficulties of this analogy, Gunton states that "a careful reading of this letter [*Ep.* 38] will reveal [that] he is chiefly interested in showing how the three persons of the Godhead are distinctively what they are in relation to each other in the being of the one God." Gunton, "The Trinity in Modern Theology," *Companion Encyclopedia of Theology* (London: Routledge, 1995), 939.
60. Gunton, *Promise of Trinitarian Theology*, 198
61. Holmes, "Analogia Personae," 43.

"relational ontology." As the letter states, "Even in objects perceptible to the senses [one] may find a similar condition" of "conjoined separation and separated conjunction."[62] Thus while Gunton must develop such ideas, the roots are present within *Epistle* 38 itself.[63] Yet if such isolated statements reveal the strength of Gunton's Cappadocian argument, then a broader reading of these thinkers reveals the *problems* with a simplistic contrast with Augustine.

Augustine and the Cappadocians: More Similar Than Gunton Notes

Upon further inspection, there are several convergences between those tendencies that Gunton critiqued in Augustine and those that exist also in the Cappadocian Fathers. In what follows, we will briefly illustrate this by highlighting three areas of trinitarian convergence: first, a generous appropriation of "Hellenistic" wisdom; second, an elevation of the rational mind (or soul) as the locus of the image of God; and third, a surprising reticence to offer what might be referred to as an overtly "personal" and univocal definition for *hypostases*. In all of this, Augustine and Cappadocians have more in common than Gunton acknowledged.

As seen previously, Gunton's claim was that Augustine's "Platonism" resulted in a myriad of theological problems. The result was an alleged monistic imbalance in Augustine's doctrine of God, and a damaging dualism in his doctrine of creation.[64] Yet in turning to the unquestionable Greek influence upon the Cappadocians, Gunton's tone was rather different. Of course there were "remnants of Platonism,"[65] but such remnants, it seems, were rarely emphasized.

---

62. *Ep.* 38.4.
63. For support, see Anatolios, *Retrieving Nicaea*, 232–33.
64. See especially Gunton, *Promise of Trinitarian Theology*, 10–11.
65. Gunton, *The Triune Creator: A Historical and Systematic Study* (Grand Rapids: Eerdmans, 1998), 79.

In light of this, it seems reasonable to ask what would have happened if Gunton had applied the same level of *Hellenistic scrutiny* to the Cappadocians as he did to Augustine? To address this question, some help may be garnered from Pelikan's expansive monograph on the Cappadocian "encounter with Hellenism."[66]

In summary, Pelikan cites Florovsky, who claimed that Basil "did not so much adapt Neoplatonism as overcome it," while for Nazianzen, "the idea which he expresses in Platonic language is not itself Platonic." Yet in turning to Gregory of Nyssa, the evaluation was rather different. In Florovsky's words, Nyssen "always remained a Hellenist."[67] As we have seen, this claim is made more interesting given Gunton's repeated usage of Nyssen's *Epistle* 38, and his claim that this work offers a clear contrast to the "insidious . . . Hellenism" of Augustine.[68] On this same subject, Maurice Wiles (whether right or wrong) could even refer to Nyssen's "radical Platonism," in which the universal was more real than the particular.[69]

It is not our goal to render an exhaustive judgment on the Cappadocian use of Greek philosophy,[70] and indeed the judgments of Wiles and others are open to dispute. Still, it seems strange for Gunton to bemoan every instance of Platonic influence in Augustine, while simultaneously brushing aside the many ways in which men like Gregory of Nyssa were equally indebted to the dreaded "Hellenists." To build upon this theme, a second convergence of

---

66. See Pelikan's, *Christianity and Classical Culture: The Metamorphosis of Natural Theology in the Christian Encounter with Hellenism. The Gifford Lectures at Aberdeen, 1992-3* (New Haven: Yale University Press, 1993). The above quote is from the subtitle.
67. Georges Florovsky, *Collected Works* (Belmont, MA: Nordland, 1972–), 7:107, 119, 147. Cited in Pelikan, *Christianity and Classical Culture*, 8.
68. Gunton, *Promise of Trinitarian Theology*, 10–1.
69. Maurice Wiles, *The Making of Christian Doctrine* (London: Cambridge University Press, 1967), 133. Cited in Coakley, "'Persons' in the 'Social' Doctrine of the Trinity," 132.
70. For his own part, Pelikan argues that Christianity's true Hellenizers were neither Augustine nor the Cappadocians, but "the Roman-Byzantine emperors Constantine, Julian, and Theodosius." Pelikan, *Christianity and Classical Culture*, 169.

this common Greek inheritance may be seen in the Augustinian and Cappadocian connection between the rational mind and the image of the triune God.

As we have seen, Gunton frequently bemoaned Augustine's treatment of the *imago Dei*. Yet upon inspection, the Cappadocians held to similar positions on the topic. As Pelikan notes, "The other Cappadocians were unanimous in affirming with Basil the doctrine of 'reason as the distinctive quality' of the human soul. 'The mind is a wonderful thing,' [Basil] said elsewhere 'and therein we possess that which is according to the image of the Creator.'"[71] For his own part, Nyssen actually preceded Augustine in seeing the human soul as a "mirror" of the triune God,[72] while Nazianzen claimed that the mind is "that within us which is Godlike and divine."[73] Thus for all of Gunton's concern over Augustine's alleged "divinising" of the human mind,[74] one wonders why the Cappadocians largely avoid a similar critique. At this point, it seems that Gunton's idealistic contrast between Western "Hellenism" and Cappadocian trinitarianism was misguided.

Still a final, and perhaps most notable, Trinitarian convergence between Augustine and the Cappadocians has to do with the meaning behind the use of *hypostasis*. As we have seen, Augustine professed a famous confusion over what "the Greeks" had meant by such language,[75] and for Gunton, this signaled a failure to affirm the

---

71. Ibid., 127–28. Citing Basil, *Hexaemeron*, 4.5; *Ep.* 233.1.
72. Pelikan, *Christianity and Classical Culture*, 124; cf. David Bentley Hart, "The Mirror of the Infinite: Gregory of Nyssa on the *Vestigia Trinitatis*," in *Modern Theology* 18, no. 4 (Oct. 2002): 541–61.
73. Pelikan, *Christianity and Classical Culture*, 315. Citing Gregory of Nazianzus, *Theological Orations*, 28.17.
74. See Gunton, "Trinity, Ontology and Anthropology: Towards a Renewal of the Doctrine of the *Imago Dei*," in *Persons, Divine and Human: King's College Essays in Theological Anthropology*, ed. Christoph Schwöbel and Colin Gunton (Edinburgh: T&T Clark, 1991) 47; Colin Gunton, *Revelation and Reason*, ed. P. H. Brazier (London: T&T Clark, 2008), 42–43.
75. Augustine, *Trin.* 5.8.10; 5.9.10–11. See also ch. 3.

particularity of triune persons. Yet as recent scholarship has noted, the Cappadocians themselves were often less than clear when explaining the meaning of this term (*hypostasis*). As Barnes argues, it is a "modern idea that ὑπόστασις means 'person.'"[76] In fact, the Cappadocians would often employ the term without attempting to define it,[77] and when a definition was set forth, it was most notable for its lack of specificity.

One of few attempts to specify the sense of *hypostasis* actually occurs within the letter that we have dealt with quite extensively already: *Epistle* 38.[78] Here, the writer rather opaquely defines *hypostasis* as "the conception which, by means of the specific notes it indicates, restricts and circumscribes in a particular thing what is general and uncircumscribed."[79] In response, as Coakley notes, "this 'definition' [if one can even call it that!] is peculiarly devoid of any overtones of 'personality', let alone of 'consciousness.' A *hypostasis* is simply a distinct enough entity to bear some 'particularizing marks.'"[80] This is not to say, of course, that the Cappadocians present an impersonal conception of the Trinity. As we have seen already, the lengthiest analogy of this epistle is exceedingly personal, and as Gunton loved to note, one of Basil's arguments for the Spirit's divinity was that it was possible to grieve him.[81]

---

76. Michel René Barnes, "Divine Unity and the Divided Self: Gregory of Nyssa's Trinitarian Theology in its Psychological Context," in *Modern Theology* 18, no. 4 (Oct., 2002): 484. This view is seconded by John Behr, *The Nicene Faith*, 2:297n93.
77. See for example, Basil, *Ep.* 125. As Pelikan notes, such apophatic theology was an attempt to avoid the arrogant error of claiming to know too much about the inner life of the Trinity. See Pelikan, *Christianity and Classical Culture*, 241.
78. See Lienhard, "*Ousia* and *Hypostasis*," 105.
79. *Ep.* 38.3: τὸ κοινόν τε καὶ ἀπερίγραπτον ἐν τῷ τινὶ πράγματι διὰ τῶν ἐπιφαινομένων ἰδιωμάτωδα χαὶ περιγράφουδα [ἔννοια]. Cited in Lienhard, "*Ousia* and *Hypostasis*," 107n40.
80. Coakley, "'Persons' in the 'Social' Doctrine of the Trinity," 133. Emphasis original.
81. Gunton, *Act and Being: Towards a Theology of the Divine Attributes* (London: SCM Press, 2002), 130; *Father, Son, and Holy Spirit*, 84. See Basil, *On the Holy Spirit*, 19.50.

What the above discussion does reveal is that Augustine can hardly be blamed for failing to define "exactly" what the Cappadocians meant by *hypostasis*. In fact, the Cappadocians themselves professed a certain apophatic ignorance upon this subject. In regard to Basil, Pelikan states that "what was common to the Three and what was distinctive among them lay beyond speech and comprehension."[82] Likewise, as Holmes notes, it was (in part) the challenge of Eunomius that would lead the Cappadocians to reject the idea that *any* human terminology could refer straightforwardly to the ineffable God; rather, "all our names for God are the result of *epinoia*."[83] This word, while difficult to translate, speaks to "the difference, but also the connection, between our perception [*epinoia*] and God's reality."[84]

Thus when a cautious definition of *hypostasis* was attempted (as in *Epistle* 38), one should not be surprised if the clarification hardly "clarifies" the matter. Perhaps this explains why Gunton never made use of this particular definition in his own work. For the Cappadocians, as with Augustine, all language must ultimately fall silent before the ineffable and triune God. Thus in one sense, no sentiment is more "Cappadocian" than the statement that Gunton found so irksome in Augustine: "When the question is asked, What three? Human language labours altogether under great poverty of speech. The answer, however, is given three 'persons,' not that it might be spoken, but that it might not be left unspoken."[85] In this most crucial of areas, Augustine and the Cappadocians were more similar than Gunton noted.

---

82. *CT*, 1:223.
83. Stephen R. Holmes, *The Quest for the Trinity: The Doctrine of God in Scripture, History and Modernity* (Grand Rapids: IVP Academic, 2012), 104.
84. Ibid., 78. For more on the significance of *epinoia* within "Cappadocian" theology (including its partial roots in Origen), see the work of Lewis Ayres, *Nicaea and Its Legacy: An Approach to Fourth-Century Trinitarian Theology* (New York: Oxford University Press, 2004), 24–25; 191–7.
85. Augustine, *Trin*. 5.8.9. For Gunton's critique of this statement, see *Promise of Trinitarian Theology*, 39–40.

Conclusion

As stated at the outset, the arguments of the past two chapters have comprised a kind of "split decision." First, with Irenaeus and the doctrine of creation, we noted several strengths in Gunton's contrast between the bishop of Lugdunum and the one from Hippo Regius. On *matter*, *time*, and *mediation* Irenaeus indeed offered consistent alternatives to Augustine's partial but pervasive dualism. Thus while Augustine read *Against the Heresies*, he often differed from Irenaeus on the treatment of created being.[86] As Gunton argued, and as chapters 5–8 within the present book have validated, these differences between Augustine and Irenaeus did, at times, contribute to certain problems within the subsequent tradition.

Yet in the Cappadocian treatments of the Trinity, we found Gunton's claims to be more problematic. First, while he appealed frequently to "Basil" in *Epistle* 38, we saw how recent scholars have tethered this work to Gregory of Nyssa, who was, by some accounts, the most "Hellenistic" of all the Cappadocian voices. Second, we also challenged Gunton's claim that the Cappadocians grant priority to the "concept" of person in their doctrine of God. In fact, it would be more accurate (though perhaps distasteful to Gunton) to say that the Cappadocians grant a logical priority not to the *concept* of person, but to the *particular person* of the Father. Here again there is a problem with Gunton's contrast between East and West.

In fairness, however, there are also certain problems with some of Gunton's critics. In Turcescu and Coakley, we noted an occasional lack of differentiation between application and projection. Thus while the Cappadocians may not distinguish between *hypostasis* and *atomon* (Gunton never claimed they did) they do *sometimes* offer intimations of a kind of relational ontology which would make

---

86. See ch. 9.

Gunton's applications more appropriate. Likewise, Gunton was also right to say that *Epistle* 38 finds a certain analogy between triune and human *koinonia*. In all of this, it is unfair to dismiss Gunton's Cappadocian insights as merely the projectionistic musings of another "social trinitarian." As Van Den Brink argues, in a statement that may be read as a correction both to Gunton and his critics: "Social trinitarians do not need to denounce Augustine's views or uphold an over-simplified construction of Eastern versus Western accounts of the Trinity. It is enough for them to point to the undeniable fact that the patristic sources contain a variety of trinitarian accounts, some of which may be more illuminating than others."[87]

Last, the real problem in Gunton's contrast between Augustine and the Cappadocians resides in a failure to acknowledge adequately the many similarities between these thinkers. Both sides made generous use of "Hellenistic" wisdom; both connected the rational mind to the divine image within the human; and both were surprisingly reticent to offer a simplistically "personal" and univocal definition for triune *hypostases*. As we found, the profoundly apophatic qualities of Cappadocian thought led to sentiments that were often similar (though not identical) to those of Augustine. Thus while Gunton often exaggerated the "poisonous" nature of Augustine's doctrine of the Trinity, he also overreached when locating an antidote within the Cappadocian Fathers.

---

87. Van Den Brink, "Social Trinitarianism," 341.

11

On "Fruit" and Free Correctors: Conclusions on Colin Gunton and the Legacy of Augustine

We began this book with a quotation and a question. As Augustine wrote, when speaking of his legacy, he desired "not only a pious reader but a free corrector."[1] With regard to the latter, we noted that he got his wish in Colin Gunton. Yet our question was as follows: To what extent was Gunton's reading of Augustine's legacy (to use Augustine's word) a "pious" one? To what extent was it fair? And with this, we set out to reevaluate the extent to which Gunton may have distorted (or perhaps elucidated) certain aspects of the Augustinian inheritance.

As we argued, Gunton was indeed unfair in decrying certain aspects of Augustine's treatment of the Trinity and creation. Yet as we have also shown, there are isolated points at which Gunton's

1. Augustine, *Trin.* 3.pr.2.

Augustinian narrative remains more viable. Among the most valid of Gunton's claims pertained to the implications of Augustine's so-called *inward turn*.[2] Yet to understand these later implications, we were forced to look not only to Augustine, but also to his "afterlife" (that is, to the selective appropriation of Augustine's thought by specific figures from the medieval era to the dawn of modern thought). To make this possible, while remaining within the confines of a single monograph, we sought the help of a noted church historian (Jaroslav Pelikan) who came to serve as the primary (although certainly not the only) arbiter between Gunton and his critics.[3] Our findings may be summed up as follows.

The Trinity

On the Trinity, Gunton was grossly unfair in claiming that "a kind of monism results" from Augustine's doctrine of God.[4] As we saw, this error was partly rooted in his uncritical acceptance of a "Greek/Latin paradigm" (often traced to de Régnon) in which Augustine and "the West" were portrayed as beginning with the one substance of God, while the Cappadocian "East" was depicted as beginning with the three *hypostases*. As we found, this idealized schema is inaccurate with regard to both Augustine[5] and the Cappadocians.[6] Thus while an anti-Arian agenda sometimes led Augustine to focus upon on the "oneness" of the immanent Trinity (especially in *De Trinitate*) it is safe to say that this Greek/Latin paradigm has now been largely discredited.

---

2. See ch. 3 for our extended treatment of Augustine's "inward turn" (that is, his conviction that one could encounter the divine, or truth, by looking inward).
3. See again O'Donnell's claim that Pelikan's multivolume *Christian Tradition* is, at least for now, the "best guide" to Augustine's theological legacy. O'Donnell, *Augustine: A New Biography*, 336.
4. Gunton, *The Promise of Trinitarian Theology* (Edinburgh: T&T Clark, 1991), 57.
5. Ch. 3.
6. Ch. 10.

Second, Gunton also failed to account adequately for Augustine's statements on the *irreducibility* of the Father, Son, and Spirit. Here Augustine was clear that "the Godhead is ineffably and inseparably a Trinity," and therefore "the essence is nothing else than the Trinity itself."[7] Third, when Gunton did present evidence for Augustine's alleged monistic imbalance, he often returned to a particularly dubious claim about Holy Spirit as the "bond of love." As Gunton argued, this conception turned the Trinity into an "inward turning circle,"[8] and thus "the Achilles' heel of all Western theology" was to be seen in "Augustine's failure to make the Spirit a person."[9] This claim is simply false. As we found, Augustine clearly affirmed the *outward-facing* work of the Spirit throughout redemptive history.[10] In all of this, Gunton often built his trinitarian critique of Augustine upon a questionable reading of isolated passages, while ignoring many other statements that reveal Augustine's non-monistic doctrine of God.

Despite such weaknesses, however, there was one area in which we found some merit in Gunton's trinitarian argument. As is well known, Augustine would come to seek out certain triune similitudes within the inward and immaterial realm of the human mind. This search was motivated, in part, by Augustine's Trinitarian reading of the plurals in Gen. 1:26 ("Let us make man in *our* image").[11] Thus it was that Augustine became convinced that God had made the individual human mind to be an image of the Trinity.[12] Yet despite

---

7. Augustine, *Ep.* 120.3.13,17.
8. Gunton, *The Christian Faith: An Introduction to Christian Doctrine* (Oxford:Blackwell, 2002), 186; cf. *Father, Son, and Holy Spirit: Toward a Fully Trinitarian Theology* (London: T&T Clark, 2003), 73, 86.
9. Gunton, *Becoming and Being: The Doctrine of God in Charles Hartshorne and Karl Barth*, 2nd ed. (London: SCM Press, 2001), 238 (2001 epilogue).
10. See, for instance, Lewis Ayres, *Augustine and the Trinity* (Cambridge: Cambridge University Press, 2010), 255.
11. See Augustine, *Gn. litt. imp.* 16.61; *Conf.* 13.22.
12. See ch. 3.

this ostensibly "biblical" motivation behind Augustine's quest, we found that there were also latent dangers, and exegetical fallacies, within his subsequent focus upon the inward and immaterial realm. In short, Augustine's focus upon the rational mind as the *imago Trinitatis* unwittingly contributed to a deemphasis of the Irenaean theme that the incarnate Christ is the true *imago Dei*, and indeed the whole human (both body and soul) should be seen as having been fashioned after the image of the Messiah.

Augustine's exegetical weakness on this matter may be seen in his rather strained handling of what was one of his favorite texts, 1 Corinthians 13. While the Scripture directed Augustine to see a dim reflection of God within the looking glass, Augustine's response was to see not a "whole person" reflecting dimly the image of Christ, but rather the internal workings of an immaterial *mind* reflecting dimly the three-in-oneness of the Trinity. Thus while such internal triads did not necessarily result in an overtly monistic view of God (because of Augustine's previously mentioned safeguards regarding the irreducibility of the Father, Son and Spirit), they did provide, as Gunton supposed, a link between Augustine's treatment of the Trinity, and the sometimes dualistic implications of his doctrine of creation. In this way, the immaterial triads that Augustine sought within his rational mind served as the hinge-points between our discussion of the Trinity and our discussion of creation.

Creation

For Gunton, Augustine's failure to value adequately created being was to be evidenced in the Platonic presuppositions that influenced his handling of *matter*, *time*, and *mediation*.[13] Yet in examining this claim, we again found certain faults in Gunton's argument. He often

---

13. See ch. 1.

took key passages out of context,[14] and he failed to account fully for the maturation of Augustine's thought throughout his lifetime. As Augustine grew older, it is clear that his biblically based appreciation of God's good creation grew more prominent, even while his early infatuation with the "Platonic books" was tempered.[15] Thus Green is right to say that Augustine's dualism was indeed "limited."[16]

Yet herein lies another contribution of the present book. For Gunton, it was precisely the limited nature of Augustine's dualism that was part of the problem. As he argued, Augustine's treatment of creation was actually "more dangerous" (that is, more transferable to the subsequent tradition) because it was "controlled" enough to avoid the outright condemnations that might be leveled against the more overtly dualistic works of Origen or Marcion.[17] Given this, we concluded that Green's praiseworthy scholarship requires some crucial supplementation as the focus shifts to the question of Augustine's legacy. On the subject of materiality, Gunton was justified to critique the dualistic nature of Augustine's hierarchy of being, and in terms of time, the *Confessions* especially come dangerously close to seeing temporality as a penalty for the fall. Thus, when coupled with Augustine's eschatology of heavenly escape, such emphases reveal that Gunton's concerns regarding Augustine's limited (though potentially influential) dualism remain viable, albeit in more limited respects.[18]

In terms of *mediation*, the results were similar. In defense of Augustine, we saw that his use of the angels and the *Logos asarkos* did not mean that the Son's divinity was discussed (as Gunton unfairly

---

14. See especially the importance of *Conf.* 12.7 as elucidated in ch. 4.
15. See again our contrast between Augustine's *Civ.* and his *Conf.* in ch. 4.
16. See Bradley G. Green, *Colin Gunton and the Failure of Augustine: The Theology of Colin Gunton in Light of Augustine* (Eugene, OR: Pickwick, 2011), 89, 96, 174.
17. Gunton, *Promise of Trinitarian Theology*, 76.
18. See ch. 4.

alleged) "in the absence of the human story."[19] Yet by granting an almost mediatorial significance to the immaterial human soul (especially in the *Confessions*) Augustine can be seen to downplay the outward realm of salvation history as the place where God is to be encountered. Thus again we saw the importance of Augustine's focus upon the interior realm. As later chapters showed, this was one area in which Augustine would exert a profound and diverse influence upon the subsequent tradition.

The Medieval Era

In turning to Augustine's "afterlife," we found that Augustine's inheritors were often selective (and at times creative) in their appropriation of his work. For Boethius, it was Augustine the philosopher whose use of Greek wisdom would provide the sanction for his own more extensive Hellenism. Thus Boethius claimed that he was bringing to fruition "the seeds of *reason* from . . . the blessed Augustine."[20] In noting this, Pelikan was sympathetic to Gunton's connection between the selective Augustinianism of Boethius and the eventual elevation of reason to the place of revelation.[21] Yet while claiming this, Pelikan was also clear that what Boethius bequeathed to the medieval scholastics was a "reinterpreted" Augustine.[22]

In Gregory the Great, the reinterpretation continued.[23] By softening Augustine's statements on predestination and the status of the human will, Gregory helped to shield his predecessor from charges that his thought was tainted by a fatalistic Hellenism.[24] Yet in

---

19. Gunton, *Act and Being: Towards a Theology of the Divine Attributes* (London: SCM Press, 2002), 135.
20. Boethius, *On the Trinity*. Cited in Pelikan, *CT*, 1:350. Italics mine.
21. *CT*, 5:107; cf. Gunton, *Revelation and Reason*, ed. P. H. Brazier (London: T&T Clark, 2008), 111.
22. *CT*, 1:350. Emphasis mine.
23. See again the comments of Reinhold Seeberg as cited in ibid.
24. *CT*, 1:319–20.

Hanby's view, such changes actually contributed to the very "modern self" decried by Gunton.[25] In response, we agreed that Gregory indeed departed from the mature Augustine on the freedom of the human will, yet we also noted Gregory's continuity with one of Augustine's early works: *De Libero Arbitrio*. Thus while Gunton was unfair in blaming Augustine for the growth of a voluntaristic rationalism, we noted the legitimate trajectory between some of Augustine's works (for instance, *Soliloquies*, *De Libero Arbitrio*, *De Vera Religione*, and *Confessions*) and a train of thinkers from Gregory the Great, to Petrarch, to René Descartes. As became a theme, the question often hinged on "which Augustine" one was reading. And in this regard, Gunton was not the only one to be selective in his usage of the Augustinian corpus.

In the High Middle Ages, theologians from Anselm to Bonaventure saw Augustine's treatment of the Trinity as the ultimate model of faith in search of understanding. Yet while Augustine was more cautious in his triune speculations, some of his scholastic inheritors were less so. Some would even use his notion of the rational mind as the *imago Trinitatis* in order to *prove* the doctrine of the Trinity "on the basis of reason alone."[26] Likewise, for Bernard, Augustine's *Confessions* provided the impetus to "turn your minds inward" in an Augustinian exploration of individual interiority.[27] At this point, Pelikan provided some crucial corroboration for one of Gunton's central arguments.

> The Augustinian combination of objective and subjective truth led Bonaventure to assert that "when the soul speculates on its triune Principle . . . which makes it the image of God, it is assisted by the lights of knowledge, which perfect and inform it. . . . Profoundly Augustinian

---

25. See Hanby, *Augustine and Modernity* (New York: Routledge, 2003), 135.
26. See *CT*, 3:263.
27. Bernard of Clairvaux, *Sermons on the Song of Songs*, 3.1.1.

and thoroughly medieval though this theology was in Bonaventure, it was to become something quite different in later centuries. As the natural theology of the scholastics eventually lost its connection with the traditional doctrine out of which it had come, so the experiential theology of Bonaventure and of Augustine was transformed into an autonomous source of truth.[28]

Yet if Gunton's narrative found some support in the line from Anselm to Bonaventure, then his link between Augustine and the supposed errors of Aquinas was seen to be more problematic. On creation, Pelikan noted that the more prominent roots of Aquinas's (1) *via negativa* and (2) hierarchical ontology should be linked to Pseudo-Dionysius and not Augustine. Likewise, on the Trinity, both Pelikan and a host of recent scholars (led by Gilles Emery) praised Aquinas for tempering the speculations of others, and for grounding even his so-called natural theology in the biblical text. In all of this, Gunton's bolder claims regarding the Trinity and the primacy of divine revelation have been roundly challenged with regard to Aquinas.[29]

Finally, in the Late Middle Ages,[30] Gunton saw Ockham as reasserting an Augustinian account of the apparently monistic and arbitrary will of God, even while he and Scotus rejected other aspects of the Augustinian inheritance. Our own research would blunt the edge to this critique, for as we noted, Augustine's treatment of God's will was also tethered to his treatment of God's redemptive *love* for his creation. Yet while Gunton's narrative faltered here, our investigation showed how it might have been bolstered with some attention to another late medieval Augustinian: Francesco Petrarch.

In Petrarch's humanistic reappropriation of Augustine's inward turn, he made great of Augustine's early works (and especially the *Confessions*) in order to uncover an "Augustine who could once

---

28. *CT*, 3:306, citing Bonaventure, *The Journey of the Mind to God*, 3.6.
29. See ch. 5.
30. Ch. 6.

more inspire and legitimate a synthesis of Christianity with classical thought."[31] Thus while Petrarch's "ghost" of Augustine held views that were often contrary to those of the mature bishop from Hippo Regius, they were not particularly out of step with the statements made in such works as *De Libero Arbitrio* and *De Vera Religione*. This early Augustine had (1) championed the postlapsarian freedom and potential of the human will, (2) displayed a marked dualism with regard to material creation, (3) imbibed heavy and more unfiltered doses of classical philosophy, and (4) topped all this off with a strong emphasis upon the divine truth to by found by looking inward.

To be sure, Augustine would later come to change his views on such matters,[32] yet even in his *Retractationes*[33] the older man would often stubbornly refuse to acknowledge the extent to which his thinking had evolved.[34] Like Gregory the Great and (later) René Descartes, Petrarch's inspiration came from this early Augustine. Thus if Gunton had focused more upon this line of influence, he might have found more support for his link between isolated aspects of Augustine's thought and the eventual growth of modern inwardness and subjectivity.[35]

The Reformation Era

In preparation for the dawn of modern thought, Gunton claimed that both Luther and Calvin evidenced the faults of Augustine's focus upon the inward (or "spiritual") realm. Yet here again we found flaws in Gunton's case. On creation, Luther famously championed the goodness of the bodily realm, while at times critiquing Augustine's Platonic presuppositions.[36] Thus, if there is any merit to Gunton's

---

31. *CT*, 4:19–20.
32. See again our tracing of this transformation in chs. 3 and 4.
33. See Augustine, *Retr.* 1.9.2, in reference to *Lib. arb.*
34. See O'Donnell, *Augustine: A New Biography*, 318.
35. See again our extensive engagement with Petrarch's *My Secret*, in ch. 6.

charge, it resides in the introspective conscience that Luther would allegedly inherit, at least in part, from Augustine. Behind this debatable phenomenon,[37] Pelikan noted a potential connection between Augustine's inwardness, and the post-Reformation "understanding of Christian faith and experience as a phenomenon based on the relation between 'God and the soul, the soul and God.'"[38]

On Calvin, the results were similar. At this point Gunton added a critique of Calvin's Augustinian doctrine of predestination. For Gunton, such abhorrent theology was seen as "tilting hellwards,"[39] while the cause was traced to Augustine's *monistic* elevation of the divine will. While we did not attempt to adjudicate all of the debates surrounding this controversial subject, we did note the apparent *insufficiency* of Gunton's charge. By choosing to frame the issue almost exclusively as a trinitarian imbalance, Gunton failed to engage sufficiently in the kind of thoroughgoing exegesis that he often demanded of others. In turning to the doctrine of creation, Gunton's charge was more viable (if only slightly). Here Calvin did, at times, evidence (and even admit to) certain *dualistic* tendencies that sometimes mirrored those of Augustine on the subject of embodiment. Yet despite this reality, we noted the obvious unfairness of attributing "all" this to Calvin's "Augustinian heritage."[40]

Descartes, and the Dawn of Modern Thought

While much more could be said of Augustine's place within the sixteenth century, it was Gunton's practice to turn quickly from

---

36. See, for instance, Oberman, *Luther: Man Between God and the Devil*, trans. Eileen Walisser-Schwarzbart (New Haven: Yale University Press, 1989), 160–1.
37. See Krister Stendahl, "The Apostle Paul and the Introspective Conscience of the West," in *The Harvard Theological Review* 56, no. 3 (July, 1963): 199–215.
38. *CT*, 5:289. Citing Augustine, *Soliloq.* 1.2.7.
39. Gunton, *Christ and Creation*, the Didsbury Lectures, 1990 (Eugene, OR: Wipf and Stock, 2005), 95.
40. Gunton, *Promise of Trinitarian Theology*, 121. See ch. 7.

the Reformers to René Descartes.[41] In Descartes's selective Augustinianism, we noted some important truths in Gunton's case. While the Reformers drew heavily upon Augustine's anti-Pelagian corpus, Descartes (with his Jesuit education at La Flèche) drew key insights from other works. Thus the relative optimism of *De Libero Arbitrio* was combined with the interiority of the *Confessions*, and the latter sections of *De Trinitate*. Thus while Augustine did not provide Descartes with a comprehensive system, he did furnish some important clues as to where one looks in order to perceive the indubitable truth. This, of course, was the opinion of some of Descartes's own contemporaries.

In the Cartesian inward turn, we noted the partially Augustinian origins of both the *cogito*, and a subsequent modern shift toward inwardness and subjectivity. Thus while Augustine cannot be blamed for the often selective and decontextualized ways in which his thought would be appropriated, this is one area in which Gunton's broad-brushed narrative retains some merit.

The "Antidotes" to Augustine? Irenaeus and the Cappadocian Fathers

In order to address the final piece of Gunton's Augustinian argument, we were forced to return to a time before Augustine. As Gunton argued, if Augustine had only appropriated the work of certain predecessors (most notably Irenaeus and the Cappadocian Fathers), then Western theology might have been different. In response to this claim, our findings were a kind of "split decision."

On creation, we found that Gunton was often justified in heralding Irenaeus as an alternative to Augustine's occasional faults on matter, time, and mediation.[42] Yet on the subject of the Cappadocians and

---

41. Ch. 8.

the Trinity, the results were seen to be more dubious.[43] As we saw, Augustine and the Cappadocians were often far more similar than Gunton noted. Both made generous use of Platonic wisdom, both connected the rational mind to the *imago Dei*, and both refused to offer a simplistically "personal" and univocal definition for triune *hypostases*.[44] Thus the profoundly apophatic qualities of Cappadocian thought often led to sentiments that were quite similar (though not identical) to those which Gunton decried in Augustine.

In fairness, however, some of Gunton's critics (and those of Zizioulas) also evidenced some imbalances in their handling of these matters. As we saw, there was at times a failure to differentiate between "appropriation" and "projection" in the modern application of the Cappadocian Fathers.[45] Likewise, we also found that Gunton was right to claim that there is indeed an intimation of what might be called a relational ontology in such places as *Epistle* 38. Here, and in keeping with the words of Jesus in John 17, the author of *Epistle* 38 draws some cautious connections between divine and human personhood. Thus the attempt to dismiss any construal of a social (or relational) Trinitarianism within the Cappadocian corpus may eventually be seen as an overreaction to the admittedly incautious claims of certain social Trinitarians.[46] In the end, however, we were forced to conclude that even *Epistle* 38 presents as many problems for Gunton's reading as it does solutions.[47]

---

42. Ch. 9.
43. Ch. 10.
44. See again the way in which *Epistle* 38.3 can speak of a hypostasis as merely "the conception which, by means of the specific notes it indicates, restricts and circumscribes in a particular thing what is general and uncircumscribed."
45. This was especially evident in the work of Turcescu, Lucian Turcescu, "Person Versus Individual, and other Modern Misreadings of Gregory of Nyssa," in *Modern Theology* 18, no. 4 (Oct., 2002).
46. See Gijsbert Van Den Brink, "Social Trinitarianism: A Discussion of Some Recent Theological Criticisms," in *International Journal of Systematic Theology* 16, no. 3 (July, 2014): 231–50.

In all of this, our study has, at times, found cause to correct both Gunton and his critics. In so doing, the primary contribution of the present book has been to supplement (and, at points, to challenge) the prior scholarship on Gunton and Augustine. As Green and others have rightly noted, Gunton's reading of Augustine was indeed unfair. Yet while Green is helpful here, his monograph consciously left aside the question as to whether "there are tendencies . . . in Augustine's thought which, over time, may [have been] exaggerated by later theologians."[48] In addressing this issue, we have sought to fill an important gap in the existing scholarship. We have done so by addressing not merely Gunton and Augustine, but also Gunton and the Augustinian legacy, for as we have seen, Augustine's legacy was always Gunton's chief concern.

Possibilities for Further Study

Despite such contributions, this book also has its limitations. In noting three of these, we will point forward to some possibilities for future research. First, given the breadth of the subject matter (from the patristic era to the dawn of modern thought), we were forced to select a primary arbiter between Gunton and his critics. Thus while the appeal to Pelikan and a selection of other specialists allowed us to adhere to the bounds of a single monograph, it also means that more specialized work remains to be done in dealing with Gunton and the particular periods of Augustine's afterlife. Indeed, as O'Donnell argues, while Pelikan remains the "best guide" to Augustine's legacy, "a wonderful book [still] deserves to be written."[49]

---

47. As we noted, it was *Epistle 38* which refused to offer an overtly "personal" definition for triune *hypostases*.
48. Green, *Gunton and the Failure of Augustine*, 10.
49. O'Donnell, *Augustine: A New Biography*, 336.

A second limitation to this work involves the decision to cease Augustine's afterlife at the "dawn" and not the "dusk" of modern thought. Indeed, Gunton's own narrative did not end with Descartes and his immediate successors.[50] By concluding here, however, we have at least begun to trace the trajectory between Augustine and the era that was often the focus of Gunton's critique: modernity.

Third and finally, our work has asked about what is (and is not) *viable* in Gunton's Augustinian narrative. Yet it should be obvious that "viable" is not the same as "proven." While this distinction may appear like an attempt to evade critique, it is in fact an effort to *avoid* the sort of historical overstatement that made Gunton's Augustinian narrative so alluring, and yet, so problematic. With such limitations of the present book now noted, we turn finally to how this study may shed some light on Gunton's own legacy.

On "Fruit" and Free Correctors

As Jesus taught, it is impossible for a good tree to bear bad fruit (Matt. 7:18). Despite the truth in this notion, it is also the case that even the best of fruit may spoil *over time*, especially if the "harvesters" mishandle it. The same is true in history. As Gunton argued, certain modern maladies could be linked to both Augustine and his "harvesters." As we have seen, this charge is only partly viable. While Augustine's doctrine of God was not overtly monistic, his decision to look inward, in order to find an echo of the Trinity, would contribute to certain unintended consequences. Some fruit, while only blemished on the tree, would grow rotten in the hands of later harvesters. This is a danger (and perhaps even a certainty) for any great figure whose work is taken up by the subsequent tradition.

---

50. See Gunton, *Yesterday and Today: A Study of Continuities of Christology* (Grand Rapids: Eerdmans, 1983), 110, 120 for the commonalities between Augustine and Kant.

Yet the irony is this: of all people, Augustine would perhaps be unsurprised by this phenomenon. After all, his most famous story involved the ruin of some perfectly good fruit![51] His *Retractationes* were written with the knowledge that his words would haunt his legacy, and his view of human nature would seem to leave the likelihood of "pious readers" somewhat in doubt.

On the other hand, it should be obvious that Gunton's way of doing history could also lead to problems over time. While his "grand narratives" convinced students of the importance of ideas,[52] they could also turn past thinkers into caricatures. Thus a further application of this work involves the tension between *engaging pedagogy* and *historical reduction*. In the words of one of Gunton's friends, "Colin was a magician as a teacher."[53] While meant as a compliment, the statement may also encapsulate the faults of Gunton's historical arguments. As Robert Dodaro notes, there are consequences from the careless use of *–isms*—as in *Platonism*, *Hellenism*, and especially *Augustinianism*.[54]

Yet if some of Gunton's students are any indication, such consequences were limited in scope. As both Green and Holmes have noted of themselves, the initial allure of Gunton's "grand narratives" led ultimately to further and more detailed study. Thus the end result was a deepening of theological inquiry, and an eventual departure from of some of Gunton's own positions.[55] The same has been true in the research and writing of the present book. In the end, Gunton was

---

51. Augustine, *Conf.* 2.4.
52. See Holmes's comments in *Revelation and Reason*, 7.
53. This comment was relayed by Bruce McCormack in personal conversation.
54. Robert Dodaro, "Scholasticism," in *Augustine through the Ages: An Encyclopedia*, ed. Allan Fitzgerald (Grand Rapids: Eerdmans, 1999), 753.
55. See Holmes's comments in introduction to *Revelation and Reason*, and *The Barth Lectures*, ed. P. H. Brazier (London: T&T Clark, 2007), 7. See also Ralph Wood's comments on how Green "set out to vindicate" Gunton's "critique of Augustine," before coming to other conclusions in time. This quote appears, among other endorsements, on an unnumbered page in *Gunton and the Failure of Augustine*. While Green was not formally one of Gunton's students at King's

too "free" in his correction of Augustine and his heirs; thus certain errors of history may lead one to suspect a form of cultural projection in his own theology.

Yet the "piety" of Gunton's reading resides *not only* in the fact that he was justified in highlighting certain problematic implications of Augustine's afterlife. The true virtue of Gunton's work resides in the fact that, like Augustine (in *De Civitate Dei*), he sought to show how the gospel provides a lens for viewing even the *grand sweep* of human history. In so doing, both Gunton and Augustine marveled at the ways in which the triune God remains at work within a fallen creation. Thus as Lewis Ayres states of all great theologians now departed, "We imagine them now . . . not as ever-present defenders of their works, but as aware of the failings of those very same texts, aware that all our searching is completed in final contemplation."[56]

College, he admits to being greatly impacted by Gunton's thought prior to beginning his doctoral dissertation.

56. Lewis Ayres, *Nicaea and Its Legacy: An Approach to Fourth-Century Trinitarian Theology* (New York: Oxford University Press, 2004), 9.

Bibliography

Adams, Marilyn M. "Romancing the Good: God and the Self according to St. Anselm of Canterbury." In *The Augustinian Tradition*, ed. Gareth Matthews. Berkeley: University of California Press, 1999.

Alexander, Philip S. "Hellenism and Hellenization as Problematic Historiographical Categories." In *Paul Beyond the Judaism/Hellenism Divide*. ed. Troels Engberg-Pedersen. Louisville: Westminster John Knox Press, 2001.

Anatolios, Khaled. *Retrieving Nicaea: The Development and Meaning of Trinitarian Doctrine*. Grand Rapids: Baker Academic, 2011.

———. "Yes and No: Reflections on Lewis Ayres, *Nicaea and Its Legacy*." *Harvard Theological Review* 100, no. 2 (2007): 153–58.

Anselm. *Monologion*. In *Anselm of Canterbury: The Major Works*, ed. Brian Davies and G. R. Evans. Oxford: Oxford University Press, 1998.

Aquinas, Thomas. *Summa Theologiae: A Concise Translation*. Translated by Timothy McDermott. Westminster, MD: Christian Classics, 1989.

Armstrong, A. H. "St. Augustine and Christian Platonism." In *Augustine: A Collection of Critical Essays*, ed. R. A. Markus. Garden City, NY: Anchor, 1972.

Augustine. *Against Julian (Contra Julianum)*. Translated by Matthew A. Schumacher. The Fathers of the Church, vol. 35. Washington, DC: Catholic University Press, 1957.

———. *City of God* (*De Civitate Dei*). Translated by Marcus Dods. Peabody, MA: Hendrickson, 2010.

———. *Confessions* (*Confessiones*). Translated by Henry Chadwick. Oxford: Oxford University Press, 1991.

———. *Eighty-Three Different Questions* (*De diversis quaestionibus octoginta tribus*). Translated by David L. Mosher. The Fathers of the Church, vol. 70. Washington, DC: Catholic University of America Press, 1982.

———. *Faith and the Creed* (*De fide et symbolo*). Translated by S. D. F. Salmond. *Nicene and Post Nicene Fathers*, first series, vol. 3. Peabody, MA: Hendrickson, 1994.

———. *Faith, Hope, and Charity* (*Enchiridion de fide, spe et caritate*). Translated by Bernard M. Peebles. The Fathers of the Church, vol. 21. Washington, DC: Catholic University of America Press, 1947.

———. *Free Choice of the Will* (*De Libero Arbitrio*). Translated by Thomas Williams. Indianapolis: Hacket, 1993.

———. *Genesis: A Refutation of the Manichees* (*De Genesi adversus Manicheos*). In *On Genesis*. Translated by Edmund Hill. The Works of Saint Augustine; A Translation for the 21st Century, part I, vol. 13. Hyde Park, NY: New City Press, 2002.

———. *Letters* (*Epistulae*). Translated by J. G. Cunningham. *Nicene and Post-Nicene Fathers*, first series, vol. 1. Peabody, MA: Hendrickson, 1994.

———. *Literal Meaning of Genesis* (*De Genesi ad Litteram*). In *On Genesis*. Translated by Edmund Hill. The Works of Saint Augustine; A Translation for the 21st Century, part I, vol. 13. Hyde Park, NY: New City Press, 2002.

———. *On the Catholic and the Manichean Ways of Life* (*De moribus ecclesiae catholicae et de moribus Manichaeorum*). Translated by Donald A. Gallagher and Idella Gallagher. The Fathers of Church, vol. 56. Washington, DC: Catholic University of America Press, 2008.

---. *On Christian Teaching* (*De doctrina Christiana*). Translated by Edmund Hill. The Works of Saint Augustine: A Translation for the 21st Century, part 1, vol.11. Hyde Park, NY: New City, 1992.

---. *On the Soul and Its Origin* (*De anima et eius orgine*). Translated by Philip Schaff. *Nicene and Post-Nicene Fathers*, first series, vol. 5. Peabody, MA: Hendrickson, 1994.

---. *Reconsiderations.* (*Retractationes*). Translated by Mary I. Bogan. The Fathers of the Church, vol. 60. Washington, DC: Catholic University of America Press, 1968.

---. *The Teacher* (*De Magistro*). Translated by Joseph M. Colleran. Ancient Christian Writers, vol. 9. New York: Newman, 1949.

---. *Tractates on the Gospel of John* (*In Johannis Evangelium Tractatus*). Translated by John Gibb. *Nicene and Post-Nicene Fathers*, first series, vol. 7. Peabody, MA: Hendrickson Publishers, 1994.

---. *The Trinity* (*De Trinitate*). Translated by Arthur Haddan. Revised and annotated by W. G. T. Shedd. *Nicene and Post-Nicene Fathers*, first series, vol. 3. New York: Cosimo Classics, 2007.

---. *Unfinished Literal Commentary on Genesis* (*De Genesi ad litteram imperfectus liber*). In *On Genesis*. Translated by Edmund Hill. The Works of Saint Augustine; A Translation for the 21st Century, part I, vol. 13. Hyde Park, NY: New City Press, 2002.

Ayres, Lewis. *Augustine and the Trinity*. Cambridge: Cambridge University Press, 2010.

---. "Augustine, Christology, and God as Love: An Introduction to the Homilies on 1 John." In *Nothing Greater, Nothing Better: Theological Essays on the Love of God*, ed. Kevin J. Vanhoozer. Grand Rapids: Eerdmans, 2001.

---. "The Cappadocians," in *Augustine through the Ages: An Encyclopedia*, ed. Allan Fitzgerald. Grand Rapids: Eerdmans, 1999.

———. "The Discipline of Self-Knowledge in Augustine's 'De Trinitate' Book X," in *The Passionate Intellect: Essays on the Transformation of Classical Traditions*, ed. Lewis Ayres, 261–96. Rutgers University Studies in Classical Humanities. New Brunswick: Transaction, 1995.

———. "The Fundamental Grammar of Augustine's Theology," in *Augustine and His Critics*, ed. R. Dodaro and G. Lawless, 51–76. New York: Routledge, 2000.

———. "Giving Wings to Nicaea: Reconceiving Augustine's Earliest Trinitarian Theology." *Augustinian Studies* 38, no. 1 (2007): 21–40.

———. *Nicaea and Its Legacy: An Approach to Fourth-Century Trinitarian Theology*. New York: Oxford University Press, 2004.

———. "On Not Three People: The Fundamental Themes of Gregory of Nyssa's Trinitarian Theology as Seen in *To Ablabius: On Not Three Gods*." *Modern Theology* 18, no. 4 (Oct., 2002): 445–74.

———. "'Remember That You Are Catholic' (Serm. 52.2): Augustine on the Unity of the Triune God." *Journal of Early Christian Studies* 8 (2000): 39–82.

———. "Response to the Critics of *Nicaea and Its Legacy*." *Harvard Theological Review* 100, no. 2 (2007): 159–71.

———. Review of *The One, the Three and the Many*, by Colin E. Gunton. *Augustinian Studies* 26, no. 2 (1995): 127–33.

———. Review of *The Promise of Trinitarian Theology*, by Colin Gunton. *Journal of Theological Studies* 43 (1992): 780–82.

———. "*Sempiterne Spiritus Donum*: Augustine's Pneumatology and the Metaphysics of Spirit," in *Orthodox Readings of Augustine.*, ed. George E. Demacopoulos and Aristotle Papanikolaou. Crestwood, NY: St. Vladimir's Seminary Press, 2008.

Barnes, Michel R. "The Arians of Book V and the Genre of *De Trinitate* I." *Journal of Theological Studies* 44 (1993): 185–95.

―――. "Augustine in Contemporary Trinitarian Theology." *Theological Studies* 56 (1995): 237–50.

―――. "De Régnon Reconsidered." *Augustinian Studies* 26, no. 2 (1995): 51–79.

―――. "Divine Unity and the Divided Self: Gregory of Nyssa's Trinitarian Theology in Its Psychological Context." *Modern Theology* 18, no. 4 (Oct., 2002): 475–76.

―――. "Exegesis and Polemic in Augustine's *De Trinitate* I." *Augustinian Studies* 30 (1999): 43–59.

―――. "Rereading Augustine's Theology of the Trinity," in *The Trinity: An Interdisciplinary Symposium on the Trinity*, ed. Stephen T. Davis, Daniel Kendall, and Gerald O'Collins. Oxford: Oxford University Press, 1999.

―――. "The Visible Christ and the Invisible Trinity: Mt. 5.8 in Augustine's Trinitarian Theology of 400." *Modern Theology* 19, no. 3 (July 2003): 329–55.

Barth, Karl. *Church Dogmatics.* Edited by G. W. Bromiley and T. F. Torrance. Translated by G. T. Thomson and Harold Knight. 4 vols. Edinburgh: T&T Clark, 1956.

―――. *Dogmatics in Outline.* Translated by G. T. Thomson. New York: Harper and Row Publishers, 1959.

―――. *Fides Quaerens Intellectum: Anselm's Proof of the Existence of God in the Context of His Theological Scheme.* Translated by I. W. Robertson. London: SCM Press, 1960.

―――. *The Holy Spirit and the Christian Life: The Theological Basis of Ethics.* Translated by R. Birch Hoyle. Louisville: Westminster John Knox, 1993.

―――. *The Humanity of God.* Translated by John N. Thomas and Thomas Wieser. Louisville: Westminster John Knox Press, 1960.

―――. *The Word of God and the Word of Man.* Translated by Douglas Horton. London: Hodder and Stoughton, 1928.

Basil of Caesarea. *On the Holy Spirit*. Translated by Stephen M. Hildebrand. New York: St. Vladimir's Seminary Press, 2011.

Bayer, Oswald. *Schöpfung als Anrede*. Tübingen: J. C. B. Mohr and Paul Siebeck, 1990.

Beeley, Christopher. Review of *Augustine and the Trinity*, by Lewis Ayres. *Scottish Journal of Theology* 66, no. 1 (February 2013): 99–100.

Behr, John. "Calling Upon God as Father: Augustine and the Legacy of Nicaea," in *Orthodox Readings of Augustine*, ed. George E. Demacopoulos and Aristotle Papanikolaou. Crestwood, NY: St. Vladimir's Seminary Press, 2008.

———. *The Nicene Faith*. The Formation of Christian Theology, parts 1–2. Crestwood, NY: St. Vladimir's Seminary Press, 2004.

———. "Response to Ayres: The Legacies of Nicaea, East and West." *Harvard Theological Review* 100, no. 2 (2007): 145–52.

———. *The Way to Nicaea*. The Formation of Christian Theology. Crestwood, NY: St. Vladimir's Seminary Press, 2001.

Behr, John and Khaled Anatolios. "Final Reflections." *Harvard Theological Review* 100, no. 2 (2007): 173–75.

Berkouwer, G. C. *The Triumph of Grace in the Theology of Karl Barth: An Introduction and Critical Appraisal*. London: Paternoster, 1956.

Blackham, Paul. "The Trinity in the Hebrew Scriptures," in *Trinitarian Soundings in Systematic Theology*, ed. Paul Louis Metzger. London: T&T Clark, 2005.

Blumenberg, Hans. *The Legitimacy of the Modern Age*. Translated by R.M. Wallace. Cambridge, MA: MIT Press, 1983.

Boersma, Hans. *Violence, Hospitality, and the Cross: Reappropriating the Atonement Tradition*. Grand Rapids: Baker Academic, 2004.

Boisset, Jean. *Sagesse et Sainteté dans la Pensée de Jean Calvin*. Paris: Université de France, 1959.

Bonner, Gerald. *St Augustine of Hippo: Life and Controversies*. Norwich: The Canterbury Press, 1986.

Bouwsma, William J. *John Calvin: A Sixteenth Century Portrait*. New York: Oxford University Press, 1988.

Bowery, Anne-Marie. "Boethius," in *Augustine through the Ages: An Encyclopedia*, Allan Fitzgerald. Grand Rapids: Eerdmans, 1999.

Bradshaw, David. "Augustine the Metaphysician," in *Orthodox Readings of Augustine*, ed. George E. Demacopoulos and Aristotle Papanikolaou. Crestwood, NY: St. Vladimir's Seminary Press, 2008.

Brown, Alan. "On the Criticism of *Being as Communion* in Anglophone Orthodox Theology," in *The Theology of John Zizioulas*, ed. Douglas Knight. Burlington, VT: Ashgate, 2007.

Brown, Peter. *Augustine of Hippo: A Biography*. New edition with an epilogue. Berkeley: University of California Press, 2000.

Buckley, Michael. *At the Origins of Modern Atheism*. New Haven, CT: Yale University Press, 1987.

Busch, Eberhard. *The Great Passion: An Introduction to Karl Barth's Theology*. Translated by Geoffrey W. Bromiley. Edited by Darrell L. Guder and Judith Guder. Grand Rapids: Eerdmans, 2004.

Calvin, John. *Commentary on John*. Translated by William Pringle. Grand Rapids: CCEL, 1847.

———. *Institutes of the Christian Religion*. Edited by J. T. McNeill. Translated by F. L. Battles. Philadelphia: Westminster Press, 1960.

Cairns, Earle E. *Christianity through the Centuries*. 3rd edition. Grand Rapids: Zondervan, 1996.

Callus, Daniel. *The Condemnation of St Thomas at Oxford*. 2nd edition. London: 1955.

Cary, Philip. *Augustine's Invention of the Inner Self: The Legacy of a Christian Platonist*. Oxford: Oxford University Press, 2000.

———. *Inner Grace: Augustine in the Traditions of Plato and Paul*. Oxford: Oxford University Press, 2008.

———. "Interiority," in *Augustine through the Ages: An Encyclopedia*, ed. Allan Fitzgerald. Grand Rapids: Eerdmans, 1999.

Chadwick, Henry. *Boethius: The Consolations of Music, Logic Theology, and Philosophy*. Oxford: Clarendon Press, 1981.

Chevalier, Irénée. *Saint Augustin et la pensée grecque. Les relations trinitaires*. Collectanea Friburgensia 24. Fribourg; Librairie de l'Université, 1940.

Clark, Mary T. "*De Trinitate*," in *The Cambridge Companion to Augustine*, ed. Eleonore Stump and Norman Kretzmann. Cambridge: Cambridge University Press, 2001.

———. "Image Doctrine," in *Augustine through the Ages: An Encyclopedia*, ed. Allan Fitzgerald. Grand Rapids: Eerdmans, 1999.

———. "Irenaeus," in *Augustine through the Ages: An Encyclopedia*, ed. Allan Fitzgerald. Grand Rapids: Eerdmans, 1999.

Coakley, Sarah. "'Persons' in the 'Social' Doctrine of the Trinity: A Critique of Current Analytic Discussion," in *The Trinity: An Interdisciplinary Symposium on the Trinity*, ed. Stephen T. Davis, Daniel Kendall, and Gerald O'Collins. Oxford: Oxford University Press, 1999.

———. "Prayer, Politics and the Trinity: Vying Models of Authority in Third—Fourth-Century Debates on Prayer and 'Orthodoxy.'" *Scottish Journal of Theology* 66, no. 4 (2013): 379–99.

———, editor. *Re-Thinking Gregory of Nyssa*. Oxford: Blackwell, 2003.

———. "Re-Thinking Gregory of Nyssa: Introduction—Gender, Trinitarian Analogies, and the Pedagogy of *The Song*." *Modern Theology* 18, no. 4 (Oct., 2002).

Coleridge, Samuel T. "On the Prometheus of Aeschylus," in *Complete Works of Samuel Taylor Coleridge*, ed. W. G. T. Shedd. Vol. 4. New York: Harper and Brothers, 1853.

Colwell, John E. "Provisionality and Promise: Avoiding Ecclesiastical Nestorianism," in *The Theology of Colin Gunton*, ed. Lincoln Harvey. London: T&T Clark, 2010.

Copleston, Frederick. *A History of Philosophy*. Volume two. Book one. Garden City, NY: Image Books, 1985.

Craig, Edward. *The Mind of God and the Works of Man*. Oxford: Oxford University Press, 1987.

Cross, Richard. "'Quid Tres?' On What Precisely Augustine Professes Not to Understand in *De Trinitate* 5 and 7." *Harvard Theological Review* 100, no. 2 (2007): 215–32.

Crouse, Robert. "'Paucis Mutatis Verbis': St. Augustine's Platonism," in *Augustine and his Critics*, ed. Robert Dodaro and George Lawless. New York: Routledge, 2000.

Cumin, Paul. "The Taste of Cake: Relation and Otherness with Colin Gunton and the Strong Second Hand of God," in *The Theology of Colin Gunton* ed. Lincoln Harvey. London: T&T Clark, 2010.

De Régnon, Theodore. *Études de thélogie positive sur la Sainte Trinité*. 4 vols. in 3. Paris: Victor Retaux, 1892/1998.

Descartes, René. *Oeuvres*. Edited by Charles Adam and Paul Tannery. Paris: J. Vrin, 1964.

Djuth, Marianne. "Will as Love," in *Augustine through the Ages: An Encyclopedia*, ed. Allan Fitzgerald. Grand Rapids: Eerdmans, 1999.

Dobell, Brian. *Augustine's Intellectual Conversion: The Journey from Platonism to Christianity*. Cambridge: Cambridge University Press, 2009.

Dodaro, Robert, and George Lawless. *Augustine and His Critics*. New York: Routledge, 2000.

Dodds, E. R. "Augustine's Confessions: A Study of Spiritual Maladjustment." *Hibbert Journal* 26 (1927–28).

Dolezal, James E. *God without Parts: Divine Simplicity and the Metaphysics of God's Absoluteness*. Eugene: Wipf and Stock, 2011.

Donavan, Mary Ann. *One Right Reading? A Guide to Irenaeus*, Collegeville, MN: The Liturgical Press, 1997.

Drecoll, Volker H. Review of *Augustine and the Trinity*, by Lewis Ayres. *Scottish Journal of Theology* 66, no. 1 (Feb. 2013): 88–98.

Drever, Matthew. "Created in the Image of God: The Formation of the Augustinian Self." PhD diss., University of Chicago, 2008.

———. "Redeeming Creation: *Creatio ex nihilo* and the *imago Dei* in Augustine." *International Journal of Systematic Theology* 15, no. 2 (April, 2013): 135–53.

———. "The Self before God? Rethinking Augustine's Trinitarian Thought." *Harvard Theological Review* 100, no. 2 (2007): 233–42.

Dunham, Scott A. *The Trinity and Creation in Augustine: An Ecological Analysis*. SUNY: Albany, NY, 2008.

Du Roy, Olivier. *L'Intelligence de la foi en la Trinité selon Sain Augustin. Genèse de sa Théologie Trinitaire jusqu'en 391*. Paris: Études Augustiniennes, 1966.

Elliott, Mark W. "Thomas Aquinas," in *Shapers of Christian Orthodoxy*, ed. Bradley Green. Downers Grove, IL: IVP, 2010.

Emery, Gilles. "Trinitarian Theology as Spiritual Exercise in Augustine and Aquinas," in *Aquinas the Augustinian*, trans. John Baptist Ku, ed. Michael Dauphinais, Barry David, and Matthew Levering, 1–40. Washington, DC: Catholic University of America Press.

———. *Trinity in Aquinas*. Ypsilanti: Sapientia Press, 2003.

Erickson, Millard J. *Christian Theology*. 2nd edition. Grand Rapids: Baker, 1998.

Evans, G.R. "Anselm of Canterbury," in *Augustine through the Ages: An Encyclopedia*, ed. Allan Fitzgerald. Grand Rapids: Eerdmans, 1999.

Farrow, Douglas. "St. Irenaeus of Lyons: The Church and the World." *Pro Ecclesia* 4 (1995): 333–55.

Ferguson, Sinclair B. *The Holy Spirit*. Contours of Christian Theology. Downers Grove, IL: IVP, 1996.

Fermer, Richard. "The Limits of Trinitarian Theology as a Methodological Paradigm." *Neue Zeitschrift für Systematische Theologie und Religionsphilosophie* 41 (1999): 158–86.

Ferrari, Leo. "Augustine's Cosmography," *Augustinian Studies* 27, no. 2 (1996).

———. "Interpretation, Assimilation, Appropriation: Recent Commentators on Augustine and His Tradition," in *Tradition & the Rule of Faith in the Early Church: Essays in Honor of Joseph T. Lienhard, S.J.*, ed. Ronnie J. Rombs and Alexander Y. Hwang. Washington, D.C.: The Catholic University of America Press, 2010.

———. "Matter," in *Augustine through the Ages: An Encyclopedia*, ed. Allan Fitzgerald. Grand Rapids: Eerdmans, 1999.

Florovsky, Georges. *Collected Works.* Fourteen volumes to date. Belmont, MA: Nordland, 1972–.

Fitzgerald, Allan, ed. *Augustine through the Ages: An Encyclopedia.* Grand Rapids: Eerdmans, 1999.

Fredriksen, Paula. "Apocalypse and Redemption in Early Christianity: From John of Patmos to Augustine of Hippo." *Vigiliae Christianae* 45 (1991).

Fuller, Peter. *Theoria: Art, and the Absence of Grace.* London: Chatto and Windus, 1988.

Gilson, Étienne. *The Christian Philosophy of Saint Augustine.* Translated by L. E. M. Lynch. New York: Random House, 1960.

Grant, Robert M. *Irenaeus of Lyons.* London: Routledge, 1997.

Grayling, A. C. *Descartes: The Life and Times of a Genius.* New York: Walker & Company, 2005.

Green, Bradley G. "Augustine," in *Shapers of Christian Orthodoxy*, ed. Bradley Green. Downers Grove, IL: IVP, 2010.

———. *Colin Gunton and the Failure of Augustine: The Theology of Colin Gunton in Light of Augustine.* Eugene, OR: Pickwick, 2011.

———. "Colin Gunton and the Theological Origin of Modernity," in *The Theology of Colin Gunton*, ed. Lincoln Harvey. London: T&T Clark, 2010.

———. "The Protomodern Augustine? Colin Gunton and the Failure of Augustine." *International Journal of Systematic Theology* 9, no. 3 (July, 2009): 328–41.

Gregory, Brad S. *The Unintended Reformation: How a Religious Revolution Secularized Society.* Cambridge, MA: Harvard University Press, 2012.

Grenz, Stanley J. *The Social God and the Relational Self: A Trinitarian Theology of the Imago Dei.* Louisville: Westminster John Knox Press, 2001.

Gunton, Colin E. *The Actuality of Atonement: A Study of Metaphor, Rationality, and the Christian Tradition.* Grand Rapids: Eerdmans, 1989.

———. "Augustine, the Trinity and the Theological Crisis of the West" *Scottish Journal of Theology* 43 (1990): 33–58.

———. *The Barth Lectures.* Edited by P.H. Brazier. London: T&T Clark, 2007.

———. *Becoming and Being: The Doctrine of God in Charles Hartshorne and Karl Barth.* 2nd edition. London: SCM Press, 2001.

———. *A Brief Theology of Revelation.* The 1993 Warfield Lectures. Edinburgh: T&T Clark, 1995.

———, ed. *The Cambridge Companion to Christian Doctrine.* Cambridge: Cambridge University Press, 1997.

———. *Christ and Creation.* The Didsbury Lectures, 1990. Grand Rapids: Eerdmans, 1992. Reprint, Eugene, OR: Wipf and Stock, 2005.

———. *The Christian Faith: An Introduction to Christian Doctrine.* Oxford: Blackwell, 2002.

———. "Christus Victor Revisited: A Study in Metaphor and the Transformation of the Meaning." in *Journal of Theological Studies* 36 (1985): 129–45.

———. "The Church on Earth: The Roots of Community," in *On Being the Church: Essays on the Christian Community*, ed. Colin E. Gunton and Daniel W. Hardy, 48–80. Edinburgh: T&T Clark.

———. "Creation and Mediation in the Theology of Robert W. Jenson: An Encounter and a Convergence," in *Trinity, Time, and Church: A Response to the Theology of Robert W. Jenson*, ed. Colin Gunton. Grand Rapids: Eerdmans, 2000.

———. "Creation and Recreation: An Exploration of Some Themes in Aesthetics and Theology." *Modern Theology* 2 (1985): 1–19.

———. "The Doctrine of Creation," in *The Cambridge Companion to Christian Doctrine*, ed. Colin E. Gunton, 141–88. Cambridge: Cambridge University Press, 1997.

———. *Enlightenment and Alienation: An Essay Towards a Trinitarian Theology*. Grand Rapids: Eerdmans, 1985.

———. "A Far-Off Gleam of the Gospel: Salvation in Tolkien's Lord of the Rings." *King's Theological Review* 12 (1989): 6–10.

———, ed. *God and Freedom: Essays in Historical and Systematic Theology*. Edinburgh: T&T Clark, 1995.

———. "Historical and Systematic Theology," in *God and Freedom: Essays in Historical and Systematic Theology*, ed. Colin E. Gunton, 119–33. Edinburgh: T&T Clark, 1995.

———. *Intellect and Action: Elucidations on Christian Theology and the Life of Faith*. Edinburgh: T&T Clark, 2001.

———. "Knowledge and Culture: Towards an Epistemology of the Concrete," in *The Gospel and Contemporary Culture*, ed. H. Montefiore, 84–102. London: Mowbray, 1992.

———. "Mozart the Theologian." *Theology* 94 (1991): 346–49.

———. "No Other Foundation: One Englishman's Reading of Church Dogmatics, chapter V," in *Reckoning With Barth: Essays in Commemoration* of *Karl Barth's Birthday*, ed. Nigel Biggar, 61–79. London: Mowbray, 1988.

———. "The One, the Three and the Many: An Inaugural Lecture in the Chair of Christian Doctrine." London: King's College, 1985.

———. *The One, the Three and the Many: God, Creation and the Culture of Modernity*. The 1992 Bampton Lectures. Cambridge: Cambridge University Press, 1994.

———. "Persons and Particularity," in *The Theology of John Zizioulas: Personhood and the Church*, ed. Douglas Knight. Burlington, VT: Ashgate, 2007.

———. "The Political Christ: Some Reflections on Mr. Cupitt's Thesis." in *Scottish Journal of Theology* 32 (1979): 521–40.

———. *The Promise of Trinitarian Theology*. 2nd ed. Edinburgh: T&T Clark, 1997.

———. *Revelation and Reason*. Edited by P. H. Brazier. London: T&T Clark, 2008.

———. Review of *Justitia Dei: A History of the Christian Doctrine of Justification*, vol. 1: *Beginnings to 1500*, by Alister E. McGrath. *Expository Times* 99 (1987): 252.

———. "Time, Eternity and the Doctrine of the Incarnation." *Dialog* 21 (1982): 263–68.

———. *Theology through Preaching*. Edinburgh: T&T Clark, 2001.

———. *Theology through the Theologians: Selected Essays 1972–1995*. Edinburgh: T&T Clark, 1996.

———. "The Trinity in Modern Theology," in *Companion Encyclopedia of Theology*, 937–57. London: Routledge, 1995.

———. "Trinity, Ontology and Anthropology: Towards a Renewal of the Doctrine of the *Imago Dei*," in *Persons, Divine and Human: King's College Essays in Theological Anthropology*, ed. Christoph Schwöbel and Colin Gunton. Edinburgh: T&T Clark, 1991.

———. *The Triune Creator: A Historical and Systematic Study.* Grand Rapids: Eerdmans, 1998.

———. "Two Dogmas Revisited: Edward Irving's Christology." in *Scottish Journal of Theology* 41 (1988): 359–76.

———. "Universal and Particular in Atonement Theology." in *Religious Studies* 28 (1992): 453–66.

———. "Until He Comes: Towards an Eschatology of Church Membership," in *Called to One Hope: Perspectives on Life to Come.* ed. John E. Colwell. Carlisle: Paternoster Press, 2000.

———. "Using and Being Used: Scripture and Systematic Theology." in *Theology Today* 47 (1990): 248–59.

———. *Yesterday and Today: A Study of Continuities of Christology.* Grand Rapids: Eerdmans, 1983.

Gunton, Colin E., and Daniel W. Hardy. *On Being the Church: Essays on the Christian Community.* Edinburgh: T&T Clark, 1989.

Hanby, Michael. *Augustine and Modernity.* Radical Orthodoxy Series. London: Routledge, 2003.

Hankey, Wayne J. "Between and Beyond Augustine and Descartes: More Than a Source of the Self." *Augustinian Studies* 32, no. 1 (2001).

———. "Mind," in *Augustine through the Ages: An Encyclopedia,* ed. Allan D. Fitzgerald. Grand Rapids: Eerdmans, 1999.

———. "Philosophical Religion and the Neoplatonic Turn to the Subject," in *Deconstructing Radical Orthodoxy: Postmodern Theology, Rhetoric and Truth,* ed. Wayne Hankey and Douglas Hedley. Burlington, VT: Ashgate, 2005.

Hardy, Edward R., ed. *Christology of the Later Fathers.* Philadelphia: Westminster, 1954.

Harnack, Adolf. *History of Dogma.* Translated by Neil Buchanan. 7 vols. 1894–1900. Reprint, Eugene, OR: Wipf & Stock, 1997.

Harris, Harriet A. "Should We Say That Personhood Is Relational?" in *Scottish Journal of Theology* 51, no. 2 (1998): 214–34.

Hart, David Bentley. "The Mirror of the Infinite: Gregory of Nyssa on the *Vestigia Trinitatis.*" *Modern Theology* 18, no. 4 (October, 2002): 541–61.

Harvey, Lincoln, ed. *The Theology of Colin Gunton.* London: T&T Clark, 2010.

Hennessy, Kristin. "An Answer to de Régnon's Accusers: Why We Should Not Speak of 'His' Paradigm." *Harvard Theological Review* 100, no. 2 (April, 2007): 179–97.

Hildebrand, Stephen. *The Trinitarian Theology of Basil of Caesarea: A Synthesis of Greek Thought and Biblical Truth.* Washington, DC: Catholic University of America Press, 2007.

Hill, Edmund. *The Mystery of the Trinity.* London: Chapman, 1985.

Höhne, David. *Spirit and Sonship: Colin Gunton's Theology of Particularity and the Holy Spirit.* Burlington, VT: Ashgate, 2010.

Holmes, Stephen R. "Obituary: Rev. Professor Colin E. Gunton," *Guardian*, June, 3, 2003.

———. *The Quest for the Trinity: The Doctrine of God in Scripture, History and Modernity.* Grand Rapids: IVP Academic, 2012.

———. "'Something Much Too Plain to Say': Towards a Defence of the Doctrine of Divine Simplicity." in *Neue Zeitschrift fur Systematische Theologie und Religionsphilosophie* 43 (2001): 137–54.

———. "Towards the *Analogia Personae et Relationis:* Developments in Gunton's Trinitarian Thinking," in *The Theology of Colin Gunton*, ed. Lincoln Harvey. London: T&T Clark, 2010.

———. "Triune Creativity: Trinity, Creation, Art and Science," in *Trinitarian Soundings in Systematic Theology*, ed. Paul L. Metzger. London: T&T Clark, 2005.

Horn, Brian L. "Person as Confession: Augustine of Hippo," in *Persons, Divine and Human,* ed. Christoph Schwöbel and Colin E. Gunton. Edinburgh: T&T Clark, 1991.

Hübner, Reinhard. "Gregor von Nyssa als Verfasser der sog. Ep. 38 des Basilius. Zum unterschiedlichen Verständnis der oujsiva bei den kappadozishen Brüdern," in *Epektasis. Mélanges patristiques offerts à Jean Daniélou*, ed. J. Fontaine and C. Kannengiesser. Paris: Beauchesne, 1972.

Inwood, M. J. "Duns Scotus," in *The Oxford Companion to Philosophy*, ed. Ted Honderich. Oxford: Oxford University Press, 1995.

Irenaeus. *Against the Heresies.* Translated by Dominic J. Unger. Edited by A. Robertson, J. Donaldson, and A. C. Cox. *Ante-Nicene Fathers*, vol. 1. Grand Rapids: Eerdmans, 1987.

———. *Demonstration of Apostolic Preaching.* Translated by Armitage Robinson. New York: MacMillan, 1920.

Irving, Edward. *The Collected Writings of Edward Irving in Five Volumes.* Edited by G. Carlyle. London: Alexander Strachan, 1865.

Janowski, Zbigniew. *Augustinian-Cartesian Index: Texts and Commentary.* South Bend, IN: St. Augustine's Press, 2004.

Jenson, Robert W. "Afterword," in *Trinitarian Soundings in Systematic Theology*, ed. Paul L. Metzger. London: T&T Clark, 2005.

———. "A Decision Tree of Colin Gunton's Thinking," in *The Theology of Colin Gunton*, ed. Lincoln Harvey. London: T&T Clark, 2010.

———. *The Knowledge of Things Hoped For.* London: Oxford Press, 1969.

———. "The Triune God," in *Christian Dogmatics*, ed. Carl E. Braaten and Robert W. Jenson, vol. 1. Philadelphia: Fortress Press, 1984.

———. *The Triune Identity: God according to the Gospel.* Philadelphia: Fortress Press, 1982.

Jüngel, Eberhard. *The Doctrine of the Trinity.* Translated by Horton Harris. Edinburgh: Scottish Academic, 1976.

———. *Zur Freiheit eines Christenmenschen. Eine Erinnerung an Luthers Schrift.* München: Christian Kaiser, 1987.

Kannengiesser, Charles. "Boethius, Cassiodorus, Gregory the Great," in *The Medieval Theologians: An Introduction to Theology in the Medieval Period*, ed. G. R. Evans. Blackwell: Malden, MA, 2001.

Kany, Roland. "'Fidei Contemnentes Initium': On Certain Positions Opposed by Augustine in *De Trinitate*," in *Studia Patristica* 27 (1993): 322–28.

Kapic, Kelly M. "Trajectories of a Trinitarian Eschatology," in *Trinitarian Soundings in Systematic Theology*, ed. Paul Louis Metzger. London: T&T Clark, 2005.

Kelly, J. N. D. *Early Christian Doctrines*. 5th edition. New York: Harper, 1978.

Kilby, Karen. "Aquinas, the Trinity and the Limits of Understanding." *International Journal of Systematic Theology* 7, no. 4 (Oct., 2005): 414–27.

———. "Perichoresis and Projection: Problems with Social Doctrines of the Trinity." *New Blackfriars* 81 (2000): 432–45.

Kloos, Kari. *Preparing For the Vision of God: Augustine's Interpretation of the Biblical Theophany Narratives*. Ann Arbor: UMI Dissertation Publishing, 2003.

Knight, Douglas. "Introduction," in *The Theology of John Zizioulas*, ed. Douglas Knight. Burlington, VT: Ashgate, 2007.

Knuuttila, Simo. "Time and Creation in Augustine," in *The Cambridge Companion to Augustine*, ed. Eleonore Stump and Norman Kretzmann. Cambridge: Cambridge University Press, 2001.

Krey, Philip. "Martin Luther," in *Augustine through the Ages: An Encyclopedia*, ed. Allan Fitzgerald. Grand Rapids: Eerdmans, 1999.

Lamberigts, Mathijs. "Predestination," in *Augustine through the Ages: An Encyclopedia*, ed. Allan Fitzgerald. Grand Rapids: Eerdmans, 1999.

Leftow, Brian. "Anti Social Trinitarianism," in *The Trinity: An Interdisciplinary Symposium*, ed. Stephen T. Davis, Daniel Kendall, and Gerald O'Collins. New York: Oxford University Press, 1999.

Leithart, Peter J. "Cappadocian Innovations?" Leithart.com. Entry posted December 7, 2009. http://www.leithart.com/2009/12/07/cappadocian-innovations/.

———. *Defending Constantine: The Twilight of an Empire and the Dawn of Christendom.* Downers Grove, IL: IVP Academic, 2010.

Letham, Robert. "The Three Cappadocians," in *Shapers of Christian Orthodoxy*, ed. Bradley Green. Downers Grove, IL: IVP, 2010.

Leupp, Roderick T. *The Renewal of Trinitarian Theology: Themes, Patterns and Explorations.* Downers Grove, IL: IVP, 2008.

Levering, Matthew. *The Theology of Augustine: An Introductory Guide to His Most Important Works.* Grand Rapids: Baker Academic, 2013.

Lienhard, Joseph T. "Augustine of Hippo, Basil of Caesarea, and Gregory Nazianzen," in *Orthodox Readings of Augustine*, ed. George E. Demacopoulos and Aristotle Papanikolaou. Crestwood, NY: St. Vladimir's Seminary Press, 2008.

———. *"Ousia* and *Hypostasis:* The Cappadocian Settlement and the Theology of 'One *Hypostasis*,'" in *The Trinity: An Interdisciplinary Symposium on the Trinity*, ed. Stephen T. Davis, Daniel Kendall, and Gerald O'Collins. Oxford: Oxford University Press, 1999.

Lloyd, Genevieve. "Augustine and the 'Problem' of Time," in *The Augustinian Tradition*, ed. Gareth Matthews, 39–60. Berkeley: University of California Press, 1999.

Luther, Martin. "The Freedom of a Christian," in *Martin Luther's Basic Theological Writings*, ed. Timothy F. Lull. Minneapolis, MN: Augsburg Fortress, 1989.

———. *Lectures on Genesis chapters 1–5.* Edited by J. Pelikan. St. Louis: Concordia, 1958.

Mackey, J. P. "Are There Christian Alternatives to Trinitarian Thinking?" in *The Christian Understanding of God Today*, ed. J. M. Byrne. Dublin: Columbia Press, 1996.

Maier, Harry. "The End of the City and the City without End: The *City of God* as Revelation." *Augustinian Studies* 30, no. 2 (1999): 153–64.

Manoussakis, John P. "Theophany and Indication: Reconciling Augustinian and Palamite Aesthetics." *Modern Theology* 26, no. 1 (Jan., 2010): 76–89.

Mann, William E. "Augustine on Evil and Original Sin," in *The Cambridge Companion to Augustine*, ed. Eleonore Stump and Norman Kretzmann. Cambridge: Cambridge University Press, 2001.

Markus, Robert A. "Augustine's *Confessions* and the Controversy with Julian of Eclanum: Manicheism Revisited," in *Collectanea Augustiniana: Mélanges T. J. Van Bavel*, ed. B. Brunning, M. Lamberigts, and J. Van Houtem. Leuven: Leuven University Press, 1990.

———. "'*Tempora christiana*' revisited," in *Augustine and His Critics*, ed. Robert Dodaro and George Lawless. New York: Routledge, 2000.

Marshall, David J. "John Calvin," in *Augustine through the Ages: An Encyclopedia*, ed. Allan Fitzgerald. Grand Rapids: Eerdmans, 1999.

Martin, Dale B. "Paul and the Judaism/Hellenism Dichotomy: Toward a Social History of the Question," in *Paul Beyond the Judaism/Hellenism Divide*, ed. Troels Engberg-Pedersen. Louisville: Westminster John Knox Press, 2001.

Marty, Martin. *Martin Luther*. New York: Viking, 2004.

Matthews, Gareth B. "Augustine and Descartes on Minds and Bodies," in *The Augustinian Tradition*, ed. Gareth B. Matthews. Berkeley, CA: University of California Press, 1999.

———. "Knowledge and illumination," in *The Cambridge Companion to Augustine*, ed. Eleonore Stump and Norman Kretzmann. Cambridge: Cambridge University Press, 2001.

———. "Post-Medieval Augustinianism," in *The Cambridge Companion to Augustine*, ed. Eleonore Stump and Norman Kretzmann. Cambridge: Cambridge University Press, 2001.

———. *Thought's Ego in Augustine and Descartes.* Ithaca, NY: Cornell University Press, 1992.

McCormack, Bruce. "Foreword," in *Trinitarian Soundings in Systematic Theology*, ed. Paul Louis Metzger. London: T&T Clark, 2005.

———. "Introduction," in *Mapping Modern Theology: A Thematic and Historical Introduction*, ed. Kelly M. Kapic and Bruce L. McCormack. Grand Rapids: Baker Academic, 2012.

McDonnell, Kilian. "*Quaestio Disputata:* Irenaeus on the Baptism of Jesus, A Rejoinder to Daniel Smith." *Theological Studies* 59 (1998): 317.

McGrath, Alister E. *Christian Theology: An Introduction.* 5th edition. Oxford: Blackwell Publishers, 2011.

McKenna, Stephen. Introduction to *The Trinity*, by Augustine. Washington, DC: Catholic University of America Press, 1963.

Menn, Stephen. *Descartes and Augustine.* Cambridge University Press, 1998.

Metzger, Paul Louis. "The Relational Dynamic of Revelation: A Trinitarian Perspective," in *Trinitarian Soundings in Systematic Theology*, ed. Paul Louis Metzger. London: T&T Clark, 2005.

Miles, Margaret. *Augustine on the Body.* Eugene, OR: Wipf & Stock, 1979.

Minns, Denis. *Irenaeus.* London: Chapman, 1994.

Moltmann, Jürgen. *The Church in the Power of the Spirit.* Minneapolis: Fortress Press, 1993.

———. "Some Reflections on the Social Doctrine of the Trinity," in *The Christian Understanding of God Today*, ed. James M. Byrne. Dublin: The Columba Press, 1993.

Morris, Colin. Review of *The Christian Tradition: A History of the Development of Doctrine.* Vol. 3, *The Growth of Medieval Theology (600–1300)*, by Jaroslav Pelikan. *Journal of Ecclesiastical History* 31, no. 3 (July 1980): 346–47.

Nausner, Bernhard. "The Failure of a Laudable Project: Gunton, the Trinity and Human Self-Understanding." *Scottish Journal of Theology* 62, no. 4 (2009): 403–420.

Noll, Mark A. "The Doctrine Doctor," in *Christianity Today*, Sept. 2004.

Oberman, Heiko A. *Luther: Man between God and the Devil.* Translated by Eileen Walisser-Schwarzbart. New Haven: Yale University Press, 1989.

O'Connell, R.J. *Images of Conversion in Saint Augustine's Confessions.* New York: Fordham University Press, 1996.

———. "Peter Brown on the Soul's Fall." *Augustinian Studies* 24 (1993).

O'Daly, Gerard. *Augustine's Philosophy of Mind.* London: Duckworth, 1987.

O'Donnell, James J. *Augustine: Confessions.* 3 vols. Oxford: Clarendon Press, 1992.

———. "Augustine: His Time and Lives," in *The Cambridge Companion to Augustine,* ed. Eleonore Stump and Norman Kretzmann. Cambridge: Cambridge University Press, 2001.

———. *Augustine: A New Biography.* New York: Harper, 2005.

———. "Augustine's Unconfessions," in *Augustine and Postmodernism: Confessions and Circumfession,* ed. John Caputo and Michael Scanlon. Bloomington, IN: Indiana University Press, 2005.

Oden, Thomas C. *Systematic Theology.* 3 vols. Peabody, MA: Prince Press, 2001.

Orbe, Antonio. "¿San Ireneo Adopcionista? En torno a *Adv. Haer.* III, 19, 1." *Gregorianum* 65 (1984): 5–52.

O'Regan, Cyril. *Gnostic Return in Modernity.* Albany, NY: State University of New York, 2001.

Origen of Alexandria. *Against Celsus.* Translated by Frederick Crombie. *Ante-Nicene Fathers,* vol. 4, edited by Alexander Roberts, James Donaldson, and A. Cleveland Coxe. Buffalo, NY: Christian Literature Publishing Co., 1885.

Osborn, Eric. *Irenaeus of Lyons.* Cambridge: Cambridge University Press, 2001.

Papanikolaou, Aristotle. "Is John Zizioulas an Existentialist in Disguise? Response to Lucian Turcescu." *Modern Theology* 20, no. 4 (Oct., 2004): 601–7.

Papanikolaou, Aristotle, and George Demacopoulos, eds. *Orthodox Readings of Augustine.* Crestwood, NY: St. Vladimir's Seminary Press, 2008.

Partee, Charles. *Calvin and Classical Philosophy.* Louisville: Westminster, John Knox, 2006.

Pecknold, C. C. "How Augustine Used the Trinity: Functionalism and the Development of Doctrine." *Anglican Theological Review* 85, no. 1 (2003): 127–41.

Pelikan, Jaroslav. *The Christian Tradition: A History of the Development of Doctrine.* 5 vols. Chicago: University of Chicago Press, 1971–85.

———. *Christianity and Classical Culture: The Metamorphosis of Natural Theology in the Christian Encounter with Hellenism. The Gifford Lectures at Aberdeen, 1992–3.* New Haven: Yale University Press, 1993.

———. *Credo: Historical and Theological Guide to Creeds and Confessions of Faith in the Christian Tradition.* New Haven, CT: Yale University Press, 2003.

———. "Foreword," in *Augustine Through the Ages: An Encyclopedia*, ed. Allan Fitzgerald. Grand Rapids: Eerdmans, 1999.

Petrarch, Francis. *My Secret Book.* Translated by J. G. Nichols. London: Hesperus Press, 2002.

Plantinga, Alvin. *Does God Have a Nature?* Milwaukee: Marquette University Press, 1980.

Plotinus. *The Enneads.* Translated by Stephen MacKenna. Abridged and edited by John Dillon. London: Penguin Books, 1991.

Polanyi, Michael. *Personal Knowledge. Towards a Post-Critical Philosophy.* London: Routledge, 1962.

Prenter, Regin. *Spiritus Creator: Luther's Concept of the Holy Spirit.* Philadelphia: Muhlenberg, 1953.

Prestige, G. L. *God in Patristic Thought.* London: SPCK, 1956.

Quillen, Carol. "Renaissance Humanism," in *Augustine through the Ages: An Encyclopedia,* ed. Allan Fitzgerald. Grand Rapids: Eerdmans, 1999.

———. "Renaissance to the Enlightenment," in *Augustine through the Ages: An Encyclopedia,* ed. Allan Fitzgerald. Grand Rapids: Eerdmans, 1999.

Rahner, Karl. *The Trinity.* Edited and translated by Joseph Donceel. London: Burns and Oates, 1970.

Rand, Edward K. *Founders of the Middle Ages.* Cambridge, MA: Harvard Press, 1929.

Ratzinger, Joseph. "The Holy Spirit as Communio: Concerning the Relationship of Pneumatology and Spirituality in Augustine." Translated by Peter Casarella. *Communio* 25 (1998): 324–37.

Reed, Esther D. "Revelation and Natural Rights: Notes on Colin E. Gunton's Theology of Nature," in *Trinitarian Soundings in Systematic Theology,* ed. Paul Louis Metzger. London: T&T Clark, 2005.

Rigby, Paul. "Original Sin," in *Augustine through the Ages: An Encyclopedia,* ed. Allan Fitzgerald. Grand Rapids: Eerdmans, 1999.

Rist, John. *Augustine: Ancient Thought Baptized.* Cambridge: University Press, 1994.

———. "Faith and Reason," in *The Cambridge Companion to Augustine,* ed. Eleonore Stump and Norman Kretzmann. Cambridge: Cambridge University Press, 2001.

Robinson, Peter M. B. "The Trinity: The Significance of Appropriate Distinctions for Dynamic Relationality," in *Trinitarian Soundings in Systematic Theology,* ed. Paul Louis Metzger. London: T&T Clark, 2005.

Rombs, Ronnie J. *Saint Augustine and the Fall of the Soul: Beyond O'Connell and His Critics.* Washington, DC: Catholic University of America Press, 2006.

Scanlon, Michael J. "Modern Theology," in *Augustine through the Ages: An Encyclopedia*, ed. Allan Fitzgerald. Grand Rapids: Eerdmans, 1999.

Schwöbel, Christoph. "The Shape of Colin Gunton's Theology: On the Way Towards a Fully Trinitarian Theology," in *The Theology of Colin Gunton*, ed. Lincoln Harvey. London: T&T Clark, 2010.

Spence, Alan. "The Person as Willing Agent: Classifying Gunton's Christology," in *The Theology of Colin Gunton*, ed. Lincoln Harvey. London: T&T Clark, 2010.

Steenberg, M. C. *Of God and Man: Theology as Anthropology from Irenaeus to Athanasius.* London: T&T Clark, 2009.

Stendahl, Krister. "The Apostle Paul and the Introspective Conscience of the West." *The Harvard Theological Review* 56, no. 3 (July, 1963): 199–215.

Stone, M. W. F. "Augustine and Medieval Philosophy," in *The Cambridge Companion to Augustine*, ed. Eleonore Stump and Norman Kretzmann. Cambridge: Cambridge University Press, 2001.

Studer, Basil. *History of Theology.* Edited by A. Bi Berardino and Basil Studer. Translated by M. J. O'Connell. Vol. 1. Collegeville: Liturgical Press, 1997.

Stump, Eleonore. "Augustine on Free Will," in *The Cambridge Companion to Augustine*, ed. Eleonore Stump and Norman Kretzmann. Cambridge: Cambridge University Press, 2001.

Taylor, Charles. *Sources of the Self.* Cambridge: Harvard University Press, 1989.

Terry, Justyn. "Colin Gunton's Doctrine of Atonement: Transcending Rationalism by Metaphor," in *The Theology of Colin Gunton*, ed. Lincoln Harvey. London: T&T Clark, 2010.

TeSelle, Eugene. "Theses on O'Connell: The Origin and 'Proper Life' of the Soul in Augustine's Thought." *Augustinian Studies* 27, no. 2 (1996): 7–19.

Teske, Roland. "Augustine's Philosophy of Memory," in *The Cambridge Companion to Augustine*, ed. Eleonore Stump and Norman Kretzmann. Cambridge: Cambridge University Press, 2001.

———. "Augustine's Theory of the Soul," in *The Cambridge Companion to Augustine*, ed. Eleonore Stump and Norman Kretzmann. Cambridge: Cambridge University Press, 2001.

———. *Paradoxes of Time in Saint Augustine*. Milwaukee: Marquette University Press, 1996.

———. "Soul," in *Augustine through the Ages: An Encyclopedia*, ed. Allan Fitzgerald. Grand Rapids: Eerdmans, 1999.

Tibbs, Praskevè. "Created for Action: Colin Gunton's Relational Anthropology," in *The Theology of Colin Gunton*, ed. Lincoln Harvey. London: T&T Clark, 2010.

Torrance, Alan J. *Persons in Communion: An Essay on Trinitarian Description and Human Participation*. Edinburgh: T&T Clark, 1996.

Torrance, Thomas F. *Karl Barth, Biblical and Evangelical Theologian*. Edinburgh: T&T Clark, 1990.

———. *The Mediation of Christ*. Colorado Springs, CO: Helmers & Howard, 1991.

Trinkaus, Charles. "Erasmus, Augustine, and the Nominalists." *Archiv für Reformationsgeschichte* 66 (1976): 274–301.

Turcescu, Lucian. "'Person' Versus 'Individual', and other Modern Misreadings of Gregory of Nyssa." *Modern Theology* 18, no. 4 (Oct., 2002): 527–39.

Vallicella, William. "Divine Simplicity," in *The Stanford Encyclopedia of Philosophy*, ed. Edward N. Zalta. Fall 2010 Edition. http://plato.stanford.edu/archives/fall2010/entries/divine-simplicity/.

Van Fleteren, Frederick. "Confessions," in *Augustine through the Ages: An Encyclopedia*, ed. Allan Fitzgerald. Grand Rapids: Eerdmans, 1999.

Vanhoozer, Kevin J. "Introduction: The Love of God—Its Place, Meaning, and Function in Systematic Theology," in *Nothing Greater, Nothing Better: Theological Essays on the Love of God*, ed. Kevin J. Vanhoozer. Grand Rapids: Eerdmans, 2001.

Volf, Miroslav. *After Our Likeness: The Church as the Image of the Trinity*. Grand Rapids: Eerdmans, 1998.

———. *Exclusion and Embrace: A Theological Exploration of Identity, Otherness, and Reconciliation*. Nashville: Abingdon Press, 1996.

Von Balthasar, Hans Urs. *The Scandal of the Incarnation: Irenaeus. Against the Heresies*. Translated John Saward. San Francisco: Ignatius Press, 1981.

Warfield, B. B. *Calvin and Augustine*. Philadelphia: Fortress Press, 1956.

Wawrykow, Joseph. "Franciscan and Dominican Trinitarian Theology (Thirteenth Century): Bonaventure and Aquinas," in *The Oxford Handbook of the Trinity*, ed. Gilles Emery and Matthew Levering. Oxford: Oxford University Press, 2011.

———. "Thomas Aquinas," in *Augustine through the Ages: An Encyclopedia*, ed. Allan Fitzgerald. Grand Rapids: Eerdmans, 1999.

Webster, John. "Gunton and Barth," in *The Theology of Colin Gunton*, ed. Lincoln Harvey. London: T&T Clark, 2010.

———. "Systematic Theology after Barth: Jüngel, Jenson and Gunton," in *The Modern Theologians: An Introduction to Christian Theology since 1918*, ed. David Ford and Rachel Muers. 3rd ed. Oxford: Blackwell, 2005.

Wetzel, James. "Predestination, Pelagianism, and Foreknowledge," in *The Cambridge Companion to Augustine*, ed. Eleonore Stump and Norman Kretzmann. Cambridge: Cambridge University Press, 2001.

Wiles, Maurice. "Attitudes to Arius in the Arian Controversy," in *Arianism after Arius*, ed. M. R. Barnes and D. H. Williams, 31–43. Edinburgh: T&T Clark, 2000.

———. *The Making of Christian Doctrine*. London: Cambridge University Press, 1967.

Wilken, Robert L. "Jaroslav Pelikan, Doctor Ecclesiae." *First Things*, Aug. 2006.

Wilkens, Steve, and Alan G. Padgett. *Christianity and Western Thought: A History of Philosophers, Ideas and Movements*. Vol. 2. Downers Grove, IL: IVP, 2000.

Williams, Rowan. "Creation," in *Augustine through the Ages: An Encyclopedia*, ed. Allan Fitzgerald. Grand Rapids: Eerdmans, 1999.

———. "*Sapientia* and the Trinity: Reflections on the *De Trinitate*," in *Collectanea Augustiniana: Mélanges T. J. Van Bavel*, ed. B. Brunning, M. Lamberigts, and J. Van Houtem. Leuven: Leuven University Press, 1990.

Williams, Thomas. "Biblical Interpretation," in *The Cambridge Companion to Augustine*, ed. Eleonore Stump and Norman Kretzmann. Cambridge: Cambridge University Press, 2001.

Wills, Garry. *Saint Augustine*. New York: Viking, 1999.

Wright, N. T. *Justification: God's Plan and Paul's Vision*. Downers Grove, IL: IVP Academic, 2009.

———. *The New Testament and the People of God*. Minneapolis: Fortress Press, 1992.

Wright, Terry J. "Colin Gunton on Providence: Critical Commentaries," in *The Theology of Colin Gunton*, ed. Lincoln Harvey. London: T&T Clark, 2010.

Zizioulas, John D. *Being as Communion: Studies in Personhood and the Church*. New York: St. Vladimir's Press, 1985.

———. "Human Capacity and Human Incapacity: A Theological Exploration of Personhood." *Scottish Journal of Theology* 28, no. 5 (1975): 401–47.

———. *Lectures in Christian Dogmatics*. Edited by Douglas H. Knight. London: T&T Clark, 2008.

———. "On Being a Person. Towards an Ontology of Personhood," in *Persons, Divine and Human*, ed. Christoph Schwöbel and Colin E. Gunton. Edinburgh: T&T Clark, 1991.

Index

Abelard, Peter, 144, 152n100
angels, 13n59, 24, 117–21, 131, 234, 246, 250, 257, 285
Anselm, 150, 151, 155, 164, 185, 287, 288
apophaticism, 143, 162, 163n163, 269, 271, 276n77, 277, 279, 292
Aquinas, Thomas, 58, 140, 150, 152n97, 153n107, 156–69, 186, 288
Aristotle, 60, 138, 141, 142n45, 163, 170; Aristotelian, 21, 140, 142, 156, 157, 161, 166, 168, 186, 192, 201
Arius/Arianism, 19n94, 24n116, 46, 75n99, 119, 131, 247

Barth, Karl, 5–12, 18–20, 25–27, 58, 59, 64, 90, 151, 154, 202, 203, 206, 208, 233n1
Basil of Caesarea, 11, 16, 43–45, 58n17, 68n70, 78, 81, 200, 259, 261–65, 274–78
Bernard of Clairvaux, 152, 183, 287
Boethius, 137–45, 149, 163, 184, 185, 190, 286
Bonaventure, 150–52, 154, 155, 164, 166, 169, 183, 185, 186, 287, 288

Calvin, John, 123n158, 148n76, 172, 189, 190, 194, 196, 198–212, 225, 232, 239n32, 289, 290
Cappadocian Fathers, 10, 11, 21, 29, 34, 35, 39, 43–46, 51, 66, 68n69, 70, 71, 158, 184n107, 233, 234, 259–82, 291, 292
Cassian, John, 146

cogito ergo sum, 148, 216, 219–21, 225, 228n78, 232, 291
communion, 11, 34, 43, 89, 260–63, 265–70. See also *koinonia*

Descartes, René, 35, 51, 137n15, 146, 147, 184, 190, 215–29, 232, 287, 289–91, 294
docetic tendency, 15, 47, 123
dualism, 1, 8, 14, 21–24, 27, 29, 31–33, 46, 51, 53, 90, 93–131, 140, 141, 156–58, 169, 179–82, 201, 206–12, 218, 220, 225–28, 231, 235, 242, 243, 254, 257, 273, 278, 285, 289
Duns Scotus, 18n87, 165–74, 186, 288

economy, divine, 1, 14, 20, 22, 27, 35, 57, 58, 66, 73, 77–79, 87, 88, 106, 194, 244, 245
Eden, 113, 248
Enlightenment, 14, 64n51, 195, 215
Erigena, John Scotus, 142n45
eschatology, 11n48, 23, 76, 79, 110–15, 130, 172, 194, 202, 241–43, 256, 285
ex nihilo, 18, 25, 35n27, 47, 168

Faustus of Riez, 146
fides quaerens intellectum, 25, 26n124, 150, 151, 163
filioque, 153

gnostic/gnosticism, 14, 108, 236, 241–45, 251, 252, 256
Gregory of Nazianzus, 43, 47, 48n82, 58n17, 68n70, 83, 250, 259, 264, 265, 274, 275
Gregory of Nyssa, 43, 44n62, 58n17, 68n70, 83n138, 183, 184n106, 259, 262–67, 270–75, 278, 292n46
Gregory the Great, 138, 144–49, 185, 224, 225, 286–89

haecceitas, 167, 170
Hartshorne, Charles, 6, 58, 59
hierarchy of being, 97, 104, 106, 130, 155n114, 169, 285
Hilary of Poitiers, 118n129, 120n142, 124
Hugh of Saint Victor, 152, 153
hypostasis, 11, 21, 35, 44, 66–68, 261–64, 267–71, 275–78, 292

imago Dei, 7n20, 12, 35n27, 83–89, 160–63, 231n90, 237–40, 248, 255n132, 275, 284, 292

imago Trinitatis, 83, 89, 96, 151, 153, 186, 219, 228n72, 234, 238, 256, 284, 287
individualism, 4, 7–9, 25, 35, 39, 41, 42, 85, 87, 140, 146, 184, 185, 192–99, 212, 218, 231, 232, 266–68
inward turn, 4, 54, 60, 62, 82, 85, 86, 89, 92, 127–29, 135, 152, 154, 155, 160, 164, 175, 183, 184, 187, 190, 198, 200, 218, 220, 226, 227, 230–32, 236, 282, 288, 291
Irenaeus, 13, 14, 23, 46, 47, 51, 89n165, 108, 114, 118–20, 155n113, 184n107, 233–60, 278, 291
Irving, Edward, 13–17, 47–49

Jenson, Robert, 6, 33–35, 45, 49, 195n30
John of Damascus, 158

Kant, Immanuel, 23, 110, 142, 219, 220, 230, 294n51
koinonia, 11, 21, 43, 264–66, 279. *See also* communion

Logos asarkos, 17, 24, 117, 123, 124, 126, 127, 131, 246, 252, 257, 285

Lombard, Peter, 128, 152
Luther, Martin, 189–206, 211, 212, 225, 232, 289

Manichaean, Manichees, 23, 56, 60, 102, 108, 109, 251n110
mediation, 6n14, 13–15, 22, 24, 27, 46, 51, 65, 94, 96, 116, 117, 121–23, 127, 131, 168, 235, 238, 246–48, 257, 278, 285, 286, 292
millennium/millenarianism, 114, 115, 136, 141, 241
modalism, 20, 21, 56n8, 92, 119
monistic imbalance, 1, 20, 21, 33, 43, 51, 53–93, 96, 140, 143, 156, 169, 201, 206, 212, 231, 234, 273, 283
monothelitism, 16

Neoplatonism, 22n106, 32, 61, 62, 64n51, 79, 86, 105, 128, 147n71, 180, 195, 226, 228, 244, 274. *See also* Platonism

Ockham, William, 75n100, 123n158, 166, 170–74, 186, 196n32, 288
Origen, 32, 106, 114, 145, 158n135, 242, 277n84, 285

ousia, 11, 21, 35, 43, 66, 68, 261, 264, 268–71

Owen, John, 13–17

particularity, 9, 11n46, 14n66, 15, 17, 21, 27, 33, 34, 38, 42, 54, 58, 66, 68, 73–77, 91, 170, 205n83, 265, 266n34, 276. See *also* substantiality

perichoresis, 9, 40, 42, 272, 314. See *also* transcendentals

Petrarch, Francesco 166, 174–83, 187, 190, 225, 232, 287, 288

Platonism/Platonic/Platonists, 14, 18, 21, 22, 26, 31, 56, 59–65, 74, 75, 81, 84–86, 90n167, 95, 99, 100, 102, 105, 107, 109, 118, 119, 126–28, 130, 140, 142, 146n67, 147n71, 152, 155, 157, 163, 166, 168, 179, 180, 186, 195, 196, 200, 207–9, 212, 227, 228, 231, 232, 240, 244, 254, 257, 273, 274, 285, 290, 292, 295. See *also* Neoplatonism

Plotinus, 22n106, 61–63, 95n10, 96, 100, 102, 110, 111, 226, 244

pneumatology, 13, 50, 77, 78, 92, 194, 199, 207, 212, 257

predestination, 145, 146, 148, 172, 173, 185, 203–5, 286, 290; double predestination, 121, 172, 201, 201–5

Pseudo-Dionysius the Areopagite, 142n45, 152n97, 158, 164, 186, 288

de Régnon, Theodore, 34, 70–71, 91, 282

relationality, 8, 9, 42. See *also* transcendentals

resurrection, 101, 102, 115, 240n39, 242

Richard of Saint Victor, 152, 153

scholasticism, 150, 152n97, 155–56, 175, 185, 192, 287, 295n55

stoicism, 36, 146, 157, 224

substantiality, 9, 66n59. See *also* particularity; transcendentals

Taylor, Charles, 19n92, 224

theophanies, 117–20, 250, 257

transcendentals, 8–10, 42

vestigia trinitatis, 9, 20, 85, 159, 183n106, 275n72

via negativa, 156–58, 167, 186, 288

voluntarism, 36, 173, 174, 182, 185, 224, 287

Zizioulas, John, 5, 10–12, 19n92, 21, 27, 43–45, 71n83, 260–68, 271n54, 292

www.ingramcontent.com/pod-product-compliance
Lightning Source LLC
Chambersburg PA
CBHW071148070526
44584CB00019B/2707